Cultural Marxism in Postwar Britain

POST-CONTEMPORARY INTERVENTIONS

Series Editors: Stanley Fish and Fredric Jameson

Dennis Dworkin

CULTURAL MARXISM IN POSTWAR BRITAIN

History, the New Left, and the Origins

of Cultural Studies

Duke University Press   Durham and London 1997

For Peter,

7/11/97

friend, teacher, generous but tough critic

Dennis

© 1997 DUKE UNIVERSITY PRESS

All rights reserved

Printed in the United States of America on acid-free paper ∞

Typeset in Bembo by Keystone Typesetting, Inc.

Library of Congress Cataloging-in-Publication Data appear
on the last printed page of this book.

Contents

Acknowledgments

In the course of writing this book I have incurred numerous intellectual debts. It was originally written as a dissertation at the University of Chicago. I wish to thank Russell Berman for his friendship, intellectual companionship, and first drawing my attention to an alternative Marxist intellectual tradition. I also would like to thank Ira Katznelson, under whose direction I initially read Perry Anderson, E. P. Thompson, and Raymond Williams. Many of the arguments in this book involving cultural studies were originally developed and tested in the University of Chicago mass culture workshop. Discussions with two friends and participants in that workshop—Arthur Knight and Loren Kruger—were especially important to the writing of the dissertation. I am grateful to the members of my dissertation committee—Leora Auslander, Keith Baker, and Jan Goldstein—for constructive criticism of my manuscript. I am especially grateful to Peter Novick, the chair of the committee, for his encouragement, for his friendship, and for being a tough and fairminded critic.

I want to thank those whom I interviewed and discussed my research with while I was in Great Britain in 1984. Space does not permit acknowledging all of them, but I could not have written either the dissertation or the book without their help. I would like to acknowledge those whom I met with on more than one occasion, who shared primary documents with me, or who invited me for meals or to pubs: Sally Alexander, Anna Davin, the late Alan Hall, Stuart Hall, Catherine Hall, Christopher Hill, Rodney Hilton, Eric Hobsbawm, Richard Johnson, Victor Kiernan, Michael Rustin, Bill Schwarz, Barbara Taylor, the late E. P. Thompson, Peter Worsley, and Robert M. Young.

I have written this book as a member of the History Department of the University of Nevada, Reno, one of the few departments in the country whose faculty are mostly cultural and intellectual historians. All my colleagues have been supportive, but three of them (also friends) deserve special recognition: Martha Hildreth for nu-

merous conversations on cultural and historical theory; Elizabeth
Raymond for intellectual and moral support and for editorial expertise; and Scott Casper for the many hours he spent reading the
manuscript, listening to me think out loud, and always asking the
right questions. In addition, I'd like to thank Jen Huntley-Smith
for her heroic work in proofreading and in creating the index for
this book.

I would like to thank Duke University Press for its professional
and respectful treatment of me and my manuscript. I am indebted
to Geoff Eley and Lawrence Grossberg for their thought-provok-
ing criticism, to Bob Mirandon for helping improve the clarity of
my prose, to Pam Morrison for providing encouragement during
the book's production, and to Ken Wissoker for having faith in the
project and bringing it to completion. I also would like to thank
Mark Poster for critically reading this manuscript when it was a
completed dissertation.

Finally, this book is dedicated to my family. My parents Grace
and Joe and my brother Kenneth have encouraged and supported
my intellectual pursuits for many years. My wife Amelia Currier
has provided love and friendship and my son Sam has furnished
indescribable joy while I wrote this book.

Introduction

In *Marxism and the Interpretation of Culture*, a collection of papers given at a 1983 conference, the editors, Lawrence Grossberg and Cary Nelson, argue that Marxism is at the center of an explosive trend in the social sciences and the humanities that cuts across traditional boundaries and takes "the entire field of cultural practices" as its subject. The editors suggest that Marxism is ideally suited for this task because it

has long been at least implicitly involved in breaking down the barriers between these domains, making each of necessity a site of interpretative activity—by politicizing interpretative and cultural practices, by looking at the economic determinations of cultural production, by radically historicizing our understanding of signifying practices—from political discourses to art, from beliefs to social practices, from the discourse of psychology to the discourse of economics—and, of course, by continuing to revise and enlarge a body of theory with multidisciplinary implications.[1]

Their volume begins with a series of essays grouped under the title, "Rethinking the Crisis in Marxism," suggesting that "the renaissance of activity" is likewise going through a "crisis of definition." Overall, the book captures the excitement, enthusiasm, and commitment that more than one generation of historians, literary critics, art historians, philosophers, and cultural theorists had come to feel about an unorthodox and critical tradition of Marxist theory as it developed over several decades.

This book, *Cultural Marxism in Postwar Britain*, is a historical account of the creation and development of one part of this unorthodox and critical Marxism: the British tradition of cultural Marxism from the mid-1940s until the late 1970s, from the founding of the Welfare State to Margaret Thatcher's transformation of it. I focus on the contributions of scholars and writers working in the field of history and cultural studies. The work of the British Marxist historians needs little introduction. Rodney Hilton's writings on the medieval peasantry; Christopher Hill's work on the seventeenth-century English revolution; E. P. Thompson's contributions to understanding eighteenth-century popular culture and the early working class; Eric Hobsbawm's many articles and books on labor history, preindustrial rebellion, and world capitalist development; and Raphael Samuel and Gareth Stedman Jones's work on the nineteenth century have been synonymous with the new social history and the history of the dominated classes. In various ways they have played major roles in creating a "history from below." Sally Alexander's writings on working-class women in the Industrial Revolution, Catherine Hall's work on the middle classes during that period, Sheila Rowbotham's numerous projects on the history of women, and Barbara Taylor's recovery of the feminist dimension of utopian socialism have been equally powerful voices in constituting a new socialist feminist history. They have been important not only in recovering the role of women in history, but they have made contributions to reconceiving more generally the relationship between men and women by focusing on the gendered nature of class and the relationship between production and reproduction, work and family.

Equally important as the historians' contributions has been the achievement of British cultural studies scholars, whose influence worldwide (especially in North America) has produced what an Australian practitioner, Meaghan Morris, has described as an "unprecedented international boom."[2] Pioneered by Richard Hoggart, Raymond Williams, and Stuart Hall, and extended by Hazel Carby, Paul Gilroy, Dick Hebdige, Angela McRobbie, and Paul Willis, among others, cultural studies has advanced critical understanding of the media, youth subcultures, literary production, the contemporary working class, the cultural construction of race and gender, popular culture, and the nature of ideology. It is distinguished by its simultaneous respect for the potentially subversive culture of dominated and marginalized classes and groups and an acute awareness of the ideological forces in society containing them. Interdisciplinary and theoretically eclectic, cultural studies has supplanted the traditional dichotomy between high and low culture, so prevalent in discussions about the mass media, with an enlarged concept of the cultural terrain.

I am neither the first to critically examine historians such as Hobsbawm, Thompson, and Hill or cultural theorists such as Hall and Williams, nor am I alone in recognizing the importance of British Marxist history and cultural studies for social and cultural theory and the new left environment associated with them. Indeed, by now, a sizable literature concerned with components of both disciplines has developed. But most writers have either attempted to publicize and explain the contributions of Marxist history and cultural studies, or they have put forth critical interpretations or defenses—frequently political in nature—from a position interior to those disciplines.[3] My account is the first intellectual history to study British cultural Marxism conceived as a coherent intellectual tradition, not limited to one discipline or one figure within it. With the death of two of the giants in this tradition—Edward Thompson and Raymond Williams—such an effort seems especially worthwhile.

I view British cultural Marxism in terms of a constructive but by no means harmonious dialogue and debate between, and within, the disciplines of history and cultural studies. At issue has been the relationship between culture and society, structure and agency, experience and ideology, and theory and practice. It is my contention that this cultural Marxist tradition cannot be viewed in isolation; it must be seen in the context of the crisis of the British Left, a crisis virtually coterminous with the postwar era. While the depths of this crisis became apparent in the 1980s in the aftermath of the Thatcher revolution, its contours began to take shape during the long Conservative rule of the 1950s. I do not argue that all of the works to be discussed were written explicitly in response to the crisis of socialism and the British Left, although this was certainly true in many cases. Rather, I suggest that much can be learned about British cultural Marxist history and cultural studies if they are viewed from this perspective.

British cultural Marxism grew out of an effort to create a socialist understanding of Britain which took into consideration postwar transformations that seemed to undermine traditional Marxist assumptions about the working class and that questioned the traditional Left's exclusive reliance on political and economic categories. Cultural Marxists were, above all, concerned with redefining the relationship between structure and agency, for it was the agency of traditional socialism, the industrial working class, that was being called into question. They attempted to identify the contours of the postwar terrain, to redefine social struggle, and to articulate new forms of resistance appropriate to a democratic and socialist politics in an advanced capitalist society. At the heart of this project was "culture." It signified both the terrain on which such a politics was to be reconceived and the recognition that this terrain was a site of political struggle. In this regard, British cultural Marxism distanced itself from the mainstream Marxist tradition—especially in its Stalinist, mechanistic, and economistic guise. Stuart Hall has characterized the relationship between Marxist theory and cultural studies as "working within shouting distance of Marxism, working on Marxism, working against Marxism, working with it, working to try to develop Marxism."[4] The same could be said of the more general relationship between Marxism and British cultural Marxism.

Possibly a more detailed picture can be drawn of British cultural Marxism by comparing and contrasting it with another Marxist-inspired tradition that has influenced contemporary discussions of culture—the Frankfurt School. Founded in the aftermath of World War I and shaped by the experience of the Russian Revolution and fascism, the Frankfurt School likewise represented a philosophical alternative to Marxist economism and Leninist vanguardism. Frankfurt School Marxists emphasized the cultural and ideological dimensions of social life; they characteristically attempted to grasp society as a "totality," and they were concerned with the disappearance of the revolutionary subject in advanced capitalist societies. Like Antonio Gramsci, they advocated a revolution against Marx's *Capital*, in other words, opposition to the simplistic belief that capitalist collapse and proletarian triumph were guaranteed by the laws of Marxist economics.[5]

Like the Frankfurt School, the British tradition was founded on a rejection of economism; it stressed the autonomy of culture and ideology in social life, and it was shaped by the failure of revolutionary movements in the advanced capitalist West. But the differences between the British cultural Marxists and Frankfurt School traditions are as striking as the similarities. First, while both recognized that that culture played a critical role in securing the masses' acquiescence to the dominant ideology and the status quo, they had very different attitudes toward modern culture. The Frankfurt School tended to see contemporary culture as the debased mass entertainments of the culture industry. It was a culture that encouraged the masses to think as passive consumers, undermined their autonomy and independence of judgment, and induced them to acquiesce to dominant social relations. The British cultural Marxist tradition, on the other hand, saw culture as more contradictory. Cultural studies regarded popular culture as potentially subversive, but, equally important, theorists attempted to understand mass cultural consumption from the point of view of the consumers rather than the producers; they concluded that the people's response was frequently creative and varied. The same held true for the historians, although they were primarily concerned with earlier historical periods. Taken as a whole, the historians' work treated the cultural domain as an arena of contestation between dominant and subservient classes over values and meanings—culture as a "whole way of struggle." And their work on earlier historical periods implied that this fight was no less visible in the twentieth century. Given this distinctive cultural Marxist attitude toward culture, it is understandable why historians universally embraced Antonio Gramsci, whose concept of hegemonic struggle paralleled and enriched their own.

Second, significant differences existed between the Frankfurt School and the cultural Marxist approaches to politics. While generalizations are difficult, the Frankfurt School believed that in a historical epoch when theory and practice stubbornly refused to come together, critical thought itself was a form of revolutionary practice. As Herbert Marcuse said of Lucien Goldmann, they were radical intellectuals who did not have the least qualm about not being workers and who thought that intellect by nature was revolutionary.[6] The majority agreed with Lenin that workers left to themselves could never achieve anything but trade union consciousness, but they rejected his concept of the vanguard party because it justified the suppression of dissent. Some even refused on principle to join radical parties.

Unlike the Frankfurt School, which tended to remain aloof from working-class politics, especially after the 1920s, intellectuals in the British tradition continuously struggled with the relationship between theory and practice. They have never had an unproblematic association with working-class and radical movements, but they tended to view their intellectual work as in some way contributing to those movements. Marxist historical and cultural theory in Britain was produced by several generations of intellectuals in the context of the most radical causes and movements of the last sixty years: the Popular Front of the thirties and forties, the New Left movement and the Campaign for Nuclear Disarmament (CND) of the late fifties and early sixties, the countercultural and student politics of 1968, and the feminist and antiracist politics of the 1970s. Cultural Marxists used their skills as intellectuals to articulate the experience and goals of dominated classes and groups, and they tried to understand the forces in society constraining the working class. A vigorous strain of populism has always been present in cultural Marxist theory and politics.

Undoubtedly many reasons can help explain why British Marxist intellectual culture has assumed such a distinct pattern, but two stand out. The British tradition of workers' and adult education, notably the Workers' Educational Association, provided a unique opportunity for intellectuals and working people to communicate, and this environment played a major role in creating cultural studies and shaping Marxist historical approaches.[7] Some of the tradition's major texts—Hoggart's *The Uses of Literacy*, Thompson's *The Making of the English Working Class*, and Williams's *Culture and Society* and *The Long Revolution*—were products of the adult education setting. The new feminist history was a product of this milieu as well. In addition, because of the gradual expansion of educational opportunities, many British cultural Marxists (though certainly not a majority) were from working-class backgrounds and attended universities on scholarships. Hoggart and Williams are undoubtedly the best-known of these figures, but they were by no means alone.

Another major distinction between the two traditions was that the majority of Frankfurt School theorists were philosophers, nurtured in Hegelianism, while British Marxists with the greatest influence have been historians and literary and cultural theorists. It has been common to attribute this difference in approach to the antitheoretical and empirical bent of the English, and indeed this assertion contains some truth.[8] But it needs qualification. Although British historians were specialists who generally wrote about specific historical periods, they were no less concerned with understanding the social totality than the philosophers of the European tradition. Indeed, they originally conceived of their work as a collective project aimed at understanding the trajectory of modern British society and history. (See discussion in chapter 1.)

Furthermore, during the sixties and seventies British Marxists engaged in a critical dialogue with advocates of European traditions of literary, philosophical, and social theory, and this dialogue left an indelible imprint on British cultural Marxism's development—a process that was simultaneous with Britain achieving membership in the European Community. Many intellectuals were attracted to these traditions and other forms of theory precisely because they represented alternatives to what they saw as the stifling effects of the English empirical idiom. But many of them also used these ideas to extend and renew, rather than negate, the English tradition. By the end of the 1970s it was still true that much of the most creative work of British Marxists was historical in nature, even if outside the historical discipline proper, but it was by no means antitheoretical.

My account of British cultural Marxism in this book is a critical history of ideas. On the one hand, I have tried to carefully reconstruct the historical development of this tradition. Because it has been so closely related to politics, I have necessarily viewed theoretical developments and major texts as inseparable from this context. This approach has often meant describing the major protagonists in relationship to radical political movements and debates. On the other hand, I am interested in this tradition's contributions to cultural and historical theory, to Left-wing intellectual debates, and to efforts at understanding contemporary society, and I have thus attempted to evaluate their achievement critically. Sometimes I have done this by re-creating theoretical debates that have arisen in response to major works at the time they appeared; at other points I have put forward my own critiques and evaluations. Here, I have often engaged in detailed textual analyses of many of the principal texts, sometimes analyzing at length those which by this point will be familiar to many readers. I have followed this course for two reasons: because it seems essential to achieving the goal of viewing this tradition as a whole, and because I hope that my account will be read by a wider audience than those already thoroughly acquainted with the major texts of the tradition that is being re-created. I do not see myself as being a disciple of any particular tendency in British cultural Marxism, but it will undoubtedly become clear that I have the most sympathy for the later approaches of the cultural studies tradition as developed by Stuart Hall and others.

This book is organized into three chronological parts. The first part (chapter 1) describes the growth of Marxist historiography in the context of the Popular Front and the Cold War; it concentrates on the Communist Party's Historians' Group that proved to be so important to the development of Marxist historical scholarship and was responsible for an embryonic version of cultural Marxism. In the second part (chapters 2 and 3) I focus on the pivotal role of the New Left of the late fifties and early sixties in creating cultural Marxist theory. Its socialist-humanist philosophy and commitment to cultural politics based on postwar changes inspired the original agenda of cultural studies and contributed to shifts in Marxist historical approaches. The third section comprises three chapters, but its divisions are somewhat artificial. I examine the achievement of the 1970s in separate chapters on cultural studies (chapter 4), history (chapter 5), and a final one (chapter 6) on the passionate and heated debate between the two disciplines over Althusserian Marxism, the centerpiece being E. P. Thompson's wholesale condemnation of it in "The Poverty of Theory" (1978). I begin this section (chapter 4) with a discussion of the social, political, intellectual, and cultural context—what for abbreviation's sake might be described as the legacy of "1968." What I have attempted is not a full-scale study of this historical moment or the wider Marxist intellectual culture that in important ways was produced by it, although I recognize such an effort is highly desirable. My goal is the more limited one of situating the cultural Marxist tradition of the 1970s.

Two final observations about method are in order. First, I am aware that there are advantages and disadvantages to undertaking a historical project that is so contemporary. Clearly, I cannot evaluate the long-term significance of British cultural Marxism with the same assurance that would be possible a hundred years from now. Nor have I been able to use some of the documents usually available to historians who study the more distant past. But I have had access to correspondence, minutes of meetings, unpublished papers, internal memorandums, and a tape recording of a debate between E. P. Thompson, Stuart Hall, and the historian Richard Johnson over "The Poverty of Theory." I hope that what I cannot achieve in terms of the long glance backward will be compensated for by the immediacy of my analysis. In addition, after the collapse of Soviet communism and the tearing down of the Berlin Wall, it is possible to argue that the post–World War II epoch is over and that the investigation of this period by historians is now overdue.

Second, although I interviewed more than thirty of the protagonists of this study from various backgrounds and generations, this book is not an oral history. My use of interviews has been uneven and unsystematic, in part because, as is so often the case, what I imagined I would write turned out to considerably differ from what I did write. As an interviewer, I was mostly concerned with reconstructing the earlier phase of this study. But I have always seen the principal sources of this book as written ones. As it turned out, the interviews mostly—I hope—saved me from innumerable mistakes I would have made had I never met those whom I have written about. Experience, as many in this study have realized, has its limits, but it has no substitute.

ONE Lost Rights

A pivotal moment in the creation of a Marxist tradition of historical scholarship in Great Britain was the launching of the Communist Party Historians' Group in 1946. The core of the Group came from the radical student generation of the 1930s and early 1940s. They became Communists in large measure because of the movement's prominent role in the Popular Front against fascism. The group included Christopher Hill, Rodney Hilton, Eric Hobsbawm, Victor Kiernan, George Rudé, John Saville, and Dorothy and Edward Thompson (though Edward Thompson played only a marginal role). It was also shaped by Communist scholars of an older generation who were not professional historians per se but were devoted historical materialists, most importantly the economist Maurice Dobb and the Marx scholar Dona Torr.

The Group's practice bore the imprint of two political moments. On the one hand, it conceived of itself as spearheading a Popular Front, a broad coalition of progressive historians combating reactionary tendencies in historiography. Its thinking was simultaneously constrained by the sectarianism already present in the 1930s but accentuated by the Cold War's polarization of intellectual and political discourse. The Group's members were relatively open-minded, considering that they were loyal Communist militants in the late 1940s and early 1950s. In spite of crippling illusions about Stalin's regime and the nature of their own party, they openly debated Marxist theory, critically examined numerous historical issues central to the study of British history, and, in conjunction with a few sympathetic non-Marxist historians, they launched the social history journal *Past and Present*. While the Group's worldview was steeped in Marxist dogma, it shared the same objectivist and empiricist assumptions about the nature of historical knowledge as did other professional historians. Such allegiances, however, were not easy to reconcile and led to internal conflicts.

In retrospect, the significance of the Historians' Group was as a kind of incubator for the development of British cultural Marxist historiography and historical theory. It represented a unique moment in the intellectual history of Marxism.

I

The Marxist historiographical tradition in Britain was rooted in Popular Front politics and the Communist culture of the 1930s. Founded in 1920 and consisting of dedicated militants, the British CP was a tiny organization consisting of no more than several thousand members that, because of its penetration into the trade union movement, exerted an influence belying its size. In the mid-thirties the Party was in flux, a consequence of the triumph of fascism in Germany and the destruction of the CP there. Following the lead of the international movement, the British CP reversed its disastrous "class against class" position, which failed to distinguish between social democrats and the extreme Right, and launched a Popular Front against fascism that came to include progressives of all kinds. Most importantly, this new direction made possible Communist support of the Spanish Republicans. Of the approximately two thousand British volunteers in the International Brigade, about half were Communists. The British CP never became a serious rival to the Labour Party, but, owing to its shift in posture, it tripled its membership and progressively dominated the small revolutionary Left.[1]

During the era of the Great Depression and fascist expansion, English intellectual culture for the first time became dominated by leftist ideas. What stands out are the flirtations with communism by poets W. H. Auden, Stephen Spender, and C. Day Lewis; fiction writer Christopher Isherwood; the technological humanism of Marxist scientists Hyman Levy, Lancelot Hogben, J. D. Bernal, J. B. S. Haldane, and Joseph Needham; the work of political writers such as John Strachey and Harold Laski; George Orwell's engagement with poverty in *Down and Out in Paris and London* and *The Road to Wigan Pier* and with Spain in *Homage to Catalonia*; the anti-fascist novels of Graham Greene; the economic writings of Maurice Dobb; and the populist historical work of A. L. Morton. Left-wing ideas were powerfully spread by Victor Gollancz's Left Book Club, which by 1938 had nearly 60,000 subscribers, a monthly newspaper *Left News*, and a national network of 1,500 Left discussion groups.[2] One of the most striking features of this intellectual culture was its enrichment by the first radical student movement in

England, drawn into politics by the Great Depression, the rise of fascism, and, most importantly, the cause of Republican Spain. Communists were a minority of the student activists, but they took the lead in supporting Spanish Republicanism, organizing the antifascist movement in the universities and progressively dominating university socialist societies, the principal medium of agitation. Communist student intellectuals saw themselves as forming a column in a great international army, fighting to preserve freedom and democracy and to establish a socialist world. They viewed Marxism as an alternative to the decadence and emptiness of bourgeois thought. It contained a compelling analysis of the historical moment, a vision of the future, and a philosophy—dialectical materialism—that unified nature and history, thought and reality, theory and practice. Armed with this new way of understanding, the rising generation was convinced of the necessity of revamping whole intellectual disciplines corrupted by bourgeois ideology: literary criticism, the sciences, philosophy, history, and anthropology.

Before the 1940s the small amount of Marxist writing on British history that existed was closely related to the broader tradition of socialist and radical democratic historiography. Typically, it was the work of intellectuals and militants, some of whom were from working-class backgrounds, who offered a historical materialist reading of known accounts. A. L. Morton exemplified this type of historian. He had been a Party member since the late twenties and a correspondent for the *Daily Worker*. His *A People's History of England*, published by the Left Book Club in 1938, was founded on a Marxist conception of class struggle but roughly modeled on the historical work of the earlier radical democratic tradition, particularly J. R. Green's *A Short History of the English People* (1877).[3]

Marxist historical writing produced in the academy during the thirties was not done by professional historians. It was written by a small number of scholars in other disciplines who used a historical materialist approach: classicists like Benjamin Farrington and George Thomson; the specialist of the German Reformation, Roy Pascal; the Communist scientists of the social relations of science movement; the Australian expatriate and archaeologist V. Gordon Childe; and the economist Maurice Dobb, who was already engaged in the historical research that culminated in the influential *Studies in the Development of Capitalism* (1946).[4]

The first Marxists to establish themselves within the historical profession came from the student generation of the thirties. Hobsbawm and Kiernan, who attended Trinity College, Cambridge, were classmates of James Klugmann, who would later be a leading Party intellectual, and the Communist poet John Cornford, who died fighting in Spain. (Dobb was a don of the college.) Rodney Hilton and Christopher Hill were radicalized while attending Balliol College, Oxford. John Saville was active in the radical student milieu of the London School of Economics. Somewhat younger than the others, Edward Thompson got involved in Cambridge student politics in the years immediately before the war. With the exception of Thompson, these historians all joined the British CP in the mid-1930s, the years that saw the coalescing of the Popular Front. Their participation in this coalition had a profound impact on their vision of politics and history and deeply influenced their perspective on the proper relationship between theory and practice.

While some of the best-known English Marxists of the 1930s, such as John Strachey and John Cornford, came from upper-class families, more typically Party members originated from the more "protestant" sections of the working class—Sheffield engineers, Clydeside shipbuilders, South Wales and Scottish miners. Party intellectuals likewise tended to be from Nonconformist middle-class backgrounds.[5] The Marxist historians from the thirties' generation were no different, the majority of them being from Nonconformist households steeped in liberal dissent.

Christopher Hill, for one, was the product of an affluent but sternly middle-class Yorkshire Methodist upbringing, one he remembered as being pious, serious, and deeply inscribed with a "puritan conscience."[6] His father, a successful solicitor, led an austere life, forbade smoking and drinking at home, and (as one of Hill's friends at Balliol recalled) was a "strict, but genial puritan."[7] Hill, who attended a grammar school and reached Oxford owing to a scholarship, acknowledged that his background played an indispensable role in preparing him for a Communist commitment. He also believed that becoming a Party member represented a decisive break with, and a reaction against, his past.[8] Victor Kiernan was from a Congregationalist background and from Northern England. His father worked for a Manchester shipping firm, translating correspondence into Spanish and Portuguese. Kiernan developed an interest in history while he attended a grammar school in Manchester, and he gravitated toward communism as a result of the influence of Klugmann and Cornford in the Cambridge Socialist

Society. He recalled that, given his background, joining the Party did not seem like a big jump.[9] Similarly, Rodney Hilton's family, though "deliberately irreligious," had all the cultural characteristics of Nonconformity.[10] Hilton was part of the mobile working class and a child of the Lancashire labor movement. His grandfather, a politically active weaver, had campaigned to abolish the House of Lords in 1884; his parents were involved in the cooperative movement and were members of the Independent Labour Party.[11] Like Kiernan, Hilton developed a love for history while attending a Manchester grammar school, and he attended Oxford on the basis of a scholarship. He remembered that participants in the Balliol CP group were mostly from similar backgrounds, often being one or two generations removed from working-class families. "In fact it was not difficult for people with this sort of background to become Communists."[12]

Eric Hobsbawm was a notable exception to this pattern. Like Hill, Hilton, and Kiernan, he attended an English grammar school and received a scholarship to study in a university, in his case Cambridge. Yet Hobsbawm was a second generation English citizen. His mother's family was Austrian, his grandfather emigrated from Russia to England in the 1870s, and Hobsbawm himself grew up in Vienna. He was one of the last products of the now largely extinct culture of Central European middle-class Jewry, a milieu that in his formative years was rapidly disintegrating. As he remembered it: "After 1914 there was nothing but catastrophe and problematic survival. We lived on borrowed time and knew it. To make long-term plans seemed senseless for people whose world had already crashed twice within ten years (first in the war, later in the Great Inflation)."[13]

For a young and precocious Jewish intellectual trying to find a political identity in a fragmented world, the choices appeared limited. Liberalism was not worth considering, since it symbolized the world before 1914. To support nationalist or Christian parties was likewise out of the question. Hobsbawm remembered the choice as being between communism, or some other form of revolutionary Marxism, and Zionism, a Jewish version of nationalism often compatible with a revolutionary socialist commitment. Hobsbawm chose communism.

We did not make a commitment against bourgeois society and capitalism, since it patently seemed to be on its last leg. We simply chose a

*future rather than no future, which meant revolution. But it meant
revolution not in a negative but in a positive sense: a new world rather
than no world. The great October revolution and Soviet Russia proved
to us that such a new world was possible, perhaps that it was already
functioning.*[14]

Hobsbawm's family moved to Berlin in 1932, and he soon joined a
Communist youth group at the age of fourteen. His commitment
to communism would be renewed when he became involved in
the radical student movement at Cambridge.[15]

II

The idea of a Party Historians' Group was discussed before the war,
but it materialized only in the aftermath of a conference held to
discuss a revised edition of A. L. Morton's popular *A People's History of England* in 1946.[16] The nucleus of the Group came from the
student generation of the thirties. Some of them, as in the case of
Hill and Kiernan, had already published historical work and had
positions in universities. Hill was a fellow and tutor in modern
history at Balliol College, Kiernan a fellow at Trinity (though soon
to join the history faculty of the University of Edinburgh where he
would remain for the whole of his academic career). Others like
Hilton, Hobsbawm, and Saville were slightly younger and were
preparing to embark upon academic careers.[17] Raphael Samuel
began attending group sessions while he was still a student at a
secondary school. The Group also included intellectuals from an
older generation. Dobb and Torr were especially influential on the
Group's direction, but others of their generation were involved—
Morton, Farrington, Alfred Jenkin of the British Museum, Thomson, and Jack Lindsay. Also, diverse intellectuals and militants,
mostly older, attended group sessions because they loved history
and were devoted Marxists.

The Historians' Group and the writings of the historians connected with it were products of the political climate. The Group
was shaped by both the triumph of the Popular Front mentality and
the distress produced by the Cold War.

Before the Second World War the Popular Front was a small but
vocal protest movement on the periphery of mainstream politics.
Its status was changed by the war. The English people's collective
struggle for survival in a total war created an unprecedented unity
and solidarity and perhaps even a partial and momentary breakdown of class barriers. As a result of their wartime experience, they

came to believe that society would have to be restructured during peacetime. Such a belief produced the Labour victory of 1945, an electoral success which gave rise to expectations that the postwar reforms would produce a more egalitarian society. Accompanying the British people's shift to the Left during the war years was a change in their perception of Stalin, the Soviet Union, and the British CP. After the German invasion of Russia and the solidification of the Anglo-Russian alliance, the days of the Nazi-Soviet pact were swiftly forgotten. Owing to its close relations with the Soviet Union and the overall shift in the climate of opinion, the British CP began to be taken more seriously. Although minuscule by European standards, the Party nonetheless claimed 65,000 members in 1942—the highest figure in its history. Communists might have been disappointed by their showing in the 1945 parliamentary elections, for the Party won only two seats. But several fellow travelers were returned as Labour candidates, and the CP continued to make inroads into the trade union movement.

After the war, then, Communists had good reason to be optimistic about the future, but their buoyant mood quickly dissipated. Both socialists and Communists were extremely disappointed by the Labour Party's performance in office, which, despite pushing through enduring social reforms, did little to disturb either the social structure or productive relations of British society. According to R. H. S. Crossman, "the postwar Labour government marked the end of a century of social reform, and not as its socialist supporters had hoped, the beginning of a new epoch."[18] Moreover, as a result of the Labour government's evolving anti-Soviet foreign policy, a visible sign of the emerging Cold War, Communists found themselves relegated to a political ghetto, looked upon by the majority as the enemy within. In the 1950 general elections the Party lost both of its parliamentary seats, the first time since the mid-thirties that it was without parliamentary representation. By 1953 it had lost nearly 30,000 members—half the number it had claimed in 1942. The Cold War in Britain never reached the hysterical frenzy of its American counterpart, but it was stamped by the same red-baiting and blacklisting.[19] Within the Left itself, the Labour Party and the trade unions launched campaigns directed at impeding Communist influence. While Communist academics rarely lost their jobs, they were unlikely to find new ones or receive promotions after 1948.

E. P. Thompson was the Marxist historian whose development was perhaps most deeply affected by Popular Front hopes and Cold War disappointments. Slightly younger than the Historians' Group's core members, his political vision was grounded in the Popular Front's culmination, not its origins—the Second World War, not the Spanish Civil War. Thompson came from a liberal and anti-imperialist background. His father, Edward John Thompson, was a novelist, poet, historian, and a champion of Indian independence. The Thompson home was the site of stimulating intellectual and political discussions frequented by "some of the most interesting men of the preceding generation," including Tagore, Gandhi, Nehru, and other Indian nationalists.[20] Thompson remembered growing up "expecting governments to be mendacious and imperialist and expecting that one's stance ought to be hostile to government."[21]

Thompson's early model for political activism was his brother Frank who joined the Party in 1939. As a major in the British Army during the war, Frank Thompson commanded a British mission to support the Bulgarian partisans in 1943—44. Captured, tortured, dragged through the streets, and finally shot by the fascists, he gave his life for a "vision of the common people of Europe building, upon their old inheritance, a new creative society of comradeship. . . ."[22] After the war, a Bulgarian railway station was named in his honor.

Thompson followed his brother's example. He joined the CP as a student at Cambridge in the early 1940s and later served as a tank troop commander in Italy and France. Thompson's strongest impressions of his army years were the men's antifascist spirit, their adherence to democratic and often socialist principles, and their resolute anti-imperialism. He remembered it as an authentic Popular Front. "I recall," he wrote in 1978, "a resolute and ingenious civilian army, increasingly hostile to the conventional military virtues, which became . . . an anti-fascist and consciously anti-imperialist army. Its members voted Labour in 1945: knowing why, as did the civilian workers at home. Many were infused with socialist ideas and expectations wildly in advance of the tepid rhetoric of today's Labour leaders."[23] Like his brother, Thompson became involved in the struggle for Eastern European socialism and democracy. Through army newspapers he followed the partisan movements with what in retrospect he acknowledged as "simplistic pro-

Soviet feelings." At the time, however, he was most of all impressed by the decisive contribution of the Soviet army and the heroic sacrifices of the Russian people.

After the war Thompson returned to Cambridge to finish his degree, but in 1947 he left England again to become commandant of a British youth group assisting the People's Youth of Yugoslavia in building a 150-mile railroad from Samac in Slovenia to Sarajevo.[24] For Thompson, the railroad signified a new socialist and nationalist spirit, an outgrowth of the partisan movement and the defeat of fascism. "It springs from the pride of ownership by the ordinary man of his own country, its sources of wealth and its means of production."[25] Thompson's participation in the building of this railroad proved to be a decisive moment in his political development; he became convinced that men "within the context of certain institutions and culture can conceptualize in terms of 'our' rather than 'my' or 'their.'"[26] His faith in socialism was sustained over the years by this and other achievements inspired by the Popular Front of the forties.

In view of Thompson's involvement in the 1940s Popular Front it should come as no surprise that he was very disappointed by the Cold War that superseded it. In "The Poverty of Theory," he talked of voluntarism "crashing" against the "wall of the Cold War," of democratic forces in East and West being silenced by two monolithic power blocs. Or in his words, "'History,' so pliant to the heroic will in 1943 and 1944, seemed to congeal in an instant into two monstrous antagonistic structures, each of which allowed only the smallest latitude of movement within its operative realm."[27] Admittedly, this judgment entailed considerable hindsight. At the time, Thompson held the United States alone responsible for the poisoned atmosphere. However, his words suggest the extent to which he experienced the Cold War as a political and personal defeat. Thompson saw the Cold War as being responsible for the decline of the socialist movement, and he argued that renewal depended on destroying its ideological grip. He spent more than thirty years in the disarmament movement to bring this about.

The dual influence of the Popular Front and the Cold War that shaped Thompson's political development can also be detected in the project of the Historians' Group. The Group's self-image mirrored the Popular Front origins of its most active members. It saw itself as the avant-garde of a broadly based, progressive coalition opposed to historical writing that either implicitly or explicitly defended conservative politics. The historians believed that Marxism alone occupied the position in historiography once held by the nineteenth-century Whig interpretation, but they closely allied themselves with the radical democratic and labor traditions—Sidney and Beatrice Webb, J. L. and Barbara Hammond, G. D. H. Cole, and R. H. Tawney.[28] As Hobsbawm put it: "We saw ourselves not as trying, say, to distinguish ourselves from Tawney, but to push forward that tradition, to make it more explicit, to see Marxism as what these people *ought* to have been working toward."[29]

The Group's defense of the progressive tradition was apparent in its involvement in the two major English historiographical controversies of the 1950s: the gentry's role in the English Revolution and the social consequences of the early Industrial Revolution. In the "storm over the gentry," Christopher Hill was the lone defender of Tawney, "the giant upon whose shoulders all historians of the 17th century stand."[30] In the "standard of living" debate, Hobsbawm offered both quantitative support for the Hammonds' bleak image of the Industrial Revolution and defended their contention that living standards were subjective. Nothing was specifically Marxist about either Hill's or Hobsbawm's positions in these controversies, although the outcomes of these debates had important implications for the Marxist interpretation of English history. At stake was Marx's contention that a revolutionary upheaval was *necessary* for the full flowering of capitalism and, by implication, socialism.

The Group's Popular Front mentality also played a role in the creation of the social history journal *Past and Present*. Originally conceived by John Morris and elaborated on in Group discussions, the journal was to be a forum for Marxist and non-Marxist historians alarmed at the growing tide of conservative historiography. In a memoir celebrating the journal's thirtieth birthday, Hilton, Hill, and Hobsbawm described it this way:

> *In short, we wished to draw the line . . . between what we saw as a minority of committed historical (and political) conservatives, not to mention the anti-Communist crusaders, and a potentially large body of those who had a common approach to history, whether they were Marxists or not. We were thus trying to continue, or to revive, in the post-war period the politics of broad unity we had learned in the days of pre-war anti-Fascism.[31]*

The name was borrowed (aside from the obvious reference to Carlyle's book) from a postwar series of history texts that included both Marxist and non-Marxist work.[32]

If originally framed as a Popular Front project, *Past and Present* was also affected by the Cold War environment. In the memoir the founders claimed that, after the early planning stages, they wanted the journal to be independent of both the Party's influence and the Group's influence.[33] Yet the Group's own deliberations do not fully corroborate this contention. According to the Group's minutes, the historians wanted non-Party historians to be involved in the project, but they were determined that the new journal would "remain firmly under the control of the Historians' Group."[34] This does not mean that the earliest non-Communist supporters of the journal were deceived, exploited, or used for some pernicious hidden agenda. But the historians would have likely resisted losing control over the venture, a fact glossed over by Hobsbawm and company in their memoir.

In fact, the Historians' Group itself never established direct control over *Past and Present*, but Marxist historians dominated the journal in its earliest years. The editor and assistant editor of the first issue were Morris and Hobsbawm, while Hill, Hilton, Dobb, and Childe were on the editorial board. The only non-Marxists involved were R. R. Betts, a historian of Eastern Europe; A. H. M. Jones, who specialized in ancient history; and Geoffrey Barraclough. (Barraclough resigned from the editorial board after the first issue, although apparently not for political reasons.) As if to compensate for their numerical domination, Communist historians were more than willing to accommodate the few non-Marxists who would work with them. Significantly, they allowed them a de facto right of veto over any manuscript, a right apparently never exercised.[35]

In 1959 the journal's internal structure was transformed. Several more non-Marxist scholars joined the editorial board, and the subtitle "a journal of scientific history" was replaced by the neutral and innocuous "a journal of historical studies."[36] The authors of the memoir cited this change as being consistent with their original aspirations.[37] This was undoubtedly true in 1959, although Lawrence Stone remembered a sustained argument with the journal's old guard over changing the subtitle.[38] But the situation of Marxist historians had changed since the project's conception. As a consequence of the 1956 crisis, many of them resigned from the Party, and the Historians' Group disintegrated. There was a void in their lives. In the early 1950s the situation was different. They might have wanted to be part of a Popular Front coalition, but only one that, at least in a broad sense, would be under their direction. As Hobsbawm suggested: "In short, we were as unsectarian as it was possible to be in those years."[39]

During the Cold War years Marxist historians felt beleaguered, defensive, and isolated. Despite their professed goal of establishing a progressive coalition of historians, they frequently felt and acted more like an embattled minority in a hostile environment. Hill recalled that members of the Oxford establishment regarded him as a "tame" and therefore acceptable Marxist, and they regarded a Communist in their midst as proof of their liberalism. They were also intent on not making the same error again and hiring another Red.[40] Hilton and Hobsbawm were certain that their failure to be offered permanent positions at Oxford and Cambridge, though they were under consideration for them, was because of their politics, not their scholarship.[41] It is noteworthy that—Hill notwithstanding—none of the Marxist historians of this generation, despite international recognition, would ever hold permanent positions at Oxford or Cambridge.

In the polarized climate of the "two camps," the Historians' Group, like all Communists, uncritically defended the Soviet Union and Stalin. Such defenses, of course, did not begin in the 1950s, but they attained new levels of rhetorical excess in the highly strained Cold War atmosphere. One particularly dramatic example was the *Modern Quarterly* issue at the time of Stalin's death. J. D. Bernal, the illustrious Nobel Prize winner, saluted Stalin's achievement as a *scientist*: both his contribution to the social sciences and his promotion of "the new, expanding and popular science."[42] Christopher Hill was no less admiring. In his contribution, "Stalin and the Science of History," he praised the Soviet leader's masterful synthesis of theory and practice. Stalin's writings on history were worthy of consideration:

> First, because he was a very great and penetrating thinker, who on any subject was apt to break through the cobwebs of academic argument to the heart of the matter; secondly, because he was a highly responsible leader, who expressed a view only after mature consideration and weighing the opinion of experts in the subject. His statements, therefore, approximate to the highest wisdom of the collective thought of the USSR.[43]

It is no wonder that Hill was later embarrassed by this essay.[44]

E. P. Thompson's writings were also replete with what he once described as "Stalinist pieties."[45] He was specifically speaking about his book on William Morris, a text that, though a pioneering study, was grounded in Cold War politics. Thompson's interest in Morris was part of a larger Communist project to create an English revolutionary tradition. But the book grew out of a paper given at a conference on the American threat to British culture, where Thompson attacked an American academic for appropriating Morris for reactionary political purposes. In the book Thompson portrayed the English poet and designer as a precursor of British communism whose utopian vision was being actualized in the Soviet Union: "[T]o-day visitors return from the Soviet Union with stories of the poet's dream already fulfilled. Yesterday, in the Soviet Union, the Communists were struggling against every difficulty to build up their industry to the level of the leading capitalist powers: to-day they have before them Stalin's blue-print of the advance to Communism."[46] Like other Communist intellectuals of the period, Thompson's work felt the effects of an uncritical acceptance of the Party's version of politics and theory, in his own words, "casuistries explaining away what one should have repudiated in the character of Stalinism."[47] It was not until 1956 that he began to openly question it.

During the Cold War, Communists were not alone in using inflammatory and divisive rhetoric. In the *Times Literary Supplement*, for instance, a ferocious anticommunist campaign distorted and caricatured Marxist positions. One writer, anonymous in the *TLS* tradition, used a review of Jack Lindsay's *Byzantium into Europe* as an occasion to condemn the pernicious influence of Marxism in universities. The reviewer argued that, because historical materialism was ipso facto impervious to empirical criticism, it violated the canons of Western scholarship. This in turn raised the question whether Communists should be given the responsibility of teaching history.[48] Though the reviewer did not answer the question, the way that it was posed amounted to a thinly disguised call for a witch-hunt aimed at Communists.

In response to letters from Hill and Lindsay objecting to the review, the *TLS* editor used the leading article of a subsequent issue to support the reviewer's main assertions.[49] He argued that, insofar as Marxists believed the purpose of understanding history was to teach the proletariat its historical destiny, they implicitly repudiated accepted norms of research and investigation—the dialogue between facts and hypotheses.[50] He was even more emphatic than the original reviewer that universities needed to reconsider whether

Marxist historians were serving the interest of education. "It is the business of teaching historians in the universities of Europe to teach the technique of historical research and thinking which is so essential a part of the culture over which they stand guard. To employ or retain in employment a teacher who, in practice as well as in theory, repudiates that technique is a dereliction of duty."[51] While the red-baiting found in these *TLS* articles occurred much less frequently in Britain than in the United States, it nonetheless serves as a reminder that not only Communists were dogmatic during the Cold War.

III

The Historians' Group was organized by periods—ancient, medieval, early modern (sixteenth and seventeenth centuries), and nineteenth century—and included a teachers' section.[52] Subgroups varied in size, composition, and importance. The nineteenth-century section, for instance, had about forty members, the majority of whom were nonacademics, while the ancient history section consisted of a small group of professional historians.[53] The most significant of them, it seems, focused on early modern times and the nineteenth century, the periods with which British Marxist historians have been most closely associated.

In a *Communist Review* article Daphne May observed that the Historians' Group had two principal functions. First, it allowed Marxist historians working in similar areas to discuss fundamental historical problems. "The argument and criticism should enable us to improve the quality of our individual writing and teaching, and—more than that—help us to make really creative contributions to Marxist theory."[54] The Group's second function was to make historical work "politically useful."[55] The Group's sustained effort at portraying the Party as the inheritor of the English democratic tradition, an extension of the prewar Popular Front agenda, was an example.[56]

A sporadic concern surfaced among party members over whether the Group was sufficiently sensitive to the practical applications of its work. At a Group committee meeting on 8 July 1950 one participant argued, "The tendency to academic sectarianism prevalent amongst the academic members must be combated sharply."[57] And clearly unhappy with the academic historians' control of the Group's agenda, Betty Grant complained of the lack of involvement of the nineteenth-century section in the affairs of the labor movement.[58] She viewed the study of local history as an alternative practice, for it would bring historians directly in touch with people in the Party and the working-class movement.[59] Defending the professional historians and the importance of specialized research, Rodney Hilton argued that historical work could be a valuable political practice, even if the dividends were not immediately apparent: "The battle of ideas had to be fought indirectly as well as directly, and especially in the universities themselves. It could change the opinions of students, future teachers, and opinion formers."[60] Despite Hilton's argument, the historians probably always felt somewhat anxious about producing historical texts for purely academic audiences—whatever the ultimate political stakes. How were they to successfully meet the demands of both professional scholarship and political militancy? How were they to bring together theory and practice? It is a quandary that has persistently plagued British Marxist debates and other Left-wing academic discussions.

Despite these disagreements over theory and practice, from the Party's viewpoint the Group was "almost certainly the most flourishing and satisfactory" of the various professional and cultural groups under the national cultural committee's authority.[61] The historians "were as loyal, active and committed a group of Communists as any, if only because" they "felt that Marxism implied membership of the Party."[62] In tandem with the leadership, Group members believed that "history—the development of capitalism to its present stage, especially in our own country, which Marx himself had studied—had put our struggles on its agenda and guaranteed our final victory."[63]

In general, the Group was not pressured to comply with some specific notion of orthodoxy; neither was it subject to overt censorship. Rather, the Group censored itself. That is, the historians intuitively seemed to have known the boundaries of their autonomy and independence and scrupulously avoided any transgression. This kind of self-censorship was partially responsible for the Group's conspicuous silence on twentieth-century history—a sensitive area of interpretation for Communists. Hobsbawm, one of the few historians from the Group to remain in the Party after 1956, continued to feel this restraint.[64]

Despite the stifling Cold War atmosphere that adversely affected intellectual debate, the Historians' Group broadened rather than narrowed the intellectual horizons of Marxist historiography. In his memoir, Hobsbawm offered several reasons why this should have been the case.[65] He argued that, even during the worst years of Stalinist orthodoxy, it was possible to debate historical issues that did not infringe directly on Party policy. He pointed out that Communist intellectuals were encouraged to critically read the classic Marxist texts, a position bolstered by Stalin's own authority. Most importantly, he observed that no official positions had been taken on long stretches of British history, while other positions, sanctioned in the USSR and Eastern Europe by Stalinist orthodoxy, were unknown in Britain. "Such accepted interpretations as existed came mainly from ourselves . . . and were therefore much more open to free debate than if they had carried the byline of Stalin or Zhdanov."[66]

Another explanation for Marxist historians' work being relatively undogmatic is their isolated position in English intellectual life. The historians were fully aware that an educated public receptive to—or even familiar with—Marxist terminology did not exist. They also realized that British academics were only too willing to dismiss their work as "dogmatic oversimplification and propagandist jargon." They were thus compelled by circumstance to rigorously adhere to the established criteria of historical scholarship and to write in a language a general readership could easily grasp.

If Marxist historians submitted to the conventions of historical scholarship, it was not only a tactical move taken to attract the attention of fellow academics. They shared with their bourgeois colleagues crucial assumptions about the nature of the historian's enterprise. Foremost among these was the belief in the objective nature of historical knowledge and an acceptance of the empirical controls established by the profession. Marxists might have believed that their own way of thinking—historical materialism—was scientific, and they perceived the thought of contending approaches as ideological, but they, no less than other historians, subscribed to the realist, objectivist, and antirelativist ideals that dominated the profession. As they expressed it in the first issue of *Past and Present*: "We believe that the methods of reason and science are at least as applicable to history as to geology, palaeontology, ecology or meteorology, though the process of change among humans is immensely more complex."[67]

For Marxist historians the Historians' Group was an immensely stimulating experience, a major source of intellectual growth and development. Christopher Hill remembered his years in the Group as the most exciting of his intellectual career.[68] John Saville recalled an atmosphere in which everything, with the notable exception of the twentieth century, was subject to questioning and criticism: nothing was sacred, including Marx.[69] In his contribution to the Hill festschrift, Rodney Hilton wrote that the Group's deliberations "emerged simultaneously and were a great stimulus to research."[70] Perhaps Hobsbawm summed it up best: "Physical austerity, intellectual excitement, political passion and friendship are probably what the survivors of those years remember best—but also a sense of equality. . . . [A]ll of us were equally explorers of largely unknown territory. Few of us hesitated to speak in discussion, even fewer to criticize, none to accept criticism."[71]

IV

Part of the reason the historians' deliberations were so fruitful was that for the fifties they had a relatively open conception of historical materialism. They were unquestionably ardent defenders of orthodox Marxism. Their thinking was limited at times by a reductionist understanding of the base/superstructure relationship, an economistic view of class relations, and a reluctance to confront countervailing evidence. Yet they appreciated the enormous complexity of the historical process and were cognizant of the many difficulties that arose from employing Marxist categories in their work. In short, Communist historians were torn between their commitment to orthodoxy and their acceptance of the profession's norms.[72]

During the era of the Popular Front, Marxists were pulled in two theoretical directions. (1) They regarded Marxism as a science guaranteeing the collapse of capitalism and the triumph of the proletariat. This conviction continued an established tradition originating in the later writings of Engels and the orthodox theorists of the Second International. (2) Yet they also saw that in the face of fascism, faith in historical inevitability was no substitute for determined political action. Indeed, Communists were—despite the obvious contradiction—equally committed to a philosophy of heroic self-sacrifice and "voluntarism." Or as James Klugmann put it: " 'There is nothing a Bolshevik cannot do,' we used to say, and therefore we would 'will' things."[73]

The conflict between "inevitability" and "voluntarism" during this period was by no means a singular event in the history of Marxism. It pervaded debates within the pre-1914 German Social Democratic Party among Edward Bernstein, Karl Kautsky, and

Rosa Luxemburg. In addition, this dichotomy may be regarded as a specific case of a wider conflict in the Marxist tradition: the opposition between "structure" and "human agency." Such an opposition and tension can be traced to Marx's own writings, notably in the immensely suggestive but profoundly enigmatic assertion, "Men make their own history, but they do not make it just as they please; they do not make it under circumstances chosen by themselves, but under circumstances directly found, given and transmitted from the past."[74] Indeed, a principal debate running through the history of Marxist theory has been between those who emphasized human agency and those who emphasized structure.

After 1956, historians and cultural theorists became acutely aware of the conflict between structure and agency, determinism and freedom in Marxism; they began to reformulate the theory so that it did not rely on historical guarantees. But in the 1940s and early 1950s, Marxists seemed less aware of apparent conflicts and contradictions. Indeed, the Communist historians adhered to two historical theories. One interpretation was determinist and functionalist, regarding historical figures as acting in accordance with the laws of history; it was founded on the inevitability of socialist triumph. The other interpretation emphasized the class struggle and recognized the significance of culture, ideas, and human agency; it was closely associated with the voluntarist mentality of the Popular Front.

Marxist historians' macro view of history was derived principally, though not exclusively, from Marx's 1859 preface to *A Contribution to the Critique of Political Economy*. According to this text, the aim of the historical process was the liberation of productive forces—an achievement that was only possible by means of a socialist transformation. For Marxist historians, history recorded human beings' progressive appropriation of nature, their growing liberation from scarcity, and their ever-widening ability to rise above contingencies. But productive forces could not be analyzed in isolation. Marxism was not a form of economic or technological determinism: "a dull record of economic changes producing inevitable changes."[75] Rather, the productive forces had to be considered in relationship to the historically specific social relations of production and the complex of superstructures to which those relations gave rise. Or in Hilton's words: "Society and its movement must be examined in their totality, for otherwise the significance of uneven developments, and of contradictions, between the economic foundation of society, and its ideas and institutions, cannot be appreciated."[76] British Marxists, no less than members of the Frankfurt School, viewed history and society as a totality.

The historians' commitment to total history simultaneously implied a critique of narrow specialist approaches and advocacy of an interdisciplinary methodology. Moreover, even during the most doctrinaire years of Stalin's rule, British Communist historians never regarded the superstructure as a mere reflection of the economic base, nor did they minimize the importance of politics and ideology. "[T]he Marxist," in Hill's words, "does not deny the influence of ideas on history because he postulates an ultimate economic origin for those ideas."[77]

Yet this "productionist" account was teleological and functionalist. The historians tended to evaluate historical actors and classes on the basis of their contribution to the growth of productive forces. Hill, for example, argued that individual freedom involved recognizing what was historically progressive and consciously cooperating to bring it about, and he viewed individual men and women as "the instruments through which social change is effected."[78] In this context, class struggle was relegated to a secondary role in the historical process, an expression of the contradictions between the forces and relations of production. Such a view was most apparent in the historians' view of the transition between feudalism and capitalism (see discussion later in this chapter).

The second theoretical framework used by Marxist historians was based on Marx's and Engels's thinking about concrete history. Although the historians were affected by several works, the one text that most influenced them was the *Selected Correspondence*, translated, edited, and annotated by Dona Torr.[79] Torr's selection of letters represented Marx and Engels as political and social theorists with an astute sense of history and a detailed knowledge of contemporary politics. They continually revised their ideas in accordance with new evidence, were preoccupied with the political forms of the class struggle in all its complexity, and were concerned with historical specificity. The *Selected Correspondence* included some of Marx's and Engels's most important theoretical reflections on historical materialism—most importantly, Engels's warning that the materialist conception of history was a "guide to study," not a formula to be rigidly applied, and his observation that the economic structure of society was the ultimate—not the only—influence on historical outcomes. In short, the text stimulated critical thinking and concrete historical research. Predominantly from this text, British Marxists derived their conception of what it meant to be Marxist historians, a fact acknowledged by several members of the Group.[80]

In the spirit of the *Selected Correspondence* and other of Marx's and Engels's historical writings, Marxist historians saw the class struggle, in Hill's terms, as "the motive force in history."[81] From this point of view, the unequal class relations that resulted from exploitative modes of production were responsible for epochal conflict. A crucial distinction here was between the "objective" and "subjective" components of class. "Objective" referred to the structural basis of class relations; "subjective" described the growth of class consciousness, the process whereby the exploited class or classes became subjectively and experientially aware of objective conditions and moved to resist them or, in highly developed circumstances, overthrow them. It was the subjective component of class that Marxist historians made the subject of "history from below." When viewed from the perspective of the contradictions between the forces and relations of production, the class struggle was accorded a secondary status. However, when examined in historically specific terms with its own consequences and effects, class struggle's importance was more central. Indeed, the focus on class struggle implied a theoretical alternative to the rigid determinism of the productionist model. This focus made possible a greater emphasis on consciousness, experience, ideas, and culture; it granted an enlarged role to human agency in the making of history; and it escaped the determinist straitjacket by seeing historical outcomes as being shaped by both social being and social consciousness. In the early 1950s Marxist historians believed in both of these historical interpretations, while being blind to the contradictions between them. It was the second to which they would eventually commit themselves.

V

Marxist historians' understanding of historical materialism provides an entry point into their conceptual universe—but no more. They were neither philosophers nor were most of them equipped to write about the methodological foundations of history. Besides, as Hill observed, the real test of Marxism "is in action, whether in the writing or the making of history."[82] The historians' theoretical outlook was most fully disclosed in the historiography itself.

One of the Group's major concerns was with the complex,

drawn-out, and turbulent transition from feudalism to capitalism, which in England culminated in the Civil War. Maurice Dobb was primarily responsible for the historians' conception of the "transition." Dobb joined the Party in 1921 and became a lecturer in economics at Cambridge in 1924. In the 1920s he was the only Communist to hold an academic position in a British university. During a fifty-year career Dobb made numerous contributions to economic history and theory, Soviet economic studies, and the history of economic thought. With Piero Sraffa, he edited the complete writings of David Ricardo.

Dobb's friends and associates remembered him as humble and humane. A former student recalled how Dobb "treated everyone with unfailing courtesy" and remembered his "kindness and modesty" as being "quite literally, legendary."[83] This corresponds with Hobsbawm's image of him at Cambridge: "most typically sitting in an armchair, rosy-faced, still elegant in an informal but carefully colour-checked shirt and disclaiming, against all probability, any special competence on any subject under discussion, diffidently intervening in conversation."[84] One foreign visitor remarked that he had only heard about English gentlemen but had never met one until he met Dobb.[85]

By the time Dobb was involved in the Historians' Group and *Past and Present*, he was one of British Marxism's elder statesmen. Although he greatly influenced the Group's work, he did not play a central role. He was an economist, not a historian, and he had other interests and obligations; thus, he was only sporadically involved in the Group's proceedings. Moreover, owing to his shyness and modesty, Dobb seldom spoke out during historical controversies or during Group sessions. He showed the same reticence to take part in *Past and Present* meetings.[86] Instead, Dobb influenced the Group through his writings, especially his *Studies in the Development of Capitalism*. That book established the agenda for the Group's debates in the late forties and early fifties, and it provided a detailed picture of capitalist development. It was, as Hobsbawm recalled, the historians' basic draft.[87]

Dobb's *Studies in the Development of Capitalism* was not based on his own historical research. Its originality consisted in his use of Marxist theory to create a new narrative out of recent scholarship on the origins and development of capitalism.[88] Most importantly, Dobb described the historical transition of the European economy (mostly in England) from its feudal to its capitalist stage.

Dobb's understanding of the transition was founded on his belief that the transition represented a transformation from one mode of production to another. In opposition to those who viewed feudalism as a system of interlocking obligations within the noble class and those who saw it as a self-sufficient natural economy, Dobb perceived it as a mode of production founded on class relations. Under feudal conditions the producers *controlled* their own means of production and subsistence but were *forced* by extraeconomic means of coercion—arms, custom, and law—to give most of their surplus—either in labor or goods—to the ruling class.

Dobb's explanation for the decline of feudalism followed from his understanding of its structural foundation. Like other presocialist modes of production, feudalism was threatened by internal, ultimately irresolvable contradictions—the conflict between the forces and relations of production. For Dobb, the ruling class's growing need for armaments and luxury goods proved to be incompatible with feudalism's inefficient productive methods and its inability to provide incentives to increase productivity. Feudal lords' efforts to extract greater and greater amounts of the surplus from the peasantry produced the fourteenth-century feudal crisis—an epoch of war, plague, local famines, agricultural decline, depopulation of the countryside and, consequently, a scarcity of labor.

Dobb regarded peasant rebellions and mass desertions from the manors as forms of class struggle that transformed lord-peasant relations, ultimately ensuring the end of the old economic system. Yet if Dobb believed that class struggle was the mechanism that overthrew or transformed feudal relations, he argued that it played only a contributory role; economic factors must have exercised the "outstanding influence" in deciding the fate of feudal relations. Or in his words: "[I]t seems evident that the fundamental consideration must have been the abundance or scarcity, the cheapness or dearness, of hired labor in determining whether or not the lord was willing or unwilling to commute labour-services for a money-payment, and whether this was a profitable or a profitless thing for him to do if he was forced into it."[89] Like the Marxist historians, Dobb adhered to a productionist model of historical development. Class struggle was an aspect, or manifestation of, the contradiction between the forces and relations of production—"necessary" but not in itself "sufficient" to overthrow the mode of production.[90]

Dobb not only explained the decline of the feudal mode of production, but he analyzed the rise of capitalism. In his account, capitalism appeared only after feudal disintegration had reached an advanced state of decay. While Dobb acknowledged that the evolution of capitalism was connected to the expansion of trade, he argued that the merchant class associated with it depended on existing productive relations, and hence trade expansion did not usher in the new mode of production. In Dobb's view the really revolutionary way to capitalism took place when "a section of the producers themselves accumulated capital and took to trade, and in course of time began to organize production on a capitalist basis free from the handicraft restrictions of the gilds."[91] The culmination of this initial stage in capitalist growth was the revolutionary age of the seventeenth century. It signaled the end of the old feudal order and the removal of the remaining obstacles preventing the free development of capitalist accumulation.

Dobb's *Studies in the Development of Capitalism* is best-known for its central role in the international Marxist debate over the nature of the transition from feudalism to capitalism initiated by his exchange with the American Marxist economist Paul Sweezy.[92] Within the context of the Historians' Group the most contentious issue raised by Dobb's conception of the transition was his understanding of the nature of Tudor and Stuart England. It was Dobb's contention, shared by Hill and Hilton, that England in the fifteenth and early sixteenth centuries was predominantly feudal and that the bourgeoisie became the dominant force in both society and state only during the Civil War.

To appreciate the resonance of this issue in Marxist historiography, we must return to the Popular Front. As a result of its policy shift in the mid-1930s, the British CP proclaimed itself the inheritor of the English democratic tradition and the party of the common people. This shift ushered in a new way of looking at history. Historical events such as the Civil War, usually downplayed because of their bourgeois inadequacies, were presented in a new light. Communists now viewed the Civil War as a pivotal moment in the creation of the English democratic tradition, as a decisive phase in socialist theoretical development, and as a revolution, not an interregnum. Joseph Needham captured this new spirit: "[I]t is of much importance to-day, that the leaders of the socialists of Cromwell's time were true-born Englishmen every one, and indeed that it was in England, our England of the game-laws and the factory children, that men first saw the vision of the co-operative social commonwealth, where the iniquity of class should for ever be swept away."[93]

Christopher Hill is the Marxist historian most closely associated with the seventeenth century. Hill's fascination with this turbulent epoch originated when as an undergraduate at Balliol College he fell in love with the Metaphysical poets—their sense of ambivalence and conflict, their "double heart." He saw their poetry as mirroring the social turmoil of the time, an age reminiscent of his own.[94] Hill soon discovered that Marxism was the only system of thought that was able to grasp the complexity of these relationships. The Marxist method "linked the 'double heart' of which the Metaphysical poets were so poignantly aware to the social conflicts, which were ultimately those of moral standards and of religious and philosophical outlook, to the deep political and social conflicts which in 1642 were to break out into civil war."[95] Originally drawn to Marxism as a method, Hill quickly embraced it as a political practice.

Hill was impatient with the Oxford environment, and he originally saw an academic career as the "ultimate defeat." But when his first career choice as a BBC correspondent never materialized, he continued his academic studies. He used a two-year advanced research fellowship from All Souls College to develop a materialist interpretation of the Civil War.[96] He began this project when Marxism was still a "dirty word" in the "unregenerate Oxford" of the early thirties. Tawney's most influential essays on the historical significance of the Civil War and Morton's preliminary discussion of the seventeenth century in *A People's History of England* were still future events. Models for Marxist historical research in England scarcely existed.[97]

Hill used his fellowship in two ways. He spent the first year studying the Marxist classics and became convinced that these texts contained a fully developed theory of the Civil War. In his words: "They never wrote a consecutive history of the period, and the niggling may be able to find verbal inconsistencies. But their view of the revolution as a whole is consistent and illuminating."[98] During the second year he traveled to the Soviet Union to see the Bolshevik regime for himself and to meet Soviet scholars whom he understood had done research on the seventeenth century.[99]

Hill's trip to the Soviet Union was a pivotal moment in his life. Deeply moved by the Russian people's optimism and egalitarian spirit, he concluded that the Revolution was succeeding, and he joined the Communist Party upon returning to England.[100] He also met the Soviet historians whom he had heard about. He found their work, though sometimes founded on inadequate evidence, to be a major step in constructing a Marxist understanding of the period. Hill was especially impressed by their sensitivity to land issues, which, he observed, were "as familiar to them as they seem obscure and remote to us."[101]

Hill's first complete analysis of the Civil War was contained in his 1940 essay "The English Revolution 1640," originally published as part of a volume commemorating the tercentenary of the revolt.[102] Written for a general audience and published under the auspices of the British CP, it was blunt, militant, iconoclastic, and polemical. Hill argued that the seventeenth-century revolution was not an interregnum, an "unfortunate accident" connecting two periods of "the old constitution normally developing" but a decisive turning point in the nation's historical development.[103] It was a "bourgeois revolution" comparable to the French Revolution of 1789.

One critical aspect of Hill's early text was his conception of "bourgeois revolution." In using this term he did not mean that the bourgeoisie were the creators of the revolution, as they had been in France. Indeed, Hill acknowledged that in the English revolt a segment of the gentry and the aristocracy were on the side of Parliament. Rather, he argued that the Civil War was a bourgeois revolution in a Marxist sense: it destroyed the old feudal regime and made possible the free development of capitalism. The bourgeois class, rather than its primary agents, was the beneficiary of the revolution. Hill defended this position his entire academic career.

Hill's English Revolution essay was not universally accepted by party intellectuals. Ironically, it was more enthusiastically reviewed in the *London Evening Standard* than in *Labour Monthly*, the official party journal.[104] The attack was initially launched by the German émigré historian, Jürgen Kuczynski, with the support of Andrew Rothstein and Palme Dutt, the guardian of Marxist orthodoxy in the Party.[105] Under the pseudonym of P.F., Kuczynski attacked Hill's thesis, arguing that capitalism was already the dominant mode of production in the sixteenth century and that the bourgeois revolution had taken place long before 1640. He viewed the Civil War as a counterrevolution launched by those remnants of the feudal aristocracy who refused to relinquish their power.

At the time of Kuczynski's attack, Hill was a young, unknown academic without enough political influence and prestige to triumph over such formidable opponents. But he found allies: Douglas Garman, Dona Torr, and, to a lesser extent, Maurice Dobb. Torr, in particular, played a leading role in championing Hill's position, and her support proved crucial to his successful defense of it. As a result of this collaboration, they developed a close and productive intellectual and personal friendship that lasted until her death in the 1950s.

The English Civil War debate was not purely historiographical. Like many Marxist controversies, the debate had political implications. As Garman argued, the *logical terminus* of Kuczynski's case was "reformist," a denial of the historical necessity of revolution. If the Civil War was not a bourgeois revolution and, in fact, the transition had happened earlier over a gradual period of time, then it was possible a socialist transition might be achieved the same way. Such a possibility, Garman suggested, was a vindication of a reformist, evolutionary position, unacceptable to any devoted Communist.[106]

The dispute arising from Hill's essay was not decided in the pages of *Labour Monthly* where the major protagonists had intervened, but behind closed doors with the Party hierarchy supervising the proceedings.[107] Hill remembered the critical moment in the conflict occurring when a supporter of the Kuczynski position invoked the authority of the historian Mikhail Pokrovsky, who in the late 1920s and early 1930s had defined correct historical practice in the Soviet Union. While introducing Pokrovsky's name was intended to indicate the stamp of orthodoxy, the strategy backfired because further discussion revealed that Pokrovsky had been subsequently discredited.[108] This revelation does not seem to have led to an immediate resolution of the conflict, but it paved the way for the acceptance of Hill's argument. Hill's views prevailed because they eventually were judged to be in harmony with orthodoxy.

After the war the publication of Dobb's *Studies in the Development of Capitalism*, in tandem with preparations for the tercentenary celebration of the English Revolution, rekindled the debate on Tudor and Stuart England. Support for Kuczynski's position had evaporated, and Hill's thesis was modified by Dobb, who stressed that merchant capital perpetuated the old order. But the thesis remained controversial.

Victor Kiernan emerged as the principal critic of what was now the majority position.[109] Ever impatient with orthodoxy, Kiernan posed difficult and probing questions based on an encyclopedic knowledge of history.[110] His reluctance to accept the majority view grew out of his skepticism that the age of Elizabeth and Shakespeare could be characterized as feudal.[111] Kiernan was uncomfortable with Marxists' insistence on a rigid dividing line between the feudal and capitalist epochs, and he was uncertain whether the Civil War affected the immediate future of capitalism as dramatically as British Marxists assumed. "The precise ways," he wrote, "in which existing institutions impeded the development of the new forces have to be defined exactly and estimated realistically. It has then to be shown precisely how the new energies were liberated by the institutional changes brought about by the revolution. These changes were not so extensive as is sometimes supposed."[112]

Kiernan's doubts about the claims made for the role of the revolution formed the point of departure for his critique of Dobb and Hill. Kiernan argued that they exaggerated the feudal and retrogressive elements in merchant capital, underestimated the role of the Tudors in advancing capitalist interests, and magnified the feudal barriers arresting capitalist development in the seventeenth century. He conceived of the bourgeois revolution as a much more gradual process—a series of transformations over a period of centuries. "This mode of thought in turn involved the argument that the bourgeois revolution in any country proceeds by distinct stages, of which in England 1485 would be one and 1832 another, and 1642 only the biggest of a number of leaps."[113] Kiernan was inclined to see 1485 as the point at which the bourgeoisie assumed control of the state.

Kiernan's critique, and the responses that it provoked, afford a rare glimpse into the conceptual world of British Marxist historians, only rarely revealed in their published writings. The debate demonstrates the extent to which their understanding of historical evidence was connected to their commitment to revolutionary theory and politics. It also suggests the conflict between, on the one hand, their awareness of the complexity of the historical process and acceptance of the norms of the historical profession, and, on the other, their desire to defend Marxist orthodoxy.

At one level the debate hinged on historiographical issues. As the principal defender of the orthodox position, Hill reiterated his view that the Tudor monarchy was essentially feudal. He acknowledged that the monarchy had formed a temporary alliance with the gentry and merchant class in the sixteenth century, but he insisted that it ultimately responded to capitalist expansion by fostering monopolies, opposing enclosures, and attacking Puritanism—the principal form of bourgeois ideology.

At another level Hill's response was theoretical and political. His defense was based on a specific conception of the "transition" and the role of the bourgeois revolution within it. Hill argued that only when capitalism had penetrated civil society, when the bourgeoisie were politically mature, and when Puritan ideology was sufficiently developed "to give the rising bourgeois class confidence for its task" did the bourgeois revolution happen.[114] Only at this historical juncture did the ascending capitalist class assume control of the main arteries of power. In other words, Kiernan was mistaken to think that the bourgeois revolution advanced by stages. Or as Hill stated it: "The Bourgeois Revolution is not a ladder up which one advances, step by step. State power at any time is either bourgeois or it is feudal."[115]

In fact, Hill viewed Kiernan's formulation of the entire period as "politically dangerous." While granting that difficulties existed in analyzing the Tudor monarchy, he believed that Kiernan's framework was incompatible with the mainstream Marxist tradition and that it had conservative political implications. Kiernan's argument offered support to bourgeois intellectuals who wanted to continually push back the origins of capitalism so as to prove it was an "eternal category." It corroborated the traditional image of English development as "peculiar, peaceful, nonrevolutionary." And Kiernan implicitly negated a tradition of Marxist thinking on the Civil War from Marx and Engels to the Soviet historians. "We, as Marxist historians," Hill pleaded, "find strong (bourgeois) resistance to the Marxist categories, naturally. All the more reason for refining our analysis *within* those categories, not for abandoning them, and with them all the revolutionary traditions of 1640 and of our own part."[116] For Hill, Marxist historians had to remain united to defeat the bourgeois enemy and to preserve the English revolutionary heritage. This meant preserving the orthodox view rather than supplanting it.

In spite of Hill's denial, Kiernan's critique posed difficult problems for Marxists trying to understand England of the sixteenth and seventeenth centuries. But Kiernan's position had problems of its own. He vacillated between thinking that the bourgeois revolution passed through a sequence of stages in which 1642 was only an "important incident" to believing that "the Revolution is the greatest transaction in English history."[117] His assertion that 1485 was a pivotal moment in the transference of state power was as problematic as the alternative position that it was 1642. Kiernan withdrew his critique, but true to form he restated his reservations "as detached comments or questions of detail, not as part of a general criticism of the point of view put forward by C. Hill, M. Dobb and others."[118] His assault on orthodoxy, and the debate that followed, signified the resiliency and constraints, open-mindedness and dogmatism, limits and possibilities of British Marxist historiography in these years. Only after a shift in the political and intellectual atmosphere was a more open and thorough critical examination possible.

VI

Marxist historians saw themselves as restoring to the working class and progressive movements their revolutionary past, a heritage suppressed by several centuries of ruling-class obfuscation. Or as Hill expressed it: "Marxism restores unity to history because it restores real, live, working and suffering men and women to the center of the story."[119] Founding their work on the theory of class struggle, Marxist historians aspired to recover the experience of the common people, to create a "history from below." The goal of recovering the political culture of the oppressed inspired many historical texts most closely associated with British Marxism, *The Making of the English Working Class* being the most famous.

Dona Torr was instrumental in developing this project. Torr was a founding member of the British CP and an acknowledged authority on Marx. She was a serious student of history, working for years on a multivolume biography of Tom Mann and his era, which was never completed but published posthumously.[120] According to Thompson, the published version did not do justice to her erudition. Torr was not a founder of the Historians' Group, but, as Hill recalled, she was "at once at home in it, for it gave her the sort of intellectual stimulus of a specifically academic historical kind that she had hitherto lacked."[121] Hill and Thompson believed that Torr used her influence with the Party hierarchy to protect the Group's autonomy.[122]

Torr's greatest impact was on Hill, Saville, and Thompson. Her admirers remembered her as an intellectual of enormous power, an exceedingly tough and severe critic who generously gave of her time. According to Saville, she would push people hard but be encouraging and supportive as well.[123] To Thompson, she was the mentor he never knew as a student at Cambridge. In the foreword to *William Morris: Romantic to Revolutionary* he wrote: "It has been a privilege and an education to be associated so closely with a Communist scholar so versatile, so distinguished, and so generous with her gifts."[124] Of her admirers, Hill perhaps best summed up their feelings: "In fact, she knew more, had thought more about history than any of us; moreover, she put her work, learning, and wisdom at our disposal."[125]

Historians in the Group were not unanimous in their feelings about Torr. Some members found her conception of Marxist theory exceedingly rigid and orthodox. Hilton felt that she pushed the Group toward defending approved Party positions.[126] Hobsbawm recognized that she was a fine scholar, but he thought she was too willing to accept the truth of Marxist theory a priori. He cited as an example her behind-the-scenes effort to guarantee the victory of orthodoxy in the Absolutism controversy and her insistence that the world fundamentally changed as a result of the Russian Revolution.[127] Hill was more sympathetic. He conceded that she was an ardent defender of Marxism-Leninism, but he believed that her defense of orthodox Marxism was not to be confused with that of a Party hack like Palme Dutt.[128] What cannot be doubted is that Torr played a major role in spurring on the historians to recover the common people's struggle against oppression and domination.

Torr's historical vision of that struggle complemented Dobb's notion of the "transition" in *Studies in the Development of Capitalism.* She recognized two historical phases in English history. The first, inaugurated by the English Peasant Rising of 1381, reached its culmination in the radical movements of the English Revolution. It was rooted in the primitive accumulation of capital, the collapse of the open field system, and the end of the village's tradition of common rights. Accordingly, the people's resistance during these years was defensive, consisting either of striving to preserve long-established customs or of protesting in the name of "lost rights." Torr saw the second phase of English history as being ushered in by the Industrial Revolution—the final stage whereby the common people were transformed from a peasantry into a working class. The memories of the village were displaced by working-class consciousness; the "conscious class struggle" displaced the theory of lost rights and assumed a revolutionary meaning. Yet Torr stressed that the working-class movement had an organic connection with the past, a theme that would recur time and again in British Marxist historiography.

Torr's historical account of popular resistance was felt both explicitly and implicitly. One of Hilton's major concerns had been to situate the English Peasant Rising in the context of a wider tradition of peasant resistance, as was apparent in his 1951 essay "Peasant Movements in England before 1381." Hilton portrayed the Peasant Rebellion as the culmination of nearly two centuries of class struggle and as anticipating the seventeenth-century revolt. He viewed John Ball as an ancestor of Colonel Thomas Rainborough, evidence in his view of a tradition of resistance "as ancient as the more publicized traditions of reverence for old-established institutions."[129]

The most compelling case for a theory of lost rights was Hill's "The Norman Yoke," an essay "stimulated by" and "greatly benefiting from" discussions with Torr and appearing in the festschrift in her honor.[130] The Norman Yoke myth was a centerpiece of the radical Whig tradition. It contrasted the free, equal, and harmonious existence of the Anglo-Saxons with the tyrannical rule of the Norman kings after the Conquest. Yet despite their subjection to the Norman Yoke, the people kept their former way of life alive as a collective memory. Their remembrance of lost rights inspired them to resist tyranny and oppression and ultimately to create English democracy.

Hill realized that this myth could not adequately explain the course of English history. Rather, he was interested in it as a "political ideology"—an embryonic theory of class politics. The Norman Yoke myth was historically important because it inspired the popular classes to resist the crown, church, and landlords. It made "the permanently valid point" that ruling class interests were inherently "alien." This was true in a double sense. In contrast to the foreign roots of the ruling classes, the people's traditions were indigenous. Correlatively, it was the culture of the common people, not their rulers', that authentically represented the English way of life. Hill was, in effect, implicitly using an organic definition of culture—the idea of culture as the whole way of life of a people. His approach foreshadowed the cultural studies and cultural Marxist history of the late 1950s and 1960s.

Hill's essay was a historical account of the theory of lost rights. He demonstrated that the Norman Yoke myth was used for various political purposes, represented the aspirations of different classes and fragments within classes, and underwent perpetual transformation in accordance with shifts in historical forces. Hill argued that interpretations of the myth were rooted in class culture and struggle, but he avoided simplistic notions of class and the base/superstructure relationship. His account of the decline of the Norman Yoke theory was clearly indebted to Torr. Like Torr, he believed that the appeal of lost rights was connected to the evaporating memory of village life. The working classes, on the other hand, had the capability to shape the future. The myth of a golden age was displaced by a theory of history, that is, scientific socialism. In short, Hill believed that the theory of lost rights was supplanted by historical materialism.

In "The Norman Yoke" Hill argued that Marxism dialectically resolved the apparent contradictions of English intellectual and political traditions. "Marxism, by combining Burke's sense of history with Paine's sense of justice, gives us an approach both to the study of the past and to political action immeasurably superior to any which preceded it."[131] Hill's attempt to "naturalize" or "anglicize" Marxism was part of a broader effort at building a native revolutionary tradition—an extension of the Popular Front agenda. Marxist historians claimed a theoretical lineage no less authentic than the people's, and they refuted the idea that Marxist theory was incompatible with Englishness. They saw Marxism as bringing together—and perhaps superseding—two traditions of dissent that had failed to converge: English popular resistance and the alternative vision of Romanticism.

Marxist historians were particularly drawn to English Romanticism. Although the Romantics failed to recognize the historical significance of the working class, their writings paralleled the protests from below. Their nostalgia for a harmonious rural past—Merry Old England—was analogous to the people's collective memories of lost rights. Like the early socialists, the Romantics opposed triumphant liberalism, utilitarianism, and laissez-faire. In its early stages, at least, they championed the French Revolution.

Victor Kiernan brought together these various themes in a 1954 essay on Wordsworth, who, in Kiernan's words, "experienced longer and more urgently" than any of the other Romantic poets "the problem of the relation between artist and people, art and life, individual and mass."[132] Kiernan praised Wordsworth's democratic spirit, his passionate hatred of government, poverty, and industrialization, his devotion to the old rural ways, and his admiration for the unadorned life of the common laborer. Yet he also emphasized that Wordsworth was incapable of more than sympathy for the oppressed: "He missed the good side because he had no faith in men's ability to control what they had created. He knew nothing of factory workers, and even when he had asserted most ardently the survival of virtue in the rustic poor, he had been thinking too much of passive resistance to life, too little of active control of circumstances."[133] Wordsworth was repelled by the new industrial society but had no understanding of how to transform it. It would be nearly fifty years, Kiernan wrote, "before Marx and Engels would open the leaden casket of the industrial slums from which Wordsworth . . . recoiled in horror."[134]

William Morris was the only writer rooted in the Romantic tradition to embrace the working-class movement and Marxism. While Morris was frequently lauded by Communist writers, E. P. Thompson's biography was most responsible for presenting him as a revolutionary Marxist. Morris's interpreters had either been primarily concerned with his artistic achievements—and derided his politics—or had heralded him as a forefather of the Labour Party. Thompson argued that Morris was a serious revolutionary. He portrayed Morris's life as an epic in which the poet and creative artist left behind the world of beauty, polite society, and material comfort to cross "the river of fire." He "was the first creative artist of major stature in the history of the world to take his stand, consciously and without shadow of compromise, with the revolutionary working class: to participate in the day-to-day work of building the Socialist movement."[135] Morris's development as a socialist would have been incomplete were it not for his discovery of Marxism. He fused a Marxist analysis of the capitalist social process, a moral critique of industrialization, and a utopian vision of the future. It resulted in "moral realism."

The historians' recovery of the Romantics for the Communist movement points toward a more general dimension of their practice—the privileged status that they attributed to literature and poetic sensibility. This is apparent in Hill's essay "Marxism and History" in which he draws connections between Marxism and poetry, not perhaps the first association that comes to mind. "But the Marxist approach," Hill wrote, "whilst thoroughly scientific—more so indeed than that of the economic determinists—can preserve the poetic element in history and the historian's right to a standard of moral values."[136] In his Wordsworth essay Kiernan pointed to a similar relationship. "Wordsworth," he wrote, "devoted the greater part of his life to the study of political and social questions, and Marx a great part of his to the study of poetry." He concluded that contemporary poetry that ignored Marxism was "irrelevant," while "Marxism also has much to learn, that it has not yet learned, from poetry."[137]

British Marxist thought was steeped in English literary culture. During the thirties—the student years of the majority of the historians—the radical culture of the Left was dominated by writers, while many of the most prestigious Left-wing journals of the period were literary magazines. One of the key Communist theoretical debates in the late forties focused on the work of Christopher Caudwell, a literary and cultural critic. And most importantly, British intellectuals were rigorously trained in the reading of English literature. Indeed, literary culture had a dominant position in English intellectual culture as a whole, a situation that, as Raymond Williams noted, reached its apex during the fifties.[138]

Among the historians, Hill was originally drawn to Marxism because it illuminated Metaphysical poetry. His rejection of the simplest versions of the base/superstructure model—even in his early work—may have partially resulted from his understanding that seventeenth-century literary sources were essential to an understanding of the period. As he wrote in 1985: "It does not seem to me possible to understand the history of seventeenth-century England without understanding its literature, any more than it is possible fully to appreciate the literature without understanding the history."[139]

Kiernan's interest in Marxist theory was inseparable from his love and respect for the English literary tradition. One of his original historical studies used the Marxist method to understand Shakespeare, a study begun more than forty years ago and completed and published in 1993.[140] Hobsbawm's relationship to literature has been less obvious than Hill's and Kiernan's but no less important. His earliest writing included short stories and criticism, and throughout his career he studied various aspects of cultural life, including literature, from a materialist point of view.[141] Thompson's entire intellectual formation was steeped in literary culture, and, like Hobsbawm, he published short stories and poetry. As a Party member, he was best-known as a literary type, and he participated more in the cultural committee than in any other intellectual group.[142] In fact, he never intended to be a historian. He became one in the process of writing his book on William Morris. "I took no decision," he recalled. "Morris took the decision that I would have to present him. In the course of doing this I became much more serious about being a historian."[143]

In the mid-seventies Thompson revised his *William Morris* and removed the political rhetoric of his Communist youth. Significantly, the substance of the book remained the same; retrospectively, he could see that it was already a work of "muffled 'revisionism.'"[144] This revisionist tendency was true not only of Thompson but of Marxist historians in general. Despite uncritically accepting the truth of Communist practice and Marxist theory, their ideas pointed beyond orthodox confinement. When they were talking about the long sweep of history, they adhered to a rigidly determinist conception of the historical process in which human agency played a subsidiary role. But when they examined historical forms of class struggle, they did so in terms that stressed consciousness, experience, ideas, and culture. In this context, Marxist historians saw the historical process as being shaped by both social structure and human volition. Such ideas did not jell until the 1960s and 1970s, but they existed in a less developed form in the earlier people's history and historical studies of literature.

In 1956–57 most of the leading participants in the Historians' Group left the British CP in protest over the Soviet invasion of Hungary and their own Party's unwillingness to reform itself. In contrast to intellectuals who had left the Party at earlier pivotal points, they remained committed Marxists who did not reject the revolutionary tradition in which British Communists claimed to be a part. They critically extended and renewed it. While there are undoubtedly many reasons why the historians remained within the Marxist fold, surely among the most important was their participation in the Historians' Group. Despite internal and external constraints, the Group expanded the parameters of Marxist historical theory in Britain and was responsible for the beginnings of a cultural Marxist historical practice.

For the intellectual Left the 1950s was a decade of defeat. It was synonymous with a stalled working-class movement, an indifferent electorate, the withdrawal of intellectuals from politics, and a resurgent Toryism whose slogan was "you've never had it so good." Leftist intellectual culture, dominant in the thirties and forties, was displaced by a stifling conservatism founded on the revival of traditional values and a defense of Western culture defined as the best that has been thought and written. The result in Leftist circles was a kind of intellectual despair that was captured by Jimmy Porter in John Osborne's play *Look Back in Anger*: "There aren't any good, brave causes left."

Radical intellectual culture began to gradually revive in the late fifties, spurred on by the emergence of the New Left political and intellectual movement.[1] The British New Left was a heterogeneous group of ex-Communists, disaffected Labour supporters, and socialist students hopeful of renewing socialist theory and practice. They came together in response to the Suez and Hungary crises in 1956 and consolidated in a shared commitment to the Campaign for Nuclear Disarmament (CND) of the late fifties and early sixties. New Left activists attempted to create a democratic socialist politics rooted in English traditions but not bogged down by the orthodoxies of the past, a politics that acknowledged postwar economic and cultural changes. They never succeeded in creating a permanent organization, but they created a new political space on the Left, and their project was critical to the development of radical historiography and cultural studies in Britain. The theoretical and intellectual work associated with the New Left period is the subject of chapter 3; in this chapter the New Left as a movement is examined.

I

The New Left was originally formed out of two groups who produced theoretical and political journals. The *Reasoner* group was composed of former Communists, predominantly from the gener-

ation of the thirties and forties, who left the Party as a result of the
Khrushchev speech on Stalin's crimes and the Soviet invasion of
Hungary in 1956. *Universities and Left Review (ULR)* was created by
a group of Oxford students active in the opposition to British
involvement in the Suez crisis. The producers of these two journals
were to find a common ground, but their distinctive formations
also help explain their conflicts and frustrated attempts at creating
anything but a precarious unity.

The *Reasoner* and its successor the *New Reasoner* evolved from an
opposition movement within the CP dissatisfied with the leadership's response to the revelations of Khrushchev's speech at the
Twentieth Party Congress. Communist historians were in the forefront of the opposition. Although they were Party loyalists, the
historians enjoyed considerable independence and freedom, debated controversial political and theoretical issues among themselves, and never submitted to a mindless orthodoxy. They played a
prominent role in criticizing the leadership because, as John Saville
wrote at the time, they were the Party's only intellectual group in
the last ten years "who have not only tried to use their Marxist
techniques creatively, but have to some measure succeeded."[2]

According to Hobsbawm, the revelations of the Khrushchev
speech produced "the political equivalent of a nervous breakdown."[3] Not only did the historians have to face their silence over
contemporary history, but they had to explain to themselves their
uncritical acceptance of Party accounts of history since 1917, most
importantly, their own Party's self-representation. This was especially true of controversial periods like the early 1930s (when
Communists opposed social democrats as fiercely as conservatives)
or during the years of the Hitler-Stalin Pact. While the historians
were deeply troubled by what had been revealed about Soviet
history, they were, above all, worried about the implications of the
crisis for the Party's future in their own country. How could British Communists recover their credibility in the labor movement?
Could the Party learn from its past and reform its authoritarian
structure?[4] The historians believed that a precondition for the
Party's revitalization was democracy within the Party.

Marxist historians were involved in three tangible forms of protest in the 1956 crisis. Christopher Hill pushed for reform through
official channels. He served on the Commission on Inner Party
Democracy, a group ostensibly created to investigate the state of
democratic safeguards in the Party, but whose actual intent was to

defuse the revisionists' critique of democratic centralism.[5] Hill and his allies failed in their effort to shape the commission's report, but they were allowed by the Party leadership to write a minority statement—a meaningless concession meant to create the impression of a democratic process. In fact, at the Party's congress in May 1957, formal discussion of the minority report was not allowed; and though Hill, as a delegate to the conference, was able to speak in defense of it, his speech was not reported in the Party press's account of the event. He soon resigned.

A second form of protest in which Marxist historians were involved was a letter protesting the Party's support of the Soviet invasion of Hungary. Hobsbawm, Hill, Hilton, and Kiernan were among those who reaffirmed their commitment to Marxist theory but denounced the "false presentation of the facts" upon which Communists were forced to rely. They described the Party's uncritical support of Soviet aggression as an "undesirable culmination of years of distortion of fact, and the failure by British Communists to think out political problems for themselves."[6] The signatories originally intended to publish the letter in the Party newspaper, the *Daily Worker*, but the paper refused to publish it—or, more accurately, the paper ignored it—and they arranged for its publication in both the *Tribune* (30 November 1956) and the *New Statesman* (1 December 1956). This was regarded by the leadership as an act of defiance; historically, critical statements outside the Party press had been viewed as violating Communist solidarity.

The *Reasoner*, edited by John Saville and Edward Thompson, was unquestionably the most influential expression of the historians' opposition to the Communist Party leadership's position. From the onset, Saville and Thompson had played prominent roles in the opposition. Saville was among the first dissidents to have a letter published in *World News*, the principal forum of Party debate. He complained that a decline of debate and a spread of conformity within Party circles had contributed to uncritical thinking; and he accused the leadership of being unwilling "to admit that we shall stand discredited before the Labour movement unless we honestly and frankly state where we went wrong and that we will ensure, as far as we can, that similar errors are not made in the future."[7] Thompson's "Winter Wheat in Omsk," also published in *World News*, was equally critical of Party policy. Thompson claimed that British Communists' obsession with imitating the Bolsheviks had resulted in their being isolated in their own country. Most importantly, they ignored a vital tradition of native moral criticism and activism, which had inspired many political struggles of the British people.

"It should be clear now to all," he wrote, "that conscious struggle for moral principle in our political work is a vital part of our political relations with the people. The British people do not understand and will not trust a Monolith without a moral tongue. It is also clear that the best formulations can conceal shame and unreason: that we must still read Shakespeare as well as Marx."[8] Thompson's critique echoed the collective voice of the historians and his own study of William Morris. He attacked the Party for only superficially identifying with the English revolutionary tradition and using it for propaganda purposes. To reform itself, the Party would have to genuinely absorb the heritage of English popular resistance and moral critique. Thompson's socialist humanism, developed during these years, was an attempt at precisely this reform.

Saville and Dorothy and Edward Thompson had been friends for years, although they were not particularly close at the time of the Khrushchev speech. In discussing the crisis they agreed that if Communists were to regain their integrity and self-respect, they must openly and honestly discuss the Party's plight. Yet their efforts at further intervention through the pages of *World News* were frustrated. The editors rejected Saville's second letter because he already had "one crack of the whip."[9] Thompson's article was forcefully rebutted by George Matthews, who accused him of unconsciously reproducing anti-Communist caricature and promoting controversy as an end in itself.[10] Thompson's efforts at replying to Matthews's rebuttal were likewise rejected. He and Saville realized that the Party executive would not sanction an open discussion; yet they were hesitant to undertake such a discussion outside the Party press, for the leadership would certainly represent it as an act of betrayal. To avoid this stigma, they conceived of the *Reasoner*, a journal produced for and by loyal Communists such as themselves, which would stimulate a debate on the Party's condition. It was a unique venture in the history of British communism.

The *Reasoner* appeared in mid-July 1956. It consisted of thirty-two mimeographed pages, produced at Thompson's home, bearing a quotation from Marx: "To leave error unrefuted is to encourage intellectual immorality." In three issues the *Reasoner* published articles by some of the most talented intellectuals in the British Communist movement, including Doris Lessing, Rodney Hilton,

Ronald Meek, and Hyman Levy. The journal articulated the feelings of many Party members dissatisfied with the leadership's response and desirous of reform.

The *Reasoner* editors themselves set the journal's tone. In their view the uncritical acceptance of Soviet policy resulted from abandoning Marx's critical and historical method. This abandonment reflected "a fear of ideas on the part of some members" and signified "the veritable crisis of theory which has resulted from this long Ice Age."[11] In his suppressed reply to Matthews, Thompson confessed that such attitudes had contaminated the very sinews of Marxist historical work: "Increasingly we have emphasized an arbitrary selection of conclusions (some derived from nineteenth century or Russian conditions) rather than the method of historical materialism: have sought to make 'correct formulations' within a schematized system of doctrine, rather than to return again and again to social realities."[12] Thompson argued that Communists must not limit themselves to regretting their past record of sectarianism and dogmatism; they had to reexamine themselves and their movement. A precondition for this self-scrutiny was inner Party democracy.

Not surprisingly, the leadership initiated steps to end publication of the journal. After failing to convince Thompson and Saville to stop publishing on their own accord, the leadership threatened them with suspension or expulsion after the second issue appeared. Thompson and Saville found themselves in a quandary. They realized that the *Reasoner* was playing a critical role in sustaining dissent but that the hierarchy used its existence as an excuse to suppress debate in the Party press. Both men remained convinced of the need for a viable Communist Party. However, they were increasingly disillusioned with the leadership, "less and less sure that they would respond in any generous or positive way," and more aware of the stifling effect of the Party's bureaucracy.[13] Thompson and Saville decided to distribute a third issue while simultaneously announcing that they would stop publication. Inevitably, they would be suspended from Party membership, but they would avoid expulsion; thus, they would be able to continue to work for Party reform. But when the leadership without hesitation supported the Soviet invasion of Hungary in November 1956, the *Reasoner* editors became convinced that the Party had discredited itself beyond repair. In a hastily written editorial for the third issue, Thompson and Saville demanded that the leadership withdraw its support of

Soviet aggression and call for a national congress. Short of taking this step, they urged Party militants to "dissociate completely from the leadership of the British Communist Party, not to lose faith in Socialism, and to find ways of keeping together."[14] Thompson and Saville soon resigned from the Party.

By 1957–58 the great majority of the Communist historians—Hill, Hilton, Kiernan, Rudé, Thompson, and Saville—had resigned (or were about to resign) from the Party. This was a difficult decision. Most of them had been members for twenty years and believed that a Marxist commitment was unthinkable without belonging to the CP. They remained Communists when it was no longer the intellectual vogue, as it had been in the thirties, and they withstood isolation and abuse during the Cold War. Earlier generations of Communist intellectuals who left the Party at major turning points, say, 1929–33 or 1939, typically became disillusioned with radicalism as well. The historians, in contrast, remained Marxists.

Hobsbawm was the only major historian to remain a Party member. He was not unsympathetic to the dissident movement. He had been one of the signatories to the *New Statesman* letter, and, in response to George Matthews's criticism of the action, he both defended it and criticized the leadership for self-satisfaction with its political record. Yet Hobsbawm believed that the CP, though seriously flawed, was the only workers' party in Britain committed to revolution and that it might eventually reestablish itself as a political force. He also realized that if it failed to seize this opportunity, it would find itself increasingly irrelevant politically.[15] What were the alternatives? Joining the Labour Party? Being a socialist academic alienated from any working-class base? Whatever one might think of Hobsbawm's decision, Marxists outside Communist parties also have found these questions difficult to resolve.

Hobsbawm's political biography provides a less tangible reason for his remaining in the Party. His decision to become a Communist had been bound to the tragedy of European Jewry; communism, in effect, was an alternative to the disintegrating world of his youth. Although it is difficult to know precisely how he was affected by this experience, a deep personal attachment to Party membership and the international movement may have intensified his reluctance to resign. As Hobsbawm himself acknowledged: "I got into the communist movement a long, long time ago as a schoolboy in Berlin before Hitler came to power, and when you got politicised at the age of fourteen, and then stayed politicised for an awful long time, it's a long part of your life." [16] As a consequence of "1956" and de-Stalinization, Party intellectuals never again were subjected to the censorship, or threat of censorship, that existed in the early fifties. As Hobsbawm observed: "It was a good deal easier to be Marxist without constantly feeling that you had to toe the line because, by this stage, it wasn't quite clear what the line was." [17] He could not have foreseen this development when he decided to remain in the Party in the late 1950s, but it certainly made his decision easier to sustain.

Continuing the *Reasoner* project was the most concrete political expression of the historians' Marxism after they left the Party. Thompson and Saville were acutely aware of the theoretical and political crisis of Marxism. They acknowledged the "shallow growth of Marxist scholarship" in Britain and their own failure to make Marxism a "body of ideas to stimulate and excite." [18] Yet they were greatly encouraged by the *Reasoner*'s reception, and they hoped that a journal which encouraged free discussion might contribute to Marxism's renewal and growth. Significantly, Thompson and Saville did not see themselves as breaking with communism but rather as reviving an older, uncontaminated tradition of English socialist thought and practice—the tradition of Tom Mann and William Morris. [19] They saw a return to this heritage, which as historians they themselves had begun to recover, as central to a socialist revival. They wanted to create an authentic English Marxism.

The *New Reasoner: A Journal of Socialist Humanism* first appeared in the summer of 1957. Its original editorial board was dominated by ex-Communists: the novelist Doris Lessing, economists Ken Alexander and Ronald Meek, and the critic Ronald Swingler. The board was eventually enlarged to include former *Daily Worker* correspondent Malcolm MacEwen, economist Michael Barratt Brown, and two intellectuals from the Labour Left, Mervyn Jones, a writer who had resigned from the Party in 1954, and Ralph Miliband, a political scientist at the London School of Economics and a former student of Harold Laski. Christopher Hill, the art critic John Berger, the philosopher Alisdair MacIntyre, and the anthropologist Peter Worsley were among the journal's contributors. While careful to keep a certain amount of distance, Hobsbawm supported the venture and wrote for the first issue, although not on an explicitly political subject. The *New Reasoner* contained art and literary criticism, short stories, and political and theoretical analysis.

E. P. Thompson articulated the *Reasoner* group's socialist-humanist philosophy. His point of departure was a critique of Stalinism. For Thompson, Stalinism was a logical and consistent system of thought. It was an ideology, "a constellation of partisan attitudes and false, or partially false, ideas" based on abstractions rather than individual experience or social reality.[20] Stalinist ideology was composed of three elements: anti-intellectualism, moral nihilism, and a devaluing of individuals. In opposition to the false consciousness of Stalinism, Thompson advocated socialist humanism: a political philosophy that combined the liberal tradition's concern for the individual and a socialist society's egalitarian goal. Socialist humanism supplanted Stalinist abstractions such as the Party, the two camps, and the working-class vanguard with concrete individuals and the revolutionary potential of "real men and women."[21] It equally emphasized "socialism" and "humanism."

For Thompson, the intellectual bankruptcy of Stalinism was rooted in its economism—the attempt to view society's political, moral, and artistic dimensions in terms of economic and class structures. In opposition to this crude determinism, Thompson reaffirmed the central role of human agency in history. Adapting Marx's famous words in the *Eighteenth Brumaire*, Thompson wrote: "But men make their own history: they are part agents, part victims: it is precisely the element of agency which distinguishes them from the beasts, which is the *human* part of man."[22] Thompson's belief in the powers of human agency to shape historical outcomes provided one of the enduring themes of his subsequent writings. Equally important, his initial defense of agency was in the context of opposition to Stalinism in the aftermath of 1956. It seemed as if whenever Thompson was confronted with a Marxist mode of thought that emphasized determinations or constraints on human volition, he situated it within this frame of reference, seeing it as a descendant of Stalinism.

Thompson was also highly critical of the Stalinist emphasis on base/superstructure. In his view it had been a "clumsy static model," even when used by Marx, a simplification of the interaction of social being and consciousness so central to historical materialism. When used by Stalinists—particularly by Stalin himself—base/superstructure had degenerated into a "bad and dangerous model." It reduced "human consciousness to a form of erratic, involuntary response to steel-mills and brickyards, which are in a spontaneous process of looming and becoming."[23] For Thompson, the scope of this theoretical degeneration was broader than Stalinism; it was symptomatic of a widespread tendency in the Marxist tradition (especially since the later writings of Engels) to ignore or minimize moral and ethical questions.

Thompson was by no means alone in criticizing orthodox Marxism from a socialist-humanist perspective, and his critique was undoubtedly inspired by the Marxist humanism of Polish and Hungarian opponents of Stalinist rule. Yet Eastern European revisionists derived their humanist understanding of Marx from the philosophical anthropology of the *1844 Manuscripts* or the Hegelian Marxism of György Lukács's *History and Class Consciousness.* Thompson's critique of orthodox Marxism was uniquely rooted in English sources—"modes of perception" learned while writing the Morris biography.[24] For Thompson, Morris's "historical understanding of the evolution of man's moral nature" was a necessary complement to Marx's economic and historical analysis.[25] Marxist renewal depended on the restoration of a moral vocabulary: implicit assumptions deeply lodged—but inadequately expressed—in Marx's own work. To restore this moral discourse, Thompson advocated a revival of the kind of utopian thinking that had been integral to the socialist tradition before the ascent of scientific socialism. Such thinking was exemplified by Morris's *The Dream of John Ball* and *News from Nowhere.* Most important, Thompson argued that Marxists must come to terms with the implications of Morris's insight that productive relations (base) did not only produce moral values (superstructure) but had a moral dimension themselves. "Economic relationships are at the same time moral relationships; relations of production are at the same time relations between people, of oppression or of co-operation: and there is a moral logic as well as an economic logic, which derives from these relationships. The history of the class struggle is at the same time the history of human morality."[26] Since human consciousness was no less central than productive relations, "the construction of a Communist community would require a moral revolution as profound as the revolution in economic and social power."[27] This perspective suggested an alternative vision of politics, while negating the base/superstructure distinction, restating the relationship between economy and culture in more complex and interactive terms.

II

The *Reasoner* group comprised former Communists radicalized during the days of the Popular Front. Their revolt against orthodoxy was inspired by Eastern European alternatives to Stalinism and what they saw as a return to authentic English radicalism. The group responsible for *Universities and Left Review* (*ULR*) were Oxford university students who tended to have shallower roots in the labor movement, and *ULR* was initiated in response to the political crisis of 1956. It was affected by the crisis in communism, but primarily it was reacting to British involvement in the Suez crisis. Moreover, *ULR* was representative of a new generation of radical intellectuals too young to have been shaped by the experience of the depression and the war. Its principal participants were mostly intellectuals and writers in their twenties, and its sensibility was closer to that of CND protestors of the Aldermaston marches than the Popular Front partisans of the 1930s. They felt an affinity, if not a direct connection, with the 1950s culture of working-class youth, who, as Stuart Hall suggested, felt the same frustrations toward postwar society but were "only less 'mature,' less polite, less conformist and restrained in giving vent to their feelings than we are."[28]

ULR was more heterogeneous than the *Reasoner* group. It included several foreign nationals. Charles Taylor, a French-Canadian Rhodes scholar, read philosophy at Balliol and All Souls College. Norman Birnbaum, important in the later stages of the journal, was an American sociology student at the London School of Economics. Stuart Hall, a Jamaican Rhodes scholar, read English at Merton. In 1956 Hall was a graduate student writing a thesis on Henry James, an early instance of his long-term interest in the relationship between modern consciousness and capitalism.[29] As an undergraduate, Hall was active in anticolonial politics, and he was interested in the anthropological approach to culture and the Marxist theory of classes. He is one of the few black intellectuals to make an imprint on socialist intellectual discussions in Britain.

Among the British participants in *ULR*, Alan Hall was from Scotland and was a Balliol graduate student in classics. Gabriel Pearson, from a London Jewish background, a Communist Party member until the Party's crisis, read English at Balliol. Raphael Samuel (at the time called Ralph) was also Jewish, grew up mostly in London's East End, and was the nephew of the highly respected Communist scholar Chimen Abramsky. Samuel was from a Communist background; his life goal was to be a Communist organizer; and his heroes were J. R. Campbell and Palme Dutt. He read history at Balliol, where he was Christopher Hill's protegé. At the time that the journal was founded, he was at the London School of Economics, writing a thesis in history on dockers in the late nineteenth century.

ULR's origins can be traced to several sources. In the early fifties the seminars of the socialist historian G. D. H. Cole, which were occasions for discussing the Left's paralysis during the Cold War era, served as a bridge (because of Cole's involvement) to Continental efforts to create an independent Left. Stuart Hall recalled that the idea of creating a "new left" in Britain was partially inspired by his own and others' contact with the French *nouvelle gauche* movement. Launched by Claude Bourdet, it envisioned a European socialist movement that opposed Cold War military alliances and leftist orthodoxies.[30] By 1954 a renewal of an open socialist discussion occurred in Oxford Left-wing circles. While such discussions were taking place on the fringes of the CP and the Labour Club, their central location was the Socialist Club, a Popular Front group of the 1930s, which had in practice died out but was revived by student intellectuals, many of whom would create *ULR*. The nature of the discussions can be ascertained by a brief inventory of books that captured their imaginations. The summer before the Suez invasion, Alan Hall and Stuart Hall contemplated putting together an edited collection of recent work analyzing the contours of contemporary capitalism. The texts that they regarded as key included C. A. R. Crosland's *The Future of Socialism*, John Strachey's *The End of Empire*, two chapters of Raymond Williams's forthcoming *Culture and Society*, F. R. Leavis's *Culture and Environment*, Angus Maude's *The English Middle Classes*, John Osborne's *Look Back in Anger*, and George Scott's autobiographical portrait of an "angry young man," *Time and Place*.[31]

While these pre-Suez discussions recognized the need for renewed political activism, it was the combined impact of the Suez invasion and crisis in the Communist world that made *ULR* possible. *ULR*'s founders regarded the events of 1956 as a warming trend in the frigid political climate and perhaps the revival of Left politics: "Hard as we try, we cannot turn back the course of events which forced de-Stalinisation on the Stalinists. Hungary is there to point the moral, and adorn that tale. Much as we would like, we cannot think our way round Suez back to that comfortable womb-world in which conservatives and socialists still held hands. The thaw is on."[32] They hoped to use the clamor over Suez and Hungary as the point of departure for a wide-ranging project whose central focus would be a journal primarily, but not exclusively, aimed at the new student audience. The title, *Universities and Left Review*, evoked the groups they were attempting to reach and the tradition of radicalism they wanted to revive (*Left Review* being one of the most successful radical intellectual journals of the thirties). Stuart Hall, Gabriel Pearson, Samuel, and Taylor were chosen as editors. Although as Hall recalled: "Too much should not be made of those particular names since, out of the ferment, almost any four people would have done."[33] In balancing ex-Communist and non-Communist influence, *ULR* was sending a clear message that the journal would not be overtaken by sectarianism. Although conceived in Oxford, *ULR* moved to London's West End, which was closer to the hub of political and intellectual life.[34]

The journal was the *ULR* project's focus, but the group also wanted to make its presence felt in daily affairs. Two projects that met this goal were the Partisan coffeehouse and the *ULR* Club. The Partisan was established as an informal meeting place for the new generation of socialist intellectuals and emulated the milieu of the Paris Left Bank. The *ULR* Club, based in London, held organized meetings, lectures, and discussions. Its aim was to promote new directions in socialist analysis and strategy. From the outset in April 1957, the club generated noticeable enthusiasm; a lecture by Isaac Deutscher on the political crisis in the Soviet Union drew six hundred people. Club participants came from various political backgrounds and were from different generations, although the majority of them were probably in their twenties. They shared a common aversion to received socialist orthodoxy and an eagerness to entertain new ideas. This willingness to be heterodox was both the source of *ULR*'s (and later the New Left's) appeal and a major reason that it had difficulty creating a cohesive political position.

In its first editorial, *ULR* spoke of itself as a "calculated risk" and insisted that it had no "political 'line'" to offer. It was convinced that socialists must recover "the whole tradition of free, open, critical debate," but it was uncertain what precise shape that discussion should take. The journal's editors spoke of socialist thinking as ossifying into two narrow and irrelevant camps: orthodox leftists "who clung to the slogans of the thirties" and revisionists who regarded the 1945 Labour reforms as having all but resolved the contradictions of interwar capitalism. Both "evaded the critical problems and the main frustrations of postwar society" and "appeared monstrously irrelevant to the postwar generation."[35]

To appreciate *ULR*'s critique of revisionism, it should be situated within the crisis of the postwar socialist movement. Despite having created the mixed economy and the welfare state, the British Left was unable to sustain its political success. Following its narrow defeat in 1951—when it actually won the popular vote—Labour suffered a seemingly endless string of political losses, unable to defeat a Tory party that had triumphed with the slogan, "You never had it so good." At the root of the problem was the postwar reshaping of working-class consciousness and culture, a consequence of full employment, real increases in income, class mobility, and spreading mass culture. These beginnings of the "Americanization" of Britain problematized the very underpinnings of the socialist project: the belief that the working-class movement would inevitably usher in a socialist world. This change marked the beginning of a crisis in the socialist movement, which, although sporadic and not strictly speaking linear, attained epidemic proportions in the 1980s and 1990s.

Throughout the fifties Labour struggled to find a way of appealing to an acquisitive and mobile working class living in a mass society. Its most imaginative response was the revisionism of Anthony Crosland, for whom the crisis of the Left was rooted in an inability to come to terms with the new postcapitalist and statist social and economic order. Crosland's advocacy of American-style liberalism and his insistence that the Left must retire the rhetoric of class struggle was enshrined as party policy after the 1957 defeat when the newly elected party leader, Hugh Gaitskell, attempted to dramatically revamp the party's image. In its official platform, *Industry and Society* (1958), Labour deployed rhetoric that broke with historical tradition; it declared that, on the whole, private industry was serving the national interest. Where nationalizations were traditionally regarded as an integral part of any Labour program, they were redefined as a last resort—a form of discipline for irresponsible firms bent on overthrowing the mixed economy.[36]

For *ULR* socialists it was insufficient to condemn the new revisionism on the grounds that it violated socialist principles. While they certainly objected to the portrayal of Britain as postcapitalist, and they strenuously disagreed that the conditions for class struggle were coming to an end, they recognized that sweeping and wide-ranging transformations had occurred in postwar British society. They rejected the politics of revisionism, but they believed that a revisionist analysis of the new society could not be overlooked. Socialists, they argued, must acknowledge the profound impact of the new consumer society and welfare state. They must create a socialist politics founded on people's everyday experiences, not outworn myths and slogans. To achieve this end, *ULR* challenged socialist orthodoxy by publishing articles on topics outside the usual boundaries and with a more penetrating style of analysis. Articles analyzed alienation in urban areas, the class basis of British education, the cultural politics of adolescence, the social impact of advertising, the transformation of mass communications, the meaning of racial strife, the Third World and postcolonialism, the power elite in Britain, and the effects of consumer capitalism on working-class culture. That *ULR* articulated and began to give shape to a new mood on the intellectual and student Left is reflected in its sales figures. The journal at its height sold about 8,000 copies—two and a half times greater than the formerly Communist *New Reasoner.*[37]

At the root of *ULR's* theoretical project was a collective belief in "the singleness of human life," its multiple facets and unity. As an editorial stated, the group wanted "to break away from the traditions which see economic or political man as separate from man in the centre of a web of human relations, which draw him into the full life of his community—which consider 'economic' or 'political' life as a lower form of existence, as an external prop to the private life of the individual, rather than as his very nature."[38] *ULR* advocated a totalizing conception of radical politics, or "socialism at full stretch," a conception in which the cultural dimension was viewed as being as important as the explicitly political. And it insisted that literature and art, no less than machines, could contribute to "a fuller life for the human person and the community."[39] For Stuart Hall, artists and political intellectuals were not only compatible but were opposite sides of the same coin:

> *The political intellectual is concerned with the institutional life of the society: the creative artist with the attitudes, the manners, the moral and emotional life which the individual consummates within that social framework. It seems to me that the beginning of a common socialist humanism is the realisation that these are not two distinct areas of interest, but the complementary parts of a complex, common experience.*[40]

To further its goal of cultural politics, the *ULR* group at an early point reached out to the simultaneously emerging Free Cinema movement, a politically committed group of film directors—notably Lindsay Anderson, Karel Reisz, and Tony Richardson—who made highly personal documentaries of working-class life. Anderson's seminal statement of its aspirations, "Stand Up! Stand Up!," which advocated making films in which "people—ordinary people, not just Top people—feel their dignity and importance," was originally published in *Sight and Sound* in 1956. At the request of Hall and Samuel, it was reprinted in the first issue of *ULR* as "Commitment in Cinema Criticism." Anderson later said of *ULR*'s overtures: "It was surprising and very, very encouraging—because it suddenly seemed as if there could really be a 'Popular Front' of political and creative principle; and in that popular front, movies and theatre could have a place and enjoy sympathetic support. For just a short time that is what actually happened."[41]

In creating a British cultural politics the *ULR* group perhaps may be regarded as prefiguring feminist efforts to break down the wall between private and public spheres; they wanted "to break with the view that cultural or family life" was "an entertaining sideshow, a secondary expression of human creativity or fulfillment." Yet if those associated with *ULR* were interested in issues that would later concern feminists, they—as well as the New Left in general—were not to create a feminist politics. Given that women played key roles in the first New Left (although often behind-the-scenes roles), it might be asked, why did feminism in Britain not materialize in the late 1950s rather than in the aftermath of 1968? While no final answer can be given, Lynne Segal has offered several plausible reasons. She argues, first, that after the war men and women on the Left, no less than in other segments of society, bought into the consensual view that women's problems had been solved and that the sexes had achieved equality. Second, Segal suggests that an "assumed biological imperative of motherhood and childhood" had emerged in the fifties such that a women's political movement would have been deemed unnatural. And, most importantly, Segal believes that at a time when men's roles were likewise being domesticated, New Left men "identified strongly with the tough, amoral, cynical, invariably misogynist heroes of Alan Sillitoe, John Osborne and others." "Women were never to be trusted but treated as part of the system trying to trap, tame and emasculate men. A stifling domesticity had killed the spirit and guts of men, these 'rebels' declared, and women were to blame. What was really happening in most of the 'Angry' literature was that class hostility was suppressed and twisted into new forms of sexual hostility."[42] One might reiterate Segal's point with regard to Osborne, whose main character, Jimmy Porter, in *Look Back in Anger*, having withdrawn from the public world of political causes, is able to repair his bruised masculinity only by physically dominating the middle-class women around him.

Like the *Reasoner* group, *ULR*'s critique of capitalist society was founded on the principles of socialist humanism. Yet *ULR*'s conception of this philosophy was more eclectic and diffuse, less affected by the experience of Eastern European anti-Stalinism. Stuart Hall characterized socialist humanism in terms that most traditional socialists would reject, viewing it as the belief in genuine equality, a sensitivity to "the capacity to feel," and "the vindication of the moral imagination." These "capacities lie dormant and unused, the stored energy and moral life of a democracy that has not made the first approach to a democratic way of life." In defining socialist humanism, he quoted the literary critic F. R. Leavis. Hall viewed Leavis's description of the nineteenth-century novel—"a vital capacity for experience, a kind of reverent openness before life, and a marked moral intensity"—as capturing socialist-humanist priorities.[43] Hall disagreed with Leavis's politics but regarded his critical vocabulary as having radical implications, especially when compared with economistic versions of Marxism. In appropriating Leavis for radical purposes, Hall was following Raymond Williams's strategy in his influential *Culture and Society* (discussed in detail in chapter 3).

Because *ULR* was so preoccupied with lifestyle, "the whole way of life," and culture, it was often referred to in socialist intellectual debates as "culturalist." There were two dimensions to culturalism. On the one hand, it was a rejection of Marxist economic determinism. Culturalists saw the social process as a complex result of economic, political, and cultural determinations, and they insisted that none of these determinations was primary. On the other hand, they saw culture in broader terms—as a whole way of life. From this point of view, culture was the social process itself, economics and politics constituent parts. One political implication of this culturalist position was that a socialist policy on advertising, the mass media, or workers' self-management could no longer be regarded as less critical than the nationalization of a steel company. In a society where the means of cultural production were themselves a major capitalist industry, the distinction between culture and economics became blurred. *ULR* believed that socialist politics must adapt to these rapidly changing conditions.

III

From 1957 until 1959 a New Left emerged in Britain. The inner circle consisted of the *ULR* and *Reasoner* groups, but the New Left became a diverse and informal political movement signifying a new mood on the Left. It included CND participants, veterans of the unions and Labour Left, radical professionals, countercultural students and artists, and dissident Communists. In general, the New Left saw itself as an alternative to the economism of the Communist and Labour Left and the revisionism of the Labour leadership. It conceived of its political position—socialist humanism—as more than just another strategy for socialism; socialist humanism represented an alternative set of priorities based on a whole way of life and the total individual. New Leftists wanted to supplant Harold Macmillan's "opportunity society" and Labour's "equality of opportunity" with William Morris's "society of equals." They accorded a privileged status to culture and the arts, for such practices were integral to human life conceived as a whole and because cultural apparatuses and institutions were playing an increasingly important role in people's lives.

The New Left also took a dim view of the traditional Left's organizational forms. They argued that both the Labour and Communist leaderships, despite obvious differences, were fundamentally antidemocratic, intent on using bureaucratic organization and procedure to stifle minority and grassroots opinion. The New Left enthusiastically supported the CND, partially because it represented a means of displacing Cold War polarities, but most importantly because it represented a democratic and grassroots alternative to the deadening authoritarianism of the labor movement. As a result, the producers of *ULR* and the *New Reasoner* were reluctant to assume leadership roles in the New Left for fear that their assumption of such roles would bring about hierarchical decision making and grassroots passivity. Yet if the original New Left severely criticized Labour politics, it stopped short of abandoning the Labour Party. It never doubted that Labour was the party of British working people or that it was indispensable to a socialist transformation. In short, New Left activists saw themselves as being both inside and outside the Labour Party, a position that evoked skepticism from both the radical Left and committed Labour veterans.

The first stage in constructing the New Left was the development of a close working relationship between the two journals. While each group advocated a socialist-humanist position and regarded the other as engaged in a common struggle, they had disagreements, a result of differences in age, political experience, and theoretical orientation. *Reasoner* activists were somewhat scornful of *ULR*'s lack of real ties to the working-class movement, their enthusiasm for artistic avant-gardes, and their attraction to what was in vogue. Thompson, for instance, was concerned that *ULR* would surrender to "precious and self-isolating" attitudes that "could be as corrosive in the socialist movement as those opportunist and philistine attitudes" that it opposed.[44] Meanwhile, *ULR* socialists tended to think of the *Reasoner* group as politically narrow and intellectually behind-the-times. Indeed, Raymond Williams, who was from the generation of the *Reasoner* group but intellectually closer to *ULR*, found the *New Reasoner* "still much too involved in arid fights with the Party Marxists," and he thought that some of its essays gave the impression that nothing at all had changed.[45]

The tension between the two groups was most apparent in their attitudes toward Marxism. *New Reasoner* socialists wanted to rejuvenate Marxist theory by removing Stalinist distortions and developing it in new and creative ways. They did not see a problem with Marxism per se, only with what had happened to it. The younger generation associated with *ULR*, on the other hand, acknowledged Marxism as a critical part of their heritage, but they questioned its relevance to understanding the complexities of contemporary society. The *ULR* socialists most interested in reading Marx were invariably drawn to the early humanistic writings that stressed "alienation." Yet even here they were ambivalent. Charles Taylor—responsible for introducing many to Marx's *1844 Manuscripts* in French translation since the work was not available in English until 1960—regarded Marxist philosophy as an "*incomplete humanism*" with a tendency toward authoritarianism.[46] And few proponents of *ULR* were enthusiastic about the *Reasoner* group's efforts at reexamining Marxism. "We Marxist dissidents in the years 1956 to 1962," Thompson recalled,

were beset not only by radical inner doubts and self-criticism, but also by a total climate of skepticism or active resistance to Marxism in any form.

This climate permeated the New Left also, at its origin, and many comrades then shared the general view that Marxism, . . . was a liability which should be dumped, while new theories were improvised from less contaminated sources.[47]

Thompson perceived the time as "a last stand amidst a general rout."[48]

These differences, however, did not inhibit an open dialogue between the two groups. From the beginning, contributors overlapped, and articles submitted to one journal might end up in the other. By 1959 the two groups offered joint subscriptions and cosponsored New Left clubs scattered throughout Britain that were inspired by the success of the *ULR* Club in London. Acknowledging the development of a close relationship, the last *ULR* editorial observed that "it has become difficult to know just who is who."[49]

Arguably the most important reason for the two groups' closer cooperation was their increasing involvement in the CND. The disarmament movement represented the historical culmination of a long and active tradition of pacifism and radical dissent in Britain.[50] It was organized in the aftermath of the Suez crisis, which, in demonstrating Britain's fall from international prominence, raised questions about the rationale for an independent nuclear deterrent. The founders of the movement hoped that Britain could recover its loss of international status and regain its role as a great power by setting the moral example of banishing nuclear weapons. The desire to recover national pride and former world power status was a major impetus behind the first CND.

Founded in 1958, the CND was supported by a broad spectrum of progressive and radical opinion, though the CP did not support the movement until well after it was off the ground. The movement's founders (including such intellectuals as J. B. Priestley, Julian Huxley, and A. J. P. Taylor) conceived of it as a pressure group to transform public opinion. Yet from the beginning, the CND contained radical factions, notably the Direct Action Committee, which advocated a more aggressive political presence through passive resistance and direct action. The CND undoubtedly would have remained a small group of committed pacifists had it not been for its adoption by the emerging student movement and youth culture of the late 1950s. Originating as a force opposed to the spread of nuclear weapons, it came to symbolize a wider discontent with the institutions of modern society. It was the only genuine mass political movement between the Popular Front of the 1930s and the student revolt of the late 1960s.

The CND was put on the political map in April 1958 when thousands participated in a protest march from London to the nuclear research plant at Aldermaston. Although the march attracted people of all ages and political backgrounds, the most conspicuous group comprised the politically conscious youth counterculture. Aldermaston, as David Widgery wrote, was "a student movement before its time, a mobile sit-in or marching pop festival; in its midst could be found the first embers of the hashish underground and premature members of the Love Generation as well as cadres of forthcoming revolutionary parties."[51] The march became the most visible symbol of the disarmament movement and was made into an annual event. It attracted 150,000 marchers in 1961 when public support for the CND was at its height.

The *Reasoner* and *ULR* groups were early supporters of the campaign. *ULR* socialists, frequently from the same generation as the most zealous antinuclear activists, sympathized with the movement's distrust of conventional politics and its reliance on grassroots protest. However, they differed from many of the more radical disarmers. They were more hopeful that the Labour Party could be pressured into adopting a unilateralist position, and their ultimate goal was to direct the energies of the movement in an explicitly socialist direction. *ULR* socialists saw themselves as possible mediators between the CND and the mainstream labor movement—a position that proved to be untenable.

Many *Reasoner* intellectuals regarded the CND as an extension of the peace movement of the early 1950s that had gained their support as CP members.[52] Even before the founding of the disarmament movement, Thompson was writing in the *New Reasoner* about the relationship between nuclear disarmament and socialist strategy: "The bomb must be dismantled; but in dismantling it, men will summon up energies which will open the way to their inheritance. The bomb is like an image of man's whole predicament: it bears within it death and life, total destruction or human mastery over human history."[53] Yet if *Reasoner* socialists were CND enthusiasts, they were unhappy with the movement's anarchist tendencies, its moral posturing, its disdain for conventional politics, and its predominantly middle-class character.

One of the most striking features of the *Reasoner* group's approach to unilateral disarmament was its effort to relate disarmament to the Cold War. They saw unilateralism as a means of breaking through the superpowers' hold on international politics: a springboard for British withdrawal from NATO, the eventual creation of a politically independent Europe, and political self-determination for the emerging Third World. The *New Reasoner* defined its position as "positive neutralism," a term conveying the dual aspiration of staying aloof from superpower politics and creating an independent foreign policy. As Peter Worsley stated: "It was a *positive* neutralism, aiming at the creation of a political space in which, globally, superpower hegemony could be dismantled and colonized peoples could free themselves—the prerequisites for ending world poverty and abolishing the bomb. For us in Britain, it meant a new opportunity to align ourselves with movements for self-determination all over the world."[54]

In retrospect, the *Reasoner* group's attempt to transform foreign policy was based on mistaken assumptions about what was possible in the international arena. Such mistakes were nowhere more apparent than in the writings of Edward Thompson. Although he was a brilliant polemicist, Thompson's analysis of contemporary events often lacked the kind of detached understanding necessary to make realistic political calculations. As a historian of eighteenth- and nineteenth-century history, he fused passionate sympathy and rigorous analysis to obtain powerful, unforgettable results. But when he turned to the contemporary world, his political analysis was frequently marred by his political hopes. A principal component of Thompson's neutralism was the role he assigned to Britain in ending the international stalemate. He argued that owing to its international influence, ties with India, undivided labor movement, strong democratic structure, and the growing CND, Britain was "the nation best placed to take the initiative which might just succeed in bringing down the whole power-crazy system like a pack of cards."[55] Such an argument was certainly part political exhortation—an effort to embolden and inspire activists by elevating the importance and significance of their activities. Nonetheless, Thompson's depiction of Britain's position in the international arena more accurately expressed his hopes for an international breakthrough than any conceivable political reality, and it was tinted with nostalgia for Britain's once preeminent role in the world.

The *Reasoner* and *ULR* groups both regarded the disarmament movement as a sign that political indifference and cynicism might have run their course and that a genuinely new socialism might materialize at the end of the decade. This spirit barely touched the mainstream working-class movement, but it could be detected among intellectuals, artists, social workers, architects, urban planners, teachers, and students.[56] Its greatest impact was on those who were—or were destined to become—the new middle-class professionals in the burgeoning public sector, many of whom were from working-class families or one generation removed from them. A *New Reasoner* editorial cautiously noted that "very slowly, and sometimes with more sound than substance, it does seem that a 'new left' is coming into being in this country."[57] This instance was perhaps the first time that a now hackneyed phrase was used in the English language. In contrast to Britain in the 1960s when the term conveyed multiple meanings, the original sense of "new left" was relatively specific: a political milieu that was neither Communist nor Labour, an alternative space on the map of the Left.

From the point of view of its founders, the merger of *ULR* and the *New Reasoner* was the greatest stimulus to creating an independent socialist movement. The idea of combining forces was, of course, made possible by the evolving relationship between the two journals. But it began to be discussed as a result of economic problems. *ULR* was on the verge of bankruptcy, owing in large part to the financial drain of the Partisan coffeehouse.[58] At the same time, following publication of the *Reasoner*, the fight inside the CP, and the more ambitious *New Reasoner* undertaking, the Thompsons, Saville, and the small group of Yorkshire radicals who ran the magazine were exhausted. The pressure of teaching, research, and long hours working on the journal (in addition to taking part in activities like the CND) was wearing them down; they needed a paid staff to assume some of the burden.

Merger discussions began because the two editorial boards saw a joint venture as a simultaneous means of solving the problems of both journals. But the main obstacles to a merger were political. Opposition on both sides was symptomatic of underlying tensions that had existed from the beginning. Where some in the *Reasoner* group continued to have qualms about *ULR's* "culturalism" and lack of labor movement connections, others in the *ULR* group were concerned about the imposition of a narrow political focus. The most vocal critic of a single journal—and the only one to actually vote against it—was Ralph Miliband. For Miliband, the

New Left was better served by two strong and unmistakable voices echoing differences than by one voice that represented a series of compromises and evasions.[59] Yet, as Thompson, Saville, and Stuart Hall have attested, the two journals could not have gone on much longer in their existing forms. A merger was the *only* real alternative.[60]

As merger discussions proceeded, it became increasingly clear to both editorial boards that much could be gained by a unified effort. Hall recalled the discussions between the two groups as among the most productive of the New Left.[61] After meetings held at Wortley Hall in late 1958, Saville noted that the two groups were moving closer to each other—personally, politically, and intellectually.[62] Thompson, not surprisingly, was the most enthusiastic. With characteristic "optimism of the will," he wrote: "We hope that our readers will never *stop* discussing and engaging in socialist education. But we think that the time has come for our readers, together with the readers of *ULR*, to pass over from diffuse discussion to political organisation. We hope that they will now engage—rapidly and confidently—in the construction of the New Left."[63] While Thompson's analysis might have lacked the requisite "pessimism of the intellect," his excitement was understandable. After a decade of Cold War polarities and political lethargy, the socialist Left appeared to be on the verge of renewal, and the appearance of a new journal giving voice to these energies might be the catalyst that was needed. As fitted such an occasion, *NLR* was launched at a celebration and rally attended by several hundred people at St. Pancras Hall in London in December 1959.

IV

At its height the New Left was a small political and intellectual network or milieu that published journals, books, pamphlets, and newsletters and was organized into a national group of clubs. Its principal theoretical organ, the bimonthly journal *New Left Review* (*NLR*), had about 10,000 readers when it first appeared, more than either *ULR* or the *New Reasoner* (but not the two combined).[64] *NLR*'s editor, Stuart Hall, sought to appeal to the various New Left constituencies, and consequently the journal was more eclectic and less cohesive than either of its predecessors. It consisted of New Left news, cultural and literary criticism, and political analysis. *NLR* analyzed contemporary capitalism, the welfare state, Labour politics, the mass media, anti-imperialist struggle, and popular culture.

It figured critically in the debate between Marxism and culturalism, which was crucial in the formation of cultural studies and the development of cultural Marxist historiography (see chapter 3). From the beginning, the journal was besieged by problems. Its editorial board consisted of twenty-six people of diverse political opinion, living in various parts of Britain.[65] The board was too large and unwieldy, and it was difficult for board members to communicate. In practice, Hall and a small group of London associates ran the journal in consultation to varying degrees with prominent figures living in other regions. However, Hall, who was engaged in numerous political activities, was often forced to hastily put together an issue at the last minute.[66]

The difficulty of Hall's task was intensified by Thompson's ceaseless pressure and criticism. Owing to his political and editorial experience and his powerful personality, Thompson was the logical choice to run the journal. For reasons discussed, he was unwilling to assume the editorship. Yet this did not prevent him from becoming one of the journal's most persistent behind-the-scenes critics. He felt repeatedly frustrated with what he perceived to be the journal's flirtations with intellectual fashion and its failure to appeal to the working-class movement. It is difficult to imagine how a New Left journal following Thompson's prescription could have been more successful, for it is unlikely that the journal could have appealed to a working-class audience without alienating the middle-class students and intellectuals who had made the New Left possible. If NLR had reached out to an even wider audience, it probably would have produced a more theoretically and politically inconsistent viewpoint than that which already existed.

A less tangible—but no less important—reason for Thompson's persistent criticism of NLR was his passionate attachment to the journal, which represented the culmination of four years of intense political activity. He apparently was frustrated at seeing what he had created being run by others, in London, away from the Yorkshire labor movement. Such feelings became even more visible in his later conflict with Perry Anderson. From the start, Thompson besieged Hall with highly critical and sometimes angry letters. Hall, who was less than thirty years old when NLR was launched, was "fathered" through this ordeal by John Saville, the first president of the New Left board. According to Hall, Saville gave valuable support to his precarious position and mediated between the two men.[67]

The New Left also established a national club network. As with the journal, the club movement contained different traditions and political tendencies, and clubs varied from place to place. In early 1960, Simon Rosenblat, secretary of the Left Clubs coordinating committee, estimated that twenty-four different groups existed, mostly in large urban areas (although many of these were closely linked to universities). Half of the clubs had formed in the six months before Rosenblat's estimate; membership totaled between 1,500 and 2,000.[68] About six months later, in October 1960, it was reported that some forty-five clubs had a paid membership of approximately 3,000.[69]

The clubs' purpose was never clearly defined. They were not meant to serve as the foundation of a political party or as mere discussion groups. NLR described them, vaguely, as places "where a demonstration of socialism can be made, and where the fragmentary sense of community and solidarity, which used to be part of the socialist movement, can be pieced together again."[70] In practice, individual clubs, left to define themselves, were frequently confused about how they should act.

One obvious solution would have been for NLR to assume a strong, explicit leadership role. Yet the journal's creators hesitated to assume a role that they regarded as opposed to their goal of reviving democratic and grassroots initiatives in the labor movement. This hesitancy was particularly true of former Communists like Thompson whose memories of authoritarian bureaucracies were vivid. NLR also was reluctant to become more active in the club movement for fear that it would be diverted from fulfilling its main purpose. Or as Saville told the editorial board: "We are in some danger of becoming involved more and more in the apparatus and thereby failing to pursue what for all of us is the main job: the development and enlargement of our ideas."[71] Similarly, NLR's first editorial named the most urgent task facing socialists as "the clarification of ideas." "The movement has never before been so short on ideas, so long on pious waffle. Not until we attain this clarity, through a decisive shift in political consciousness throughout the movement, will we be able to work with a revolutionary perspective in view." It went on to observe that the New Left would have to resist the pressure to "cease talking and begin doing," for it would be judged by the "strength of its ideas."[72] This assessment perceptively defined the outer limits of what the New Left could hope to achieve in the early sixties.

To facilitate the dissemination of its ideas and to accommodate intellectual work that was either too large in scale or did not fit into *NLR*'s format, the New Left created its own book series and published several pamphlets. New Left Books owed its inspiration to the Left Book Club of the 1930s, yet, unlike its forebear, it never found a publisher as sympathetic as Victor Gollancz. Despite plans to publish several volumes, only a reprint edition of Irving Howe's *Politics and the Novel* and a collection of essays edited by Thompson, *Out of Apathy*, ever materialized.

According to Thompson, the purpose of *Out of Apathy* was to demonstrate the intimate connections between apathy, affluence, and the Cold War, and "to suggest that tensions and positive tendencies were present which might—but need not necessarily—lead people out of apathy and towards a socialist resolution."[73] To the disappointment of many readers, the book did not break new ground, but it did serve as a kind of summation of New Left thinking up to that time.[74] It included essays by Raphael Samuel on the structure of the new capitalism, Stuart Hall on consumerism, Peter Worsley on imperialism, Alasdair MacIntyre on Marxism, and Ken Alexander on Labour.

The most provocative essay in the volume was Thompson's own "Revolution."[75] Simultaneously published in *NLR*, the essay was an attempt to develop a New Left theory of revolution drawing on the insights of both the *Reasoner* and *ULR*. Thompson's theory of revolution was framed in opposition to two historical alternatives: the evolutionary or gradualist perspective, and the orthodox Marxist, or cataclysmic, model. Thompson portrayed the gradualist tradition as believing that capitalism would terminate and socialism would come into existence when state control of the economy would be greater than private ownership. He found this premise narrowly economic and a moral capitulation to politics as defined within capitalism. Meaningful public ownership had to be accompanied by a transformation in moral values and social attitudes: the abolition of the profit motive, the democratization of the labor process, and the creation of a society of equals.

Thompson noted that the cataclysmic model owed more to Lenin, Trotsky, and Stalin than to Marx, who had observed that countries like Britain and the United States, with developed democratic traditions, might effect peaceful transitions to socialism. The cataclysmic theory held that socialist forms, however embryonic, were attainable only after the capitalist system collapsed and the state was overthrown. Reforms achieved under capitalist rule were seen as either a means of bribing the proletariat or part of a master plan by the bourgeoisie to defuse working-class pressure. From this point of view, reformist struggle might prepare the working class for the final assault but was not capable of achieving genuine gains under capitalism. Thompson argued that this theory ignored the revolutionary potential of reform *inside* capitalist society, the fact that various components of contemporary capitalism—welfare services, the public sector, trade unions—were (to use John Strachey's term) "countervailing forces." Late capitalism was an unstable socioeconomic system, a site of struggle between dominant and emergent forms.

The countervailing powers are there, and the equilibrium (which is an equilibrium within capitalism) is precarious. It could be tipped back towards authoritarianism. But it could also be heaved forward, by popular pressure of great intensity, to the point where the powers of democracy cease to be countervailing and become the active dynamic of society in their own right. This is revolution. [76]

For Thompson, the revolutionary breakthrough, though likely triggered by a political event (his example being British withdrawal from NATO), would not in itself be political but would be a "confrontation, throughout society, between two systems, two ways of life." (This reformulation of Raymond Williams's cultural theory is discussed in chapter 3.)[77] The breakthrough would happen when challenges to advanced capitalism's values and structures could no longer be contained. While Thompson argued that the point of breakthrough was unknowable in advance and could be discovered only in practice, he stressed that it did not need catastrophe in order to materialize. Since the 1940s, embryonic socialist forms had evolved within capitalism, making possible a peaceful revolution with far more continuity than had ever been thought possible. As in his writings on positive neutralism, Thompson reiterated that Britain was uniquely positioned to achieve this transformation: "The equilibrium here is most precarious, the Labour movement least divided, the democratic socialist tradition most strong. And it is *this* event which could at one blow break up the log-jam of the Cold War and initiate a new wave of world advance. Advance in Western Europe and, in less direct ways, democratisation in the East, may wait upon us."[78] Although he acknowledged that a British socialist transformation was not inevitable, Thompson insisted that it was foolish to "underestimate the long and tenacious revolutionary tradition of the British commoner," a tradition that "could leaven the socialist world."[79] The problem was that the revolutionary tradition of the British commoner had never been dominant, and there was little reason to believe that it would become so in the early 1960s.

"Revolution" is another instance of how Thompson's passionate yearning for political change stood in the way of his analysis of the real possibilities. Beyond the fact that Britain in the early 1960s was clearly not on the brink of a socialist transformation or *overripe* for a revolution, Thompson's portrayal of revolutionary breakthrough was founded on erroneous assumptions about the instability of advanced capitalist social formations. He seriously underestimated the ability of institutions that reproduced the dominant ideology—such as the media—to appropriate and neutralize countervailing forces, and he failed to consider either the hegemonic or repressive power of the capitalist state. In response to his critics, Thompson acknowledged that the New Left had failed to develop a theory of the state "and that we need not only think in detail about the kind of institutional change and democratic transformation of the machinery of State which are desirable, but also begin to press for these changes now."[80] Yet he might well have asked how the popular movement would confront the state without a theoretical understanding of the way that it worked.

If Thompson mistakenly believed that Britain was on the edge of a revolutionary situation, his concept of political struggle was a theoretical breakthrough. It possibly represented the first tangible evidence of a developed cultural Marxism. Thompson unknowingly advocated what Gramsci would have called "a war of position," and he outlined a "national-popular" politics challenging bourgeois hegemony.[81] As he wrote in "Revolution Again," "It is the business of socialists to draw the line, not between a staunch but diminishing minority [the industrial proletariat] and an unredeemable majority, but between the monopolists and the people—to foster the 'societal instincts' and inhibit the acquisitive."[82] Thompson reverted to the impressionistic rhetoric of the Popular Front, but he articulated a New Left Marxist politics based on a cultural struggle over values.

V

From the beginning, the growth of the New Left was deeply intertwined with the expansion of the CND. With the growth of the

Aldermaston marches and the continued multiplication of disarmament supporters, a growing constituency existed for an alternative socialist politics. The growth of this constituency perhaps reached its height during the struggle to win the Labour Party over to a unilateralist position. CND activists undoubtedly played a role in creating the necessary atmosphere for such a shift in Labour's position, but it became a real possibility when several influential trade union leaders agreed to support unilateralism at the party's annual conference at Scarborough in the summer of 1960. The Labour Party voted 3,303,000 to 2,896,000 in favor of the unilateral renunciation of all nuclear weapons in Great Britain.

The CND's victory at Scarborough was its most tangible political achievement, but, even at the time, it was more apparent than real. First, since the unions voted in blocs at party conferences, the vote was more indicative of the views of the union leadership than of its members. Second, union leaders' support for unilateralism was part of a wider power struggle in the party. Following Labour's third consecutive loss at the polls in 1959, Hugh Gaitskell intensified his campaign to break with the party's past. Most importantly, he sought to remove the fourth clause of Labour's constitution—its commitment to achieving the common ownership of the means of production. While Labour's pledge to Clause IV was largely symbolic, the attempt to abolish it provoked considerable indignation and resentment. Many at Scarborough might have been unilateralists deep down, but, most importantly, they used the issue as a means of venting their anger and showing up the leadership. After Gaitskell abandoned hope of removing Clause IV, his critics were eager to repair the breach in the party, and they were willing to make concessions on disarmament. At its next conference at Blackpool in 1961, Labour reversed its stand.[83]

Labour's about-face on unilateralism had a significant impact on the direction of the CND. With the failure of the strategy of working through established channels, the stage was set for a frontal assault by supporters of direct action, which by this point had congealed in the Committee of 100 initiated by Bertrand Russell. While Russell saw direct action as a symbolic gesture, other members of the committee saw the CND as an all-embracing protest movement whose eventual goal was a general strike. They equated mass civil disobedience with revolution, and they were as antagonistic to the labor movement as they were to the government. Such a position anticipated certain trends in student politics during the late sixties and early seventies. The most famous action sponsored by the Committee of 100 was a sit-down in Trafalgar Square on 17 September 1961. Some 1,300 of a total of 12,000 demonstrators were arrested. Many participated in this event because they were angered by the imprisonment of almost a third of the Committee of 100— including the nearly ninety-year-old Russell—two weeks before the demonstration. The arrested demonstrators were charged with inciting a breach of the peace under the Justices of the Peace Act of 1361. While Russell's sentence was reduced to seven days, others on the committee were imprisoned for as long as two months.[84]

As the contingent within the disarmament movement that, according to CND secretary Peggy Duff, "provided a political leadership and a hard background of political analysis to what was basically a moral crusade," the New Left played a significant role in agitating for a shift in Labour's stance at the Scarborough conference.[85] Although encouraged by the outcome, the New Left was cognizant that the change was achieved by bloc voting rather than by grassroots politics. However, when the victory turned out to be hollow, the New Left found itself in a difficult position. New Leftists saw a coalition between the CND and Labour as a precondition for socialist renewal. Their hopes were seriously deflated when Labour reversed its position on unilateralism, and a majority of New Left members were less than enthusiastic about the shift inside the CND. Although some activists associated with *NLR* became involved in the Committee of 100, most saw it as disruptive to the movement's unity and regarded it as increasing the difficulties of moving the CND in a socialist direction.[86] Yet the New Left also found it difficult to support Labour candidates who defended the leadership's position on nuclear weapons. Thompson advocated that the Committee of 100, the CND magazine *Peace News*, the New Left, and Labour dissidents sponsor a slate of independent candidates in electoral districts where Tories had no chance of being elected, but he was unable to convince CND supporters, like Michael Foot of the Labour Left, that such a strategy would not damage the Labour Party.

The New Left was just as unsuccessful in influencing the Labour Party. Not only did the New Left fail to influence Labour's defense policy, but the party never incorporated other New Left positions. A clear signal was sent when Labour adopted as its party platform *Signposts for the Sixties* in 1961. A document containing more traditional rhetoric than its 1958 predecessor, *Industry and Society*, it failed to integrate New Left approaches to social issues. Indeed, earlier versions of Labour's platform included New Left concerns such as culture, the media, and the democratic control of industry, but these issues were absent from the final text.[87]

By 1962–63 the New Left was in visible decline. Its rise had been closely connected to the CND's, and the disarmament movement was spent. The CND could survive only so long without a tangible political success, and the Nuclear Test Ban Treaty of 1963 soothed public anxiety and successfully killed the disarmament issue. As early as 1961 the New Left club movement showed signs of disintegrating. At the New Left's Stockport conference, Bob Alston observed that "if there were not more 'sense of movement' in the journal very soon, then there might cease to be any Clubs: already 20 of the 40 listed Clubs show few signs of activity: only 10 Clubs were actually represented at Stockport."[88] Later that year NLR likewise admitted the decline of club activism. While few clubs formally disbanded, many "became quiescent."[89] In 1963 NLR still published a list of clubs, but the clubs no longer met.

The journal likewise fell on hard times. After an initially enthusiastic reception, its sales declined—a thousand readers were lost in the first year—and the journal was openly criticized within the movement.[90] Some critics complained that NLR was written for an intellectual audience rather than for the movement's activists. Others were frustrated by the poor communication between the editor and the editorial board, which led to Stuart Hall making too many decisions on his own. In a circulated memorandum Raphael Samuel and Dennis Butts objected that the journal did not pay enough attention to the movement, not only the journal's relationship to the club movement, but to "a sense of the movement of life" in Britain.[91] In such a climate Hall found his position increasingly untenable, and, in the spring of 1961 he threw up his hands in disgust and offered his resignation.[92] Although he was talked out of it, he resigned as NLR editor at the end of 1961.

In spite of the many problems surrounding his editorship, Hall's resignation was a setback to New Left unity. He was an adept mediator who had many friends throughout the CND and the New Left, and he was skillful at building bridges and coalitions. He was among the very few individuals trusted by both activists of the younger generation and the ex-Communist old guard. After his resignation, the fragile bonds between the different elements in the New Left became increasingly strained. Many years later, Hall still regarded the editorship of *NLR* as the greatest opportunity in his life, one of those rare instances when an intellectual is able to play a visible role in political life. After his resignation he experienced a prolonged period of depression and withdrawal.[93]

Following Hall's resignation, various makeshift groups produced the journal, but none was successful in reviving *NLR* or the New Left's sagging fortunes.[94] By 1962–63 *NLR's* total circulation per issue had dwindled from 10,000 to 3,500, and many of the journal's founders were exhausted. They had either resigned, withdrawn from meaningful involvement, or were ready to resign as soon as *NLR* could be placed on a firm footing. The journal needed new blood and creative energy, a means of paying off its accumulated debts, and a financial plan to assure its future.[95] It was at this moment that Perry Anderson surfaced as the only candidate capable of filling the void.

Anderson was slightly younger than the *ULR* group, and during the first years of the New Left he was a prominent radical student intellectual at Oxford. He played a leading role in the student publication *New University*, and he was known as an intellectual of enormous power and range. By this time he had edited and written for the *New University* issue on the Cuban Revolution (the first sustained analysis to appear in the British Left-wing press), and he had published articles on Swedish social democracy, the Common Market, and Portugal. He was fluent in philosophy, psychoanalysis, political theory, and literary criticism. Where most New Left activists were from middle- or working-class families, Anderson was from a wealthy Anglo-Irish background. He tended to be less involved in the daily grind of politics than his predecessors and was closer to being a traditional academic than were Hall or Samuel. Anderson's idea of a radical journal was not *Left Review* but *Les Temps Modernes*. He modeled himself, not after someone like Tawney, who was both an academic historian and a WEA teacher, but after an engagé intellectual such as Jean-Paul Sartre. The *NLR* office under Hall's editorship had been the hub of the movement, an informal, hectic place for both socializing and political activism. When Anderson took charge, the mood became more businesslike and orderly.

The old guard might have found Anderson's political style less than ideal, but they admired his intellect, and they believed that he had the requisite energy to revive the journal. Moreover, he was willing to pay *NLR's* debts and invest the money necessary to establish it on a firm basis—£9,000 as Alan Hall recalled.[96] As Thompson admitted in a letter written in May 1962, the *NLR* board had few options. *NLR* could either be formally sold to Anderson, and he could run it as he pleased, or it could be signed over to him while a board of directors or trustees acted as a backstop. Another possibility was that Anderson, having recapitalized *NLR*, could have a free hand in running it, while the old board could use *NLR*'s assets to further "Fabian-type" activities. Thompson apparently meant that Anderson could pay rent to the New Left board who were shareholders in New Left Review Ltd., which owned the building that housed the journal. They in turn could use this money to launch their own political projects. Thompson acknowledged that this course of action was unlikely: "[O]ur morale is *so* low that I don't know if this is possible."[97] After a long and acrimonious board meeting on 6 and 7 April 1963, Anderson obtained intellectual and financial control of the *Review*, and the board was disbanded. "After a number of possibilities had been explored, it was found that the Board had no clear function in the present situation, and was felt by the Editor to be a 'constitutional built-in irritant and distraction.'"[98] With the transfer of ownership of *NLR* to Anderson, the first New Left lost its principal vehicle of communication, but at the same time, for all practical purposes, it was a spent force.

VI

The New Left created a distinct location on the political map; it fused the cultural and political protest characteristic of the CND and youth subcultural revolt with the older socialist traditions of the labor movement. Theoretically, its politics represented a decisive break with fundamental assumptions inscribed in the socialist Left's history, particularly the belief that a socialist transformation was guaranteed by the laws of history. New Leftists began to supplant a politics founded on the triumph of "socialist man" with a more complex analysis of human roles and possibilities in contemporary society—what might in more contemporary terms be described as the beginnings of identity politics.[99] Yet if the New Left was preparing to discard the obsolete mythology of the socialist heritage, in other respects its politics were founded on a recovery of neglected dimensions of the socialist past—particularly the revival of utopian thought and a renewed appreciation of historical traditions of popular resistance. Here, the writings of the Communist historians and Raymond Williams were of great importance.

Yet the New Left was never able to translate its intellectual breakthroughs into a permanent organization. The movement consisted of numerous tendencies with different priorities and agendas; the ties keeping them together were always fragile. In acknowledging the perspectives of its various constituencies, the New Left satisfied none of them. It suffered from a multiplicity, rather than a lack, of purposes. Its strategy of keeping one foot inside and one foot outside the Labour Party was conceivable only when Labour was in opposition. When Labour had a chance to assume power, such distance was nearly impossible. The choice between the Tories and Labour might have been, as Stuart Hall once said, between black and dark gray, but it was a choice none-theless, and the New Left could not stay on the sidelines.[100]

Even had the New Left defined itself and its goals more rigor-ously, and even if it had organized itself into a more cohesive and structured organization, it probably would have been equally un-successful. At a time when the Cold War was still a tangible reality, the Conservative Party in firm control, and the traditional working-class movement in active flux and in the initial stages of decomposi-tion, the revival of socialism en masse was not on the agenda. Most important, the New Left was a movement whose audience con-sisted mainly of middle-class students and professionals (though not infrequently from working-class backgrounds), many of whom were entering the growing public sector in positions where cultural issues were of great importance. The most tangible connections to the labor movement, as Mike Rustin observed, were "characteristi-cally effected through the channel of workers' education—through trade union colleges, research departments, and links with a few significant trade-union leaders, such as Lawrence Daly of the Na-tional Union of Mineworkers."[101]

The founders of the New Left disagreed among themselves whether the New Left's first priority should be building an inde-pendent political movement or creating the theoretical ground for such a possibility. In retrospect, those who saw the New Left as an incubator of ideas had the greatest foresight. For ultimately the original New Left's legacy was not that of a political movement in the traditional sense, but in its creation of a space for cultural politics and theory in Britain—an achievement that requires fur-ther examination.

THREE Culture Is Ordinary

One of the most far-reaching consequences of the New Left experience was the pivotal role it played in creating cultural Marxism in Britain. British cultural Marxism grew out of the effort to generate a socialist understanding of postwar Britain, to grasp the significance of working-class affluence, consumer capitalism, and the greatly expanded role of the mass media in contemporary life. These changes posed a threat to the traditional Marxist assumption that the working class would inevitably usher in a socialist society. They also undermined the traditional Left's exclusive reliance on political and economic categories, for postwar transformations affected "the whole way of life" of working people and were reshaping their identities in new and complex ways. Cultural Marxists attempted to identify the contours of this new terrain and, in doing so, redefine social struggle. In opposition to orthodox Marxists who reduced culture to a secondary status—a reflection of real social relations—and conservatives who saw it as the best that has been thought and written, they viewed culture in anthropological terms, as an expression of everyday life and experience.

The development of a cultural Marxist perspective was critical to the creation of cultural studies and the development of "history from below." Richard Hoggart, Raymond Williams, and Stuart Hall played pioneering roles in conceiving of cultural studies, an interdisciplinary critical approach to contemporary cultural practices that owed much to discussions and debates in and around the New Left. This effort was greatly advanced by the founding of the Centre for Contemporary Cultural Studies at the University of Birmingham in 1964. E. P. Thompson played a prominent role in producing a distinctive cultural Marxist history. His influential *The Making of the English Working Class* viewed the popular struggle of the common people in cultural terms, providing a New Left inflection to the tradition of Communist historiography. Although writers in both disciplines shared common theoretical and political oppositions and were deeply affected by the New Left context, they did not share a unified approach. Rather, they engaged in a constructive debate and dialogue that reproduced some of the fundamental tensions characteristic of the original New Left as well as creating new ones. Their collective efforts produced a new theoretical terrain.

I

Unlike Marxist historiography whose roots were in the Popular Front of the mid-thirties, cultural studies did not begin to take shape until the late 1950s. It was an outgrowth of English literary criticism, a field that played a unique and pivotal role in intellectual life. Not only was it the heart of the humanities and the core of university education, but only criticism produced a totalizing vision of English society. In France and Germany, sociology and historical materialism originated as efforts to understand the fragmentation of modern society and to formulate implicit and explicit solutions restoring social unity. Britain never produced its own classical sociology, but writers and critics such as Matthew Arnold, Thomas Carlyle, Samuel Coleridge, T. S. Eliot, F. R. Leavis, William Morris, George Orwell, and John Ruskin developed its English equivalent. What Raymond Williams described as the "culture and society" tradition had no political philosophy in common; its exponents were located on both sides of the political divide. Yet they agreed that a cohesive organic culture had been eroded by an artificial industrial and political civilization. That erosion had resulted in the modern crisis, whose resolution depended on the recovery and extension of community or cultural values.[1]

Although cultural studies was predominantly socialist and Marxist, two of its key influences—T. S. Eliot and F. R. Leavis—were cultural conservatives with roots in this intellectual tradition. Eliot was preoccupied with cultural decline. He believed that democracy and mass education were incompatible with cultural values and would inevitably produce a faceless mass society. In opposition to social planning advocates who backed governmental support for the spread of culture, Eliot argued that culture evolved only "naturally" and under certain conditions. In his view these conditions consisted of a hierarchical social order founded on orthodox Christian principles, a society where each order had clearly defined functions. Cultural development depended on the existence of an intellectual elite that transcended class interests and a hereditary ruling class that supported this elite.

Like Eliot's, Leavis's thought was haunted by the cultural deterioration of modern times. For Leavis, an organic society, a harmonious social order where the arts expressed the life of the community, had existed until the seventeenth century. This society was decisively destroyed by the Industrial Revolution, the cash nexus, and middle-class materialism; it was supplanted by a vacuous social order that debased and stultified the human spirit. The last residue of the old culture, the surviving literature, was threatened with extinction by the erosion of standards, manifest in both the mass media and metropolitan literary culture.

Leavis's thought represented a counterpoint to thirties' Marxism. Like the Marxists, he recognized the pivotal role of the seventeenth-century revolution in accelerating the disintegration of the rural community, and he deeply hated the capitalist mentality. Early in his career he expressed some vague commitment to communism, and in the thirties the *Scrutiny* circle developed a Marxian fringe.[2] However, Leavis and his associates believed that Marxists were not radical enough. They viewed the Marxist emphasis on economic production and class hatred as part of the same system of values as capitalism, and they believed that Marxists misconstrued the crisis of modern society. For Leavis and *Scrutiny*, the roots of the contemporary social crisis were not material but spiritual and cultural.

For Leavis, the salvation of society was contingent upon a rehabilitation of the values of the old organic order. However, in contrast to preindustrial society when these values emerged spontaneously, an organized effort was now needed to keep them alive and restore them to preeminence. Leavis saw literary critics as being in the avant-garde of this renewal. With I. A. Richards and others, he helped transform literary studies from a gentleman's amateurish pursuit to a disciplined profession of "practical criticism," an aesthetic and moral practice based on the stringent training of one's sensibility. Leavis regarded professional critics as possessing special powers of insight into the workings of society and a responsibility for transforming it. They were to uphold literary standards, preserve "the tradition" from further erosion, and bring the "play of the free intelligence" to bear upon "the underlying issues" of the modern world. Leavis and *Scrutiny* never spelled out a political position, but they clearly saw education as the primary site from which to oppose materialism. They advocated the reform of university education so that it produced "misfits" rather than "spare-parts."

Taken together, Eliot and Leavis helped establish the terrain of cultural studies. Although Eliot was mainly interested in high culture, he believed that its existence could not be separated from the whole way of life. In a famous passage in *Notes Towards the Definition of Culture* (1949) he wrote: "[C]ulture . . . includes all the characteristic activities and interests of a people: Derby Day, Henley Regatta, Cowes, the twelfth of August, a cup final, the dog races, the pin table, the dart board, Wensleydale cheese, boiled cabbage cut into sections, beetroot in vinegar, nineteenth-century Gothic churches, and the music of Elgar."[3] Eliot's list, of course, was principally confined to sports, entertainment, and food—hardly the whole way of life. Yet his expansion of the meaning of culture to include practices outside literature and the arts was a major step toward the study of popular culture.

Similarly, *Scrutiny's* transformation of the profession of criticism pointed beyond literary studies. First, its contributors, if concerned mainly with literature, used critical methods to examine social and cultural practices more generally, making possible the critical examination of advertising, popular music, the mass media, and consumerism. Second, Leavis's interest in the tangled relationship between community, culture, language, history, and tradition raised issues that could not be easily handled in existing disciplines. This interest paved the way for a field concerned with more general cultural questions. Third, *Scrutiny's* commitment to educational reform, although chiefly aimed at creating an enlightened minority, offered itself to being extended in more democratic directions. The democratization of education could potentially break down the class barriers that stood in the way of a genuine common culture.

Richard Hoggart and Raymond Williams were principally responsible for creating cultural studies. Both of them were trained as Leavisite literary critics, and throughout the fifties they were adult education teachers in the Workers' Educational Association. Williams was a staff tutor in the Oxford extramural program at Hastings, Hoggart a senior staff tutor in literature in the department of adult education at Hull University. Most important, Hoggart and Williams belonged to that unusual breed of socialist intellectuals who were actually from working-class backgrounds and attended universities as "scholarship boys." Williams was from the Welsh border country and received his degree from Cambridge, while Hoggart grew up in the industrial town of Leeds and attended

Leeds University. Being from working-class backgrounds, yet attending universities when they were virtually off-limits to working
people, both men were acutely aware of cultural differences; further, they were in a good position to observe continuities and
changes in working-class patterns of life.

Hoggart's *The Uses of Literacy* (1957) was a contribution to both
the debate about mass culture and the controversy over the implications of working-class affluence. Hoggart disagreed with those
who believed that working-class people automatically became
more middle class as a consequence of a higher standard of living
and increased educational opportunities. He also differed with traditional Marxists who saw the working class as a fixed and static
entity, invulnerable to the pressures of a changing world. Hoggart
suggested that continuities and changes in the working-class way of
life could be understood only through a comparative analysis. In
The Uses of Literacy he described both traditional working-class
culture and the impact of the mass media on its way of life.

In "An 'Older' Order," Hoggart painstakingly re-created traditional working-class culture. For him, working-class life was distinguished by ties of solidarity, commitment to community, home,
and neighborhood, and the sense of "us" versus "them." He acknowledged that culture's limitations: its provincialism, its stubborn resistance to change and innovation, its suspicion of nonconformity. Yet he implicitly maintained that it was only because of
class prejudice that critics mistook the working-class way of life for
mass culture. Traditional working-class life was as "organic" as that
of the old rural society for which *Scrutiny* hopelessly yearned.

If the Leavisites underestimated the value of working-class culture, Marxists romanticized it. Hoggart argued that class struggle
was not integral to working-class life and that the politically conscious minority—the fixation of Marxists and labor historians—
was unrepresentative of the culture as a whole. Sticking together,
in his view, "does not develop into a conscious sense of being part
of 'the working-class movement': the 'Co-ops' are today less typical of the outlook of the majority in the working-classes than the
small privately-owned corner-shops serving a couple of streets."[4]

In the second part of *The Uses of Literacy*, "Yielding Place to
the New," Hoggart argued that mass culture—one dimension of a
complex web of social, political, and economic change—threatened traditional working-class culture. "These productions," he
wrote, "belong to a vicarious, spectators' world; they offer nothing

which can really grip the brain or heart. They assist a gradual drying-up of the more positive, the fuller, the more cooperative kinds of enjoyment, in which one gains much by giving much. . . . A handful of such production reaches daily the great majority of the population: the effect is both widespread and uniform."[5] Hoggart was not without hope. First, he believed that the working class frequently resisted the appeals of advertising and the mass media and still could draw on "older promptings." Second, he saw the shift in the political debate from economic to cultural questions as a sign of social progress.[6] Yet if Hoggart welcomed the change in the debate, he felt that important segments of the Left still saw such issues in older terms; frequently, socialists approached culture either in a philistine way or tenaciously resisted evidence of social change. "If the activite minority," Hoggart warned Left-wing readers, "continue to allow themselves too exclusively to think of immediate political and economic objectives, the pass will be sold, culturally behind their backs."[7] Society will be dominated by a vast new classless class that was defrauded of its inner freedom but would never know it.

Hoggart's account was based mainly on his own experience. It was overtly autobiographical and depended on childhood memories even when using the third person. He re-created the smells, sounds, tastes, and feelings of working-class life. It was at once sociology and criticism, sustained by the special powers that his training as a critic bestowed on him. In one passage Hoggart re-created a working-class district through the eyes of an eleven-year-old boy: "Here he passes a shop where they never grumble at being asked to sell pennyworths of sweets, here a pal's father smoking in the doorway in his shirtsleeves, after the last shift before the weekend; here a broken-down wooden fence out of which large spiders can be teased; here the off-licence with its bell clanging as someone comes out with a small jug of vinegar."[8] The powerful impact of *The Uses of Literacy* resulted from this blend of autobiography, literary imagery, and critical sensibility. Readers received a concrete image of working-class life from the perspective of an insider whose broader experience allowed him some detachment. Yet if Hoggart's account was based on childhood memories, it purported to be about the working class as a whole. He never considered the effect of regional, ethnic, and religious differences or the uneven effects of social change in Britain. His experiential approach might have been more vibrant than a sociological study based on surveys, but his failure to situate his subject in a larger social context was a real limitation. In addition, one of the most striking oddities and weaknesses of Hoggart's book was the asymmetry between its two parts. *The Uses of Literacy* purported to be a comparative analysis of two periods in working-class life. But the first part was a semiautobiographical ethnography, the second mostly critical readings of mass cultural texts. The two eluded comparison.

Hoggart's reading of popular publications and the evocative ethnography of working-class life were the most direct influences on the development of early cultural studies. First, he extended *Scrutiny*'s critical approach. He used literary-critical methods to understand the meaning of cultural experience, reading lived experience as if it were a text. This approach was a breakthrough in the analytical study of popular culture. Second, *The Uses of Literacy* was interdisciplinary, blurring the distinction between sociology, literary criticism, and politics.[9] Yet if Hoggart's approach represented a significant advance, his condemnation of new cultural trends was reminiscent of Leavis. While Hoggart regarded the older forms of popular entertainment as valid expressions of the "full rich life," he saw the newer ones as "puff-pastry literature, with nothing inside the pastry, the ceaseless exploitation of a hollow brightness."[10] Hoggart turned Leavis's historical mythology upside down, displacing the organic society of Merry Old England with the working-class culture of his youth. The problem was that the working class of the 1930s was itself subject to the pressures of mass culture. If examined from the perspective of an earlier historical period, it undoubtedly would have appeared no less diluted than contemporary working-class culture did from the point of view of Hoggart's childhood memories. Indeed, Hoggart's celebration of authentic working-class experience virtually free of the influence of mass culture was not the only way to represent the cultural experience of working people in the interwar period. The architectural critic Reyner Banham, like Hoggart a Left-wing intellectual from a working-class background, remembered (with great fondness) growing up in Norwich under the spell of American popular culture: *Mechanix Illustrated*, Betty Boop, the films of Chaplin and Keaton. "Thinking back," he recalled, "the cultural background against which I grew up was a very curious one indeed, if one is to believe the sort of things in Hoggart."[11]

Raymond Williams holds a central position in British Marxism. He was one of the most prolific and influential socialist thinkers since the Second World War, and the scope of his work is unparalleled in Anglo-American Left-wing culture. It includes political writings, cultural theory, intellectual history, literary criticism, historical linguistics, and critical and historical examinations of dramatic forms, the novel, television, and the cinema. He also published several novels.

During the Cold War years Williams was extremely isolated and thought of as a political maverick. Like the Communist historians, he was a product of the Popular Front, a Cambridge undergraduate who joined the Party on the eve of the war. However, on returning to Cambridge in the late forties, he allowed his Party membership to lapse. He approved of the Party's militancy, but he was troubled by its subservience to the Soviets and regarded it as oblivious to the realities of postwar Britain. As an adult education teacher in the fifties, Williams found himself in the middle of bitter disputes between Labour and Communist colleagues involving intrigue and witch-hunting. At the most difficult moments he was the only person to whom both contingents would speak,

> the Communists because I shared their intellectual perspectives and most of their political positions; the non-Communists—but there's the rub— because I, like almost all of them, was from a working-class family and had the same tastes in food and drink and enjoyment, whereas most of the Communists (Marxists) were public school boys to whom much of our incidental behavior was vulgar.[12]

Williams could never fully align himself with either side.

Williams's theoretical direction was no less individual. At a time when literary and cultural theory were deeply polarized along ideological lines, he drew on both Marxism and *Scrutiny*, avoiding Marxists' economistic reading of literary texts and the Leavisites' narrow concern with the fate of minority culture and antipathy for the masses. This direction was visible as early as 1947–48 in *Politics and Letters*, a journal that Williams edited with Clifford Collins and Wolf Mankowitz. *Politics and Letters* was a Left-Leavisite magazine that aspired to bring "the best that is thought and known in the world" to bear on social issues, a fusion of the critical sensibility of letters with the active engagement of politics. The editors advocated using the critical methods of literary studies to analyze the cinema and popular literature "in which the absence of the qualities that go to make a civilization is now obvious."[13] Like the Leavisites at that time, Williams and his colleagues were troubled by the corrosive effects of mass culture. However, they were concerned not only with the threat it posed to literary values, but they were worried that it would poison working-class culture.

An early example of Williams's efforts at finding a "third way" was his article, "The Soviet Literary Controversy," published in the first issue of *Politics and Letters*. The essay was a response to an English debate on the Soviet Communist Party's censorship of two Russian writers—the humorist Zoschenko and the poetess Akhmatova—for crimes of Western decadence, bourgeois individualism, and failure to educate the masses. Whereas British Communists supported the action on the grounds that it benefited the general social welfare, journals such as *Horizon* defended the writers' freedom of speech, a right, they hastened to point out, that was guaranteed in the capitalist West. The implication was that socialism in Britain would similarly limit artistic freedom.

Williams found it difficult to affiliate with either side. He found Communists unable to understand the function of literature and criticism; state intervention in literary life could only produce cultural impoverishment. However, he was equally dismayed by the smug response of *Horizon*. He argued that the commercialization of popular literature, the pernicious effects of advertising, and the growing number of writers consumed by monetary gain was as deleterious to a culture as state intervention. In this context, self-proclaimed guardians of minority culture—like *Horizon*—were no less culpable than the companies that made the profits. "To take refuge in the value of the by-product—minority culture—and to ignore the commercial process which has sustained it amounts to sanctioning the commercial process which, grown sick, is destroying the living values by which the minority culture survives."[14] In *Culture and Society* Williams would make a similar criticism of T. S. Eliot.

The lifetime of *Politics and Letters* was brief. By 1948 it had collapsed after only four issues because of financial difficulties and personal conflicts between the editors.[15] The experience left Williams devastated. "For a period," he recalled, "I was in such a state of fatigue and withdrawal that I stopped reading papers or listening to the news."[16] For nearly a decade Williams withdrew from the intellectual world and wrote in nearly total isolation. During this period he completed *Culture and Society* (1958) and conceived of *The Long Revolution* (1961).

According to Williams, the idea for *Culture and Society* began to materialize as part of an adult education course he taught in 1949. He was responding to interest in the concept of culture resulting from discussions generated by Eliot's *Notes Towards the Definition of Culture*, and he was interested in "the concentration of a kind of social thought around this term which hadn't before appeared particularly important."[17] In *Culture and Society* he traced the idea of culture from its origins during the period of the Industrial Revolution to the present day. For him, the historical development of this idea registered shifts in our common experience of the social consequences of industrialization. In the Industrial Revolution's earliest phase "culture" referred to moral and intellectual practices antithetical to an evolving mechanical civilization, to alternative standards and values used to judge, criticize, and transform society, and to a domain of private experience and feelings. It subsequently came to mean "a whole way of life," although the earlier meanings were retained. Despite being heterogeneous, the intellectual tradition responsible for articulating and developing the idea of culture was unified by the fact "that they have been unable to think of society as a merely neutral area, or as an abstract regulating mechanism. The stress has fallen on the positive function of society, on the fact that the values of individual men are rooted in society, and on the need to think and feel in these common terms."[18] For Williams, the "culture and society" tradition represented a critical opposition to classical liberalism, an effort to overcome the centrifugal forces unleashed by bourgeois society.

The significance of *Culture and Society* is twofold. First, it was a brilliant history of ideas. Williams recovered a tradition whose scope, if by now common knowledge, was scarcely appreciated at the time. When Williams began to research the book, he was unaware that cultural discourse existed before Matthew Arnold. By his own admission it was a makeshift operation.[19] Second, Williams's critical evaluation of these thinkers "was oppositional—to counter the appropriation of a long line of thinking about culture to what were by now decisively reactionary positions."[20] His recovery refuted the idea that culture was incompatible with democracy, socialism, and popular education. Like Hoggart, but in a different way, he turned "the tradition" on its head. However, it was symptomatic of the time in which *Culture and Society* was written that Williams found conservative critics such as Leavis and Eliot more relevant to a socialist understanding of postwar transformations than the approved list of progressive writers. Ironically,

Williams at times seemed more sympathetic to reactionary critics than socialist ones.

We can see the oppositional nature of *Culture and Society* in Williams's critical assessments of Eliot, Leavis, and Marxism. Williams acknowledged Eliot's contribution to the expansion of the idea of culture. Yet he found Eliot's vision of an alternative order simplistic, static, and unrelated to modern conditions, and his conservative philosophy contradictory and self-defeating. Ironically, the economic system that made Eliot's cultural elite possible was likewise responsible for the atomization and standardization that he deplored. According to Eliot's own view of culture, the two could not be separated. Eliot intended to expose the illusions of liberalism, but his thought, if taken to its logical conclusion, exposed the illusions of conservatism as well.

Williams respected and admired Leavis. He regarded him as the most interesting critic of his generation, an important influence on the period's best work, and a major contributor to English culture.[21] He was initially drawn to *Scrutiny*'s militant defense of cultural standards and the journal's account of those standards' decline, in part because *Scrutiny*'s views did not contradict his own experience. "It did not tell me that my father and grandfather were ignorant wage-slaves; it did not tell me that the smart, busy, commercial culture (which I had come to as a stranger, so much so that for years I had violent headaches whenever I passed through London and saw underground advertisements and evening newspapers) was the thing I had to catch up with."[22] Williams found freeing himself from Leavis's influence an extremely difficult task that consumed several years.

Williams's critique of Leavis and *Scrutiny* had two components. He agreed with Leavis that the most nuanced and fragile parts of tradition were embodied in language and literature, but he rejected the idea that language and literature represented the entire cultural heritage. According to Williams, Leavis ignored forms of knowledge, institutions, manners, customs, and family memories, and, conversely, he exaggerated the importance of English studies. For Williams, "the difficulty about the idea of culture" was "that we are continually forced to extend it, until it becomes almost identical with our whole common life."[23] As a consequence of this wider understanding, it was inconceivable that a group of enlightened intellectuals could serve as the guardians of cultural inheritance. Culture was intrinsically democratic.

Williams likewise found Leavis's view of historical development one-sided. Williams was not opposed to the idea of an organic society per se, and he observed that the values it embodied might be fruitfully compared to those found in the modern world. "But it is misleading," he wrote, "to make this contrast without making others, and it is foolish and dangerous to exclude from the so-called organic society the penury, the petty tyranny, the disease and mortality, the ignorance and frustrated intelligence which were also among its ingredients."[24] Correlatively, he suggested that Leavis's image of contemporary life suffered from the same problem. Williams acknowledged that while Leavis called attention to many regrettable features of modern society, he ignored what were genuine gains: new forms of gratifying work, social improvements, educational opportunities, and progressive forms of social organization. In the end, Williams found the Leavisite longing for the organic community to be part of an urban fantasy of the past. By definition, the world that was yearned for was irretrievably lost.

In the essay "Culture Is Ordinary," Williams compared Leavis's thought to Marxism. If Leavis knew more about the relationship between art and experience, Marxism had a deeper understanding of English society and history.[25] Although Williams was not a Marxist at this time, he accepted the Marxist idea that a culture "must be finally interpreted in relation to its underlying system of production." He had intuitively known this from childhood experience. "Everything I had seen, growing up in that border country, had led me towards such an emphasis: a culture is a whole way of life, and the arts are part of a social organization which economic change clearly radically affects."[26] Yet Williams objected to the tendency of Marxist cultural theory to reduce cultural practices (superstructure) to the relations of production (base). If the base was determining (a proposition that Williams was skeptical of), it would affect the "whole way of life," and it was to this way of life—not the base—that cultural practices must be related. Similarly, Williams rejected the Marxist contention, popular in the thirties and forties, that the culture of the last several hundred years was bourgeois, and that it would be supplanted by a proletarian culture following the workers' revolution. From this point of view, intellectuals should help clear the debris of the "dying culture" and champion the emerging one, for instance, by promoting socialist realism or the proletarian novel. For Williams, culture was certainly subject to bourgeois power (notably through education), but it contained contributions from other classes and challenges to the dominant ideology by those who were bourgeois themselves. It represented a valuable heritage: a common property to be learned from, evaluated, criticized, and transformed, but certainly not one rejected wholesale or written off as withering away. In terms reminiscent of Eliot, Williams argued against anticipating a future socialist culture: "My own view is that if, in a socialist society, the basic cultural skills are made widely available, and the channels of communication widened and cleared, as much as possible has been done in the way of preparation, and what then emerges will be an actual response to the whole reality, and[,] so[,] valuable."[27] Like Eliot, Williams advocated creating the conditions for cultural growth, but he thought that this growth was possible only within a democratic socialist society.

In *Culture and Society*, Williams was more sympathetic to the political aspirations of Marxists than to those of Eliot and Leavis. However, in one crucial respect Williams believed that all three were alike: their thought was founded on a disabling conception of the people as the masses. Williams acknowledged that the term "masses" had been justified as a way of describing the unprecedented "massing" of people in cities, factories, and political organizations. However, when used in other contexts—to characterize a type of democracy, depict forms of art and entertainment, or portray a mode of opinion—it was an extension of the earlier term "mob." In response to the question "who are the masses?," the answer was always somebody else, those that were unknown or "other." It was not an objective social description but an ideological category. "There are in fact no masses; there are only ways of seeing people as masses. In an urban industrial society there are many opportunities for such ways of seeing. . . . The fact is, surely, that a way of seeing other people which has become characteristic of our kind of society, has been capitalized for the purposes of political or cultural exploitation."[28] Williams believed that the idea of the masses justified a minority's manipulation and control of the majority. This minority control was true of Marxists, for whom the people were helpless and ignorant, and of conservatives who saw the people as a threat to cultural standards. Opposing both sides simultaneously, Williams put forth an alternative conception of society that emphasized growth rather than manipulation, democracy rather than domination, a common culture rather than a restrictive one. He regarded this conception as the necessary and logical outcome of the "culture and society" tradition. As will be seen when Williams's critique of Hoggart is examined, this conception of society's material embodiment was working-class democracy. As part of his examination of the usage of "the masses," Williams discussed the relationship between mass and popular culture. For him, the revolutionary transformation of the media was not only technological, that is, new means of transmission and distribution, but capitalist. The new forms of mass entertainment were not an authentic expression of working-class life, for they were neither produced nor exclusively consumed by working-class people. They represented, instead, an extension of the ideological construct of the "masses" in conjunction with the capitalist drive for maximizing profits. Yet if Williams believed that mass culture was not organically connected to the working-class way of life, he recognized that the working class derived enjoyment and pleasure from it, that it was a form of popular culture. This recognition raised a problem. Was it "mass" or "popular" culture? If mass culture was not an authentic expression of people's experience, what was their relationship to it? Williams found it difficult to understand how people whom he had a high regard for could be satisfied by a low quality of entertainment. He was caught between his own background and populist politics and his literary training. Acknowledging that current explanations were inadequate, he observed that "there is something in the psychology of print and image that none of us has yet quite grasped."[29] While not offering an answer, he was clearly beginning to ask the right question. He was implicitly acknowledging the inadequacy of making generalizations about people's experiences from textual analysis, and he was alluding to the importance of analyzing the experiences themselves. This analysis included the recovery of mass cultural consumption from the point of view of the consumers and studying it in the context of changing social relations and institutions. Williams's overall view of these problems was a crucial, if tentative, step forward in the development of cultural studies.

In *Culture and Society*, Williams came to terms with the mainstream tradition of English cultural criticism. Written during a period of "disgusted withdrawal," the book articulated an approach to culture displacing the elite-mass polarity. *The Long Revolution*, published only three years later, was written under the influence of the late fifties' socialist revival, including New Left discussions about *Culture and Society*, and it was a tangible sign of Williams's reentry into political and intellectual debate.

Williams coined "the long revolution" to describe the industrial, democratic, and cultural transformations of the last two hundred years. It was an oxymoron simultaneously conveying the radically innovative and protracted nature of the process. "It is a genuine revolution," he wrote:

> *transforming men and institutions; continually extended and deepened by the actions of millions, continually and variously opposed by explicit reaction and by the pressure of habitual forms and ideas. Yet it is a difficult revolution to define, and its uneven action is taking place over so long a period that it is almost impossible not to get lost in its exceptionally complicated process.*[30]

In Williams's terms, the cultural and democratic revolutions were not the automatic consequence of economic transformations but were part of a seamless social whole. From this point of view, the creation of the steam printing press was as fundamental as the steam jenny or steam locomotive.

Williams's conception of the long revolution was founded on a more general theory of social organization. He distinguished between four interrelated systems in society: decision (politics), maintenance (economics), education and learning, and generation and nurture. Williams's model was framed in opposition to Marxism. He refused to ascribe primal determinacy to any of these levels, and he insisted that they were separable only analytically. He created his own vocabulary as a means of distancing himself from tainted Marxist terms like "economy," "politics," and "ideology," and he simultaneously avoided dismissal by mainstream critics. In terms similar to Thompson's rejection of Stalinist ideology, Williams justified his conception of the social process by appealing to experience. This approach was most forcefully stated in the introduction to *Communications*, published in 1962: "We are used to descriptions of our whole common life in political and economic terms. The emphasis on communications asserts, as a matter of experience, that men and societies are not confined to relationships of power, property, and production. Their relationships in describing, learning, persuading, and exchanging experiences are seen as equally fundamental."[31] Here, Williams seemed to suggest that Marxist and other forms of economic determinism simplified social life. "Experience" taught that our lives were affected by numerous elements—economic and political, but also cultural, linguistic, and symbolic.

Williams's view of the long revolution and the social process more generally was founded on a complex attitude toward culture. From an anthropological perspective, culture signified the meanings, values, and institutions of a society—what Williams frequently described as the "whole way of life." Culture could also convey a more limited sphere of human activity, the body of intellectual and imaginative work representing the creative response. A limited number of these practices contributed to an ideal form of culture, that is, the finest artistic and intellectual productions that a society had to offer—the "cultural heritage" or the "great tradition." Williams was unconcerned that culture could be variously defined, for it conformed to real aspects of experience. Indeed, he suggested that the task of cultural analysis was to establish the relationship between the three levels. For Williams, the theory of culture was the study of relationships between elements in a whole way of life, while cultural analysis was "the attempt to discover the nature of the organization which is the complex of these relationships."[32]

Williams was acutely aware of the limits to the new discipline that he was proposing. He admitted that an intangible component of cultural life could be known only experientially. Just as he believed that it was through experience that we could understand the totality of the social process, he insisted that the members of a culture had a privileged knowledge of their way of life. Outsiders to the cultural situation, whether because of history or geography or both, could only imperfectly and abstractly re-create it.

Williams attempted to overcome these difficulties by means of his own conceptual vocabulary. Two concepts in particular were fundamental to his analysis of culture: social character and structure of feeling. By "social character," Williams meant a system of values and ideals taught formally and informally. It became the "dominant social character" when referring to the value system of the most influential and powerful social class, a usage similar to the Marxist concept of ideology. Williams's notion of "structure of feeling" was one of his most original contributions to cultural analysis. It was a means of characterizing the inner experience of individuals who shared a common way of life. "It is as firm and definite as 'structure' suggests, yet operates in the most delicate and least tangible parts of our activity." It was most concretely revealed in a period's cultural artifacts, particularly the arts: "the particular living result of all the elements in the general organization."[33]

Williams used these concepts to analyze England in the 1840s. He distinguished between three social characters: the "dominant" or "middle class," rooted in individual effort and hard work, the values of thrift and sobriety; the "aristocratic," which assumed that birth was more important than money and leisure as important as work; and the "working class," which was based on neither birth nor status but mutual aid and cooperation. Although Williams acknowledged that the dominant social character put its stamp on the whole society, he asserted that it was the interaction between the three social characters that gave the social process in 1840s England its distinction.

> *The aristocratic ideals tempering the harshness of middle-class ideals at their worst; working-class ideals entering into a fruitful and decisive combination with middle-class ideals at their best. The middle-class social character remains dominant, and both aristocrats and working people, in many respects, come to terms with it. But equally, the middle-class social character as it entered the forties is in many respects modified as the forties end.*[34]

Williams stressed, then, the complexity of ideological interaction, the difference between ideology in theory and ideology in practice. Yet as E. P. Thompson pointed out in a famous critique (discussed in section II of this chapter), Williams overlooked that disputes between the social characters signified not only a dialogue between competing value systems, but a class conflict over political and economic power. Williams's portrayal of ideological conflict was closer to being an amiable conversation than a struggle between unequal social forces.

Williams acknowledged how difficult it was to disentangle the structure of feeling from the social characters of the 1840s. On the one hand, he suggested, the structure of feeling was equivalent to the dominant social character and was most frequently articulated by the most prominent group in society. He likewise viewed the structure of feeling as the interaction between middle-class, aristocratic, and working-class ideals, distinguishable from the social characters in that it involved not only publicly stated ideals but equally important omissions and silences. It seemed as if Williams, though believing that the structure of feeling was connected to the deepest level of social experience, was groping to define what it in fact represented. He never explained why there was only one structure of feeling or why different generations during the same period or different classes necessarily shared the same one.

Williams's *The Long Revolution* was a landmark in the theorization of culture, a decisive break with the Leavis-Eliot tradition. It was the first sustained theoretical attempt in an English context to understand the multidimensional nature of culture, to comprehend its interdependence with other social practices, and to argue that the understanding of culture involved the creation of a new interdisciplinary approach. At the book's core, as in other of Williams's early work, was the privileged status accorded to "experience." He defended his concept of the social totality on the basis of "experience," and he argued that an intangible component of a culture always remained and was accessible only to those who experienced it. In both cases, Williams seemed to be arguing that the knowledge gained through experience was superior to that achieved through theory or abstract thought. This position was similar to that of critics such as Leavis and, more importantly, was reminiscent of Thompson's critique of Stalinism. Thompson invoked working-class experience in opposition to Stalinist distortion; he counterposed the category of "experience" to that of "ideology." Williams defended the authenticity of experience against efforts at systematizing it. Like Thompson, he was probably thinking that the experience of working people was a more reliable guide to an understanding of society than the ideological grid imposed by orthodox Marxists. While Williams and Thompson were by no means theoretical twins, the close attention they gave to "experience" helped shape the founding of cultural studies in the late 1950s and early 1960s. It was likewise central to theoretical debates between historians and cultural theorists in the late seventies.

II

Since Hoggart and Williams developed similar approaches to interpreting cultural practices and their most influential work was published at virtually the same time, it was often assumed that they developed their ideas in tandem. Williams once whimsically observed that their names were so frequently linked that it sounded as if they formed a joint firm.[35] However, when Hoggart was writing *The Uses of Literacy* and Williams was working on *Culture and Society*, they had not even met. Until the late fifties they exchanged only a dozen letters, none while the two books were being written.

Rather, their ideas were formulated in response to the same cultural and political situation, from roughly equivalent class positions, and conceived within, and against, a common intellectual tradition.[36] In different ways they shifted the socialist debate on working-class affluence and the impact of the mass media on working-class life to the realm of culture.

Hoggart's *The Uses of Literacy* provoked a wide-ranging discussion in New Left circles. *ULR* described it as "rich and disturbing," and it introduced a series of critical responses to it by asking (among other things): "What are the most effective barriers to the encroachment of 'the candy-floss world'?"[37] Among the respondents was Williams himself, who proved to be one of Hoggart's most perceptive critics. His critique of Hoggart was later incorporated into the influential conclusion of *Culture and Society.*

After criticizing Hoggart's concept of working-class culture, Williams offered his own alternative. He found Hoggart's portrayal of the working class idealized, and he was skeptical that the working-class way of life was threatened with extinction. Williams argued that the reason working-class culture was still an alternative to bourgeois society was neither because of its everyday activities (Hoggart) nor its literary output (orthodox Marxists); it stemmed from its political culture—the collective and democratic institutions of the labor movement that represented an extension of the primary relationships of family and community. Where Hoggart conceived of a binary opposition between "working-class culture" and "majority" and "labor movement" and "minority," Williams maintained that those who were politically active articulated the majority's values, interests, and goals. "It is not isolated, but is the articulate representation of an extension of primary values into the social fields. It is not self-defensive, for it seeks consistently to operate in the majority's behalf and interest. It is not opposed to majority values, but seeks to define them in wider terms and in a different context."[38] Williams acknowledged that numerous working-class people felt pressured to take advantage of the "opportunity state" and that individual members had climbed the ladder offered them. Yet he was convinced that the collective democratic idea, the foundation of working-class experience, remained unimpaired. While liberal reform was ultimately based on the maintenance of inequality and exploitation, the extension of working-class values would produce a genuine democracy. "There are no masses to capture, but only this mainstream to join. May it be here that the two major senses of culture—on the one hand the arts, the sciences, and learning, on the other hand the whole way of life—are valuably drawn together, in a common effort at maturity."[39] In short, the material realization of the *Culture and Society* tradition was working-class democracy.

Although they were not prominent in the founding of the New Left, Hoggart and Williams were both supportive of the general aims of the new socialist politics, and they contributed to New Left journals. Indeed, Williams was an original member of the *NLR* editorial board and played a pivotal role in mediating disputes that arose when the journal was transformed in 1963. Most important, Hoggart and Williams were two of the most important influences on New Left efforts at reframing socialist priorities, and they were instrumental in establishing the parameters of the debate on working-class culture.

Their influence is apparent in Stuart Hall's "A Sense of Classlessness," published in *ULR* in 1958. Hall's essay was an intervention into the debate on the contemporary working class, which *The Uses of Literacy* so powerfully provoked. He affirmed both Williams's rejection in the conclusion to *Culture and Society* of a simplistic cause-and-effect relationship between material goods and working-class consciousness and his claim that the basis of working-class culture was its values and institutions. However, Hall insisted that "a way of life cannot be sustained without a certain pattern of relationships, and outside of certain physical, economic and environmental pressures."[40] And he argued that to understand working-class culture it was necessary to establish the relationship between changing objective circumstances and subjective responses, in other words, the links between base and superstructure. Of course, Hall was not promoting a return to Marxist orthodoxy; he believed that a "freer play" must exist between the two terms, and he suggested that transformations in the superstructure were no less determining than those in the base. As a result, Hall advanced the economic and sociological analysis alluded to in Hoggart's interpretation of contemporary working-class life and absent in Williams's. In reaching his position, Hall drew from many sources, not least from the sociologist C. Wright Mills, who, in *The Power Elite*, called attention (1) to the new elites who shared a common ideology, style of living, and economic interest in the "mutual care" of corporate private property and (2) to an exploited and alienated mass of consumers who were being proletarianized in an upward direction.

Hall's analysis of working-class consciousness was founded on his understanding of transformations in the capitalist mode of production. These can be broken down into three principal components. First, the old entrepreneurial capitalism was being supplanted by the "organized irresponsibility" of corporations, the anonymity of the managerial revolution, and a system of production increasingly founded on skilled labor and automation. Second, alienation in the classical Marxist sense was on the decline, but under the guise of "joint consultation" and "personnel management" it was being built into the structure of firms themselves. Third—and most important—the new system was increasingly based on consumption (rather than production), low unemployment, and relatively high wages. Unprecedented amounts of disposable income and consumer demand resulted, kept high, in part, by the growing sophistication and prevalence of advertising.

What did these changes mean for working-class consciousness? In answering this question, Hall distinguished himself from Williams who he believed had underestimated the impact of the consumer revolution. Under consumer capitalism, working-class people conceptualized themselves more as consumers than producers, and they were more aware of exploitation in the marketplace than at the workplace. While working-class culture was not equivalent to the objects that it owned, "it may now be less and less true, because the 'new things' *in themselves* suggest and imply a way of life which has become objectified *through them*, and may even become desirable because of their social value."[41] For Hall, working-class culture was breaking down into several styles of living not unlike those of the middle class. It was not that the objective determinants of class inequalities were any less real, but that they were experienced as a sense of class confusion or a false sense of classlessness, "the tragic conflict within a working class which has freed itself only for new and more subtle forms of enslavement."[42]

Edward Thompson was the most incisive Marxist critic of the culturalism of Hoggart and Williams and the Marxist inflection given to their work by Hall. In crucial respects Thompson was unique among the Marxist historians. The historians played a major role in "1956," and they supported the *Reasoner* effort and the formation of the New Left. In the years following their departure from the Communist Party (or, as in the case of Hobsbawm, renouncing Marxist dogmatism), their writings were more cognizant of the cultural dimension of history. This awareness was especially true of their recovery of the experience of oppressed groups, or "history from below." Yet the historians' interest in culture preceded the New Left socialist revival of the late 1950s. Their greater interest in cultural practices resulted more from freeing themselves from the straitjacket of Communist orthodoxy and thus being able to pursue this aspect of their work in greater depth. They might have been affected by the change in the political and cultural climate, but not because of any specific New Left influence. Thompson, on the other hand, was one of the founders of the New Left and one of the movement's most influential writers. He was the only historian to develop a specifically New Left theoretical perspective: a cultural Marxism fusing the new approaches to culture and the Communist tradition of the Historians' Group.

Thompson's critique of Hoggart, Hall, and the *ULR* approach, in general, was historical and political. He acknowledged that they had contributed to an understanding of changes in working-class life and were responsible for bringing to light critical areas of concern for socialists. As a humanist and critic of the base/superstructure model, he approved of their interest in culture, and he was enthusiastic about their wider understanding of human existence. However, Thompson found Hoggart and Hall's sociological approach to working-class culture devoid of the more general historical context of working-class history and the class struggle. He pointed out that the working class had been lured by social climbing and status since the middle of the nineteenth century, that the working class had supplied the original consumers during the Industrial Revolution, and that church and state agencies had fought to control the people's minds as persistently as the purveyors of mass culture. Throughout its history the working-class movement, especially the militant activists of the trade union and labor movement, resisted forms of manipulation and control and struggled in turn for democratic and social reforms.

For Thompson, the pessimistic analysis contained in the work of so many cultural researchers was attributable to ambiguous attitudes toward the place of working people in the struggle to create a socialist society and an insufficient appreciation of working people's "creative potential" in the present. Their analysis was rooted in "a tendency to assert the absolute autonomy of cultural phenomena without reference to the context of class power: and a shame-faced evasion of that impolite, historical concept—the class struggle." Such views were counter to the proper role of intellectuals in the labor movement. " 'The power to compel,' " Thompson wrote, "must always remain with the organised workers, but the intellectuals may bring to them hope, a sense of their own strength and potential life." [43]

Thompson's critique of Hoggart and Hall was a decisive intervention in the "working-class culture" debate. He injected a much-needed historical perspective into the discussion. His contention that the cultural approach be joined to the Marxist concept of class struggle was a major step toward the elaboration of his own cultural Marxist position. Yet his invocation of history cut two ways. In stressing the continuity of working-class history, and suggesting that the working-class situation was neither unique nor radically different than during earlier periods, Thompson, in effect, avoided considering the unprecedented changes after 1945. Under the circumstances, his questioning of New Left intellectuals' commitment to class struggle and his insistence that they should inspire workers to activism represented a refusal to come to terms with the rapidly changing cultural and political terrain. In an open letter to the British New Left, the American sociologist Mills was critical of the New Left's attachment to a "labor metaphysic"—continued faith in the working class as *the* revolutionary agent despite "the really impressive historical evidence that now stands against this expectation." [44] Whether Mills had in mind a specific individual or individuals or a collective mood is difficult to know. But his observation certainly held for Thompson's intervention in the classlessness debate.

Thompson's critique of Williams consisted of a dual review of *Culture and Society* and *The Long Revolution*, published in *NLR* in 1961. [45] Thompson was originally reluctant to write it. He found his theoretical disagreements with Williams so pronounced, that if the article was honestly written, it would exacerbate divisions in the New Left. However, Stuart Hall, who was the *NLR* editor, persuaded him that it was better to openly air theoretical differences than to act as if none existed.

Thompson's essay was more than an important critique of Williams and his allies; it was a major statement of his own theoretical position. It was founded on an appreciation of Williams's achievement. The great majority of socialist intellectuals during the Cold War had either submitted to apathy and withdrawal or dogmatism and blind devotion. But Williams, Thompson suggested, had remained steadfast. He yielded to neither the self-satisfied rhetoric of the cultural elite nor the sectarianism of the Communist and Labour Left. "He held the roads open for the young, and now they are moving down them once again. And when, in '56, he saw some of his socialist contemporaries coming back to his side, his smile must have had a wry edge."[46]

Despite his admiration for this accomplishment, Thompson claimed that Williams had not escaped the decade's strains and pressures. As a consequence of his solitary struggle against the literary establishment, he had appropriated some of the assumptions and perspectives of his opponents, adopting a reverential tone toward a tradition of mostly reactionary thinkers. The negative effects of this attitude were apparent in Williams's continual reference to "the whole way of life." Thompson realized that Williams used the term to avoid Marxist reductionism and to convey that the social process was an irreducible totality. Yet Thompson believed that it was irrevocably tainted by its original context, Eliot's *Notes Towards the Definition of Culture*, in which it denoted a "style of living." Thompson argued that even when "a whole way of life" was used to suggest a larger sense of the social process, it fell short. In practice, the concept frequently neglected inequality, exploitation, and power relationships, and it inadequately expressed conflict and process. In other words, it lacked a sense of history. For Thompson, "culture" was not "the whole way of life": it was "the whole way of struggle," an image incorporating the concept of totality with the theory of class struggle.

Similarly, Thompson maintained that the categories of "struggle" and "confrontation" were absent from Williams's description of the long revolution. While finding the wish for a common culture admirable, Thompson argued that cultural expansion in a capitalist society inevitably produced an intensification of class conflict as the real divisions of interest and power became more visible. Even in a long revolution, Thompson suggested, those social forces working toward common ownership, a common culture, and an organic community must eventually confront the realities of class power. "My own view of revolution (I am often assured)," he wrote, "is too 'apocalyptic': but Mr. Williams is perhaps too bland."[47] Without some theory of revolutionary transformation—a conspicuous silence in *The Long Revolution*—the socialist project would be ultimately frustrated.

Thompson found Williams's books not only too respectful of

"the Tradition," but insufficiently concerned with the intellectual achievements of the working-class movement.

The Labour movement is credited from time to time with the creation of new institutions: but it is never credited with a mind. On the one side the "older human systems," on the other side "expansion," "growth," and new institutions, and in the middle The Tradition, savouring the complexities dispassionately and trying to think out the right thing to do in response to "industry" and "democracy." [48]

Thompson believed that one unfortunate consequence of Williams's partial disengagement from the socialist tradition was that he never critically examined the thought of Marx—as opposed to that of English Marxist critics. Several places in both books cried out for an engagement with Marx's ideas, even in opposition; and Williams's brief and isolated references to him were not nearly as insightful as his observations on contributors to the tradition. Despite the current New Left mood, Thompson remained convinced that Marx could no longer be ignored.

There was a certain irony in Thompson's critique of Williams. Though a product of a Welsh working-class background, Williams was the author of the most insightful socialist critique of a tradition of mostly upper-class figures. Thompson, whose background was closer to the thinkers of the *Culture and Society* tradition, was to be the preeminent historian of the early working class. The relationship between Williams's background and his intellectual practice was alluded to by Thompson, who compared Williams to *Jude the Obscure.* Despite loyalty to his own background, and conscious of the stifling class basis of Christminster, Jude could not help but romanticize it. [49] That Thompson was born and bred there adds to the potency of his observation. It was as if Williams's move to Cambridge was such a momentous transition in his life that he savored its culture in a way that Thompson, who was a product of that world, never could. Thompson, on the other hand, could be seen as a classic instance of the middle-class intellectual who idealized the working-class movement. What for Thompson was a continual source of inspiration was for Williams everyday life. It is noteworthy that Thompson saw the New Left as potentially transforming the Labour Party, while Williams would have been satisfied with the more modest achievement of a new socialist understanding of contemporary Britain. [50]

Williams never responded to Thompson's critique, but in the 1979 *Politics and Letters* interviews he discussed the review at some length. He recalled how it appeared at a time when *The Long Revolution* was being simultaneously criticized by the Right and thus added to his feelings of being under attack. Williams defended his original position. He believed that Thompson tended to confuse "class conflict" (a structural component of the capitalist mode of production) and "class struggle" (an active and self-aware form of contestation). The social process as "a whole way of struggle" might have been an appropriate description for heroic moments of resistance, but it inadequately conveyed "all the periods in which conflict is mediated in other forms, in which there are provisional resolutions or temporary compositions of it."[51] The fifties were just such a time: "a very base period, which appeared to have neutralized and incorporated many of the very institutions of struggle to which appeal was being made."[52] Still Williams could see how some of his formulations might have glossed over class conflict, and he admitted that Thompson prompted him to rethink his position on the nineteenth-century popular press. There was, however, a more important way in which Williams acknowledged the validity of Thompson's criticism, at least implicitly. In the seventies he recast his conception of the social process in terms of Gramsci's notion of hegemony, thereby seeing society as an arena of conflict among dominant, residual, and emergent cultural forms.

Thompson did not see his essay on *The Long Revolution* as a rejection of Williams's cultural theory, but as an effort at airing differences and launching a dialogue between the two major theoretical tendencies in the New Left. Thompson suggested what might be the foundations of that dialogue. If Williams reconsidered his "diffuse pluralism"—denial of the primacy of any of the elements in a social formation—and Marxists abandoned the mechanical image of base/superstructure, then both might agree that the modes of production and the relations of production associated with those modes produced a core of human relationships that determined the historical process in an "epochal sense." "Within the limits of the epoch there are characteristic tensions and contradictions, which cannot be transcended unless we transcend the epoch itself: there is an economic logic *and* a moral logic and it is futile to argue as to which we give priority since they are different expressions of the same kernel of human relationship."[53] This position was to be the foundation of *The Making of the English Working*

Class, the most influential statement of the cultural Marxist position in the historical discipline.

III

Thompson's *The Making of the English Working Class* (1963) is one of the best-known works of social history in the English language. His re-creation of the formation of working-class consciousness and culture in the early Industrial Revolution is perhaps the classic expression of "history from below." In the volume's preface Thompson made it clear that the book was written in opposition to two approaches to the working class. It countered structural-functionalist sociologists, whom Thompson characterized as seeing the working class as a "thing," or a component of the social structure, and its class consciousness as "an unjustified disturbance-symptom." The book was also antagonistic to orthodox Marxists, whom he portrayed as perceiving the working class exclusively from the point of view of productive relations. "Once this is assumed it becomes possible to deduce the class consciousness which 'it' ought to have (but seldom does have) if 'it' was properly aware of its own position and real interests."[54] In a famous formulation, Thompson argued that creation of the working class was a historical and cultural process founded on evolving experience and consciousness: "The working class did not rise like the sun at an appointed time" but "was present at its own making."[55] It made itself as much as it was made.

A more submerged dimension of *The Making of the English Working Class* was its relationship to New Left discussions on culture, the writings of Williams, and the wider socialist debate on working-class affluence. Thompson did not polemicize against New Left positions as overtly as he did against more obvious targets, but he was writing the book while engaged in a dialogue with New Left culturalism and responding to the new work on the working class. From this point of view, the book represented an alternative to the pluralism of Williams and the *ULR* contingent of the New Left as well as to labor revisionism. It was a major statement of his cultural Marxism, drawing on both his Communist heritage and the new approach to culture associated with New Left politics and theory.

From this point of view, it is possible to see *The Making of the English Working Class* as an intervention in the debate on working-class consciousness, a response to theorists like Crosland for whom postwar changes implied classlessness and an erosion of socialist consciousness. Thompson did not need to be convinced of the far-reaching consequences of these transformations, and he acknowledged that working-class life was in flux, but he refused to accept that these changes meant the end of class consciousness and socialism. In *Revolution Again* (1960) he argued that such thinking assumed

> that the working-class is a given entity with a "fixed" characteristic consciousness which may wax or wane but remains essentially the same thing—a working-class which emerged as a social force somewhere around 1780, with steam and the factory system, and which has thereafter grown in size and organisation but has not changed significantly in form or in relationship to other classes.[56]

Bearing such factors in mind, it is possible to see *The Making of the English Working Class* as refuting socialist revisionists' claims in contemporary politics by showing how misleading their thinking was when applied to the early Industrial Revolution. Thompson argued that the first working class could not be exclusively comprehended as an effect of industrialization, nor could its consciousness be derived from economic changes. Its evolving experience was rooted in hundreds of years of resistance to agrarian capitalism and political oppression as articulated in the tradition of the "freeborn Englishman." The implication of this tradition for contemporary politics was that, just as it was impossible to understand the first working class exclusively through economic changes, the meaning of contemporary working-class experience could not be derived from the facts and ideology of affluence. The working class in the postwar era was founded on more than 150 years of evolving struggle and culture. It was neither the working class of the Industrial Revolution nor of the thirties, and its relationship to other classes had changed over time. But its culture and aspirations were enriched by its past, and it was in the process of achieving not classlessness but a new form of class consciousness.

Thompson's attempt to portray working-class experience in the widest possible terms clearly identified his approach as New Left. This affinity was apparent in his contribution to the "standard of living" controversy, the historiographical debate over whether the conditions of working people had improved or deteriorated during the first phase of industrialization. During the fifties the principal disputants—the Marxist Eric Hobsbawm and the conservatives T. S. Ashton and R. M. Hartwell—defended the respective pessimist and optimist views. They argued about the existing data on wages, prices, and consumption levels, differing mostly as to the quantitative methods for attaining and analyzing these data. Thompson's intervention in the debate shifted its ground. He acknowledged that between 1790 and 1840 a slight improvement in material standards came about, which was an unequivocal admission that the quantitative case for declining living standards had been unsuccessful. Yet in language akin to many New Left articles, and especially the writings of Williams, Thompson argued that the standard of living could not be adequately measured, for it neglected the quality of life. "From food we are led to homes, from homes to health, from health to family life, and thence to leisure, work-discipline, education and play, intensity of labour, and so on. From standard-of-life we pass to way-of-life." More generally, he suggested that the quantitative approach suppressed "a sense of the whole process—the whole political and social context of the period."[57]

Thompson both employed New Left language (and especially Williams's) in "the standard of living" controversy and used it in the chapter on popular agitation in the 1790s, characterizing the new millenarian visions of the poor as a shift in the "structure of feeling." But if he acknowledged the force of culturalism, he clearly distinguished himself from it. Where Williams used metaphors of "growth" and "communication," stressed a slowly expanding long revolution, and talked rather politely of an interaction between "social characters," Thompson portrayed the formation of working-class culture and consciousness in terms of conflict and strife: the "whole way of struggle" rather than the "whole way of life."

To better understand the contrast that Thompson's work suggested, we must return to his critique of Williams's *Culture and Society*. Williams did less than justice to the achievements of the labor movement, Thompson asserted, and he further objected to Williams's notion of "the tradition," for it included thinkers who stood for diametrically opposed political ideals. "I am of the opinion that there is not one but two major traditions under review in *Culture and Society*, with sub-traditions within both, and that the extraordinarily fine local criticism from which this book is made up becomes blurred just at those points where this notion of The Tradition obtrudes."[58] In this context, Thompson's portrayal of popular radicalism in *The Making of the English Working Class* can be seen as an alternative to Williams's "procession of disembodied voices" and an exemplification of Thompson's own notion of culture as a "whole way of struggle."[59] What made it possible to talk of Thomas Paine, William Cobbett, Robert Owen, Luddism, and the artisan culture of the 1820s as part of the same tradition of radicalism was their commitment, in various ways, to the liberty and equality of the people and their opposition to views of society based on restricted rights and hierarchy. Thompson pointed to connections between this tradition and the concurrent Romantic critique of utilitarianism, and he observed that "in the failure of the two traditions to come to a point of junction, something was lost."[60] Yet in lamenting that this convergence never happened, he implicitly reiterated his differences with Williams, for whom Owen and Coleridge were part of the same tradition, not parallel ones.

Thompson's historical view of the class struggle and his image of popular radicalism was founded on the practice of the Communist historians. Although his socialist-humanist position was opposed to Stalinism and orthodox Marxism, he spoke with pride of that part of the British Communist tradition associated with William Morris and Tom Mann. Indeed, the *New Reasoner* had been launched to rediscover the democratic and libertarian strain of British communism suppressed or silenced during the Stalin years. One accomplishment of the Communist historians had been their ability to remain faithful to orthodoxy while at the same time developing the beginnings of a cultural approach to history. When Thompson argued that the working-class response to the Industrial Revolution should be seen in the context of hundreds of years of popular struggle, he was referring to the tradition of lost rights, one of the principal concerns of the Historians' Group. This shared concern was apparent when he stated that "the changing productive relations and working conditions of the Industrial Revolution were imposed, not upon raw material, but upon the free-born Englishman. . . . The factory hand or stockinger was also the inheritor of Bunyan, of remembered village rights, of notions of equality before the law, of craft traditions."[61] Thompson's notion of the history of popular resistance was based on the theory of lost rights found in Dona Torr's *Tom Mann and His Times*, Christopher Hill's essay on the Norman Yoke, and the work of many others who had been part of the tradition of Communist historiography. His critique of Williams echoed that of another Marxist historian, Victor Kiernan, who argued that "if the Tradition meant more than mere self-complacency it was because England had a record never long interrupted of popular resistance to society as it was, and of writers ready to put the feelings of the people into language."[62] Williams's concept of a unitary tradition obscured the real process of struggle.

IV

In the early 1960s, Edward Thompson was unquestionably the most forceful defender of Marxism and socialist humanism within the New Left. However, with the collapse of the movement and its fragmentation into various new left groupings, it would not be long before Thompson's Marxism was under challenge: not from a culturalist approach skeptical of Marxist theory in the first place, but from a more rigorous and philosophically based Marxism rooted in European traditions. His principal critic was the new editor of *NLR*, Perry Anderson.

When Anderson and colleagues such as Robin Blackburn and Tom Nairn began to overhaul *NLR*, they were in their early twenties, younger and less politically experienced than the group that preceded them, particularly those associated with the ex-Communist *New Reasoner*. They inhabited a space reluctantly vacated by its previous tenants but one that appeared to be the only viable alternative to extinction. In such a situation it is not surprising that the reconstituted journal was initially, in Robin Blackburn's words, "a tentative and transitional magazine," which, following the fragmentation of the New Left as a political movement, was of more "restricted scope."[63] Yet if the journal struggled to achieve a distinct identity, two characteristics immediately distinguished it from its predecessor. First, its publication of articles by such writers as Claude Lévi-Strauss and Ernest Mandel signaled a characteristic preoccupation with social theory from the Continent. Second, the first *NLR* was primarily concerned with British politics, although this focus does not mean that it lacked an internationalist perspective, as its positive neutralist position testified. *NLR*'s successor, by contrast, was drawn to the politics of the Third World, hopeful of a revolutionary breakthrough outside the European theater. As Anderson observed: "We viewed the East European turmoil of '56 with sympathy, but without finality. The Cuban Revolution of '59 appeared to us more important and hopeful for the future."[64]

The contrast became more dramatic when *NLR* turned its gaze to Britain, as the Tories' nearly fifteen-year dominance of British politics was broken by a revived Labour Party led by Harold Wilson. *NLR* analyzed the first New Left, the historical trajectory of British capitalism, the ideology of Labourism, and the English working class in a series of essays written by either Anderson or Nairn from 1964 until 1966. What became known as the Nairn-Anderson thesis was most cogently articulated in Anderson's historical analysis of the political consequences of Britain's distinct pattern of capitalist development, "Origins of the Present Crisis."[65] The "crisis" had two distinct but interwoven meanings. In one case, Anderson was responding to the first signs of British decline, documented in books such as Andrew Shonfield's *British Economic Policy Since the War* and Anthony Sampson's *Anatomy of Britain*. Here, Anderson argued that, while such works set forth the symptoms of the British crisis, they never analyzed its historical roots or foundation. In the second case, he saw the crisis in terms of the inability of the socialist Left to generate any mass following in Britain, and the failure of the Left—whether old or new—to analyze the historical forces that worked against it. The Left was thus no different from the analyses of Shonfield or Sampson; their inability to analyze the historical underpinnings of the current historical moment was symptomatic of a deeper cultural malaise. Anderson was particularly frustrated with the New Left movement, which he castigated (in a related essay) for not breaking out of this mold. For him, the New Left's "almost complete failure to offer any structural analysis of British society" represented "a major failure of nerve and intelligence." Indeed, Anderson rejected the New Left's intellectual style, thought their efforts at building a movement muddled and confused, and dismissed socialist humanism as being "populist" and "presocialist."[66]

"Origins of the Present Crisis" was a provisional effort at a structural analysis of British historical development, that is, the kind of analysis that Anderson believed had not been undertaken. It was pervaded by a loathing for English intellectual traditions and culture and a passionate attachment to European Marxism and thinkers such as Lukács and Sartre. But the real spirit behind Anderson's essay was that of the founder of the Italian Communist Party, Antonio Gramsci. Indeed, Anderson's essay represented the first sustained attempt in English to use the ideas of Gramsci in historical analysis, in large part because of the influence of Nairn who had become acquainted with Gramsci's writings while he attended the Scuola Normale in Pisa in the early sixties.[67] Anderson was inspired by Gramsci's attempt to view Italian history as being distinct from a general pattern of bourgeois historical development. Anderson argued that the course of modern English history was exceptional in nature; it failed to follow general Marxist expectations of modern capitalist development.[68] The precocious growth of English agrarian capitalism in the sixteenth century produced an incomplete bourgeois revolution in the seventeenth. It was "a supremely successful *capitalist* revolution," which transformed the base but not the superstructure of English society.[69] This process culminated in the late Victorian era when the aristocracy and bourgeoisie fused into a single bloc.

In Anderson's schema the failure of the bourgeoisie to successfully oppose and supplant the aristocracy and impose its own stamp on society proved to be an impediment to English capitalist development in the twentieth century. Most importantly, this occurrence had disastrous consequences for the working-class movement. Historically, working-class movements partially constructed their own ideologies by appropriating the bourgeois revolutionary heritage. "In England," wrote Anderson, "a supine bourgeoisie produced a subordinate proletariat. It handed on no impulse of liberation, no revolutionary values, no universal language."[70] Unlike in France, where the working classes had fought with the bourgeoisie to supplant the old aristocratic class and were allies until 1848, the world's first proletariat "fought passionately and unaided against the advent of industrial capitalism; its extreme exhaustion after successive defeats was the measure of its efforts."[71] "The tragedy of the first proletariat," wrote Anderson, "was not, as has so often been said, that it was immature; it was rather that it was in a crucial sense *premature*."[72] Its first blossoming occurred before the existence of socialism as a structured ideology. By the time the working-class movement recovered its strength in the late nineteenth century it was too late for it to be substantially shaped by the one social theory capable of challenging the dominant ideology—Marxism. Instead, it became permeated by the ideology of Labourism.

Using Gramscian terminology, Anderson regarded the dominant class, though the product of a "peculiar morphology," as "hegemonic." It controlled the means of production, and it was "the primary determinant of consciousness, character and customs throughout the society."[73] In contrast, the working class had only a "corporate" status; it attained a distinctive identity at the expense of being unable to extend its goals and aspirations to the rest of society. Ironically, it was the working class's deeply felt class consciousness that was the overwhelming obstacle to constructing a hegemony of its own. To overcome the limits imposed by this "corporate consciousness," Anderson insisted that it was necessary to create a revolutionary consciousness that challenged the dominant ideology of the ruling classes—a task to which intellectuals like himself could make decisive contributions.

Thompson was the most vocal critic of the new *NLR* and of Anderson's theoretical approach. He had been critical of the journal from the beginning. When it was under Stuart Hall's direction, he had feared that it would be dominated by London intellectuals without ties to the labor movement and that the *Reasoner* tendency would become a marginal force in the New Left. His discontent deepened following Hall's resignation. By then president of the New Left board, he had to mediate an ever-growing number of petty disputes as well as oversee the transition of the journal. And he had to do all of these things while living hundreds of miles from London. By the time Thompson resigned as president in January 1963, he was so opposed to the direction of *NLR* that he felt reluctant to defend it publicly.[74] He was willing to remain on the editorial board, but only as a passive member.

Thompson was especially upset at Anderson, whom he believed had pressed the editorial board into dissolving itself. He wrote to him: "Although you in effect dismissed the Board at our last meeting, this does not mean that its members are dismissed from political life. Some of us intend to continue our work."[75] Anderson has denied that an "editorial coup" ever took place, and he defended himself in *Arguments within English Marxism* (1980). "It is untrue that the old board was 'dismissed' by myself or by the new [editorial board], as any participant of the time can testify. No such action was ever possible: as Thompson in effect concedes . . . when he speaks of the old New Left 'electing for its own administrative dissolution'—which is an accurate description."[76] Anderson did not literally dismiss the New Left board, but he probably pressured it to vote for its own extinction. According to the minutes, the board was dissolved because the editor found it a "constitutional built-in irritant and distraction."[77]

Thompson also was offended by the new team's refusal to divide the journal's remaining assets, which primarily consisted of the building that housed *NLR* and the Partisan. From his point of view, even a small sum of money could help fund a future political project, and he was angered by the new group's "failure to offer the simplest courtesies, or suggestion as to a division of assets."[78] Thompson's position was untenable. Anderson had saved *NLR* from disaster, had invested enough capital to keep it solvent, and hence could reasonably maintain that he was entitled to the assets that remained. Alan Hall was of this opinion, as was Raymond Williams, who attempted to mediate the dispute.[79] In the end, Thompson grudgingly accepted it himself; he admitted that nothing was to be gained politically by pressing the claim, although he continued to believe that a legal case could be made.[80]

Thompson's decision to publicly break with *NLR* was precipitated by the collective's decisive turn in the mid-sixties. Anderson's characterization of English history could be seen as a wholesale rejection of the Communist historiographical tradition, which had always argued that the English and French Revolutions played analogous roles in their country's historical development. Anderson's interpretation implicitly viewed French history as the "normal" pattern of development, English history as a "deviation." In addition, Thompson could justifiably interpret *NLR*'s patronizing attitude toward British Marxism, dismissal of socialist humanism, denial of an English revolutionary tradition, and preference for "theoretical rigor" over "sentimental populism" as a rejection of his own intellectual and political practice. As Anderson later admitted, "it could indeed be read as a tacit dismissal of the work of the older New Left, or rather of that part of it (not necessarily majoritarian) which was attached to Marxism."[81] Who fit this description more perfectly than Thompson? Already angered by Anderson's actions during *NLR*'s transition, he became infuriated when *NLR* refused to publish an open letter in which he criticized the narrowing perspective of the journal and what he perceived as the exclusion of the old New Left from its pages. Even before Anderson had become editor, Thompson had reservations about what his intellectual style would mean to the life of the review. In a letter to Alan Hall, he wrote: "If unchallenged they [Anderson's theoretical assumptions] will reduce the review to a certain uniformity in which the academically reputable, or the sophisticated-Marxist, will displace other styles, and (hence) other ways of perceiving and important values and attitudes which (we once thought) were intrinsic to a socialist humanism."[82] Now he had proof. Frustrated and angered by being excluded from the journal that he had helped to found,

Thompson wrote "The Peculiarities of the English," a scathing condemnation of the Nairn-Anderson thesis and its philosophical and political assumptions.[83] Anderson replied with equal force in "Socialism and Pseudo-Empiricism" (1966).

The exchange between Anderson and Thompson represented a conflict between two conceptions of radical intellectual theory and practice. At one level it was a dispute about how to conceive of society and history. Anderson discussed classes in structural and abstract terms; he focused on the hegemonic and coercive function of the state, and he talked about "ideology," a term with impeccable Marxist credentials, rather than "culture." Thompson argued that classes were historical and cultural formations and the product of human agency. As a socialist humanist and cultural Marxist, he distrusted Anderson's preoccupation with state power and his lack of interest "in the quality of life, the sufferings and satisfactions, of those who live and die in unredeemed time."[84] While Anderson saw historical events from the perspective of the broad sweep of history, Thompson investigated small slices of time to get at more general social and historical processes.

Besides their different approaches to understanding society and history, Thompson and Anderson brought to the debate different notions of their roles in the socialist movement. Anderson's concept of intellectual practice was modeled after Continental traditions. He saw himself as part of a barely existing radical intelligentsia, a distinct stratum whose primary function was to produce theoretical analysis for the radical movement and to build a socialist intellectual culture. Anderson once admitted that "innumerable damaging consequences" to the socialist movements of Europe resulted from the existence of "a separate pariah-elite of intellectuals divorced from society." But he argued that if intellectuals attempted to build a socialist movement before the proper time—as the New Left had—the results would be "paralyzing confusions" and an "unconscious creeping 'substitutionism.' "[85] Thompson took a different approach, defending a more typically English notion of radical intellectual practice based on the widest possible interchange between intellectuals and workers. Intellectuals were located "inside" the struggle; they used their position to articulate the experience and aspirations of the subordinate classes; and their work was often conceived in terms of the movement's immediate needs. The adult education teacher in the Workers' Educational Association perhaps exemplified this practice.

The two of them also had allegiances to different intellectual traditions. Anderson argued that the blend of empiricist and literary sensibility so typical of New Left writers and indicative of English socialist and intellectual traditions in general was incapable of producing a totalizing vision of English society. "As long as our history remains fragmentary, our political analysis will remain jejune. This is the real charge against Thompson's kind of socialist culture."[86] Anderson contrasted Thompson's brilliant analytic achievements as a historian with his impressionistic and inspirational political writings. His New Left essays typically could be recognized by "their uniform abstraction, their wandering subjectivism, their inflated rhetoric, their utter renunciation of any attempt to analyze rather than merely invoke present realities."[87] Anderson acknowledged that the English idiom contained creative elements and that Thompson was not personally responsible for its limitations. Yet Thompson and his associates had produced neither a theoretical analysis of the downfall of the New Left nor anticipated Britain's present crisis, the first visible signs of Britain's economic decline and social paralysis. "The old melange contained few facts at all—only personifications like Apathy, Smoke and Squalor, Natopolis, or New Community. We have tried to move beyond this *pseudo-empiricism*, by looking at actual empirical reality—and reinterpreting it through concepts. There is no other way to advance social science, or socialist thought."[88] For Anderson, it was not enough to evoke the revolutionary tradition of the British commoner when the real challenge was to explain why no serious revolutionary movement had ever coalesced.

Thompson responded to Anderson's enthusiasm for Western Marxism and his condemnation of English culture by defending English socialist and intellectual traditions, particularly the "English idiom," a mode of thought that might be defined as a partiality toward concrete examples, facts, and ordinary language, a distrust of metaphysical speculation, abstraction, and systematic theorization. Acknowledging that it could foster "insular resistances" and "conceptual opportunism," he argued that the English idiom possessed "a conceptual toughness which is immanent rather than explicit; at best it has carried the realism of the English novel, and has served—notably in the natural sciences—as an idiom superbly adapted to the interpenetration of theory and *praxis*."[89] And he insisted that the English would never capitulate to "a self-sufficient Marxist system, even if this system has been tarted-up with some neologisms."[90] Indeed, Thompson interpreted Anderson's aloof tone, persistent transformation of cultural practices into Marxist categories, and dismissal of the English experience as a replay of his (Thompson's) own past. "It was against that tone—that sound of bolts being shot against experience and enquiry (and the remoter sound of more objective bolts)—that a few of us manned our duplicators in 1956. If this is where we are in 1965, then the locust has eaten nine years. . . . There are some of us who will man the stations of 1956 once again."[91] It was true that Anderson's concern with power was rooted in an interest in a more classical Marxist understanding of the state, that he developed a synthetic analysis stressing structural determinations over human volition, and that he was interested in developing a more systematic and rigorous Marxist theory.[92] But while these concerns might have seemed to Thompson like a return to high Stalinism, Anderson's overall project was rooted in a discourse virtually unknown in English Marxist circles. It was not a return to the years before 1956—it looked ahead to the days after 1968.

V

In his critique of Williams, Thompson had called for a dialogue between the different theoretical tendencies in the New Left. Although such a dialogue never took place during the movement's high tide, the New Left cultural and political debate continued. It was kept alive by the emerging field of cultural studies, which in the 1960s transformed New Left cultural politics into a program of politically engaged academic research.

While it is perhaps true, as Stuart Hall suggested, that cultural studies had no "absolute beginnings," a critical moment in its formation was the founding of the Birmingham Centre for Contemporary Cultural Studies in 1964.[93] The Centre was originally part of the school of English. It subsequently achieved an independent status and was established as a postgraduate research center. Its first director, Richard Hoggart, appointed Stuart Hall to be his assistant and fellow faculty member.

The Centre's original goal was to use the methods of literary criticism to understand popular and mass culture and to develop criteria for critically evaluating specific texts. In his 1964 inaugural address, Hoggart defended this method on the grounds that it could contribute to answering broader questions about the nature of society: "in co-operation with other relevant disciplines, it can help to set the phenomena of mass communications in a fuller social and historical context than any of us, working alone, have so far managed."[94] Cultural studies was thus not to be a discipline that could stand by itself, but "a useful—and essential—adjunct" to social-scientific analysis. Yet Hoggart's modest claims notwithstanding, the Centre found itself under attack from two directions. Guardians of elite culture believed that mass culture was unsuitable for serious study. Sociologists viewed cultural studies as unscientific and an intrusion on their turf, even if they had little interest in exploring the terrain. Stuart Hall recalled that the Centre received a letter from two social scientists warning it not to move from the analysis of texts to the study of social practices generally.[95]

Hall and Paddy Whannel's *The Popular Arts* (1964) exemplifies cultural studies at this time. When it was being written, the authors were secondary school teachers who were closely in touch with the emerging generation of young people and were enthusiastic about the new media and popular culture. The book fell somewhere between being a theoretical and practical guide to understanding contemporary media, and a handbook for teachers who wanted to use popular culture and the issues it raised in their classes. In this respect it recalled Leavis and Denys Thompson's attempt in *Culture and Environment* to provide educators with methods for teaching critical practices, but *The Popular Arts* did not embrace their tendency to dismiss the value of mass culture.[96] Indeed, the authors rejected such thinking, finding it typically consisting of sweeping, unfounded generalizations made by writers only casually familiar with the new media and popular art forms. Here, they seem to be particularly responding to discussions launched by the National Union of Teachers, resulting in the passage of a resolution at its 1960 conference condemning "the debasement of standards" produced by the "misuse" of the mass media. This resolution led to a special conference sponsored by the NUT, "Popular Culture and Personal Responsibility," which brought together teachers, critics, and media producers, both artists and controllers. "One of the reasons why the Special Conference itself was only a partial success," they wrote, "was that many teachers present were too eager to think in terms of censorship and control, to defend the *restrictionist* approach, and to attribute to education a purely passive role."[97]

In *The Popular Arts*, Hall and Whannel rejected the rigid dichotomy between high and mass culture, a distinction based not only on an intellectual prejudice but one that tended to fall apart under close scrutiny, particularly in the analysis of movies and jazz. For Hall and Whannel, popular and sophisticated art were not competing; they had different aims and aspirations comprehensible only in their own terms. At the same time, within the popular arts the authors distinguished between "mass" and "popular" culture. Popular culture was a genuine expression of the urban and industrial experience, an authentic rendering of known feelings immediately recognizable to interested audiences. Mass art, in contrast, embodied a high degree of personalization, not an honest expression of individual feeling; the embellishment of a stock formula known to manipulate the emotions, not the imaginative and probing use of conventions; an art that pandered to its audience, not one that was born out of a deep respect for it.

Hall and Whannel's approach to analyzing popular art was to pay close attention to style and form and to focus on the ways in which ideas and feelings were conveyed. In effect, they proposed to extend the critical and humane reading method of the *Scrutiny* tradition—"with its attention to a whole response and its concern for the life of the mind and the tone of civilization"—to new forms of cultural expression.[98] Yet they also sought to situate popular art forms in a larger social and cultural context. This overview is apparent in their analysis of youth culture and its most salient expression—pop music. They viewed the spontaneous, improvised, and anarchic nature of youth culture as a reaction to a society whose dominant values were disintegrating but that offered no alternative to replace them. In terms recalling Hall's New Left articles, they saw the younger generation "as a creative minority, pioneering ahead of the puritan restraints so deeply built into English bourgeois morality, towards a code of behaviour in our view more humane and civilized."[99] Equally important, youth culture had to be understood in the context of the new media and consumer capitalism. Teenagers were not simply a new sociological category but an economic one, a major market for the new leisure industry. From this point of view, the music and fashion of teenagers could never be an authentic popular culture in the sense defined; it was a contradictory synthesis of authentic and manufactured elements.

Hall and Whannel cited the popularity of the dance the Twist to illustrate the dynamics of youth culture in contemporary society. Although originally manufactured from above and only gradually embraced by teenagers, Chubby Checker's original version of "The Twist" did not take the teen world by storm. His second release,

"Let's Twist Again," became popular only when the music industry bombarded teenagers with Twist skirts, Twist books, Twist shoes, Twist movies, and Twist necklaces. Yet Hall and Whannel argued that when teenage audiences finally accepted the dance it was not out of gullibility. "The twist appeals to them through the natural entertainment channels, it offers a pattern of popular activity closely linked with their interests in going out, dancing, parties and social occasions of many kinds. It was personalized through the medium of young singers and entertainers. But it has also been made to connect."[100] The story of the Twist exemplified the contradictory nature of youth culture.

Hall and Whannel generally appreciated popular music. They also recognized its lack of variety, its endless recycling of the same musical ideas, and its rhythmic monotony. The pop music industry, they claimed, was incapable of giving artists the chance to genuinely express themselves, to make that deep connection with an audience characteristic of genuine popular expression. In contrast, jazz, they asserted, was an authentic popular art. Though an art form whose history was inextricably bound up with the mass media, it was an immeasurably richer and more varied form, containing levels of personal expression and imagination inconceivable in pop music. In making such comparisons, Hall and Whannel were not attempting to "wean teenagers away from the juke-box heroes," but only to make them aware of the limits of their musical experience. In language reminiscent of Raymond Williams, they observed: "It is a genuine widening of sensibility and emotional range which we should be working for—an extension of tastes which might lead to an extension of pleasure."[101] Pop music was not vulgar or morally reprehensible, but much of it was mediocre.

The Popular Arts was one of the earliest surveys of popular culture written from a sympathetic perspective and based on a detailed knowledge of its many forms and genres. Hall and Whannel's argument, that youth culture was a contradictory synthesis of authentic and manufactured elements, represented the first articulation, however embryonic, of the Centre's distinctive approach to subcultures. Yet looking at the book more than thirty years later, the limitations of its analysis are evident. In the first place, their critical judgments appear dated. While the authors found it difficult to conceive of pop music as a vital form of popular or creative expression, they did not consider rock-'n'-roll pioneers deeply rooted in blues and gospel traditions, for instance, Big Joe Turner, Fats Domino, Ray Charles, and Ruth Brown. Nor has the privileged status that they accorded to jazz over rock music held up. Rock music in the sixties and seventies came to express the experience of a generation as powerfully as any form of artistic expression in the twentieth century; during the same period, jazz was more acclaimed in art circles than in the urban neighborhoods in which it originated.

However, the real difficulty with *The Popular Arts*—and, in a more general sense, the model on which cultural studies was founded—was not in any of its specific judgments, but its methodology. First, while it was undoubtedly a genuine gain to reformulate the high/low culture distinction as a tripartite division—mass, popular, and high culture—it ultimately was based on the same assumptions as earlier works. Hall and Whannel were undoubtedly attracted to jazz because of its roots in popular experience, but they justified its value in terms derived from their training as critics: jazz was preferable to rock 'n' roll because it was as creative as classical music. Despite their best efforts, the authors reflected the standards defined by high culture. Second, their commitment to fostering the popular arts was framed in much the same terms as *Scrutiny*'s defense of the tradition. Their belief that mass culture was suppressing the authentic voice of the people was ultimately based on the same historical mythology as Leavis's; it contained the same nostalgic glance backward, though their conception of the golden age differed. Hall and Whannel's "organic community" was, loosely speaking, urban popular experience between the late nineteenth century and the Second World War: the working-class music hall, Charlie Chaplin movies, and the singing of Billie Holiday. Yet these artifacts were disembodied, analyzed apart from the social context of poverty, discrimination, and resistance in which they were rooted. It was in this context that E. P. Thompson's notion of "culture as a whole way of struggle" was so important for any future development of cultural studies. For the relationship between popular culture and social struggle was precisely what *The Popular Arts* never considered. Indeed, Thompson's approach suggested an entirely new way of conceiving of cultural practices, displacing the polarities of "high" and "mass" with a view of popular culture as an expression of resistance mediated by the dominant class's attempt to circumscribe and control it. The critical reading of isolated texts was displaced by an approach that viewed them as one kind of evidence among others and by seeing popular and mass culture as linked to historical and social conflicts. Literary criticism was supplanted by historical and critical theory.

Indeed, this is the path followed by the Centre for Contemporary Cultural Studies in the late sixties. In Centre group projects and seminars, Hoggart's original blueprint was continually refined and modified. Centre researchers continued to see their distinctive contribution as providing "close readings" of cultural artifacts, but they began to place a greater stress on discovering cultural meaning. This emphasis was manifested in the Centre's first tentative working procedure: a three-part division of labor involving the interpretation or critical reading of a text, the examination of its effect on an audience, and the analysis of its social context and cultural significance.

> *We believe that, for the purposes of a cultural analysis, both kinds of work have to be done: no rough division of labour will suffice. Such a broken-backed procedure only leads to fragmentation: close studies of texts and events here— "social background," "history of ideas" or "conditions of production" there. Useful work has been done in this way before, but it is our intention to try to develop a different, more integrated style of work.[102]*

Yet this approach depended on a theoretical understanding of culture and society beyond the scope of literary criticism. The Centre was thus drawn into the realm of social theory.

However, the Centre soon discovered that no social theory in its current state could simply be appropriated wholesale. This discovery was felt to be particularly true of the structural-functionalist paradigms that dominated the field of sociology. Centre researchers found the universal claims of these paradigms to be transparently based on the American society of the 1950s, and they rejected the view of culture as the social realm in which the individual personality was integrated into the social system. Under such conditions they were compelled to create their own social theory.

The Centre's initial movement into the realm of social theory, its second phase, was a transitional and eclectic period devoted to broadening its theoretical foundation. It might be described as its "idealist" period, for Centre researchers grappled with a set of questions raised by the idealist tradition in social thought—what Alan Shuttleworth called the German "culture and society" tradition.[103] In *Two Working Papers in Cultural Studies*, Shuttleworth argued for broadening the Centre's theoretical approach by enriching it with German idealism. The German critique of positivism was analogous to the attack of literary criticism on political economy and utilitarianism; it also was founded on a conception of men and women as expressive, evaluative beings; and both traditions regarded human action as embodying subjective meaning and values. Yet as Shuttleworth pointed out, notable differences existed. Sociology, unlike criticism, was a generalizing mode, primarily concerned with groups, organizations, and institutions. What it had to offer was "not so much the 'facts'—because the literary mind has its own ways of acquiring knowledge—but a classificatory, topological way of organising knowledge, and a way of making ideas explicit and theorising about them."[104] In this context, Shuttleworth argued that Weberian sociology was particularly important to the future of cultural studies. It simultaneously linked subjective judgments and objective understanding in the social sciences, and it was self-reflective about the nature and limits of theoretical models and explanation. But most importantly, it proposed a method for going beyond the phenomenal world and discovering the values that ordered it. In Shuttleworth's words:

> Its aim is to move beyond that fixed perception of the world which convention and common-sense and ordinary language makes self-evident and yet to show the world, not as a chaos, but as an order. . . . We show by ideal type analysis, or value-interpretation, that within the apparent chaos of particular actions, immediate purposes and local situations, there are principles, values, attitudes to life. . . .[105]

The Centre's engagement with the German "culture and society" tradition was the initial stage in a much broader dialogue with modes of thought outside its original orbit of discourse. Centre researchers were attracted to those trends in contemporary sociology that were likewise involved in creating alternatives to structural-functionalist sociology, many of which were reviving the classic themes of social thought. This included an interest in ethnomethodology, its focus on the common sense or ideological foundations of everyday knowledge, and its tendency to see language and "conversational analysis" as a model of social activity. It also explored American social-interactionist sociology that used an ethnographic approach to recover the self-definition of deviant subcultures.[106] The Centre's interest in the idealist tradition was furthered through its enthusiasm for Peter Berger and Thomas

Luckmann's "social construction of reality" perspective, which was founded on the revival of Alfred Schutz's phenomenological sociology. The Centre saw their approach as relevant to understanding how "the subjective meanings of actors, who share a common social world, become expressed or 'objectivated' in cultural artifacts, in social gesture and interaction."[107]

Perhaps more important, given the Centre's subsequent history, Centre researchers were becoming interested in structuralism and semiology.[108] Although aware of "the totalizing methodology and the omnivorous, indeed terroristic, formalism" characteristic of much structuralist thought, they recognized the momentous shift contained in the structuralist conception of culture as a "field of significations."[109] This concept called into question whether culture was a text that had been authored, and it suggested, on the contrary, that culture spoke through individuals, a major critique of the original liberal-humanist foundations of cultural studies. First signs of how some of these theoretical interests were manifested can be seen in the Centre's initial group project, *Paper Voices*, an analysis of two newspapers, the *Mirror* and the *Express* from the mid-thirties through the mid-sixties.[110] The Centre research team of Anthony Smith, Elizabeth Glass, and Trevor Blackwell approached the newspapers as texts containing embedded structures of meaning revealed through style, rhetoric, form, and language. *Paper Voices* was less interested in the newspapers' explicit political views, more in how their underlying linguistic, visual, and ideological assumptions— their structure of feeling—represented daily events, constructed an ideal reader, and reacted to and smoothed the way for social change. *Paper Voices* linked the ideas of thinkers like Williams with an interest in fields like semiotics.

By the end of the sixties, then, cultural studies was in flux. It had emerged from literary criticism as one of the few disciplines in Britain that allowed for the moral and critical examination of society. It subverted the tradition of Leavis and *Scrutiny* and Eliot by establishing a radical academic discipline committed to understanding contemporary culture. But if cultural studies was grounded in literary practice, those studies felt the pressure to expand the project, to develop an integrative style of work that was as dependent on social theory as on the close reading of texts. This project began to take shape in the late 1960s—a time of social, political, and intellectual turmoil—and began to bear fruit in the 1970s. Central to this transformation was the Centre's distinctive appropriation of Western European Marxist theory, a tradition that, like cultural studies, sought to overcome the crude determinism of orthodox Marxism. In these years the Centre made major contributions to an understanding of contemporary media, youth subcultures, working-class life, the modern state, historical theory and the theory of ideology, and the relationship among race, class, and gender in society.

In the early 1960s, Marxist and New Left intellectual culture in Britain consisted of handfuls of scholars and writers who worked as individuals in hostile university environments or as adult education teachers. The journals *Past and Present*, though it was not explicitly radical, and *New Left Review* were the only two intellectual vehicles for socialist scholars. By the 1970s, however, owing to the extension of higher education, the growth of the student movement and counterculture in the late sixties, and the emergence of the British social and economic crisis, socialist intellectual culture underwent a remarkable expansion. From a collection of scattered individuals, the intellectual Left developed into many thriving groups, within a variety of disciplines, guiding their own publications and organizations. Radical culture was supported by a number of mainstream and academic publishers, which published substantial numbers of books in the social sciences and the humanities and had a more visible presence in university life. This presence was apparent in increased numbers of Marxist and feminist faculty members, especially in universities that were formerly polytechnics, and in the growth of left-wing-oriented programs and organizations either sponsored by, or connected to, academic institutions: the Centre for Contemporary Cultural Studies at the University of Birmingham, the Social History Centre at the University of Warwick, and History Workshop associated with Ruskin College, Oxford.

The principal figures in this intellectual culture were by and large older than the generation of 1968, but many of them were affected by the libertarian, countercultural, and antiauthoritarian spirit so prominent in the late sixties. This revolt was political, but not in any traditional sense. It was, most importantly, a cultural revolt against the dominant ideological structures of society, making possible, for instance, movements like feminism that grew out of a critique of patriarchal power.

The Marxist intellectual culture of the seventies was influenced in a double sense by this revolt. Not only did this intellectual culture make the cultural and the ideological dimensions of social life its primary focus, but in certain respects it resembled an alternative culture itself. As with participants in the sixties' subcultures, radical intellectuals created their own semiautonomous culture founded in opposition to bourgeois norms. They escaped what they saw as the stifling effects of English bourgeois culture by introducing new discourses—French structuralism, poststructuralism, semiology, and Western Marxist thought—into English radical discussions. The result was a radical intellectual culture larger than anything that had existed before, but one that systematically excluded those unschooled in its intricate and sometimes obscure philosophical language. Michael Rustin has observed that it became possible for radical intellectuals to live their entire lives within the confines of this culture, though in much narrower and more inward terms than existed before.[1]

Since the 1950s a major debate among socialist intellectuals in Britain was whether the working class and its primary political expression, the Labour Party, were potential agents of a radical transformation of society. Despite vigorous expressions of working-class militancy that erupted in the seventies, as witnessed by the miners' strikes of 1972 and 1974, as the decade progressed a power-ful body of evidence suggested that the labor movement was, as Eric Hobsbawm forcefully argued in 1978, stagnant and in crisis, the result of long-term structural transformations.[2] While the New Left of the 1950s hoped to radicalize the Labour Party, the various new lefts that succeeded it regarded Labour's relationship to capital-ism as barely distinguishable from that of the Tories. This view was not confined to Trotskyist sects such as the International Marxist Group (IMG) that grew out of the student movement of the late sixties and, like the evolving Marxist intellectual culture, had clear affinities with the counterculture. It was likewise true of the found-ers of the original New Left whose 1968 *May Day Manifesto* was based on the idea that Labour was not only an inadequate vehicle for a socialist transformation, but that it was an active and willing contributor to the maintenance of capitalist social relations.

If the Marxist intellectual culture of the 1970s had an affinity with the counterculture(s) and was founded on the energies un-leashed in 1968, it was overdetermined by the crisis in the socialist movement that was becoming acutely evident by the end of the seventies. Theoretically, this crisis was most clearly expressed as an implicit and explicit debate over the relationship between structure and agency, experience and ideology, and theory and practice. We shall look at this crisis in the present chapter on the growth and development of cultural studies, in chapter 5 on Marxist and socialist-feminist history, and in chapter 6 on the debates between history and cultural studies.

I

Cultural studies in the seventies developed in the context of the student and countercultural revolt that coalesced in "1968" and the greatly expanded radical intellectual culture that was its consequence. The British radical milieu in the late sixties resists neat and compact divisions; it was a spontaneous explosion of political and cultural opposition converging in the same turbulent and unruly historical space. It included new left activists, avant-garde artists, alternative rock musicians, revolutionary theater groups, underground poets, and anarchist squatters. Many people assumed more than one of those roles. The British revolutionary and countercultural left was never associated with an event of the magnitude of May 1968 in Paris, the Democratic convention in Chicago, the Columbia University protests, or Prague Spring. Yet it created a radical culture in Britain whose scope was without historical precedent.

Numerous instances of the unruly spirit of late-sixties culture could be cited, but in the present context two examples might suffice. The first involves the revolutionary underground newspaper *Black Dwarf*, which was founded by three people with distinct personalities. Clive Goodwin was a wealthy left-wing literary agent from a working-class background who originally conceived of the idea. Sheila Rowbotham was a middle-class socialist activist involved in Trotskyist politics and the Agitprop collective (a radical political group that produced posters and street theater). She forced feminist ideas into *Black Dwarf*'s agenda before she left the paper to devote herself to the emerging women's movement. (For her contributions to feminist history, see chapter 5.) Tariq Ali, the paper's editor, was a political activist from a Pakistani landowning family who was gravitating toward the IMG and (like Rowbotham) had graduated from Oxford. *Black Dwarf*, which took its name from a nineteenth-century working-class newspaper, was launched during the excitement over the French May events.[3] Its goal was to bring together the political and the alternative Left by focusing on anti-imperialist politics (particularly the anti-Vietnam War move-

ment), radical student and labor activism, and the countercultural
revolt. The editorial board was multisectarian, including International Socialists (IS) and IMG Trotskyists, *NLR* contributors, anarchists, and independent radicals.[4]

In *Black Dwarf*, explicitly political articles were juxtaposed with
contributions from counterculture artists and musicians. Its in-
clusiveness attracted such writers as John Berger, Eric Hobsbawm,
and David Mercer. The paper printed Mick Jagger's handwritten
copy of "Street Fighting Man." David Hockney and Jim Dine
produced paintings for reproduction. And when John Hoyland
challenged John Lennon's politics in an article, the Beatle replied in
a subsequent issue that he and *Black Dwarf* were making different
contributions to a common pursuit. The paper's demise resulted
from an editorial board split over whether to take a more aggressive
political line. The IMG contingent broke away and formed *Red Mole*,
an explicitly Fourth International publication whose goal was to
create a revolutionary youth organization. *Black Dwarf* ceased publication in 1970.[5]

A second example of 1960s culture is the Anti-University of
London, which in a lifetime of only several months sought to break
down the bourgeois distinctions between teacher and student and
set out to abolish the arbitrary divisions between disciplines and art
forms, theory, and practice.[6] Anti-University courses represented
the full sweep of the emergent culture. The counterculture was
represented by the artist John Latham who offered a course on
"antiknow," the LSD-inspired novelist Alexander Trocchi who lectured on "the urgencies of the invisible insurrection," and Yoko
Ono who was billed as giving an "irregular course" bringing individuals in touch with themselves through "brain sessions and rit-
ual." Revolutionary left intellectuals who participated included
C. L. R. James who gave a course on the workers' movement
in history, the feminist Juliet Mitchell (one of its founders) who
taught literature and psychology, and Robin Blackburn and Nicholas Krassó (like Mitchell, members of the *NLR* editorial board)
who lectured on the Cuban Revolution.

The Anti-University was possibly the only British academic institution to be wrecked by the impact of May 1968. By its nature it
encouraged revolutionary activity, and the actions of students emu-
lating their Parisian counterparts threatened its tenuous stability.
According to Roberta Elzey (involved in its administration), "Although this mini-revolt fizzled out after a few weeks, it left a bad

taste in many mouths, particularly as the instigators never assumed any responsibility, did any 'dirty work,' paid fees or contributed to the common cause."[7] By July the Anti-University had degenerated into a crash pad.

The radical culture of the late sixties existed in a chronic state of disarray, its frenetic energy arguably among its principal achievements.[8] Yet if as a culture it defied cohesion, a continuous—or near continuous—thread ran through it: a mass student movement that, if smaller and less vocal than its French or American counterparts, provided a focus for the political and cultural opposition of the time. One form taken by this activism was the Vietnam Solidarity Campaign (VSC), many of whose principal supporters and leaders were drawn from the ranks of students or those closely tied to the student milieu. The VSC, as Perry Anderson observed, was "the most important single political mobilization of the British Left in the 60s," at its height organizing mass demonstrations on the same order of magnitude as the earlier CND, in important ways an inspiration and a model.[9] Yet the VSC went beyond the reformist and neutralist politics of the disarmament movement, asserting its solidarity with the National Liberation Front's attempt to defeat American military forces in Vietnam.[10]

The VSC was founded in June 1966 at a national conference supported by almost fifty organizations and groups. It resulted from the initiative of the Bertrand Russell Peace Foundation, his International War Crimes Tribunal (which subsequently withdrew its support), and the Trotskyist IMG, which viewed the VSC as a means of building a wider political movement. The VSC saw its peak support at a mass demonstration in London in October 1968, organized by an ad hoc committee representing a wide spectrum of left opinion (including Tariq Ali, Vanessa Redgrave, and Mike Martin). Estimates ranged from 50,000 to 100,000 demonstrators. The London rally took place in a highly strained atmosphere, amid bitter disputes among the organizers and a flurry of groundless accusations in the established press. In a September issue of the *Times*, an article bore the headline, "Militant Plot Feared in London"; another article suggested that "a small army of militant extremists plans to seize control of certain highly sensitive installations and buildings in Central London next month."[11] Yet the event proved to be relatively tranquil, resulting in a minimum of arrests and injuries. This outcome in part resulted from the restraint shown by the London police, but it also occurred because the ad hoc committee was primarily interested in making a principled statement about the war rather than provoking a wider confrontation.

The student movement also expressed itself through numerous protests, demonstrations, sit-ins, and confrontations with authorities that took place in universities and colleges throughout Britain. These included the universities of Birmingham, Essex, Hull, Leister, and Warwick; the London School of Economics (LSE); and the art colleges of Hornsey and Guildford. In general, student protests had two frequently inseparable dimensions. They challenged the hierarchical and authoritarian structure of colleges and universities, and they demanded meaningful student participation in their governance. Or they represented attacks on universities' connections with industry, the military, and the state—what was portrayed as the presence of capitalist imperialism in higher education. At first, protests were rarely supported by a majority of students, but disruptive actions by a small group of militants tended to produce disciplinary actions, which in turn provoked a wider student involvement. This occurred in the May 1968 uprisings at Essex, where events were precipitated by a small group of militant students, who, inspired by the activities of Parisian radicals, disrupted a lecture by T. A. Inch, a specialist in germ warfare. Their suspension from classes by the authorities provoked a more generalized student action that led to the school's closing, attacks on the authoritarian structure of the university, demands for wider student participation in university affairs, and the brief emergence of an alternative university, which at its peak involved a thousand faculty members and students.[12]

Of the many sites of student protest, the LSE saw the most prolonged and perhaps intensive conflict, combining both student demands for a voice in university affairs and students' outrage at the impact of capitalist imperialism on school policy. The friction between students and school authorities originated in 1966 following the announcement that the school's new director was to be Walter Adams. At the time, Adams held a comparable position at University College, Rhodesia, and was accused of having actively worked with the racist and illegal Rhodesian government to expel and arrest opposition students and faculty. Despite repeated student initiatives, school officials adamantly defended their right to hire Adams without either consulting students or opening up the process to public scrutiny, and he assumed his post in a highly strained atmosphere. The conflict reached a climax in early 1969 when a group of student militants, armed with sledgehammers, crowbars, and pickaxes, broke down a steel gate. Arrests followed. The school was closed for four weeks. Further protests ensued over disciplinary actions brought against those responsible for breaking down the gate. A LSE in exile materialized while the school was closed. And two radical faculty members—Robin Blackburn and Nicholas Bateson—were dismissed for allegedly promoting violence, despite explicit university guidelines protecting freedom of speech. In the end, David Caute has suggested, the administrative structure changed very little.[13]

The majority of student protestors were neither revolutionary nor radical, and they tended to become involved either because of a passionate belief in a specific issue, for instance, opposition to the Vietnam War, or because of the general oppositional mood of the time, or both. The new left, like the Communist students of the thirties, was the vanguard of the movement; it shaped the movement's political discourses, developed its strategies, and led its protests and demonstrations. The new left's ultimate goal, as David Fernbach suggested, was to convince the mass of students to embrace revolution as a way of life: "to communicate with the mass of students at a deeper psychic level—finding ways to show them the bankruptcy and vacuity of the bourgeois career, the bourgeois home, the bourgeois family, helping them liberate their repressed sexuality and aggression, helping them discover the alternative lifestyle that is involved in being a 1. revolutionary fighter 2. a comrade 3. sexually emancipated. . . ."[14] The New Left of the fifties and early sixties had a loosely agreed upon political philosophy, a network of clubs, and a journal, *NLR* (which more or less spoke for it). Its successor comprised a multitude of political positions, factions, and tendencies as expressed in numerous interrelated journals, parties, and sects. In contrast to the earlier movement's absorption in British labor traditions, the new left—or new lefts—of the late sixties, frequently inspired by cultural and political developments outside Britain, became preoccupied—the May events in Paris notwithstanding—with the revolutionary politics of the Third World. A brief inventory of its component parts would include *some* but not all of the following: independent Marxists, anarchists, old New Leftists, black power advocates, situationists, dissident Trotskyists, Maoists, socialist feminists, and even Communists. Generalizations about the new left are difficult to make. But perhaps what those people who were involved shared was a common opposition to the style and substance of old left politics.[15] They rejected what they perceived as the old left's integration into the corporate and bureaucratic capitalist state, its rigid adherence to the centralized machinery of the labor movement, its advocacy of conventional lifestyles, its reverence for existing institutions, its preoccupation with managed technological and industrial growth, and its attachment to a mode of politics that stifled grassroots spontaneity. The old left and its politics were rooted in the class politics of the trade unions and the Labour Left, while the new left's politics stemmed from the more loosely structured activism of the civil rights movement, student protests, and, somewhat later, women's liberation (see chapter 5).

NLR in the late 1960s never achieved the same degree of authority as its predecessor in speaking for the movement that bore its name. Given the fractured nature of the new left of the late sixties, it is hard to conceive of any journal assuming an authoritative role. In any event, although several of the journal's producers were politically engaged, NLR itself was more concerned with establishing theoretical priorities than addressing the daily grind of political organization.[16] Some critics, following the lead established by Edward Thompson, represented the journal as being intellectually remote, divorced from everyday life, and condescending in its attitude toward ordinary working people. David Widgery of the IS, for example, wrote of NLR in 1975: "Underlying the apparent sophistication of the analyses was the extraordinarily arrogant belief that it is the role of the intellectuals to make the theory, the job of the workers to make the revolution and that what is wrong in Britain is that the latter are too backward to understand the former's instructions."[17] Such criticisms notwithstanding, the second incarnation of NLR represented a major achievement, produced by some of the most brilliant intellectuals of their generation (between twenty-five and thirty years old in 1968).[18] NLR played a central role in shaping the radical intellectual culture that materialized in the 1970s, which in the present context—understanding cultural Marxist history and cultural studies—is our major concern.[19]

From the mid-sixties on, NLR aspired to create a socialist intellectual culture that would formulate the theoretical vocabulary enabling a corporate working class to challenge the power of the dominant classes and the capitalist state. NLR saw the political radicalism of the decade's final years as expanding the parameters of this culture and challenging the classical models of revolution in the West. This view was especially true of the May events in Paris, of which Tom Nairn wrote: "Every existing theory becomes inadequate before it. Every sacred truth is shown up as partial, in the face of it, and ideas must patiently reform around it until our awareness has caught up with reality."[20] Although mostly older than the generation of "1968," the second *NLR* group viewed students as "a potentially insurgent force." And, inspired by the spirit of Maoist political practice, they advocated establishing "red bases" in colleges and universities. "By their struggles," an *NLR* editorial stated, "students can undermine an important bastion of ruling class power (higher education) and help to detonate wider social conflicts."[21] Such a view reflected the blurring of lines between *NLR* and the Fourth International IMG. For the leading theorist of the movement, the Belgian Marxist Ernest Mandel, the subordination of universities to capitalism, the increased demand for higher education, and the proletarianization of postgraduate occupations created a situation ripe for a revolutionary student movement of international dimensions. At the same time, Mandel viewed "the traditional organisations of the workers' movement" as "profoundly bureaucratised and long since co-opted into the bourgeois society."[22]

NLR enthused about the revolutionary potential of students, but it realized that Britain, as Anderson pointed out in 1968, was the only major industrialized country to have failed to produce a "coherent and militant student movement," although—he added hopefully—"it may now be only a matter of time before it does."[23] Anderson's explanation as to why Britain lagged behind France and Germany was that it lacked an intellectual heritage capable of fostering revolution. "Only where revolutionary ideas are freely and widely available—forming part of their daily environment—will large numbers of students begin to revolt."[24] For Anderson, a revolutionary culture could take root only if the ties binding students to the university system, and ultimately to bourgeois culture, were severed. To achieve this goal, he and his *NLR* colleagues launched a direct assault on "the reactionary and mystifying culture inculcated in universities and colleges."[25]

This assault took various forms, but in general it dramatized the poverty of cultural and intellectual life in Britain, and it laid bare the political and ideological underpinnings of nascent modes of thought. Writing in *NLR*, Richard Merton found Britain to be "a society stifling for lack of any art" that expressed "the experience of living in it." He acknowledged the "authentic expressive vitality" of English pop music, while portraying its theater as anachronistic, its novel as dead, and its cinema as "a mere obituary of it."[26] Robin Blackburn discovered in the dominant mode of empiricist and value-free social science a covert political agenda that consistently upheld "the existing social arrangements of the capitalist world" and that suppressed "the idea that any preferable alternative does, or could exist."[27] Such ways of thinking, Blackburn argued, had been superseded by Marxist dialectical thought: "the only viable alternative to the confusion and sterility into which post-classical bourgeois social theory has fallen" and "the theory of the practice which is changing the world."[28]

Gareth Stedman Jones's "History: The Poverty of Empiricism" attacked the liberalism and (as the essay's title suggested) empiricism of the historical profession, lamented its virtual obliviousness to modern European social thought, and defended the centrality of theory to the historian's enterprise. Stedman Jones argued that isolated attempts to challenge the dominant empiricist ideology of the profession, for instance those of R. H. Tawney and Sir Lewis Namier, had been absorbed and neutralized, and individual efforts in the present conjuncture would inevitably suffer the same fate. He thus called for a *collective* reconstruction of historical practice, one that would establish its theoretical foundations, be totalizing in its ambitions, and "advance into the structure and history of the ruling class, into the interpretation of the historical morphology of whole cultures."[29] Stedman Jones's thought was clearly inspired by historical materialism, but the model that he advocated was not that of the British Marxist historiographical tradition; rather, it was the historical practice of the French Annales school, "the most successfully revolutionary group of modern historians." He admired the Annales school's "aggressive" and "iconoclastic" nature, and he advocated a British equivalent. "Only vigorous intellectual imperialism and collective assault will make a mark. Otherwise the limp ghosts of long departed liberal mandarins will forever 'weigh like a nightmare on the brain of the living.'"[30]

Undoubtedly the pivotal essay in *NLR*'s critical examination of English bourgeois culture was Anderson's own highly influential, "The Components of the National Culture." Anderson's article was a sweeping panoramic survey of the achievement—or, perhaps more accurately, lack of achievement—of the human sciences in twentieth-century Britain, including economics, sociology, literary criticism, political science, art history, history, and anthropology. But more important, it was a theoretical attempt to explain why Britain alone among major European countries had failed to produce a major totalizing social theory on the order of Durkheim's, Weber's, or Pareto's, let alone a Marxist one as found in Adorno, Sartre, Althusser, or Lukács—what he described as the "absent centre" of British society and culture. Here, Anderson did not simply lament British thinkers' absorption in myopic forms of empiricism; he offered his own way of thinking as an alternative to their narrow-mindedness. In terms borrowed from Lévi-Strauss, Anderson's goal was to explain the interrelationship among British intellectual disciplines rather than the characteristics of any one discipline. Or, as he stated, "It is not the content of the individual sectors that determines the essential character of each so much as the ground-plan of their distribution."[31]

Anderson's explanation for this "absent centre" recapitulated the argument of his earlier "Origins of the Present Crisis." First, he argued that because the English bourgeoisie fused with, rather than supplanted, the old aristocratic ruling class, it was never compelled by dint of historical circumstance to conceptualize society as a totality. "It consequently never had to rethink society as a whole, in abstract theoretical reflection. Empirical, piece-meal intellectual disciplines corresponded to humble, circumscribed social action."[32] Second, Anderson believed that sociology's emergence on the Continent was connected to the growth of a mass socialist movement, sociology from this perspective being a counterweight to the threat of revolutionary Marxism. But in Britain, where the culmination of the nineteenth-century working-class movement was a *labor* party rather than a *socialist* party, the dominant class was never forced to produce an alternative or opposing totalization of society. Ironically, when Britain eventually did experience the impact of Continental thought, it was transmitted by émigrés escaping the instability of their homelands, attracted to British culture by and large precisely because of its traditionalism and empiricism: Ludwig Wittgenstein in philosophy, Bronislaw Malinowski in anthropology, Lewis Namier in history, Karl Popper in social theory, Isaiah Berlin in political theory, and Ernst Gombrich in aesthetics among them. (The categories are Anderson's.)[33] Where British empiricism was largely instinctive, haphazard, and "shunned theory even in its rejection of theory," the achievement of the expatriates was to launch the first systematic refusal of systematic thinking.

"They codified the slovenly empiricism of the past, and thereby hardened and narrowed it."[34] Anderson and *NLR*'s critique of English bourgeois thought was a precondition to creating the theoretical underpinnings of a revolutionary socialist culture. But once the ground was cleared, no guarantee could be made that such a culture would flourish. Believing socialist theory in Britain to be impoverished—where it existed at all—the *NLR* group sought to provide the theoretical foundations on which a revolutionary culture could be built. In accordance with this goal they began to make available the most creative Marxist work since the classical writings of Marx, Engels, and Lenin—the Western Marxist tradition—in order to stimulate interest in and critical reflection on alternative modes of thought. Virtually unknown in the English-speaking world, this tradition included such important Marxist thinkers as Theodor Adorno, Louis Althusser, Lucio Colletti, Lucien Goldmann, Antonio Gramsci, Karl Korsch, György Lukács, Sebastiano Timpanaro, and Galvano Della Volpe. *NLR* made the thought of these and related thinkers accessible by means of an ambitious program of translations and critical evaluations in both the journal and a revived book series—New Left Books (NLB), later renamed Verso. It followed this venture with an equally ambitious project aimed at spreading interest in, and reflecting on, the classics of historical materialism. *NLR* published a series of new translations and editions of Marx, including the first publication of the *Grundrisse* in English and the first complete English translation of *Capital*. In retrospect, *NLR*'s publishing project was a major step in the expansion of Marxist intellectual culture in Britain. More generally, it helped facilitate the dissemination of European Marxist theoretical discourse throughout Anglo-American intellectual circles in the 1970s.

Many writers associated with *NLR* contributed to the discovery, revival, and assessment of European Marxist theory, but Anderson provided the most extensive treatment and critique in *Considerations on Western Marxism* (1976).[35] Originally intended as an introduction to an anthology of *NLR* writings, the essay represented a sweeping overview of the topography of Western Marxism, a highly compressed survey outlining the historical conditions of its production and the characteristics and preoccupations defining it as a mode of thought. Anderson's understanding of Western Marxism was in terms of the classical phase of historical materialism—the writings of Marx, Engels, Lenin, and Luxemburg. Anderson contrasted the organic relationship between theory and practice characteristic of classical Marxism with the fact that Western Marxism developed within the academy rather than as part of the workers' movement, an unprecedented entry of Marxist intellectuals into the citadels of bourgeois culture. Anderson understood this shift historically. Western Marxism was the product of defeat, isolation, and despair; it surfaced in the aftermath of working-class defeat, fascist triumph, and Soviet isolation in the interwar years; its primary achievements took place against a backdrop of ossifying Communist ideology during the Stalin era and capitalism's stabilization and subsequent unprecedented growth in the years following World War II. The result was a displacement of the theoretical agenda of classical Marxism. The classical thinkers were primarily concerned with the historical, political, and economic dimensions of society, while their Western Marxist descendants were preoccupied with the philosophical, cultural, and aesthetic—not just a shift from base to superstructure, but a redefinition of superstructure itself. In this regard, they were frequently attracted to the Hegelian or idealist roots of historical materialism. And they recast Marxism, emphasizing that it was a method. In Anderson's words:

> No philosopher within the Western Marxism tradition ever claimed that the main or ultimate aim of historical materialism was a theory of knowledge. But the common assumption of virtually all was that the preliminary task of theoretical research within Marxism was to disengage the rules of social enquiry discovered by Marx, yet buried within the topical particularity of his work, and if necessary to complete them. The result was that a remarkable amount of the output of Western Marxism became a prolonged and intricate Discourse on Method.[36]

For Anderson, Western Marxism opened up a new intellectual terrain, but the cost was its estrangement from revolutionary politics. Its adoption of highly specialized philosophical vocabularies—frequently impenetrable to the uninitiated—was one gauge of this isolation.

Twenty years after its publication, *Considerations on Western Marxism* is a classic text of intellectual history, a work of dazzling breadth and scholarly virtuosity that transformed discussions of twentieth-century Marxist theory. In this respect, Anderson achieved for Western Marxism what Raymond Williams had accomplished for the "culture and society" tradition. Yet a consequence of the book's global aspirations was an (inevitable) blurring of differences between a group of thinkers who were by any accounting highly individualistic. In *The British New Left*, Lin Chun has observed that Anderson's macro approach smoothed over antagonisms between the scientific Marxism of Della Volpe, Colletti, and Althusser and "the humanistic or Hegelian mainstream."[37] But more generally it must be asked: how is Western Marxism a tradition at all? Western Marxists, loosely speaking, developed their thought against a shared historical backdrop, and common theoretical patterns can be detected in their work. But if a tradition involves the handing down of beliefs or values or the transmission of an inherited way of thinking, Western Marxism does not qualify. As Anderson himself admitted, the exponents of this tradition were not organically connected.

> *Yet in fact, the philosophers of this tradition—complex and recondite as never before in their own idiom—were virtually without exception utterly provincial and uninformed about the theoretical cultures of neighbouring countries. Astonishingly, within the entire corpus of Western Marxism, there is not one single serious appraisal or sustained critique of the work of one major theorist by another, revealing close textual knowledge or minimal analytic care in its treatment.[38]*

Yet if Western Marxism was not a tradition in the usual sense, why did Anderson conceive of it in these terms? Western Marxists might have shared few if any organic connections, but for a cultural outsider, discovering them as a constellation of thinkers, it probably appeared otherwise. From this perspective it was precisely because Anderson was not *within* Western Marxism, because he read these thinkers virtually at the same time, and because he thought about them as an alternative to an impoverished English tradition that he represented them as constituting a tradition. In other words, Western Marxism was a construction from a particular vantage point within the British new left.

Such a view gains plausibility if we consider the book's conclusion. By the time that Anderson wrote *Considerations on Western Marxism*, Western Marxism was no longer the theoretical anchor that it once had been in his life. Indeed, the conclusion reads as if he is coming to terms with—and putting to rest—his theoretical past. Here, Anderson argued that just as Western Marxism was made possible by the rupture between theory and practice in the interwar years, it was superseded when that breach was repaired, a process initiated by the radical movements of the late sixties and early seventies. In this new situation, while Western Marxism failed to capture the imagination of the radical Left, there was "another tradition of an entirely different character" that "subsisted and developed 'off-stage'—for the first time to gain wider political attention during and after the French explosion."[39] This tradition was Trotskyism.

Anderson was of course right to point out that Trotsky's internationalism and anti-Stalinism proved attractive to a significant contingent of the radical generation of "1968." But whether it "subsisted and developed 'off-stage' " while Western Marxism "occupied in many respects the front of the stage in the whole intellectual history of the European Left" is a complex question, its answer depending on making it explicit what theater housed the stage and who was in the audience, a task in which Anderson never engaged.[40] Yet in taking for granted rather than exploring this point, Anderson conveyed a great deal about himself and *NLR*. For while he might have been preoccupied with Western Marxism in the early and middle part of the sixties, the Trotskyist historian, Isaac Deutscher, was likewise a "formative" if not the primary influence on him. The balance between the impact of these two traditions on his thought began to shift with the growing importance of thinkers like Mandel on his and *NLR*'s direction in the later sixties. From this point on, Anderson recalled in 1980, the *NLR* collective "never lost sight of the centrality of Trotsky's heritage, even while its own editors varied widely among themselves in their particular assessments of it, and none was ever uncritical of it."[41] He described Trotskyism as "a central and unevadable pole of political reference" and the encounter with Trotsky "as an inevitable process in the attempt to recover a coherent revolutionary Marxism." In the world of Perry Anderson, Trotskyism—like Western Marxism before it—had appropriated center stage.

NLR's hopes that a mass student movement would provoke a wider assault on bourgeois society and the state never materialized. But the generation of new left radicals that these hopes were pinned on did not abandon the radical cause, and the energy unleashed by "1968" took on new forms. Politically, these energies were channeled into a series of interconnected movements: feminism, gay rights, community activism, environmental politics, anti-

racism, and, somewhat later, disarmament. Here, the importance
of "1968," as Hilary Wainright observed, was that it brought forth
new forms of political power. "The sort of social transformations
that working-class people, women, black people need can't come
through a purely parliamentary route to power—a power which
turns out to be illusory—not even from an extra-parliamentary
process that's finally consummated in parliamentary fashion."[42]
Intellectually, the political aspirations of the late sixties' student
movement provided the impetus for the creation of a radical intellectual culture unprecedented in scope in a British context. Or as
Robin Blackburn suggested in retrospect:

> *The movement encouraged the growth of a radical, anticapitalist current
> of thought, brought an interest in theory and ideas—look at the number
> of radical and Marxist sociological, economic and political and philo-
> sophical journals that have come into being since then—which went
> against the grain of the philistine antiintellectualism of British society in
> general and the British left and Labour movement in particular.*[43]

Some of the journals that come to mind include *Capital and Class,
Economy and Society, Feminist Review, History Workshop, Ideology and
Consciousness, M/F, Marxism Today, Race and Class, Radical Philosophy, Radical Science Journal, Screen, Screen Education, Theoretical Practice,* and *Working Papers in Cultural Studies.* They were not necessarily
committed to Marxism, but Marxism played a major determining
role—in Raymond Williams's sense of exerting "pressures" and
"limits"—on them.

A full analysis of this culture is beyond the scope of this book,
but, in the present context, what stands out is this culture's frequent
acceptance of *NLR*'s position that a revolutionary intellectual culture in Britain must look beyond indigenous ways of thinking. We
can observe this trend in the credo of the *Radical Philosophy* collective: their belief that contemporary British philosophy was at a
"dead end," that a pressing need existed to examine its ideological
role within the wider society, and that "positive alternatives" included phenomenology, existentialism, Hegelianism, and Marxism.[44] It was apparent in the *Radical Science Journal*'s aspiration to
subject the notion of "scientificity" to political criticism by drawing on aspects of the work of Gramsci, Lukács, and Marcuse.[45] It
was the underlying inspiration of *Theoretical Practice,* which "enthusiastically adopted Althusser's programme of work."[46] It was crucial
to the shape and direction of cultural studies, which, as Stuart Hall

observed, had "been a bewildering series of theoretical explosions with the appearance, assimilation and familiarization of one continental theoretician after another."[47]

II

Cultural studies was transformed by the events of the late sixties and early seventies. The leading theorists and writers who expanded the field were affected by, and participants in, these events, and their experience of them influenced the way that they saw culture and ideology and presented them with both objects to investigate and theoretical problems to solve. They attempted to understand both the emergence of subcultural and radical practices and the means by which the dominant ideological structures defined and defused them. This attempt to understand contemporary social and political conflict included the process by which an independent media helped to secure the hegemony of the ruling class and the state. Most importantly, cultural theorists were haunted by the crisis in socialist and radical thought that, though first surfacing in the 1950s, was thrown into sharper relief by the failures and disappointments of the late 1960s and early 1970s, and they grappled with both the theoretical and political implications of the crisis: the problematic relationship between structure and agency, experience and ideology, theory and practice.

By the late 1960s cultural researchers at the Birmingham Centre had grown dissatisfied with the theoretical foundations of their project. They recognized that if their method of close reading was to illuminate contemporary culture, it must be anchored in a wider understanding of society, an understanding that could come only from social theory. The Centre's initial encounter with social theory had been transitional and eclectic, devoted to finding alternatives to structural functionalism, which, in any event, was being undermined by both internal and external developments in sociology. Centre researchers were initially drawn to German idealism, but this interest proved short-lived when they came to view it as an inadequate tool for understanding the cultural upheavals of the late sixties and early seventies, for it was unable to conceptualize power, ideology, and class relations in contemporary society. In the end, the Centre looked elsewhere to find a means of analyzing contemporary culture: to Marxism and structuralism.

A founding principle of cultural studies was opposition to orthodox Marxism, and Marxism did not play a particularly significant role in the Centre's early years. Indeed, although the study of alternatives to the mainstream Marxist tradition took place in the late sixties, such study intensified after Richard Hoggart went on leave in 1969 and Stuart Hall became acting director.[48] Hall, who had considered himself a Marxist since his student days, closely followed the British debates on Western Marxist thought that were going on in *NLR*, among other places. As early as 1968, he demonstrated the influence of their discussions, analyzing from the Marxist humanist perspective of Sartre and Goldmann the "phenomenological" and "structural" moments in the hippie movement—the disparity between subjective intentions and experience and "situated meanings."[49]

Under Hall's influence, Centre research entered into a new and closer relationship with Marxism.[50] Not Marxism in its orthodox guise, which had treated culture as a reflection or mechanical consequence of the base, nor Marxism in the socialist-humanist version of the original New Left, which, though cognizant of the specificity and irreducibility of culture, had conceptualized culture exclusively in terms of "experience." Rather, cultural studies drew on Western Marxism, which, however heterogeneous, was unified by both its opposition to the orthodox formulation of the relationship between base and superstructure and its insistence that the base/superstructure model was indispensable to Marxism. Without abandoning the idea that the mode of production had its own distinct structure and was responsible for the fundamental conflicts of society, Western Marxists saw politics, ideology, and culture as having their own specificity and logic.

Marxism became central to the Centre's theoretical repertoire in the seventies, but, it was, as Hall observed, viewed as a way of posing and thinking about questions rather than providing a set of answers.

> *And when, eventually, in the seventies, British cultural studies did advance—in many different ways, it must be said—within the problematic of Marxism, you should hear the term problematic in a genuine way, not just in a formalist-theoretical way: as a problem; as much about struggling against the constraints and limits of that model as about the necessary questions it required us to address.[51]*

Of Western Marxists, the two thinkers to have the greatest impact on the Centre were Althusser and Gramsci. Although the Centre's understanding and appropriation of Gramsci changed over the years, briefly stated he offered a view of power relations in advanced capitalist societies that (1) avoided the reductionism of the classical model; (2) viewed the cultural and ideological field as an arena of conflict between dominant and subordinate groups within historically constituted relations; (3) resisted seeing hegemony as a simplistic equivalent of ruling-class domination; and (4) understood both the centrality and complexity of the production of "consent" in Western democracies.

Cultural studies was also greatly influenced by—some might say obsessed with—what may loosely be described as "structuralism." Founded on the thought of Ferdinand Saussure, structuralism understood social reality linguistically. It saw culture not as the objectified experience of a social group, as it had been for the founders of cultural studies, but, in Graeme Turner's words, "as the site where meaning is generated and experienced . . . a determining, productive field through which social realities are constructed, experienced, and interpreted."[52] In short, culture produced social actors as much as it was created by them.

Although cultural studies in the 1970s felt the impact of several theorists within the structuralist ambit, it was above all influenced by two of them—Roland Barthes and Althusser. Barthes's contribution to the founding of semiology, which stressed the denotative and connotative dimensions of signs, suggested a way of systematically understanding the ideological underpinnings of everyday life. His own unforgettable analysis of cultural products provided a model for critical work. Althusser, who straddled both the structuralist and Western Marxist traditions, redefined ideology by combining Marxist and structuralist concepts. Basing his definition on Saussure's distinction between *langue* and *parole*, and the Marxist differentiation between science and ideology, he saw ideology as the imaginary forms and representations through which men and women lived their real conditions of existence. Adapting the thought of Lacan, Althusser stressed the "unconscious" or "forms," not the "content" or "surface manifestations," of ideological practices. He saw individuals' perceptions of autonomy as imaginary, the result of interpellation by ideological discourses. Althusser's theory provided a way of grounding ideology in material conditions yet treating it as a discrete process that was semiautonomous and overdetermined. The theory suggested that culture or ideology was not merely the expression of lived experience but its precondition, the foundation of consciousness and subjectivity.

To better appreciate the theoretical contribution of the Birmingham Centre, it is necessary to briefly consider separate alternatives as well as alternative approaches to cultural studies in the 1970s.[53] At one extreme, Graham Murdock and Peter Golding's research into the political economy of mass communications was an alternative to cultural studies; their research was founded on a reaffirmation of the traditional understanding of the base/superstructure relationship.[54] Opposing what they saw as cultural Marxist tendencies to push economic determinations to the background and view cultural practices as relatively autonomous, they argued that the media must above all be seen from the perspective of the monopoly capitalist organizations that produced them. Murdock and Golding did not regard cultural producers as being wholly determined by the structure of the capitalist media, and they acknowledged that their professional practices need not conform in any strict way with the views or policies of ownership. Yet they believed that the scope of these practices was determined by the profit motive and that their ideological function could be grasped only in relationship to the needs of large-scale commercial enterprises. Reminiscent of the Frankfurt School, they attributed the uniformity and standardization of much popular culture to the capitalist structure of the culture industry.

The Centre's work recognized the crucial importance of the mediating effect of capitalist relations on cultural production. Yet it rejected the instrumentalist and economistic implications of Golding and Murdock's political economy of mass communications, and it argued that the ideological domain of social life had a determining effect of its own. While Golding and Murdock's emphasis on production might explain certain general tendencies of the mass media, the Centre found their approach unable to account for differences between specific texts and practices or the development of particular cultural forms.

Golding and Murdock's emphasis on political economy was in diametric opposition to critical approaches loosely associated with the film journal *Screen*, an alternative approach to cultural studies that paid careful attention to the ideological dimension of cultural practices, texts, and genres. Published by the Society for Education in Film and Television, and financed by the British Film Institute, *Screen* in the 1970s sought to revolutionize the practice of writing about film, transforming it from a "subjective taste ridden criticism" to a "systematic approach" founded on the most recent

Marxist, structuralist, and semiological thought from the Continent. It attempted, as Anthony Easthope observed, to create a scientific basis for film analysis in the Althusserian sense of "a process without a subject," "the identity of individual contributions to the journal" merging "into a genuinely impersonal and developing theoretical coherence."[55] It derived its political justification from Althusser's notion of the relative autonomy of practices in a social formation. According to Colin MacCabe, a *Screen* contributor and editorial board member: "Put crudely, Althusser enabled one to take institutions and ideas seriously while still genuinely retaining a belief in the reality of class struggle and revolution. . . . one might say that Althusser provided a way of taking seriously the reality of the institutions within which one worked without forgetting the reality of the desire to transform society."[56]

Where traditional Marxist accounts of literature and culture focused on their ideological content, *Screen* writers emphasized the ideology of form. They followed Russian formalist thinking, which viewed form and style as the producer rather than the vehicle for meaning, and they applied this insight to film, analyzing the formalist techniques that produced meaning in cinematic practices. *Screen* viewed form as nothing more than the materiality of the signifier and films as signifying practices, active processes of the production of meaning in relationship to their audience. Those involved in the journal were particularly interested in how these practices contributed to the reproduction of the dominant order through Althusserian and especially Lacanian notions of the interpellation of subjectivity. Reminiscent of Barthes's classic treatment of the realist novel in *S/Z*, they focused on how realist or conventional cinema positioned the reader or viewer into a fixed relationship to the narrative. *Screen* theorists argued that the very "naturalness" of a narrative produced assent to the "common sense" or dominant ideological meaning and foreclosed subordinate and alternative discourses, interpretations, and political perspectives. In opposition to the terrorism of realism, they championed Brechtian aesthetics and the experimental techniques of the avant-garde cinema that placed viewers in different relationships to narratives and thus resisted textual closure.

Laura Mulvey's analysis of the gendered nature of audiences in her highly influential "Visual Pleasure and Narrative Cinema" (1975) captures an important dimension of *Screen*'s project.[57] Mulvey fused a feminist appropriation of Lacanian accounts of the formation of individual subjects and Freud's analysis of scopophilia as "taking other people as objects, subjecting them to a controlling and curious gaze." For Mulvey, one of the central forms of pleasure found in conventional movies was derived from the central but subordinate role accorded to women. She contrasted the passive role assigned to women, who were meant to be looked at, with the active position of men—both as actors and as viewers. "Traditionally, the woman displayed has functioned on two levels: as erotic object for the characters within the screen story, and as erotic object for the spectator within the auditorium, with a shifting tension between the looks on either side of the screen."[58] What is central here is the connection forged between the male character in the film and the one in the audience, in Mulvey's view, a connection produced by the cinematic codes themselves and understandable from the point of view of the Lacanian concept of the mirror phase.

As the spectator identifies with the main male protagonist, he projects his look on to that of his like, his screen surrogate, so that the power of the male protagonist as he controls events coincides with the active power of the erotic look, both giving a satisfying sense of omnipotence. A male movie star's glamorous characteristics are thus not those of the erotic object of the gaze, but those of the more perfect, more complete, more powerful ideal ego conceived in the original moment of recognition in front of the mirror.[59]

This subject position is not offered to the female viewer, and thus Mulvey was, in effect, suggesting that the pleasures offered by conventional films to women resulted in the negation of women's female subjectivity. Deconstructing how this process took place was the precondition for overturning it. Its transformation involved freeing "the look of the camera into its materiality in time and space and the look of the audience into dialectics, passionate detachment."[60] Mulvey would attempt this transformation in a series of films in collaboration with Peter Wollen.

The Centre's work was informed by many of the same intellectual currents as *Screen*. However, it opposed *Screen*'s fetishization of the text, the privileged status that the journal accorded to avantgarde strategies, and its concept of the subject. Some of these differences surfaced in an exchange provoked by Rosalind Coward, a former Birmingham student, who in "Class, 'Culture' and the Social Formation" (1977) challenged from perspectives derived from *Screen* the foundation of the Centre's work. (That the essay was published in *Screen* implied that Coward's attack was endorsed more generally by the film journal.) Centre researchers—including Ian Chambers, John Clarke, Ian Connell, Lidia Curti, Stuart Hall, and Tony Jefferson—responded to Coward's critique in a later issue of *Screen* in "Marxism and Culture" (1977–78). Coward briefly responded to their reply.

Perhaps the principal theoretical issue in question was the relationship between ideology and the social formation and whether that relationship could be adequately expressed within a Marxist problematic. From Coward's *Screen* perspective, the Centre's attempt to link productive relations with ideological expressions—however semiautonomous ideology was construed to be—was simultaneously idealist, empiricist, and reductionist. Coward argued that the Centre saw culture "as the product of consciousness, . . . which is free from the action of the structure"; yet it conceived of the social formation as founded on "an essential division between capital and labour" which was "directly reflected in the economic classes, which themselves are reflected at the level of culture and ideology."[61]

For Coward, the Centre failed to understand the implications of *Screen*'s Lacanian understanding of signification and the subject: the idea that signifying practices were not founded on class practices but that they inscribed ideological positions. For the Centre, Coward's conception of signification was outside the "limit-position" of Marxism, for it suggested that ideology was completely detached from material practices. Or as they stated: "This is indeed the hub of the issue between us: the emphasis on the *absolute autonomy* of signifying practice. This stress seems to us to preclude the referencing of Language-in-general to any particular language, and to refuse any attempt to analyze signifying practices as part of the 'material factors which determine the cultural formation.'"[62] Coward viewed this critique as a defense of traditional Marxism, which from her feminist perspective was founded on the primacy of class relations and accorded gender a secondary status. "The contemporary implications of this notion are also clear: members of the women's movement are to crawl back into their corners suitably reproved for attempting to theorise those things which Marx never bothered with."[63]

A principal difference between the Centre and *Screen* was clear in their views of human agency. While the film journal saw individuals and groups as subjects interpellated by ideological discourses, the Centre believed that no necessary correspondence was obtained between a text's dominant encoded meaning and the meaning that the audience decoded. Within limits, audiences could negotiate or subvert as well as assent to the intended or unintended meaning of the text's producers. In part, this reflected the Centre's Gramscian view of cultural and political struggle. But it also was grounded in the socialist humanism, culturalism, and cultural Marxism of those who shaped its original agenda.

In the tradition of Williams, Thompson, and Hoggart, cultural researchers "listened" to and re-created the lived experience of cultural consumers and producers, especially the experience of oppressed groups. The Centre's recovery of the experience of youth subcultures showed as much respect for its subjects as any work within the tradition of *The Making of the English Working Class* and incorporated the method of close reading associated with *The Uses of Literacy.* Yet the Centre's approach was irrevocably altered by the Althusserian challenge to the humanist tradition's impulse to conceptualize culture in terms of experience. Centre theorists rejected both Thompson's counterposing of experience to ideology and Williams's contention that a particular culture could be truly known only by those who lived in it. The Centre saw cultural practices as being pulled by both experience and ideology, a relationship that could only be negotiated theoretically. The Centre's practice might be regarded as a continuous attempt to elaborate on Marx's famous words in the *Eighteenth Brumaire*: "Men make their own history, but they do not make it just as they please; they do not make it under circumstances chosen by themselves, but under circumstances directly found, given and transmitted from the past." [64] Centre researchers and writers bent this statement in one direction and then the other. They struggled to hold both of its parts in a balance that could never be anything but precarious.

While the Centre's work in the 1970s represented a critique of its own theoretical foundations, it is important to remember that the founders of cultural studies themselves did not stand still. For instance, Raymond Williams, whose work crucially defined its original project, reformulated his cultural theory during the 1970s in response to the social upheavals of the late sixties and in recognition of a kind of Marxism unknown in Britain during the Cold War years. His later writings also influenced the theoretical vocabulary of cultural studies during the decade.

Although a Labour supporter for much of his adult life, Williams was deeply disappointed by the Wilson government's record in office, and he left the party over the government's handling of the 1966 seamen's strike. He viewed the government's conduct as symptomatic of the Labour leadership's authoritarian cast of mind and bourgeois style of thinking. For Williams, there was an alternative:

> The key to our future, I firmly believe, is the extension of politics beyond the routines of the parliamentary process, as CND, more than any other movement has already shown to be possible. Not all our campaigns will be of that size or character, but what we have to do, in open practice, is to define politics differently, in every kind of popular institution and demonstration, so that we can go on changing consciousness (our own included) in ways that are intrinsically of a participating, extending and therefore democratic kind.[65]

Williams's own involvement in this alternative politics was most conspicuously expressed in the *May Day Manifesto* movement, which in the last part of the sixties attempted to reconstitute and extend the "third way" of the original New Left.[66] The movement brought together dissident Communists, left-wing Catholics, dissatisfied Labour Left supporters, and *NLR* contributors, among others. The *Manifesto* appeared in two editions—the second one a Penguin Books special edition. The first edition was written by Williams in collaboration with Edward Thompson and Stuart Hall. Hall's earlier essay, "The Condition of England Question," in *People and Politics* (1967), had already created a framework for critiquing the Wilson government. The second edition drew on a wider range of Left analysis and scholarship, particularly the economic expertise of Michael Barratt Brown and Bob Rowthorn, but it was finally written by Williams. In brief, the *Manifesto* recapitulated several themes sounded by the original New Left—poverty, housing, the health service, mass communications, and workers' control. But central to its argument was its portrayal of the Labour government as not merely failing to go beyond capitalism, but creating new capitalist forms appropriate to an international system dominated by the United States.

Discussions of the *Manifesto* in London and elsewhere led to the creation in April 1969 of the short-lived National Convention of the Left, with Williams as its chair, its goal to make an impact on the upcoming parliamentary elections based on the principles embodied in the *Manifesto*. But, like the original New Left before it, the National Convention of the Left could not adequately resolve its relationship to the Labour Party. Was it to be a pressure group within it? Or was it to act as an alternative to Labour and run the risk of contributing to a Tory victory? Discussions took place of running a slate of candidates, but such talks led nowhere, and the National Convention of the Left collapsed. When the Labour Party was defeated in 1970 by the Conservatives of Edward Heath, Williams actually welcomed it.

At the same time as Williams was immersed in the *May Day Manifesto* movement, he was familiarizing himself with Western Marxism, now made available by *NLR* and others. In the fifties Williams had of course been critical of Marxist cultural theory, and he acknowledged that in the 1930s' debate between Marxism and *Scrutiny*, Marxism had failed to hold its own.[67] But as a consequence of his encounter with alternative ways of conceiving Marxism—and previously unknown writings of Marx—Williams came to describe himself as a cultural materialist, a position conceived as "a theory of the specificities of material, cultural and literary production within historical materialism."[68]

The shift in Williams's thought first became apparent in "Literature and Sociology: In Memory of Lucien Goldmann" (1971), an essay based on a lecture given at Cambridge earlier in the year and appropriately enough published in *NLR*. Here, Williams broadly aligned himself with a tradition of materialist cultural analysis that he identified with Lukács but that was refined, in his view, by Goldmann.[69] He found in Goldmann's "genetic structures" a concept that he had developed in the idea of "structures of feeling." He believed that, despite their belonging to distinct traditions, both he and Goldmann were interested in discovering the homologous relationship among literary, philosophical, and sociohistorical structures. Goldmann, like Williams, was interested in establishing the relationship between the "mental structure" of the most coherently conceived literary work and the collective mentality of the group of which the work was an expression—an idea that recalled Williams's view of cultural analysis as being concerned with the relationship between elements in the whole way of life. Also like Williams—especially in a work such as *Modern Tragedy* (1966)— Goldmann gave priority to the forms rather than the content of cultural practices. Yet despite the congruity of his own and Goldmann's interests, Williams conceded the limits of the tradition in which he was trained. "Much that has to be proved, in our own tradition—and especially the very existence of significant primary relations between literature and society—can there be surpassed, in general philosophical and sociological terms, before the particular analyses begin." This was, in his view—and in language echoing Anderson's—because the English tradition "lacked a centre, in any developed philosophy or sociology."[70]

Williams's encounter with Western Marxism was further developed in "Base and Superstructure in Marxist Cultural Theory" (1973), an essay that became the basis for parts of *Marxism and Literature* (1977). Williams had always been critical of the base/superstructure model, but the importance of his treatment here was to make a critique of it that opened up new possibilities in cultural theory. Williams's objections to the model were twofold. First, he argued that where most analysts had been preoccupied with the superstructure, the model's real problem was with the base, which was frequently conceived in a static and objectified way, in his view inconsistent with Marx's own dynamic mode of analysis. As Williams stated: "Moreover, when these forces are considered, as Marx always considers them, as the specific activities and relationships of real men, they mean something very much more active, more complicated and more contradictory than the developed metaphorical notion of the 'base' could possibly allow us to realize."[71] If the base defined "the primary production of society itself," then the characteristics that distinguished it from what was usually thought of as superstructure—with its connotation of being "secondary"— were highly problematic.

Second, Williams accepted the fact that at the heart of any version of Marxist cultural theory was a notion of "determination": the "base" or "social being" "determining" the "superstructure" or "social consciousness." Yet he rejected the concept of "determination" as Marxists conventionally conceived it: "a subsequent content" being "essentially prefigured, predicted and controlled by a preexisting external force."[72] Williams argued for a sense of "determination" that involved "the predominance of objective conditions at any particular moment" in a process, a sense that stressed "setting limits" and "exerting pressures."

Determination of this whole kind—a complex and interrelated process of limits and pressures—is in the whole social process itself and nowhere else: not in an abstracted 'mode of production' nor in an abstracted 'psychology.' Any abstraction of determinism, based on the isolation of autonomous categories, which are seen as controlling or which can be used for prediction, is then a mystification of the specific and always related determinants which are the real social process.[73]

Williams's critique of the base/superstructure model was the point of departure for his own dynamic alternative to it, in crucial respects a shift from his earlier work of the late fifties and early sixties. His critique placed a greater emphasis on both cultural and political struggle (a tacit response to Thompson's original critique) and on the "ideological" or, what was a preferable term to his mind, the "hegemonic." Williams, in effect, expanded his idea of culture—and his own idea of "structures of feeling"—by viewing the social formation as a totality and critically adapting Gramsci's concept of hegemony: "a whole body of practices and expectations, over the whole of living: our senses and assignments of energy, our shaping perceptions of ourselves and our world. It is a lived system of meanings and values—constitutive and constituting—which as they are experienced as practices appear as reciprocally confirming."[74] Hegemony was a process of cultural domination that was never static or total but was continually defended, challenged, reformulated, and reproduced. Indeed, hegemony was in continuous conflict with "alternative" and "oppositional" forces: "residual" cultural forms of earlier periods that could be construed as challenges to society's dominant values; and "emergent" ones—"new practices, new significances and experiences"—that were being created continually and were either incorporated by the dominant culture or prefigured new social forms. Williams stressed the dynamic quality of hegemony and rejected accounts of it that were either totalizing or static, but he was under no illusion as to its potential reach in contemporary society.

But I am sure it is true of the society that has come into existence since the last war, that progressively, because of developments in the social character of labour, in the social character of communications, and in the social character of decision, it [dominant culture] extends much further than ever before in capitalist society into certain hitherto resigned areas of experience and practice and meaning.[75]

The result was that what constituted an "alternative" or "oppositional" practice was defined within a narrower compass than in the past.

Centre researchers acknowledged Williams's continuing contribution to the field of cultural studies, especially his attention to cultural contestation. In language derived from Williams, the eighth annual report (covering 1974–76) discussed the importance of a historical perspective for the study of culture: "It poses, in the centre of the field, questions of cultural power and hegemony; of domination and subordination through the exercise of cultural power, and the transmission of cultural skills and competences; of what is residual or emergent . . . and thus, questions about the general relation of cultures to power, to ideologies and to forms of social consciousness."[76] Yet Centre analysts regarded his later work as a modification, rather than a transformation, of his original project. And by the end of the 1970s they distanced themselves from Williams's conception of the social totality. For Stuart Hall, Williams viewed society as an indissoluble whole, founded on a single contradiction—capital and labor—linked to the various cultural and political practices by a series of "correspondences" or "homologies." Under the influence of Althusser, Hall emphasized the "specificity" and "autonomy" of practices in a social formation, their unity based on "difference" rather than "correspondence," linked together through "articulations." He argued that the conception of the social formation as a "structured totality" made it possible to understand "how specific practices (articulated around contradictions which do not arise in the same way, at the same point, in the same moment), can nevertheless be brought *together*."[77]

From outside looking in, then, the Centre's approach to culture might be thought of as embodying a unified perspective. It occupied a distinctive space within the field of cultural studies as a whole, although a space whose definition crucially depended on opposition to and negation of available positions. Yet the perspective from within the Centre revealed a very different picture. The Centre's work was shaped by many intellectual traditions, and these traditions were felt differently by individual Centre researchers. Subgroups, such as the media or subcultures, were themselves influenced by traditions and controversies specific to their own domains of inquiry. The practice of cultural studies was deeply affected by political controversies. The rise of the women's movement, in particular, was responsible for conflicting definitions of cultural studies at the Centre. In sum, if cultural studies at the Centre occupied a distinctive space, it was a space that contained different, even opposing, definitions and directions. Much of the Centre's most important work was collectively produced, but there was no homogeneous Centre position. Its work was inscribed with important differences within and between its various subgroups, differences that were most importantly expressed over time.

III

The Centre's two principal areas of research and analysis were the intertwined domains of "youth subcultures" and "the media." The study of youth subcultures was always among the Centre's primary concerns. If not directly a model, Hoggart's *The Uses of Literacy*, which recovered the lived character of working-class culture, presaged attempts by cultural researchers to read style and experience as if they were a text. Hoggart's reliance on his own life experience to re-create traditional working-class culture was a tangible forerunner of the Centre's subsequent ethnographic research. Hall was no less an influence on the Centre's subcultural studies. As early as the *ULR* days, he observed that the postwar youth experience represented a new and significant cultural pattern, a condensation of postwar contradictions and disaffections. His analysis of youth culture in *The Popular Arts* sounded many themes pursued by cultural researchers during his tenure at the Centre.

In its original phase, subcultural studies at the Centre simultaneously reflected the socialist-humanist impetus of its original project and adjacent developments within the sociology of deviancy and criminology. The Centre's work was part of a wider network of radical scholarship that exploded on the scene in the late sixties and early seventies. Its focus was the National Deviancy Conference, an umbrella group of radical sociologists, criminologists, and social workers dissatisfied with the conservatism of English criminology and "turned on" by the entirely American field of the sociology of deviance.[78] Rooted in the transactional approach, the new criminologists and deviancy theorists were as concerned with how society determined deviancy as to how social actors, who were labeled as deviants, responded to it. They saw the symbolic world of deviant cultures as not merely an affront to a common system of values, but as a legitimate response to conformist pressures in mainstream society. They were committed to a "naturalistic" approach, that is, they attempted to re-create deviant cultures from their own point of view through participant-observer ethnographic techniques.

The original members of the National Deviancy Conference had all been involved at one time in radical politics, whether as anarchists, anti-Bomb activists, Communists, or International Socialists. But by 1968, the year of the first conference, their hopes for radical change were pinned, not on the organized groups of the radical Left, but on the cultural revolt: "hippies, druggies, squatters, and, above all, everything that was happening in the American campuses and ghettos."[79] Founded on deep sympathies with the politics and the values of the deviants, the new radical deviancy theory was often the product of firsthand experience, filtered through scholarly, academic, and theoretical discourses. In short, these theorists attempted to bridge the gap between theory and practice, academic research and countercultural revolt.

One dimension of the Centre's work on subcultures, particularly Paul Willis's, was rooted in the tradition of participant observation. In one of the Centre's earliest studies of youth subcultures, *Profane Culture* (1978), a revision of his 1972 dissertation, Willis produced an ethnographic analysis of two subcultures: working-class motorbike boys and hippies. As a researcher, Willis was clearly more than a disinterested observer, at times barely able to mask his partisan involvement. "We would stay in the 'pad' talking, playing records and, if it was available, smoking cannabis, until two, three, or four o'clock in the morning."[80] He saw the hippies and bikeboys, in very different ways, as challenging the everyday values of the dominant order, and, in the case of the hippies, the cultural politics of the organized Left. Although lacking either the means or desire to topple the system, the hippies' efforts were "profoundly premature," that is, "post-revolutionary cultural responses to pre-revolutionary social, political and organizational problems."[81] Willis's utopianism was mitigated by an awareness that the subcultures of the late sixties never really mounted a political challenge to the dominant order, that their radicalism had been defused and appropriated. Yet in defeat the subcultures provided a valuable political lesson. "A genuine politics must come from the people, from cultural politics, as well as down from theory, or the political party."[82] No less than the radical intellectuals connected with the National Conference on Deviancy, Willis romanticized the youth subcultures of the late sixties and early seventies. His later work, notably *Learning to Labour*, discernibly shifted from explaining the subcultures' radical potential to understanding how they became appropriated.

Like other researchers associated with the new radical deviancy theory, Willis was significantly influenced by the American sociological tradition of social interactionism, particularly the writings of Howard Becker whose *Outsiders* exemplified participant observation ethnography. Willis's analysis of the hippies' drug culture, for instance, extended Becker's classical work on marijuana smoking. For Becker, the drug experience was not merely a series of physiological effects: it was inseparable from the cultural meanings associated with drug use. Similarly, Willis argued that "the importance of drugs did not lie in their direct physical effects, but in the way they facilitated passing through a great symbolic barrier erected over against 'straight' society. . . . He [the head] is defined not simply by drug use, but by his *existential presence* on the other side of the symbolic barrier."[83]

Yet Willis's approach to studying subcultures in general and drug use in particular was influenced by others as well as by Becker. Like the media group, Willis owed an intellectual and political debt to the socialist-humanist tradition and cultural Marxism. He attempted to reveal the inner meaning or structure of feeling of the two subcultures as revealed in their style and material practices. These practices resulted from what he called "the dialectic of cultural life": the reciprocal interaction between their structural location and subjective experience of it. In terms reminiscent of other socialist-humanist writers, Willis argued that subordinate groups were not the passive victims of an oppressive social system dominated by a manipulative mass media. Rather, they were the authors of their own "profane culture," modes of living that contested dominant ideological forms and presaged radical cultural change.

Willis's debt to the socialist-humanist tradition—and particularly Thompson's famous preface in *The Making of the English Working Class*—was apparent in his analysis of drug use. Like Thompson, Willis argued that social experience could not be grasped from the standpoint of technological functionalism. Just as the working class was more than a structural effect of the Industrial Revolution, drug use could not be reduced to chemical properties. Again like Thompson, Willis advocated understanding a culture in its own terms. Of the mystic feeling that hippies felt when taking acid, he wrote:

> [E]ven assuming for a moment that the chemical determinant of consciousness was a more powerful factor than the cultural one, it still does

not invalidate the experiential integrity of the mystic episode. No matter what its causes, it is still experienced as real. Experience cannot be judged on the basis of its causes; it can only be judged by its nature and effectiveness in life.[84]

There is an unmistakable parallel between Thompson's rescuing of the poor stockinger and Luddite from the "condescension of history" and Willis's celebration of the hippies and motorbike boys. Both groups were oppressed, and their subversive activities occurred outside the borders of what the dominant culture deemed respectable. Willis's work may be thought of as cultural studies from below.

The appeal of *Profane Culture* was its humanism. Shaped by the interactionist and humanist traditions, Willis convincingly evoked the creative process of group self-definition: the means by which a group signified both itself and its relationship to society. Yet Willis's early work experienced the same problems as the two traditions from which he borrowed. Similar to the social interactionist approach in general, he conceived of subcultures in a historical and ideological vacuum, ignoring both the impact of the shifting social and political terrain and the power relations mediating signification. Like other socialist-humanist writers, Willis persuasively conveyed the creative and subversive dimension of marginalized groups at the expense of the countervailing forces immobilizing them. He was certainly aware that youth subcultures had failed to challenge the dominant order, but he had no theoretical means of grasping the nature of the process. It would not be long before he and other Centre researchers began to answer such questions by looking at subcultures through the combined perspectives of historical materialism and structuralism. Willis's own *Learning to Labour* (1977) and the collectively produced *Resistance Through Rituals* (1974), originally a double issue of *Working Papers*, were the result.

These two texts can usefully be thought of in terms of the research strategy mapped out in the introduction to *Resistance Through Rituals*, a strategy that advocated a three-layer approach combining individual biographies, the cultural response of groups, and structural determinations. *Learning to Labour* was an ethnographic account of individual biographies and the cultural response of groups. Structural determinations were seen as resonating through everyday life. *Resistance Through Rituals*, on the other hand, attempted to capture the political, ideological, cultural, and economic dimensions of subcultures within the framework of a historical perspective. Its "ethnography section" consisted of predominantly critical readings of style, much of the raw data being derived from secondary accounts.[85]

A primary inspiration for *Resistance Through Rituals* was Phil Cohen's "Subcultural Conflict and Working-Class Community," originally published in the second issue of *Working Papers*. Cohen's essay was informed by a complex Marxist understanding of the relationship between economic and cultural change. He saw the emergence of working-class youth subcultures as part of a wider process involving economic transformations, the fragmentation of the traditional working-class community, and the decline of the family as the center of working-class life. Working-class youth experienced these changes in terms of their class position and as a generational conflict with the parent culture. According to Cohen, the latent function of subcultures was to "magically" or "ideologically" resolve contradictions inherent in the parent culture that could not be resolved materially. Subcultures were "so many variations on a central theme—the contradiction, at an ideological level, between traditional working-class puritanism and the new hedonism of consumption; at an economic level, a future as part of the socially mobile elite or as part of the new lumpen proletariat."[86] In practice, their style combined vanishing elements of working-class culture with elements from other class fractions.

If *Resistance Through Rituals* was indebted to Cohen's theoretical framework, it did not uncritically accept his thesis, arguing for more precise historical analysis and greater care in distinguishing the experiences of youth and parent cultures. John Clarke's work on the skinheads typified this analysis. Though part of the ethnography section, it was more accurately a historical and stylistic analysis based on published sources. Clarke saw the skinheads as being doubly determined; they were reacting to the deteriorating circumstances of the unskilled working class in the late sixties, while their stylistic evolution was conceived as a negation of the middle-class countercultures from which they felt excluded. In language derived from Williams, Clarke wrote: "The resources to deal with this sense of exclusion were not to be found within either the emergent or incorporated elements of youth sub-cultures, but only in those images and behaviours which stressed a more traditional form of collective solidarity."[87]

For Clarke, the skinhead style was an ideological attempt to salvage the rapidly vanishing working-class values of community and solidarity. "They were the 'dispossessed inheritors'; they received a tradition which had been deprived of its real social bases. The themes and imagery still persisted, but the reality was in a state of decline and disappearance."[88] Skinheads clung to the working-class values of their fathers through the celebration of masculine virtues, as expressed by violence at football games and "Paki" and "queer" bashing. Ironically, the skinheads' active conception of the meaning of being football fans occurred at a time when older working-class men felt more integrated into society, a consequence of participation in the postwar consensus. Thus, where the content of the skinhead style continued that of the parent culture, its form differed from it. For Clarke, this suggested a theoretical point.

> [T]he parent culture and the youth culture evolve their own sets of negotiations to the same structural 'crisis,' while the youth culture can be seen to be reproducing (although in a distinctive form) and resolving some of the tensions of the parent culture's own changing situation, and it can be seen that these differing responses between the parent and youth culture create their own tensions and ambivalences.[89]

Clarke did not believe that the skinheads were political in a conventional sense. But in a society where ideology and the struggle for hegemonic control were fundamental, their style *became* political. It signified their rejection of the dominant cultural order and their refusal to acquiesce passively to a subordinate role.

Clarke's recovery and celebration of the skinheads exemplified the contradictory nature of the Centre's project. While persuasively explaining the skinheads' Luddite behavior within the context of class and generational struggle, and making a plausible case for seeing them as cultural subversives, Clarke's portrayal was one-sided. As a result of his sympathetic recovery of skinhead practices, he failed to critically examine their hatred of Asians and homosexuals and their violent treatment of women, and thus implicitly he ended up condoning practices such as racism and sexism to which he was opposed. It was not that he was unaware of the skinheads' limitations as political agents. Following Cohen's appropriation of Althusser, he saw subcultural response as ideological, magical, and hence imaginary, by definition unable to penetrate the real class contradictions that it resolved at another level. Yet Clarke's essay along with the work of other Centre researchers were founded on the hope that working-class youth would eventually understand

and act upon their real situation. This romanticism was sometimes expressed as a defense of, or a silence toward, practices that in other contexts, undertaken by other social agents, would have met resounding condemnation.

Like other Centre researchers and theorists, Clarke strove to overcome the dichotomy between theory and practice. His analysis of the skinhead style was political not only because it demonstrated that practices conventionally signified as deviant were in fact subversive, but because his critical reading redefined the nature of the political. Or, as he expressed it in a coauthored paper:

> *Our use of "political" here is a broad one, but one we feel is all the more justified by the increasing narrowness of its normal usage. We wish to emphasise that this attempt to define and express one's own situation and to break with dominant cultural representations is a very real political struggle, both for those attempting to do it, and for those of us attempting to analyze and understand such phenomena from a distance.*[90]

Alternatively, Clarke's compassion for the skinheads' bold, aggressive, and dramatic style might be thought of in relationship to the postwar crisis of the Left. From this point of view, Clarke's analysis—like the Centre's more generally—represented an effort to resolve the crisis in historical agency that beset the radical movement, to find alternative revolutionary social agents at a time when the traditional working class was politically passive and in active decomposition. Furthermore, such identification could be seen as an effort by the Centre's cultural researchers to overcome their own passive, sedentary, and protected position in an academic institution—the widening gap between radical intellectuals making their way into the academy in increasing numbers and the people on the street whom they viewed as their "natural" allies. In either case, Centre subcultural theorists no less than the objects of their study "magically" resolved deeply rooted conflicts that could not be resolved materially.

One of the most glaring weaknesses of *Resistance Through Rituals* was its exclusive focus on leisure activities, though Centre researchers had criticized Cohen for the same thing.[91] This failing was certainly not true of Paul Willis's *Learning to Labour*, which explored the interdependence of leisure, school, and work.

Learning to Labour was a major contribution to a debate in the field of education. It was both an extension and critique of what might be termed "reproduction theory," radical American and Eu-

ropean work, predominantly structuralist in inspiration, which attacked the liberal idea that the schools were the principal means of
achieving equal opportunity and a more democratic society. In one
of the pioneering works in the field, *Schooling in Capitalist America*
(1976), Samuel Bowles and Herbert Gintess argued that the primary task of schools was to produce a compliant and obedient
labor force, that is, to reproduce rather than obliterate unequal
relations.

Willis's response was twofold. While agreeing that the outcome
of the schooling process was to reproduce capitalist relationships,
he saw reproduction theory as rigidly determinist. In many cases
the schools genuinely tried to improve the life chances of working-
class students. It was the youth themselves who, rejecting the well-
meaning attempts of educators, *chose* a path that reproduced their
class position. They were not passive victims of inevitable circumstances but active agents in the process. "It is they, not formal
schooling, which carry 'the lads' over into a certain application to
the productive process. In a sense, therefore, there is an element of
self-domination in the acceptance of subordinate roles in western
capitalism. However, this damnation is experienced, paradoxically,
as a form of true learning, appropriation and as a kind of resistance."[92] In beginning from the known outcome of a stable capitalist system and working backward, reproductive theorists had obscured the critical intervention of human choice in social practices.

Willis's theoretical analysis was founded on an ethnographic
study of a group of "lads"—white, working-class, teenage boys
from the industrial heartland who were living through the crucial
transition from school to work. Where "the ear'oles" (the conformist group of working-class boys at the school) accepted the
authority of the official school culture and its promises of social
mobility, "the lads" saw it as a means of manipulating and controlling them. They understood better than the school authorities
their own subordinate role in the labor process, recognizing that
only scattered individuals could move up the social ladder, while
the structural position of the working class as a whole would not
change. Their response was to forge their own way of life, contesting bourgeois values and authority and creating a nonconformist
culture founded on drinking, womanizing, running the streets, and
hanging out. Ultimately, the lads *did* accept jobs as manual laborers,
but not because they produced self-fulfillment. They became manual workers because they needed the money to sustain their life-

style and because they regarded physical work as "masculine." (This pride in physical labor did not arise out of the structural logic of capitalism but was rooted in patriarchal gender relations, which, among other things, defined the sexual division of labor.) Thus, in the very act of opposing the dominant ideology of capitalist society, the lads eventually accepted a role that guaranteed their oppression.

Learning to Labour dramatically captured the contradictory nature of the reproductive process by telling the story of the lads' creative confrontation with the social agents of capitalism. However, it left some unanswered questions. First, the significance of Willis's account of the lads' experience was that it provided a concrete instance of the process of social reproduction. Yet Willis never offered any evidence suggesting that the lads' experience was typical of working-class youth. He might have indicated, for instance, how many young men like the lads and how many like the ear'oles attended the school, and thus he might have provided tangible proof that the experience of the lads, rather than that of the ear'oles, was more emblematic of the class as a whole. Furthermore, Willis never explained theoretically why the experience of the nonconformists should be regarded as more significant or typical. If he had presented the ear'oles in their own terms rather than in relationship to the lads, he might well have reached different conclusions about working-class confrontation, opposition, and resistance to capitalism.[93] Yet this approach deprived more than the ear'oles of an independent existence: the lads' girlfriends were also seen only from the perspective of the lads. If Willis had demonstrated a more explicit awareness of the unique plight of working-class young women, he might have been less tolerant of—and openly condemned—the sexual abuse, both symbolic and physical, that they experienced at the hands of their boyfriends. As Angela McRobbie has succinctly stated: "Shop-floor culture may have developed a toughness and resilience to deal with the brutality of capitalist productive relations, but these same 'values' can be used internally. . . . They can also be used, and often are, against women and girls in the form of both wife and girlfriend battering."[94] Willis might have produced a more balanced account if he had expanded his ethnographic study to include the family as well as school, leisure, and work.

While Willis's study of working-class youth was situated within a debate on education, its perspective reflected the Centre's unique theoretical stance in contemporary debates on Marxism. Willis steered a middle course between the extremes of structuralism and humanism. His recovery and celebration of contemporary working-class culture—his insistence that working people shaped their lives in the process of struggle—recalled the spirit of Thompson's *The Making of the English Working Class*. However, Willis's celebration of human agency (unlike Thompson's) was founded on a theory of reproduction. Indeed, his acceptance of the close relationship between the educational sphere and the ideological reproduction of the social formation was, in effect, an endorsement of the Althusserian concept of ideological state apparatuses. Yet it was not a wholesale endorsement. Willis echoed the socialist-humanist critique of structuralist theory, attacking its functionalism and impoverished conception of human agency. For Willis, social agents were not merely bearers of structural forces; their experience of the social world was not reducible to external determinations; and the outcome of collective projects was not a foregone conclusion. Structuralist interpretations needed to be supplemented by a conception of the "cultural," the semiautonomous domain through which social agents lived the meaning of structure, understood and represented it, resisted and transformed it, and frequently reproduced it. From this point of view social reproduction was not a "structural effect" but a complicated process in which the "penetrations" of social agents into their objective circumstances were mediated by complex forms of "limitations" or mystifications. As a structuralist, Willis acknowledged the pivotal role of ideological reproduction in advanced capitalism; as a culturalist and humanist, he emphasized the uncertain, contradictory, and precarious nature of the process.

If *Resistance Through Rituals* and *Learning to Labour* were very different texts, taken together they represented the view of subcultures and working-class youth for which the Centre became best-known. *Resistance Through Rituals* was more historically grounded and conceived from a broader perspective, and *Learning to Labour* had a more obvious affinity with the original socialist-humanist impetus of cultural studies, but they shared the common aspiration of fusing structuralism and humanism.

The two books also shared a common view of the meaning of subcultural style, which bore the imprint of Raymond Williams's thought. Following Williams, they postulated a homological relationship between the structural position of a group, its experience, and its stylistic expression. Reflecting its historical viewpoint,

Resistance Through Rituals was more sensitive to the complicated process of subcultural "diffusion" and "defusion." However, both books shared the conviction that a style, at least in its original form, was the authentic voice of the people, the cultural space where human agents creatively made sense of and constructed their lives. This conviction was most fully developed in the introduction to *Resistance Through Rituals*, which defined "culture" as Williams did: "the peculiar and distinctive 'way of life' of the group or class, the meanings, values and ideas embodied in institutions, in social relations, in systems of beliefs, in mores and customs, in the uses of objects and material life."[95] And the same text recalled Williams's approach when it declared: "A crisis in the dominant culture is a crisis for the social formation as a whole. Of course, opposition and resistance will assume different forms. Movements which seem 'oppositional' may be merely survivals, traces from the past. . . . Some may be merely 'alternative'—the new lying alongside the old."[96] This was a clear reference to Williams's appropriation of Gramsci's concept of "hegemony."

Centre researchers' understanding of the homological relationship between structure, experience, and style was founded on an analysis of the social formation in its most abstract form. Thus, despite its specificity and semiautonomy, cultural life was, in the end, determined by the structural contradictions of the capitalist mode of production. If this view of cultural practices was not specifically based on an essentialist notion of class, at the least it gave priority to class relations. The problem with this view, as Rosalind Coward polemically observed, was that

> *the social division of labour (political and ideological effects) has had a definite effectivity in producing the current very complex and contradictory class relations. Reducing these problems to a basic division labour/capital which has corresponding forms of consciousness eradicates the complexity of the political and ideological instances and falls back on a mythology of class.*[97]

From Coward's *Screen* perspective, "signification is not referred back to the conditions of existence of the means of representation. It is never a question of what class produces what form or what content of a signifying practice, but rather how systems of representation inscribe (ideological) positions."[98]

Resistance Through Rituals has often been taken to embody the Centre's quintessential statement on subcultures, but Centre researchers themselves did not long remain content with it. Hebdige's *Subculture* (1979)—the most popular book ever written within the Birmingham tradition—was a product of a different intellectual and social atmosphere from the Centre's earlier work. By the time it was written, poststructuralist theory had begun to make its way into socialist intellectual circles and was seriously challenging Marxism's hegemony. The political and cultural energies of the late sixties, though dispersed, had been felt in narrower but no less important "movement politics"—feminism, gay rights, antiracism, ecology. The appearance of punk culture marked a radical break in the history of subcultural movements and suggested the need for a new kind of analysis.

Hebdige was greatly influenced by these new currents. He used theoretical ideas that had barely been felt in subcultural studies, depending as much on Genet, Barthes, and Kristeva as on Althusser, Gramsci, Marx, Thompson, and Williams. Like his punk subjects—subcultural *bricoleurs* who "attempted through 'perturbation' and 'deformation' " to disrupt and reorganize meaning—Hebdige effortlessly stitched together apparently incompatible approaches in his own distinctive yet recognizably Birmingham style. Yet he differed radically from others in Britain who had been attracted to semiology. Unlike the *Screen* theorists, he did not think that avant-garde art was more inherently revolutionary or progressive than popular cultural forms. *Subculture*, at least at a submerged level, was an attack on the political and theoretical elitism that had permeated semiological practice in Britain. Hebdige wanted to subvert semiology as much as to recover subcultural developments. He wanted to show that popular forms could be as subversive as avant-garde ones.[99]

Subculture differed from earlier Centre work in at least three important respects. First, *Resistance Through Rituals* had established that subcultural style in its original form was an authentic expression of working-class youth. It was only in the later stages of "diffusion" and "defusion" that it was mediated and transformed by external forces such as the media. Hebdige refined this idea. For him, style was rooted in experience, but it did not arise in some pure state; it was affected by the ideological images—the preferred readings of social life—provided by the media, including images of the subcultures themselves. Hebdige was not saying that subcultures were exclusively defined by the dominant ideology. On the contrary, they simultaneously contested and accepted images of themselves; their struggle for self-definition was part of the continual struggle for cultural hegemony. Second, Hebdige demonstrated that class experience was not the only component of subcultural response. A central component of his argument was the fact that the history of subcultures in Britain not only reflected changes in capitalism and the state, but relations between white working-class youth and their black immigrant counterparts. The significance of this insight can be seen when it is applied to the skinheads. Hebdige argued that Clarke's portrayal of the skinhead style suppressed a critical dimension. "It was not only by congregating on the all-white football terraces but through consorting with West Indians at the local youth clubs and on the street corners, by copying *their* mannerisms, adopting *their* curses, dancing to *their* music that the skinheads 'magically recovered' the lost sense of working-class community."[100] In Hebdige's view, black immigrant culture and musical forms represented the "hidden dimension" of subcultures, an ongoing source of inspiration and appropriation. This influence was true not only of the skinheads, but of the punks, who viewed black youth as kindred outcasts and participated with them in political campaigns such as "Rock against Racism" to curb the increasing influence of the National Front in working-class areas. Even when punk bands expressed themselves in aesthetic opposition to black musical forms, their response to the influence of black music was significant. Black culture could be viewed as an "absent presence" in relationship to which punks created their self-identity.

Third, where *Resistance Through Rituals* and the work of Willis theorized a homological relationship between experience and style, Hebdige argued that, at least with the punks, such an argument could not be sustained. While punks were a product of working-class experience, their style did not magically resolve the contradictions of the parent culture as much as it represented the experience of contradiction itself. Punks extricated themselves from the parent culture, relating to it as if from the outside. "In this way, although the punks referred continually to the realities of school, work, family and class, these references only made sense at one remove: they were passed through the fractured circuitry of punk style and re-presented as 'noise,' disturbance, entropy."[101] Punk had a unity, but it was rupturing, dislocated, ironic, self-conscious, and in a constant state of flux. "It introduces a heterogeneous set of signifiers which are liable to be superseded at any moment by others no less productive."[102] Following Julia Kristeva, Hebdige saw punks engaged in a signifying practice whose goal was to continually subvert the dominant sign system. Punks did not create an alternative system of meaning; they questioned whether meaning could exist at all.

In *Subculture*, Hebdige continually fluctuated between celebrating the creativity and subversiveness of the various groups he dealt with and emphasizing that in the end they were economically and politically appropriated. This ambivalent stance has been seen in all of the Centre's work on subcultures. Researchers such as Willis and Clarke at times opted for a "magical" solution. However, Hebdige openly confronted his position in relationship to his object of study: he acknowledged that an unbridgeable gap existed between radical intellectuals and the subcultures that they wrote about. Indeed, radical intellectuals faced a paradox. For the very act of recovering the subversion and rage of youth culture turned subcultures into respectable academic subjects and hence contributed to their appropriation, the opposite of the researchers' original intention. Subcultures were thus wise to greet such efforts with contempt or indifference. In addition, by demythologizing and exposing unnatural, arbitrary cultural practices, intellectuals were condemned to what Barthes described as "theoretical sociality." "The study of subcultural style which seemed at the outset to draw us back towards the real world, to reunite us with 'the people,' ends by merely confirming the distance between the reader and the 'text,' between everyday life and the 'mythologist' whom it surrounds, fascinates and finally excludes."[103] Hebdige was thus resigned to an inevitable gap between theory and practice. We are a long way from the hopeful days of 1968.

IV

Like the study of subcultures, media studies played a pivotal role in the Centre's history. In *The Uses of Literacy*, Hoggart worried about the corrosive impact of the modern media on working-class patterns of life, and his original blueprint for the Centre targeted media studies as a critical area of investigation. Likewise, Hall frequently wrote about the popular media in the 1950s, and in the coauthored *The Popular Arts* he analyzed the new media through the Leavisite method of close reading. The Centre's first funded research project, *Paper Voices,* was a semiological analysis of the *Mirror* and the *Express* from the 1930s until the 1960s.

The Centre's studies of youth subcultures had stressed the creativity of human response: people's capacity to free themselves from their mundane and oppressive surroundings through subversive, disruptive, and "profane" practices. Painfully aware of the power of late capitalism to absorb and assimilate cultural opposition—the process of social reproduction—Centre researchers celebrated the rebellious spirit of subcultures whose practices seemed to them at times to presage an alternative society. As it turned out, this resolution to the crisis in radicalism was "imaginary." In contrast, media studies at the Centre stressed structural determinations on the communication process. Audience reception was circumscribed by the ideological field, relations of domination and subordination, and hegemony. Human agency could never be discounted, but it was constrained by asymmetrical power relations. Within this framework, structural determinations often seemed to overpower alternative practices. The Centre's study of the media accorded human agency a highly mediated role.

Centre media studies in the seventies were, in part, founded on its own involvement in the student upheavals of the period—notably, the University of Birmingham sit-in of 1968. That protest was rooted in conflicts simmering since 1966 that boiled over in the intensified climate of 1968. The core issue was the right of students to participate in the decision-making process of the university. An administration study, "Student Role," acknowledged that students should be allowed a role in policy making; yet the board of governors imposed its own definition of what that input should be. Both campus radicals and the more moderate elected student representatives were infuriated at not being consulted. As a result, some five hundred students occupied the Great Hall of the university for about a week until a meeting of 4,500 students voted to end the sit-in.[104]

By American or even British standards, the Birmingham protest was not a major event. The school was never shut down; no destruction of property or political violence occurred; and the sit-in attracted no attention outside the local and provincial press. Yet despite its relatively minor status, the protest was important for those involved and left a deep imprint on Stuart Hall and others at the Centre who supported it. They were particularly impressed by the fact that the local press, university officials, and local government portrayed the protest as the work of a reckless minority bent on obstruction and revolution. Such a portrayal suggested the potential and limits of human agency, the specificity of ideological struggle, and the power of the media to shape events.

Centre researchers explored the relationship between politics, protest, and the media as expressed in the Birmingham protest. The first issue of the Centre's journal, *Working Papers in Cultural Studies*, included Paul Willis's "What Is News: A Case Study," which reflected discussions at the Monday afternoon seminar. Willis analyzed the *Birmingham Evening Mail's* representation of the sit-in as seen in the paper's news reporting, editorials, photographs, and letter columns. For Willis, there was a discrepancy between the paper's publicly stated commitment to objective standards of journalism and fair editorials and its more private or latent belief that the student minority should be silenced and repressed. He argued that the newspaper's commitment to professional standards of journalism helped produce a representation of the events according to a submerged vision of social order. Willis's general conclusion was that "news is selected as reinforcement and amplification of a particular view of life, and there is a sense in which news is manufactured, almost as an event in itself, in support of this world view."[105] In other words, news was structured by ideology.

While the Centre's research on the media, as on subcultures, was a collective effort, Stuart Hall was largely responsible for developing and articulating its theoretical positions. Hall's writings on the media, though varied, addressed a few basic questions. What was the role of the media in late capitalist societies? What was the relationship between the media and the state? What was the connection between the transmission and reception of media messages?

In "Deviancy, Politics and the Media" (1971), originally a paper given at the National Deviancy Conference, Hall understood the role of the media in contemporary society from within a Marxist framework as one of the principal vehicles for reproducing the dominant ideology. However, he rejected the orthodox Marxist position that the media either consciously represented or were coerced into representing the interests of the ruling class. He viewed the media as being part of the "control culture": governmental, political, and social actors and institutions, which, sharing vested interests and a common worldview, took the lead in signifying dominant ideological meanings. According to Hall, the media were particularly effective "where no 'traditional wisdom,' no firm networks of personal influence, no cohesive culture, no precedents for relevant action or response, and no first-hand way of testing or validating the propositions are at our disposal with which to confront or modify their innovatory power."[106]

This argument had important implications for understanding the signification of "deviant" politics. In Hall's view, in conjunction with professional politicians and "agents or representatives of face-to-face control," the media distinguished between "acceptable" and "deviant" interpretations and practices. In labeling "minority" and "majority" opinion over a broad field, the media divided reasonable and permissible (within the consensus) from reckless and irrational (oppositional) politics. In the current situation the control culture used "minority" to lump together the younger generation, opponents of Britain's policies in Northern Ireland and supporters of the IRA, and workers and unions that questioned government attempts to control wages. Hall was not claiming that such ideological strategies must succeed, but he recognized the advantages that the ruling bloc had in deploying them.

Hall's understanding of the conflict between deviant politics and the control culture was rooted in a theory of ideology largely derived from Althusser and Gramsci. Rejecting any direct relationship between ideology and ruling-class interests, he argued that ideological practices were relatively autonomous yet reproduced the dominant relations of society. Most importantly, he saw ideology (as Gramsci did) as the means by which the dominant classes won consent to their moral leadership and acceptance of their worldview as "the natural mental environment and horizon of the whole society." Ideology, from this point of view, was not simply imposed from above, but was fought over, negotiated, and continually subject to challenge. This process, however, did not mean that ideological struggle was waged between equals.

> The process of emending and revising known definitions, or of constructing new ones, is a societal process, and like all processes in society, is "structured in dominance." . . . They contain or make use of their own "logic-in-use," which serves as a set of loose generative rules which governs the way the "explanation" can be used. Such normative definitions contain strong predispositions to "see" events in certain ways: they tend to "rule in" and "rule out" certain kinds of additional inferences.[107]

Reminiscent of Gramsci, Hall saw ideology as never being complete, total, or encompassing. But the struggle to redefine it typically took place in what Althusser would describe as a "structure of dominance," which implied asymmetrical power relationships.

Hall thus acknowledged both the possibility of radical change and the formidable barriers preventing it.

If Hall's analysis of the media, ideology, and state power tended to minimize the role of human agency, his work in other contexts attempted to recover a space for human actors in ideological production. In "Encoding/Decoding" and other related essays, Hall used semiology and Marxism to understand the communication process. His model was founded on Marx's concept of production. He saw communication as a chain of discrete moments, each with its own modality and form. Although "structured in dominance" and subject to asymmetrical power relations, the production of media messages, or "encoding," and audience reception, or "decoding," were two moments that were subject to their own structural logic. Producers strove to gain assent to preferred meanings, "to enforce, win plausibility for and command as legitimate a *decoding* of the event within the limit of dominant definitions in which it has been connotatively signified."[108] Audiences, in contrast, were capable of interpreting these messages in their own terms, either because they did not understand the preferred meaning, were indifferent to it, or because they chose to use a different code. Their interpretative strategies resulted from their social position and experiences. Based on Frank Parkin's work on social meaning systems,[109] Hall distinguished three types of decoding. Viewers could accept the preferred meaning of the "dominant-hegemonic position." They could negotiate it, that is, accept the authority of a global hegemonic reading but dissent from particulars within it. Or they could fully understand the connotations of the dominant coding yet reformulate the message from an alternative perspective. Hall described this reformulation as an "oppositional code." He was not suggesting, however, that readers could construct media messages as they pleased. Indeed, in normal circumstances, he wrote, "encoding will have the effect of constructing some of the limits and parameters within which decodings will operate."[110] Rather, he was suggesting that media messages were polysemic and that it was unjustifiable to infer from semiological analysis what audiences thought.

Hall's encoding/decoding model was greatly influenced by the work of the Russian linguistic philosopher and semiotician, V. N. Vološinov (thought by some to be Mikhail Bakhtin). For Vološinov, linguistic signs were polysemic, mediated by historical and social struggles and subject to the class struggle in language. Signs often appeared to have a single meaning, but this resulted (as Hall observed) from "a practice of closure: the establishment of an *achieved system of equivalence* between language and reality, which the effective mastery of the struggle over meaning produced as its most pertinent effect."[111] The same signs also could be deployed within other ideological chains with different and opposed political implications. The signs' dominant meaning resulted from the relative strengths of the contending forces at a given decisive moment. It was historically constituted.

The encoding/decoding model represented a pioneering attempt to conceptualize the transmitting and receiving of media messages in complex industrial societies without treating "the people" as passive dupes, a tacit assumption of most forms of communications theory. Hall's belief that human beings played an active role in the reception of media messages—whether to resist, tune out, partially accept, or assent to preferred readings of texts—echoed the original socialist-humanist impetus of cultural studies. Yet Hall stressed that experience was mediated by ideology, limited by the dominant hegemonic relations of late capitalist society. In this view, Hall was clearly indebted to Gramsci's notion of hegemony as adapted by Althusser. Hall thus attempted to fuse structuralism and humanism while resisting the extremes of both, a position, as we shall see, that he would adopt in the debate over "The Poverty of Theory."

Yet the encoding/decoding model had its problems. First, while Hall's approach represented an important critique of the sender-receiver model of communication, he never escaped its original assumption that messages existed before their being coded. He distinguished between the form (the code) and the content (the message), in effect, seeing language as a neutral medium, the material substance in which the message was sent. Yet coding did not perform operations on inert material; form, as *Screen* and others had so powerfully demonstrated, played an active role in the creation of content and meaning. Second, there were problems with Hall's understanding of both the coding and the decoding process. He argued that the coding process created a preferred meaning, but he did not specify whether its creation was intentional, intrinsic to the message, or the result of semiological analysis. His analysis of decoding hinged on the extent to which audiences assented to preferred meanings. Equally important was the degree to which they understood the message in the first place. Third, Hall's encoding/decoding model was based on the transmission and reception of news programs. Did it have the same purchase when applied to programming whose intention was to entertain: drama, comedies, quiz programs, and talk shows?

The encoding/decoding model inspired several efforts by Centre researchers to study audience responses to television. In the 1970s the most important of these was David Morley's ethnographic analysis of audience interpretations of the British news program *Nationwide*. Based on interviews with and observations of diverse groups of students, *The "Nationwide" Audience* (1980) attempted to empirically demonstrate the polysemic nature of the television text and the impact of class position on its deciphering. Morley was able to show clearly that audiences were not an inert mass that assented to a uniform meaning, but he was unable to find any correlation between social position and interpretation. This was not surprising, given the complexity of the determinants that produce decodings as well as the problems of creating an experimental design that reproduces everyday life. Later, reflecting the impact of feminism, Morley attempted to overcome such problems by shifting his attention from individuals' construction of texts to the domestic context of television watching, the environment in which interpretation generally took place, particularly the family.

Of the Centre's many projects in media studies, the most ambitious was the collectively produced *Policing the Crisis* (1978), a shift in crucial respects from earlier work in the decade. Stimulated by the "Handsworth Case" in which a black youth received a twenty-year sentence for his role in a "mugging attack," Centre researchers analyzed the mugging scare that apparently emerged spontaneously in the early seventies. The Centre research team argued that, far from being spontaneous, the mugging scare resulted from a lengthy and complicated process of ideological preparation, ultimately connected to the British social crisis and the state's assumption of a coercive pose. The state exploited fears of race, crime, and youth to create a "moral panic," which in turn justified an augmentation of state power at a time when it saw itself to be under siege. Although the media were by no means a state agency, they helped to make the state's version of political and social reality dominant. Despite their general independence, the media in this case relied on the state, the primary definers, for its framing of events. This process was made possible by the structure of the media themselves. As Hall and his associates wrote: "Hierarchical structures of command and review, informal socialisation into institutional roles, the sedimenting of dominant ideas into the 'professional ideology'—all help to ensure, within the media, their [the dominant ideas] continued reproduction in the dominant form."[112] The media were not so much in league with the state as indirect but powerful organic links to it. The importance of *Policing the Crisis* was threefold. First, it anticipated the conservatives' domination of British politics since the late 1970s. For Hall and his associates, Britain in the early seventies had experienced a crisis of hegemony, the roots of which could be found in Britain's poor economic performance in the postwar years. Britain's decline had been obfuscated by Harold Macmillan's ideology of affluence in the fifties and Harold Wilson's "managed consensus" in the late sixties, but by the early seventies the glue binding the social fabric of British society was no longer adhering. Faced with the perceived threat of the counterculture's attack on middle-class values and institutions, a revived labor militancy, an increasingly disgruntled black population, and civil war in Northern Ireland, the British state replaced management by consent with outright force. It exploited the public's fears of crime and the breakdown of traditional British values as embodied in youth and race. The state did not so much go beyond the scope of the law as it created the conditions to justify using the legal means of coercion. The analysis of the breakdown of the postwar consensus was accompanied by an all but prophetic reading of future trends.[113] Hall and his associates argued that the crisis in hegemony was fertile ground for the emergence of "authoritarian populism"—a new hegemonic bloc founded on free-market ideology, patriotism, the traditional family, and attacks on socialists and minorities.

Second, *Policing the Crisis* was the first Centre project to explore the articulation of race and class in contemporary Britain. While in retrospect it seems like a logical direction in the Centre's work, at the time it represented a major departure and "interruption."[114] According to Centre researchers, the distinctive trajectory of black culture in Britain was related both to transformations in capitalism affecting the working class as a whole and to changes that related only to black workers. But this did not mean that the cultural and political response of blacks could be understood simply in class terms.

Race enters into the way black labour, male and female, is distributed as economic agents on the level of economic practice—and the class struggles which result from it; into the way the fractions of the black labouring class are constituted as a set of political forces in the theatre of politics—and the political struggle which results; and in the manner in which that class is articulated as the collective and individual subjects of emergent ideologies and forms of consciousness—and the struggle over ideology, culture and consciousness which results.[115]

The authors viewed race as part of an Althusserian structured totality. They stressed "the problem of the discontinuities, the discrepancies, the divergences, the non-correspondences, between the different levels of the social formation in relation to the black working class—between the economic, political and ideological levels."[116] Adoption of this framework made it possible to analyze the relationship between race and class in more complex terms than the simpler base/superstructure model. However, as with Althusser's thought more generally, the framework tended to minimize the role of human agency. Social actors were produced by determinations taking place behind their backs.

Third, *Policing the Crisis* pointed to a new direction in cultural studies. The book represented a shift from the communication model of "encoding/decoding" and the emphasis on recovering the subjective dimension of experience, whether conceived as audience response or subcultural style. Instead, the volume manifested what Lawrence Grossberg has described as "a greater emphasis on popular languages and common sense, on the construction of a field of meanings and differences" that were "linked, on the one hand, to hegemonic projects and, on the other, to certain conditions of possibility."[117] *Policing the Crisis* contained an idea of the social formation as conceived by Althusser, but its originality resided in its innovative reading of Gramsci. It was not so much shaped by Williams's concept of "hegemony" as the relationship among the "dominant," "residual," and "emergent." Rather, the concept underlined Gramsci's emphasis on historical specificity, the "non-necessary" correspondences between practices, and the "discipline of the conjuncture." This new reading viewed "hegemony" as involving both the production of consent and as providing ideological horizons defining the limits of cultural and political struggle. A central arena where this struggle took place was, as Stuart Hall suggested in another context, over "the popular"—not in the sense of summoning up the energies of an already constituted "people" but in "the capacity to *constitute* classes and individuals as a popular force."[118] Such a radical contextualism, which saw the constellation of social forces and their antagonisms as being "produced" rather than "given," was first sketched out in *Policing the Crisis*. It was to be notably developed in Hall's writings on Thatcherism in the late seventies and throughout the eighties—writings which he thought of as representing a "Marxism without guarantees."

V

The Centre's work in the 1970s occupied a distinctive space within the field of cultural studies. However, no homogeneous Centre position ever came into being. As noted, projects that revolved around the articulation of race and class, such as *Policing the Crisis*, originally challenged and disrupted already existing Centre positions. The same holds true for the challenge of feminism, which, as Stuart Hall recalled, "broke, and broke into, cultural studies." "As the thief in the night, it broke in; interrupted, made an unseemly noise, seized the time, crapped on the table of cultural studies."[119]

Like virtually all institutions in the early 1970s, the Centre was dominated by men. Only two or three of the more than twenty students were women. In the first ten issues of the Centre's *Working Papers* a mere four articles were about topics having to do with women.[120] Women students "found it extremely difficult to participate in CCCS groups and felt, without being able to articulate it, that it was a case of the masculine domination of both intellectual work and the environment in which it was being carried out."[121] Such dissatisfaction gave rise to the Women's Studies Group that aspired to connect a feminist critique of the Centre's theory and practice with the wider feminist struggle in society.

We are all involved in some way in challenging both the existing understanding of society, and the role and construction of sex/gender within this [society], and the ways in which this understanding is achieved and transmitted. It is through the questions that feminism poses, and the absences it locates, that feminist research and women's studies are constituted as one aspect of the struggle for the transformation of society which would make "women's studies" unnecessary.[122]

The Women's Studies Group was responsible for the eleventh issue of *Working Papers*, published in book form as *Women Take Issue*. Not only was the women's group "taking issue" with sexist practices at the Centre and throughout society, but it literally took over the eleventh issue.

Feminism's impact on the Centre's work was significant. It redefined what the Centre studied, called into question its exclusively "public" and "class" conception of power, and problematized its way of conceiving subjectivity and subject position. We can see this impact in feminist work on both the media and subcultures.

Feminist work on the media is traceable to the Women's Studies Group's original project, *Images of Women in the Media*, which described and criticized the ideological subject positions reserved for women in the media: housewife, mother, sex object, insatiable female, career woman. Although relatively untheoretical, the essay questioned "how women appropriate modes of negatively-defined subjectivity from a male-dominated culture, which, in general, excludes them from the relations of production, and thus enter into a culture of difference. It is these relations of production which to some extent define 'identity' in bourgeois culture."[123]

However, the field of cultural studies as constituted was unable to pursue such questions. The media group had been preoccupied with television news, current affairs programs, and newspapers, texts that were consumed by, and aimed at, a mostly male audience. This concentration resulted in a conspicuous omission and marginalization of media texts that most intimately touched the lives of women: soap operas, women's magazines, romance literature, and melodramas.

Feminist researchers analyzed this expanded field of media texts in terms derived from the encoding/decoding model. They were simultaneously interested in the way that the media constructed feminine sexuality and women's position in the sexual division of labor and women's own response to cultural texts created with them in mind.[124] Dorothy Hobson, for instance, produced an ethnographic account of housewives' relationship to the media, considering the women's experience of their favorite radio and television programs—soap operas, afternoon disc jockeys, and comedy programs. She analyzed both women's selective and differential responses to these programs and the strategies employed by the media to shape and reinforce gendered identities. In Hobson's view, women used radio and television programs as a means of overcoming their oppressed existence at home, but ultimately their consumption of them was not liberating.

The programmes which the women watch and listen to, together with the programmes which they reject, reinforce the sexual division of spheres of interest, which is determined both by their location in the home and by

the structures of femininity that ensure that feminine values are second-
ary (or less "real") than those of the masculine world of work and
politics, which the women regard as alien, *yet* important.[125]

The reinforcement of "the sexual division of spheres and interest" was especially true with regard to television. According to
Hobson, programs chosen by women were seen as being relevant
to a woman's world, while programs that were passed up—frequently public affairs programming—were seen as relating only to
men. Yet women did not feel free to choose the programs they
preferred. "[T]here is also an acceptance that the 'real' or 'man's
world' is important, and the 'right' of their husbands to watch
these programmes is respected."[126]

Hobson expanded her analysis of soap operas in her ethnographic study of the low-budget television program, *Crossroads,* a
show centered on life in a motel in the Midlands, shown on commercial television rather than on the BBC. The originality of Hobson's approach was to gather evidence through more naturalistic
methods than those found in studies such as Morley's *The "Nationwide" Audience.* She watched television with groups of viewers in
their own homes and elicited their responses through unstructured
discussions. Inspired by feminist theory, she reconstructed the domestic context in which television viewing took place. First, she
found that viewers often were less concerned with individual television texts (single episodes) than with the series as a whole. Second, she discovered that family contexts had a major impact on the
experience of, and attitude toward, a program. In her words: "To
watch a programme at meal time with the mother of young children is an entirely different experience from watching with a
seventy-two-year-old widow whose day is largely structured
around television programmes. Family situations change both the
ability to view with any form of concentration and also the perspective which the audience have [*sic*] on a programme."[127]

Like its critique of media studies, the feminist attack on subcultural investigations pointed to a series of "absences" and "silences" that resulted from masculine prejudice. Angela McRobbie
and Jenny Garber raised this question in a preliminary form in their
contribution to *Resistance Through Rituals.* Their critique was twofold. First, they observed that women, though certainly not the
principal producers of youth subcultures, had nonetheless made
significant contributions. Female hippies, female mods, and female

punks played important, if subordinate, roles in their respective subcultures. More importantly, they suggested that young women tended to express themselves in forms that were difficult to penetrate from outside. Girl culture insulated and protected itself from boys, adults, teachers, and researchers. This particular behavior could not be explained in class terms. "We feel," they wrote, "that when the dimension of sexuality is included in the study of youth subcultures, girls can be seen to be negotiating a different space, offering a different type of resistance to what can at least in part be viewed as their sexual subordination."[128]

In "Settling Accounts with Subcultures," McRobbie produced a more developed feminist critique of the Birmingham tradition. She passionately condemned male theorists' exclusive concern with male subcultures: men's problems at work and school, their pub life, their activities at football games. Not only did theorists ignore the experience of women, but they suppressed relationships between the sexes and the sites where they were acted out.

> *If we look for the structured absences in this youth literature, it is the sphere of family and domestic life that is missing. No commentary on the hippies dealt with the countercultural sexual division of labour, let alone the hypocrisies of "free love"; few writers seemed interested in what happened when a mod went home after a weekend on speed. Only what happened out there on the streets mattered.*[129]

This bias was as true of Hebdige as it was of Clarke and Willis. Indeed, McRobbie was particularly disappointed with Hebdige. Despite his subtle probing of the complexities of punk style, and his less class-oriented perspective, he ignored the conspicuous oppression of female punks as revealed in fashion and dance.

For McRobbie, the obverse side of male subcultures' subversion of bourgeois values was the continuing subordinate position of young women in the sexual division of labor in the family. In celebrating the oppositional nature of punks, skinheads, and teds, male researchers were thus tacitly contributing to the oppression of working-class young women. In opposition to this trend, McRobbie and other feminists inverted the strategies of male researchers. They investigated the close relationships between young women as revealed in their shared experience of reading romances, watching soap operas, consuming makeup, buying clothes, and listening to music. They turned the lens of subcultural studies on domestic and family life.

In her attack on Birmingham subcultural studies, McRobbie expressed a deep ambivalence about the relationship between women and subcultures. She argued that male subcultural experience was poisoned by sexism, and women, owing to their structural position in the sexual division of labor, could not share the same space as men. Yet she shared the same identification with, and hopes for, subcultures as did Birmingham men. "As a pre-figurative form and set of social relations," she wrote, "I can't help but think it could have a positive meaning for girls who are pushed from early adolescence into achieving their feminine status through acquiring a 'steady.'"[130] Like her male counterparts, McRobbie saw subcultures as an alternative to bourgeois society. In her vision, however, they had the power to "magically" resolve both gender and class contradictions.

Feminist theory represented an important criticism of the Centre's work and a major source of inspiration for its projects, but Centre feminists were themselves divided, a major division being the result of race. The Centre's understanding of race and class, which began with *Policing the Crisis*, was extended in *The Empire Strikes Back: Race and Racism in 70s Britain* (1982), a collection of essays published after the Thatcher victory of 1979 and the race riots of the early 1980s. In a collectively written introduction, John Solomos, Bob Findlay, Simon Jones, and Paul Gilroy argued that racism in Britain must be neither reduced to economic determinations nor seen as purely autonomous. Rather, racism must be situated in relation to both the specific forms of struggle by black people in their efforts to throw off oppression and the dominant bloc's attempts to manage the organic crisis of the British state. "In this context, race relations have become the central aspect of attempts to orchestrate politically—and therefore to manage—the effects of organic crisis. We must locate the pertinence of 'race' within this *hegemonic* struggle and assess its articulation by and with the processes which secure economic, ideological and political power and domination."[131] While the authors believed that racism in the seventies must be viewed in relationship to the crisis of the state, they were not suggesting that this would be true of other periods. Extending the line of the thought marked out in *Policing the Crisis*, they advocated seeing race as historically specific "in order to see how it articulates—or not—with other social relations."[132]

In *The Empire Strikes Back*, Hazel Carby launched a critique of white feminism that, though not specifically directed against feminists at the Centre, by implication included them. In Carby's view, white feminists used theoretical categories that, though intending to promote universal sisterhood, had the effect of marginalizing and silencing the historical experience of black women. While white middle-class women might experience the nuclear family as an unproblematic site of oppression, black women's position—owing to the impact of racism on the family dynamic—was more complex.

> *The immediate problem for black feminists is whether this framework can be applied at all to analyse our herstory of oppression and struggle. We would not wish to deny that the family can be a source of oppression for us but we also wish to examine how the black family has functioned as a prime source of resistance to oppression. We need to recognise that during slavery, periods of colonialism and under the present authoritarian state, the black family has been a site of political and cultural resistance to racism.*[133]

In short, black women could recover their own "herstory" only by refusing universal categories of gender analysis that mystified rather than shed light on their experience.

In a sense, Carby's critique of white feminism pushed the theoretical insights of Centre projects like *Policing the Crisis* and *Women Take Issue* to their theoretical conclusion. While she was immediately concerned with finding a space for the voices of groups of black women, wider ramifications could be drawn from her contention that social and cultural experience represented the complex result of contradictions of class, race, and gender. Carby's argument signaled a new direction in what by the early 1980s was a rapidly expanding field of cultural studies, one in which social identity was viewed in increasingly complex "multicultural" terms. While in certain respects this move represented a departure from the class model that had inspired the Centre's earlier work, it was clearly rooted in it. Carby was interested in both recovering the experience of historically marginalized groups and in seeing culture as rooted in material and historically specific "antagonistic relations of domination and subordination."[134] She articulated a complex, nonessentialist conception of social and cultural identity that extended, rather than broke with, the cultural Marxist foundations of cultural studies. In both Carby's work and *The Empire Strikes Back* more generally, cultural studies entered a new theoretical phase.

British cultural studies was eclectic, interdisciplinary, and in the process of defining itself. It was shaped by contact with numerous theoretical traditions and discourses; it borrowed, appropriated, and combined the practices of several intellectual disciplines; and it developed in a multiplicity of directions. Marxist historiography in the 1970s was affected by the political, social, and cultural upheavals of the late sixties and early part of the decade, particularly the development of the feminist movement. But it developed within the framework of an established tradition inherited from the British Marxist historians, and it was greatly indebted to a single work within it.

Thompson's classic book, *The Making of the English Working Class*, must be the point of departure for any discussion of socialist history in the late sixties and seventies. Seldom has a scholarly work dominated the consciousness or imagination of radical intellectuals or thrust its author into such a central position. It came to define the field of radical history as a whole and exerted a major influence on socialist thought and practice. R. H. Tawney once observed that all economic history after Marx was post-Marxist, meaning that historians followed in his footsteps, whether in support of or in opposition to his views. Similarly, socialist history in Britain in the late sixties and seventies may be regarded as post-Thompsonian and post-*The Making of the English Working Class*.

There were several reasons for the book's widespread influence. Thompson's impassioned recovery of the radical aspirations and resistance of working people made a major contribution to defining "history from below." The book redefined the field of politics. His defense of the concept of class struggle was a welcome contrast to conservatives' proclamation of the end of ideology, while, at the same time, he did not conceive of class struggle in conventional Marxist terms. He saw it from a distinctly New Left perspective as a conflict between two cultures, two ways of life, "culture as a whole way of struggle." Most importantly, in opposition to the rigid determinism of orthodox Marxism, Thompson argued that human agents were not passive victims of historical circumstances but active makers and creators of their own history.

Less tangible, but no less important, was the book's timing. For the rising generation of young radical scholars and their older associates whose sympathies lay with the grassroots, student, and countercultural movements of the sixties, the book's celebration of working people's spontaneous forms of protest alluded to an alternative politics. Scholars could identify, for instance, with both Thompson's sympathetic portrayal of the Luddites and his critique of the organized labor movement's suppression of their memory. This identification was enhanced by Thompson's own practice as a radical and scholar. The book was not the product of an academic environment, but one written when Thompson was an extramural lecturer in the Workers' Educational Association and deeply immersed in New Left politics. It was openly partisan, engaged, and aimed at a Left-wing and trade union audience. As Alan Dawley observed, *The Making of the English Working Class* "resonated perfectly with the hopes of a generation of radical scholars that common people could make their own history, and that sympathetic historians could write it."[1]

Thompson's book made a significant impact on the historical practice of both the older and younger generation of radical historians, but its resonance cannot be measured in any simple way. It was not experienced in isolation but as part of a cultural and political milieu that included the new left, the student movement, and the counterculture.

For the older generation of Marxist historians, *The Making of the English Working Class* was a milestone in the evolution of Marxist historiography. John Saville, for one, saw it as transforming historical knowledge and representing a breakthrough in the historiography of the popular classes.[2] Christopher Hill regarded it as having recaptured "the imaginative sympathy of the pioneer historians while profiting by subsequent advances in knowledge and historical method."[3] Eric Hobsbawm believed that it would have been read by a wider audience if it had been shorter, but he recognized its central role in radical history and observed that it "instantly and rightly became a classic."[4] Thompson's book did not literally transform the vision of the historians of the older generation, but it probably stimulated them to focus more specifically on the experience of popular movements. Although Rodney Hilton for many years had conceived of medieval society through the eyes of the peasantry, his first full-scale study of medieval peasant movements did not appear until the early 1970s.[5] By his own admission, he was responding to the political turmoil of the late sixties and the protests of the student movement, and he acknowledged his debt to the example of *The Making of the English Working Class.*[6]

Christopher Hill had been concerned with recovering the perspective of the oppressed and had been a major contributor to "history from below" and the growth of the Marxist historiographical tradition. Yet his most important work in this field, *The World Turned Upside Down* (1972), a historical recovery of the most radical groups during the twenty years of the English Revolution, reflected both his intellectual affinity with Thompson and an atmosphere that had been partially transformed by *The Making of the English Working Class.* Hill shared Thompson's humanist attitude toward human agency. He saw himself as recovering the common people's attempts to impose their own solutions on the problems of their times. He aspired to rescue historical subjects whom his "predecessors arrogantly and snobbishly dismissed as the 'lunatic fringe.' " And he thought it "no longer necessary to apologize too profusely for taking the common people of the past on their own terms and trying to understand them."[7] It was not that Thompson had been a major influence on Hill's work; if anything, it was the other way around. But it might be said that they shared a "structure of feeling" that was given its definitive form in *The Making of the English Working Class*, and the success and influence of the book stimulated Hill to pursue more vigorously his own study of the popular classes.

I

Marxist historians of the older generation, then, were affected by the changing intellectual atmosphere that Thompson's book helped to produce, and they were stimulated by his articulation of positions they already endorsed. The younger generation of Marxist intellectuals—formed by the experience of the various new lefts—were more manifestly shaped by Thompson's project. This was especially true of the History Workshop collective, one of the most important vehicles for the development and spread of socialist history in the 1970s.

History Workshop was a distinctly English formation with roots in the labor movement, the counterculture, the women's movement, and the Marxist historiographical tradition—especially the writings of Thompson. The Workshop was created in 1966 by an informal group of professional and worker-student historians who first met in Ruskin College history seminars. As Raphael Samuel, the driving force behind the Workshop, recalled: "It was an attempt to create, within a very limited compass, an alternative educational practice, to encourage Ruskin students—working men and women, drawn from the labour and trade union movement—to engage in research, and to construct their own history as a way of giving them an independent critical vantage point in their reading."[8] Since the beginning, the group has held a series of "workshops"— informal conferences where both worker-historians and full-time socialist researchers could discuss specific topics in radical historiography. Papers given at these meetings were often published by History Workshop in books, as pamphlets, or in the group's journal.

The Workshop should be seen in the context of Ruskin College's history and connection to the labor movement. Founded in 1899, the college was established to create a cadre of union functionaries and other labor officials drawn from the working class. But after only nine years, its purpose was called into question in a series of protests launched by a group of radical Ruskin students known as the Plebs League. Committed to the principle of independent working-class education, the league was opposed to the college's expanding relationship with Oxford University and with plans to implement an examination system. Following a strike in 1909 over the exclusion of Marxist economics from the college curriculum, the disgruntled students left Ruskin, established their own institutions called labor colleges, and began to produce a journal, *The Plebs Magazine.* The labor colleges saw themselves as teaching workers a theoretical vocabulary that was grounded in their own experience, educating them on the origins of social and economic injustice, and providing them with the strategic weapons to overthrow capitalism.

The Workshop began as a kind of modern-day Plebs League protesting the innate conservatism of Ruskin College. Dave Douglass, a coal miner and one of the original contributors to the Workshop, found out what his radical forebears at the school had known sixty years before.

[T]hat under the auspices of an institution designed to serve working-class politics and trade unionism, Ruskin's major role is to take working-class militants away from their jobs and communities to "re-educate"

them. It attempts to cut off their class roots and fill them instead with notions of competitive achievement, and generally renders them useless for anything except full-time service in the ranks of union or management bureaucracy.[9]

Douglass identified his own experience with that of his hero, George Harvey, a coal miner and radical leader from his village who had been a student at Ruskin, a member of the Plebs League, and a participant in the 1909 strike.

Just as the Plebs League stood for independent working-class education, the Workshop's founders argued that "adult students, so far from being educationally underprivileged—the working definition adopted by the College authorities—were peculiarly well-placed to write about many facets of industrial and working-class history."[10] But the idea that students could engage in primary research, let alone research their own families and surroundings, angered officials who believed that the college should be teaching history, not helping to produce it. The Workshop's first seminar on the English countryside in the nineteenth century was nearly canceled because the school's principal felt that it did not involve questions germane to the examination syllabus. As a result, Ruskin faculty members and their students resorted to covert methods to escape the attention of antagonistic school officials. Tutorials supposedly devoted to weekly essays were used by working-class students to engage in original historical research. From this form of underground pedagogy came the Workshop's initial series of thirteen pamphlets.

History Workshop reached back to the example of the Plebs League, but its protest against Ruskin educational practices was also part of the countercultural and radical assault on the hierarchical structure of higher education and the rigidities of academic life. Indeed, the group's commitment to workshops—"a deliberate attempt to escape from the conventions and the coldness of the research seminar"—owed as much to the politics and culture of the new left as working-class populism.[11] Owing to its trade union connections, the Workshop strongly supported the revival of labor militancy as expressed in the seamen's strike of 1966 and the miners' strikes of the seventies. But it was no less excited by the May 1968 events in France. History Workshop was a rare example of working-class militants and new left radicals finding a common ground.

The Workshop's project drew on several intellectual sources that achieved prominence in the late 1960s and early 1970s. Workshop historians were influenced by contemporary radical theorists of criminology for whom deviants were social actors whose values and modes of living conflicted with the dominant ideology. They adapted the participant-observation techniques of ethnographers and cultural anthropologists to capture the lived quality of history. Their work developed in the context of a critical dialogue with the rapidly expanding discipline of sociology. But most importantly, work associated with History Workshop was shaped by the British Marxist and socialist historiographical tradition, particularly as embodied in *The Making of the English Working Class.*

One way to gauge the privileged position that History Workshop accorded Thompson's book is through its own declarations. Raphael Samuel observed that the Workshop profited from "the change which has taken place in the climate of historical opinion under the impact of *The Making of the English Working Class.*"[12] The *History Workshop* editorial committee wrote: "[A]nd does anyone believe that English social history would be in its present flourishing state without the enormous impetus given to it by E. P. Thompson's *The Making of the English Working Class*?"[13]

Yet it was not only through its statements that the impact of Thompson's book on History Workshop can be traced, for the Workshop was deeply influenced by his approach and extended it in directions that he had not explicitly recommended. Like Thompson, the Workshop blended moral intensity and an imaginative use of evidence with a passion for concrete detail. Workshop historians attempted to recover the experience of the oppressed, saving them from the scorn of bourgeois historians, and they viewed the people as "makers" rather than as "victims" of history. Yet if Thompson was interested in "experience," it was not in as wide a sense as that of the Workshop. "We have been guided, in the first place, by the intrinsic interest and importance of our subjects, as fundamental elements in social life—work and class relations, sex roles and family life, popular culture and education. They are an attempt to bring history closer to the central concerns of people's lives."[14] While the wish to bring history closer to people's lives was not new, Thompson and the older generation of Marxist historians were mostly interested in the daily life of the popular classes in terms of its relationship to forms of protest and resistance. The Workshop historians thought of the culture of the oppressed as a virtual alternative culture, a way of life whose values opposed those of the dominant classes. Among other developments, under the influence of the revived feminist movement, History Workshop evinced an interest in people's private as well as public lives.

As a result of extending Thompson's concept of experience, Workshop projects often were narrowly conceived. Despite his interest in the experience of ordinary people, Thompson was ultimately concerned with working-class contributions to the national political culture; *The Making of the English Working Class* was deeply embedded in arguments over British economic and political history. Workshop historians applied Thompson's method of sympathetic re-creation to seemingly smaller and smaller geographical and social spaces: a historical account of an Oxfordshire village or the life of a Durham pitman, the story of slate quarrymen in North Wales or an analysis of nineteenth-century country work girls, guides to railway men or coal miners' slang.[15] Perhaps this method reached its culmination in Jerry White's *Rothschild Buildings*, a lengthy study of Jewish immigrants in one block of London's East End around the turn of the twentieth century. Or as Samuel stated in the foreword: "Historians have long since recognised that in the city every stone can tell a story, just as in the countryside there is a history in every hedge. What Jerry White has shown is that every street—if historians were able imaginatively to reconstitute it—could be the subject of a book."[16]

Numerous obstacles confronted the production of such work. Workshop historians understood that they could not simply reread primary sources from a Marxist or socialist perspective. In many cases the sources were sparse or scattered and had to be creatively assembled, while those sources that were available seldom were neutral. As Samuel wrote: "The magistrate's clerk—or the police officer—guides the researcher on his journey into crime, the senior partner takes him by the arm when he looks at business, the temperance advocate leads him in and out of the pubs. Unless he is careful the historian may end up as their mouthpiece."[17] Workshop historians employed many techniques to circumvent the ideological distortions inherent in primary documents and to cull evidence from untapped sources. They used visual and physical evidence to convey a tangible sense of locality, searched people's homes for photographs, handbills, posters, and diaries, and used business records, family papers, wills, and deeds. Personal recollections also had a special place in the Workshop's methodological repertoire. Such evidence made it possible to fill gaps in the record, and it could be used to redefine historical inquiry itself. "Instead of allowing the documents to structure the work . . . the historian can make his touchstone the real life experience of people themselves, both domestically and at work."[18] As noted, Workshop historians believed that worker-historians, owing to their social experience, could offer invaluable insights into the nature of historical reality. Similarly, Workshop participants saw working people's testimony as a form of historical evidence that was, by definition, free of bourgeois and therefore ideological contamination. Like Thompson, the Workshop accorded a privileged position to the experience of the people; the idea that working-class experience was also mediated by ideology was less important.

Such microscopic research might have been, to use Samuel's metaphor, like traveling by foot over territories that were familiar from the vantage point of an armored car or tractor.[19] Yet just as the informed observation of a peripatetic traveler is curtailed by an inadequate map, so a historian without a clear vision of the larger picture easily loses sight of the significance of a specific detail. Workshop historians became so consumed with tracing the smallest aspects of social practices that they at times lost sight of the broader landscape. As a consequence of their preoccupation with specificity, Workshop historians tended to inflate the significance of individual incidents of working-class resistance and struggle and to magnify the dimensions of the people's culture. They were characteristically nostalgic and sentimental about the independent artisan or village laborer and the virtues of the traditional moral economy, producing an idealized image of the people's way of life that glossed over their less appealing features, such as their racism or sexism. Believing that the "people" were "creators" of their own history, they were less concerned with the structures of domination that mediated their consciousness. They took seriously Thompson's contention that the working class made its own history, while they often neglected his warning that working people also were subject to "conditioning." Thompson thought that the Workshop was an important manifestation of the libertarian tradition, but he expressed concern that the Workshop's detailed studies of people's history entailed abandoning "whole territories" of economic and political history.[20]

Dave Marson's *Children's Strikes in 1911* exhibited some of these characteristics. The essay was one of the original contributions to the pamphlet series, the work of a docker who was a student at Ruskin in 1970–72. While researching the 1911 Hull dockers' strike, Marson uncovered an event in radical history that had faded from popular memory and also had escaped the attention of mainstream historians. He discovered a series of strikes in which children of all ages protested the harsh treatment they had received at school. Beginning in a militant working-class area of Hull, the strikes spread with varying degrees of intensity to cities throughout Britain. Marson acknowledged that the children never won any concessions, but he argued that they at least experienced a few moments of freedom and the satisfaction of having challenged an institution that oppressed, smothered, and mistreated them. "These children, despite their stifling schooling showed their minds had not been overwhelmed by the gray monotonies of the class-room. They still retained imagination with ideas like the colours in a paint-box."[21]

Originally, the Workshop accorded a privileged position to working-class experience and consciousness, as was apparent in its contention that worker-historians were "peculiarly well placed" to write their own history. For the same reason, it viewed oral evidence as a means of direct contact with the people, of salvaging their own insights into their lives. This is what Samuel had in mind when he suggested that interviews could preserve the "real life experience of people as a whole." Marson's pamphlet combined these. As a docker, his theoretical understanding was free of bourgeois mystification, for by definition he had a special knowledge of the historical process. Yet he was more than a historian; he was an invaluable source of primary evidence. His childhood recollections supplemented missing links and gaps in the historical record and helped to overcome the ideological distortions inherent in newspaper accounts. His original hunch that the children's strikes might be more than curiosities resulted from an emotional response to an account of policemen charging the children, produced by his own childhood fear of the police. By the same token, his research was inspired by his experiential identification with his subjects. "It was a photograph that really affected me—it was a picture of the children picketing the gates of Courtney Street Primary School, the same school I had been to myself. I identified myself with those strikers—some of them might have been the parents of the children I went to school with."[22]

Marson unearthed a fascinating episode from the radical past.

Yet the children's revolt must ultimately be regarded as a relatively insignificant event in the history of radicalism. It was of considerable antiquarian interest, but it played no role in socialist history as a whole. More generally, the Workshop's early work seems to have been founded on the tacit assumption that the sympathetic portrayal of the lives of the subordinate classes was by definition a radical act, guaranteed by the people's "natural" propensity to resist, revolt, and transform the social order. It conformed to that version of socialist history which, as Ken Worpole pointed out, acted as if "once every moment of past working-class experience has been noted and analysed, then all the forms and structures of capitalist relationships will powder and disintegrate leaving at last, pure, unmediated working-class authentic being."[23]

In a similar vein, Samuel's view of the Victorian economic landscape emphasized both the persistence of preindustrial values associated with artisans' independence and control of the productive process and resistance to a wage labor system that threatened to destroy them. For Samuel, the British path to industrialization was not an "unbound Prometheus" inescapably pushing toward a mechanized economy, but a case study of "combined and uneven development" whereby the exploitation of labor power was as prevalent as the increased use of capital equipment. He imagined a less orderly picture than the one conceived by mainstream economic historians:

> bearing more resemblance to a Bruegel or even a Hieronymus Bosch than to the geometrical regularities of a modern abstract. The industrial landscape would be seen to be full of diggings and pits as well as of tall factory chimneys. . . . Agricultural labourers might take up the foreground, armed with sickle or scythe, while behind them troops of women and children would be bent double over the ripening crops in the field, pulling charlock, hoeing nettles, or cleaning the furrows of stones. . . . Instead of calling his picture "machinery" the artist might prefer to name it "toil."[24]

Samuel portrayed nineteenth-century laborers as living hard and difficult lives, subject to the ruthless exploitation of Victorian capitalism. Yet he saw the people's lives as continual demonstrations of nobility, strength, and moral courage. Samuel's painstaking recreation of life and work in Headington Quarry, a suburb of Oxford, paid tribute to unalienated labor and a preindustrial life, and he stressed these laborers' stubborn persistence into the twentieth century. He differentiated between the village's moral economy, which was founded on "use" and respect for available resources, and encroaching capitalism, whose primary aim was to milk the surplus regardless of the social consequences. The villagers, he explained, "lacked the capitalist instinct for getting rich at other people's expense, or on the basis of other people's labour. They made the best of their environment, but they did not overstep its limits, or treat it as a point of take-off."[25]

Samuel's portrait of nineteenth-century life thus emphasized the perseverance of the most residual characteristics in Victorian economic and social life. He stressed the continuous tradition that linked independent artisans and rural producers with workers of modern times. Thus, in capturing the complexity and unevenness of economic and social development, he extended the historical narrative of "lost rights" into the twentieth century. His depiction of a prolonged transition to a more rationalized and regulated capitalist system was tinted by nostalgia, sadness, and remorse. Samuel's portrayal of people's history represented a socialist variant of the conservative yearning for the organic community. What distinguished his portrayal from the efforts of thinkers like Leavis and Eliot was that he attributed the evils of modern times to the triumph of wage labor or capitalism rather than industrialization per se. He could imagine an alternative social order whereby the virtues of the past were reaffirmed in a more egalitarian society of the future.[26]

II

History Workshop was founded on an idealistic and nostalgic conception of the "people" in history. Its work celebrated the artisan's and the rural laborer's control of the productive process and their attachment to a moral economy based on use. However, there was more to the Workshop than celebration; the new feminist historians, though a minority, played a crucial role in its development.

Like an important segment of the American women's movement, the new British feminism grew out of the student movement, the counterculture, and the anti-Vietnam War campaigns of the late sixties.[27] Forced to accept subordinate positions in male-dominated protest movements, and feeling oppressed by sexual roles dictated by the male-controlled counterculture, women appropriated the logic of the civil rights movement and the counterculture to understand their own social position. They came to realize that, like blacks and other disadvantaged minorities, they constituted an oppressed group—the "longest revolution" as Juliet Mitchell described them in a 1966 pioneering text of the emerging feminism.[28]

The women's movement in Britain initially surfaced from several sources.[29] Lil Ballocha's battle for trawler safety in Hull and Ros Boland's efforts to achieve equal pay for women machinists at the Ford plant in Dagenham were rooted in an industrial and working-class context. Women's issues began to be discussed among revolutionary socialist groups, with *Black Dwarf* bearing the headline "1969, Year of the Militant Women?," and the IMG launching *Socialist Woman*. As a result of the spread of workshops, such as the women's group in Tufnell Park in North London, confederated women's groups formed the London Workshop and launched the first women's liberation paper, *Shrew.*

Just as historians in Britain played major roles in defining Marxist social theory, socialist feminist historians with roots in the Marxist tradition and adult education helped shape the development of feminist theory and practice. Indeed, historians and students connected with History Workshop were the ones responsible for launching a nationwide women's movement. At a Ruskin workshop on working-class history in the autumn of 1969, female participants became frustrated by the meeting's exclusive preoccupation with male workers and by men's dominant position in the group. The women decided to hold their own informal session on women's history, a move greeted with "a gust of masculine laughter."[30] Initially, the breakaway group met to plan a workshop that would be about women, but their discussions gradually became broader, and they ended up planning the first national women's liberation conference in Britain. Five hundred people—four hundred of them women—attended the sessions at Ruskin in February 1970. The women's conference adopted a platform and established a national coordinating committee, but most importantly it produced a sense of solidarity among women. As Sally Alexander recalled: "All those women! Women I've become very close friends with since . . . we just spent a lot of time talking, talking about our kids and laughing. And walking round Oxford in gangs of women. It was wonderful!"[31]

Although feminist history existed in Britain before the 1970s, it led a sporadic existence, appearing at historical moments when women's issues were being passionately debated and fading from view when interest in them receded. A historian such as Alice

Clark, whose important *Working Life of Women in the Seventeenth Century* (1919) coincided with the early twentieth-century debate on women's suffrage, founded neither a school nor a tradition and was by and large forgotten until her rediscovery by the current generation of feminist historians.[32] In this respect, feminist historiography during the 1970s signified a new phase. Sheila Rowbotham's writings on the history of British socialist feminism and women in revolutionary movements, Catherine Hall's research on early nineteenth-century middle-class gender and class relationships, Sally Alexander's work on working-class women in nineteenth-century London, Barbara Taylor's recovery of the feminist dimension of the early socialist movement, Jill Liddington and Jill Norris's study of working-class women in the suffragette movement, and (though of an older generation) Dorothy Thompson's examination of working-class women's radicalism during the Chartist period, all of them taken together established the beginning of a tradition of socialist feminist historical writing in Britain.[33]

As the name suggested, socialist feminist historians attempted to bring both socialist and feminist theoretical approaches to bear on an understanding of the past. They saw socialism and Marxism as providing a point of departure for understanding the subordination of women under capitalism, but they argued that such modes of thought had at best only implicitly suggested ways to analyze women's position in society and must be rethought in light of questions raised by feminist theory and practice. Socialist feminists advocated that historians not just fill in the gaps of existing historical accounts with sections on women but that they situate women at the center of socialist and labor history. As Sally Alexander and Anna Davin wrote in *History Workshop*:

> For women are workers too, both waged and unwaged; and capitalism is as dependent on its 'unskilled' sweated labour force as on its skilled engineers. It is important for an understanding of the development of capitalism to examine changes in how workers themselves were produced and maintained, as to know about the production of goods: feminism not only demands a history of the family but also seeks to explain why women's work as the reproducers of labour power, and their servicing of labour power in the home, has remained invisible for so long. By bringing women into the foreground of historical enquiry our knowledge of production, of working class politics and culture, of class struggles, of the welfare state, will be transformed.[34]

Socialist feminist historiography was rooted in the cultural and political milieu of the sixties and influenced by the older generation of Marxist historians, especially Thompson. Of the feminist historians, Sheila Rowbotham perhaps came closest, especially in her early writings, to producing historical work that was inspired by the spirit of *The Making of the English Working Class* and that reflected the atmosphere surrounding the book.[35] Rowbotham was a product of the counterculture and the last phases of the first New Left, and she recalled being particularly drawn to the Committee of 100, the CND breakaway organization that advocated direct action. Although she became a socialist as an Oxford undergraduate, by her own admission she was initially more of a bohemian who thought of socialists as being Oxford types—snobbish, arrogant, and power-hungry. Whereas older New Left intellectuals, such as Thompson and Williams, were hostile to the spreading influence of American culture in Britain, Rowbotham was part of a new generation whose consciousness was partially formed by American music, lifestyles, and politics. She was "turned on" by the movies of Marlon Brando and James Dean, the sounds of traditional jazz and blues, and the rhythms of Beat literature. She was attracted to the more informal kind of activism and organizing strategies characteristic of the civil rights movement and the American New Left, and she was profoundly affected by the Vietnam Solidarity Campaign, which, although opposed to American imperialism, was in significant ways inspired by, and modeled after, the U.S. student movement.

Like most aspiring radical historians of her generation, Rowbotham was shaped by the works of the older generation of Marxist historians. She read *Primitive Rebels* in her first year of college and strongly identified with the forms of political resistance that were the subject of Hobsbawm's book.[36] (Later, Hobsbawm became her thesis adviser at Birkbeck College, although the relationship was not to be a happy one.)[37] It was also during her undergraduate years that Rowbotham first read Christopher Hill, who, in conjunction with Keith Thomas, was the major source for her chapters on the seventeenth century in *Hidden from History*. Yet of the older generation of historians, Dorothy and Edward Thompson exerted the most powerful influence on Rowbotham's life and work. She was deeply affected by the way in which they combined political activism and historical research, and her own blend of scholarship and Workers' Educational Association teaching was partially inspired by their example. They greatly encouraged her in her pursuits, and they were tough critics of her work, especially Dorothy, whom for Rowbotham had no less a historical mind than her more famous husband.

Rowbotham's own historical work grew out of her involvement in the women's movement in the early seventies. Her earliest efforts were both broad in their sweep and largely based on secondary sources, suggestive of this initial stage in women's history in which whole historical epochs had to be rethought while secondary literature relevant to women was in the process of being discovered and appropriated. Rowbotham's first book, *Women, Resistance and Revolution* (1972), was probably the first historical account of feminism to come out of the feminist revival. It traced the historical connection between feminism and revolutionary socialism in countries as diverse as England, France, the United States, Russia, China, and Cuba. Shortly afterward, Rowbotham published *Hidden from History* (1973), an account of women in Britain from the seventeenth century until the 1930s. The book attempted to give activist women a historical understanding of the problems and issues that confronted them. Rowbotham brought to both books a commitment to the precarious union of socialism and feminism and an awareness that their historical linkage had most often resulted in the suppression of the feminist agenda. Yet she remained optimistic. "The revolutionary reawakening in advanced capitalism since 1968 has brought in its wake wider movements which are attacking capitalism in new areas. . . . Women's liberation is part of this reawakening and a socialist feminism is again possible in the world."[38] Reflecting the upbeat mood of the counterculture and the radical movement in the late sixties and early seventies, Rowbotham believed that the moment might be ripe for revolutionary socialism and feminism to join forces. To take advantage of that possibility, it was important to grasp their historical relationship.

Like so many others, Rowbotham acknowledged the importance of *The Making of the English Working Class* for radical historians of her generation. She described the book as "the most massive single work" of the new labor history, exerting "a tremendous influence, not only in its particular theme, but in making the undergrowth of consciousness and organisation a subject for enquiry."[39] For Rowbotham, the significance of the new radical historiography, exemplified by Thompson's book and the subsequent work of *History Workshop*, with respect to women was that: "Implicit within this history, which in various ways focused on work and community struggles, popular action and the submerged consciousness of people without power, was the possibility of studying the position and action of women, but the contours of the female historical experience were still only glanced at."[40] From this point of view, we may understand Rowbotham's historical investigation of the women's movement and socialist feminism as striving to achieve for women what Thompson and his followers had accomplished for the working class. Yet Rowbotham in this analogous project also was confronted by a unique set of problems. While women were "hidden from most history in the same way as the lives of men or the poor are obscured," they were simultaneously ignored as a sex. According to Rowbotham, only a feminist consciousness could fully come to grips with the implications of this indifference.

We can observe both Rowbotham's extension of the Marxist historiographical tradition and the expression of her feminist consciousness by looking at two of her historical works. In *Women, Resistance and Revolution*, Rowbotham attempted to rescue the contributions of women to the Russian Revolution from the distorting lens of male prejudice and to demonstrate that revolutionaries of both sexes strove to transform the family, marriage, love relationships, and sexuality. She did not achieve this objective by rewriting the Revolution's social history, which in any event was beyond her expertise, but by taking another look at intellectual trends. First, she showed that Lenin and Trotsky realized the importance of female emancipation and sexual liberation and, at least in the early stages of the Revolution, placed them near the top of the agenda. This discovery was particularly significant for feminists associated with the radical, mostly Trotskyist Left who found it difficult to defend their interest in sexual liberation. They were being accused by their male comrades of harboring bourgeois political sentiments, it being self-evident that working-class women had more important things to worry about than their sexuality. Feminists could now defend themselves on the grounds that the fathers of the Russian Revolution had similar concerns.[41] Second, Rowbotham was among the first of her generation to rediscover Alexandra Kollontai, the great Marxist and feminist who devoted herself to the cause of both social and personal liberation. Rowbotham saw Kollontai's commitment to sexual liberation, free love, and the end of the bourgeois family as part of a wider commitment to a new morality. "Instead of presenting people with a new formula, she thought always in terms of growth. She saw the new morality being created, not imposed, in the process of development towards a communist society. Communism was about the releasing of the potential for responsibility; it implied widening the scope for the practical self-activity of masses of people."[42] In much the same way that Thompson used William Morris to support his critique of orthodox Marxism, Rowbotham invoked Kollontai to demonstrate the importance of socialist feminism in the history of revolutionary practice.

In *Hidden from History*, Rowbotham attempted to chart the complex impact of male oppression and capitalism on the lives of workingwomen. Like Thompson, she argued that women were not only the product of structural conditions but the makers of their own history. This status can be seen in her portrayal of workingwomen in the early twentieth century. Citing a 1906 study, she described how women had internalized their inferior sexual status, accepting, for instance, that men deserved to make higher wages. They could not sell labor power on the same terms, and in domestic service and shopwork they were subjected to paternalistic employers who felt responsible for their spiritual and moral well-being. Yet if women workers accepted their subservient status in relation to men, they did not passively accept their working conditions. Rowbotham likened their response to that of workers in the initial phase of capitalist development. "Women workers had all the strengths and weaknesses of a labour force that has not been broken in to capitalism. They were erratic in their commitment to the union but capable, once they began to move, of an infectious militancy which spread rapidly beyond the confines of economic issues. When the women resisted they turned strikes into festivals."[43] Her portrait of women workers echoed the tradition of research that included Hobsbawm's work on "primitive rebels" and "laboring men" and Thompson's writings on the eighteenth-century crowd and the early working class.

If British feminist historians in the 1970s saw themselves as deepening the tradition of people's history pioneered by the older tradition of Marxist historians, they were likewise aware that they must distance themselves from that tradition. As Catherine Hall observed:

But the engagement with that historiography, the challenge that it presented in terms of the things that were not said and were not explored, the refusal to consider seriously the woman question, the conviction that

*class was gender blind—only slowly and tentatively articulated by us—
also moved us to reject our fathers and to attempt to do a different kind of
work, write different histories, inspired by a different set of political
imperatives.* [44]

A compelling instance of this rejection can be found in Sally
Alexander, Anna Davin, and Eve Hostettler's response to Eric
Hobsbawm's "Man and Woman in Socialist Iconography" (1978),
the original essay and the critique of it both appearing in *History
Workshop.* [45] In his essay, Hobsbawm acknowledged that male historians, including Marxists, had ignored the history of women, but
his subsequent attempt to rectify this omission only compounded
the problem. At issue was Hobsbawm's portrayal of working-class
women in the second half of the nineteenth and early twentieth
centuries as typically giving up working for wages in the public
sphere once they were married, and his representation of them as
being largely absent from the labor movement aside from supporting the activism of their husbands. While Alexander and her colleagues were pleased with Hobsbawm's admission that historians
had ignored women as historical subjects, they argued that his own
efforts at compensation reproduced the male bias found in conventional labor history. As a result of his dependence on trade union
records—and his failure to engage with the work of feminist historians—he was oblivious to a more complex picture that had
materialized in recent historical writing of married working-class
women as wage laborers and activists. For Alexander, Davin, and
Hostettler, Hobsbawm's blindness was especially troubling because
of his impact on their own intellectual formation.

> *His work in the history of capitalism and the labour movement has been
> fundamental for most younger historians and rightly commands attention
> and respect. We do not dissociate ourselves from the general admiration
> for his work, but we are disappointed that in relation to feminism he loses
> his sure touch. Instead of responding to feminist argument and research—
> including them in the advance of historical thought or disputing them in a
> properly argued (and supported) way—he dismisses them.* [46]

It was precisely because of his importance in radical history that
feminist historians felt compelled to launch a critique of his work.

Although feminist historians were careful to note the importance
of Thompson's attention to cultural determinations, much of the
general tenor of this criticism applied to him as well. He was part of

a male-dominated tradition of labor history, and, though his approach could be extended to recover other marginalized historical subjects, he did not give sufficient attention to the role of women in the making of the working class. For Thompson, class happened when "some men"—and not "some women"—became aware of their own interests and their conflicts with other groups. He saw the class experience as largely determined by productive relations, but he ignored the fact that these relations were lived differently by men and women or that "reproduction" also influenced class relations. Thompson, in effect, equated class consciousness with the male workers who eventually created the labor movement; working-class women were assigned subsidiary roles. Working-class women were represented as being supportive of, and loyal to, their male comrades, but ultimately they were too concerned with immediate grievances to contribute to the development of class politics.

In addition, as Joan Scott has persuasively argued, feminist historians could not simply supplement Thompson's narrative with a fuller treatment of women workers in the hope that a more comprehensive understanding of class formation might eventually emerge. Feminist historians were doomed to reinforce women's marginalized role in working-class history, if they never questioned the conceptual edifice on which a book like *The Making of the English Working Class* depended. According to Scott, Thompson's account of evolving class consciousness was founded on an unstated duality. "Work, in the sense of productive activity, determined class consciousness, whose politics were rationalist; domesticity was outside production, and it compromised or subverted class consciousness often in alliance with (religious) movements whose mode was "expressive." The antitheses were clearly coded as masculine and feminine; class, in other words, was a gendered construction."[47] Scott argued that given the gendered nature of Thompson's conception of class formation, women could never play anything but a marginal role. Despite Thompson's own belief that he was sympathetically re-creating the objective experience of working people, he had in fact created the working class as much as its numbers had created themselves. If feminists were to reframe working-class history, they had to create a narrative structure of their own, one that was founded on an understanding of how written history itself played a crucial role in constructing individual and collective, class and gender identities.

Perhaps it is possible to discern two directions in the feminist historiography of the 1970s that represented departures from the approach of Thompson and the older generation of Marxist historians. First, feminist historians began to rethink the historical period on which Thompson and other historians of his generation had placed their stamp. Sally Alexander analyzed the impact of the Industrial Revolution on the sexual division of labor—the making of the female working class. To achieve this analysis she passed over the industries that had revolutionized the instruments of production and focused instead on the London slop and sweated trades—businesses that resisted the factory system, depending on a minute division of labor, rock-bottom wages, and mostly female labor. She also studied the position of workingwomen who were altogether outside the manufacturing sector—prostitutes and thieves, needlewomen and domestic servants, costermongers and charwomen. Although these women did not organize against capital and their voices had escaped the attention of labor historians, they still were part of the working class. Alexander argued that while capitalism revolutionized the position of workingmen, it reinforced the sexual division of labor, "a division sustained by ideology not biology, an ideology whose material manifestation is embodied and reproduced within the family and then transferred from the family into social production."[48] She argued that class experience was gendered, and that gender-neutral assumptions about working-class formation obscured the differential experience of women in the early Industrial Revolution.

Barbara Taylor's work in the late 1970s, culminating in *Eve and New Jerusalem* (1983), was indebted to historians such as Thompson and represented a critique of the tradition of labor history of which he was a part. Taylor recovered the centrality of women's issues in the early socialist movement by focusing on the utopian socialism of the Owenites in the 1830s and 1840s; she argued that they were just as interested in liberating women from their enslavement to men as liberating the working class from the economic oppression of its capitalist masters.

> For the Owenites, like the earlier Puritan reformers and all the Romantics of the period, it was the establishment of a right order in sexual relations which was the key to general moral re-organisation. Communism found its first and foremost expression in the liberated male-female relation. Feminism was therefore not merely an ancillary feature of the socialist project, but one of its key motivating impulses.[49]

Taylor's attempt to revive the utopian tradition followed a path established by Thompson in his biography of William Morris, which was implicitly acknowledged by Taylor herself.[50] Like Thompson, she argued that Engels's distinction between "utopian" and "scientific" socialism—in conjunction with the wider development within the labor movement of an exclusively class outlook—had resulted in an incalculable loss to the socialist movement of richness and breadth. She argued that socialism must recover this lost feminist dimension in the present as well as in the past.

Second, feminist historians began to explore the historical development of middle-class culture. In one sense, this effort was part of a more general movement in radical theory which acknowledged that the dominant classes had successfully contained the protest movements of the late 1960s and early 1970s. This understanding was symbolized by a redirection of energies from celebrating the forces of opposition to comprehending the workings of "hegemony." More specifically, this new direction in feminist historical research acknowledged that neither women's oppression nor the women's movement was class-specific. Socialist feminist historians originally followed the path carved out by the Marxist historical tradition; thus, they tended to study working-class women, the working-class family, and the relationship between the feminist and labor movements. These historians eventually began to examine the oppression of women in the dominant classes as well.

Catherine Hall was central to this development in socialist feminist historiography. Hall's intellectual and political formation was deeply affected by her association with the older generation of Marxist historians, the new left, and the women's movement. Her decision to be a historian, which began to take shape while she was still a girl, became fully articulate when, as an undergraduate at the University of Birmingham, she studied with the Marxist medievalist Rodney Hilton. Her initial involvement in radical politics was through the New Left of the early 1960s, and she would meet her husband, Stuart, on an Aldermaston march. Although she was active in the politics of "1968," Hall's involvement was curtailed by being pregnant with her first child and, less tangibly, by an ambiguous relation to the politics of the time—what she has described as the "familiar discontent" of being "a woman active in left politics." She was an early participant in the women's movement, joining the first women's liberation group in Birmingham in 1970, an experience she recalled as being devoted to conversations with other women, mostly mothers, about "the things that felt wrong with our lives, especially our isolation."[51] Hall's decision to become a historian of the nineteenth century was an outgrowth of her involvement in feminist politics. She pursued a master's degree at the University of Essex in the mid-seventies (the only place in England where it was possible to do graduate work on the history of women) and embarked on a career as a historian, first as an adult education teacher, later as a reader in cultural studies at East London Polytechnic, in 1996 as a professor of cultural studies at the University of Essex.

Hall's earliest work extended the tradition of the older generation of Marxist historians while subjecting their insights to the lens of feminist theory. In "The History of the Housewife" (1980), a reworking of a 1973 essay, she achieved for women in the domestic sphere what the tradition of Marxist historiography had done for the British commoner. It was a history of the "lost rights" of women that charted their diminishing stature from the center of the medieval economic household to subservient status as housewives or exploited workers in the Victorian era. As Hall recalled, it was an implicit challenge to the grand Marxist narratives that concentrated on the separation of workers from the means of production without any reference to the experience of women. She achieved this perspective by a feminist reworking of traditional Marxist categories: an insistence on the centrality of the family as well as production, an emphasis on the reciprocity of home and work, a reinterpretation of the thesis of the dominant ideology to take into account its differential impact on men and women, and use of the concept of the sexual division of labor.[52]

While one part of Hall's project was to reexamine the experience of the working class in the Industrial Revolution, she devoted most of her attention to the lives of the middle classes. This focus culminated in her major work, coauthored with Leonore Davidoff, *Family Fortunes: Men and Women of the English Middle Class, 1780–1850* (1987). The project was a product of the late 1970s, a time that Hall has described as the end of the "utopian moment" of the women's movement and the beginning of the "long haul."[53] The book's thesis was founded on an awareness of the resiliency and strength of the dominant cultural and ideological apparatuses in English society, a desire to come to grips with her own middle-class origins, and a realization of the limits of radical histories that celebrated the resistance of the oppressed.[54] Hall challenged the dominant strain of socialist history inspired by works such as *The Making of the English Working Class*. In a 1979 paper given at History Workshop, she observed:

> *For most socialists it is clearly more attractive to work on material which offers some assertion and celebration of resistance rather than on material which documents the continuing power, albeit often challenged, of the bourgeoisie. . . . Any discussion on the "making of the English middle class" for example, is infinitely less well documented and theorized than it is on the working class.*[55]

Hall's own work on the formation of the middle class was based on her belief that the history of women could not be conceived apart from the history of men, that class relationships were gendered, and that sexual identity was produced at every level of the social formation. In the coauthored *Family Fortunes* she summed up her views on sexual identity:

> *As a generation of feminists has argued, every individual's relation to the world is filtered through gendered subjectivity. That sexual identity is organised through a complex system of social relations, structured by the institutions not only of family and kinship but at every level of the legal, political, economic and social formation. Neither these identities nor institutional practices are fixed and immutable. "Masculinity" and "femininity" are constructs specific to historical time and place.*[56]

In her work Hall linked the increasing economic dependence of middle-class women on their husbands and their intensified marginalization in public affairs to the creation of clearly delineated spheres appropriate to men and women. She argued that the middle-class home resulted from transformations in capitalist production, but the way that the home was structured and the gender roles that it created and that created it were constructed through an ideology in large part derived from the Evangelical movement of the early nineteenth century. While this ideology was middle-class in its origins, its naturalization of sexual difference had more general implications.

> *The bourgeois family was seen as the proper family, and that meant that married women should not work. The ideology of the family thus obscured class relations, for it came to appear above class. The ideology also obscured the cultural definition of the sexual division of labour, since the split between men and women came to be seen as naturally*

ordained. Nature decreed that all women were first and foremost wives and mothers.[57]

Hall implied that ideologies governing middle-class gender relations were framed in such ways that they could have an impact on working-class men and women.

History Workshop initially glorified the male working class and, at least at the outset, was hostile to feminism and the idea of women's history. Yet the Workshop over the years became generally well-disposed toward feminist ideas. The privileged position that the Workshop accorded to the study of the family, childhood, and everyday life certainly resulted from feminist influence. And when the Workshop began to produce its own journal in 1976, it was subtitled a journal of socialist and feminist historians—an indication of the rapidly growing influence of feminist historians on the Workshop's direction. Most importantly, the Workshop's involvement in the Althusserian debate (discussed in chapter 6), while often appearing to be motivated by a contempt for theory, was part of a process of self-reflection whereby Workshop historians began to question their relation to the historical text and the basis of empiricist methodology. Such rethinking was a consequence of several factors, but it can be attributed, in part, to feminists' acceptance of their own subjectivity and feelings ("the personal is political"), their skeptical attitude toward objectivity, and their attraction to Althusser's attention to the sphere of reproduction and the semi-autonomy of ideology.[58]

III

E. P. Thompson's many admirers and disciples, many of them countercultural and new left intellectuals, were moved by his celebration of human agency and self-activity and his belief that human actors could overcome structural constraints and become the makers of their own history. They were inspired by Thompson's portrait of an improvisational, creative, and insurgent working-class culture. Yet while many of Thompson's followers were swept up in the euphoria of the late sixties, Thompson himself was less sanguine. Indeed, after the collapse of the original New Left, he was only sporadically optimistic about the prospects of the Left; he felt estranged and alienated from what he saw as the dominant radical intellectual trends; and, by the late seventies, he feared that British democracy—indeed, the world—was coming to an end. In attacks on the radical Left, Thompson reaffirmed his faith in the democratic impulse of the "people," but his confidence in the socialist movement appeared shaky. In this period he did not give up on human agency, but in particular contexts he saw its field of operation as occupying a reduced space.

Thompson's pessimistic appraisal of the political and intellectual scene was, in large part, derived from his relationship with the radical culture of the late 1960s and early 1970s. While he recognized the importance of the anti-Vietnam War movement and the struggle to democratize the universities, in general he felt alienated from the student movement and the intellectual counterculture.[59] The origins of this estrangement can be traced to Thompson's own political history. A product of the Popular Front, he pinned his hopes for a socialist transformation on a coalition of working-class activists and middle-class sympathizers like himself—a coalition that at times he seemed to believe was the embodiment of the "people." Like other traditional socialists, he saw the social order of the future as an extension of the institutions and culture of the English working class. Thompson's image of the working class was particularly affected by the skilled workers whom he taught in the Workers' Educational Association and associated with in the CP. His conception of socialist brotherhood was derived from his wartime experiences, culminating in the experience of building the Yugoslavian railroad in the late forties.

No less than other socialists, Thompson was deeply concerned about the socialist movement's lack of progress in the fifties. For Thompson, the Cold War was responsible for the defeat of libertarian movements in both Eastern and Western Europe; democratic advance was impeded by the distorting lens of the American-Soviet confrontation. Thompson's thirty-year involvement in the nuclear disarmament movement was based on the belief, however romantic, that the end of the Cold War deadlock would liberate democratic socialist energies worldwide. Second, Thompson acknowledged that working-class life was being reshaped by the spreading influence of American culture, the extension of the mass media, the growth of consumer capitalism, and a rising standard of living. Yet he argued that cultural shifts could not be inferred from the facts of economic change, and he insisted that an increased standard of living did not mean that working people would become bourgeois or that the socialist project was doomed. Yet, like Hoggart and Williams, he was clearly worried about the effects of postwar changes on working-class culture and politics. In New Left debates on classlessness, he assumed a defensive posture.

Thompson found a temporary resolution to the postwar socialist crisis in the politics of the first New Left. He saw the movement's active role in defining the priorities of the CND, especially positive neutralism, as a harbinger of an international breakthrough. He regarded the New Left's advocacy of a value system partially in-debted—in large part because of his own influence—to the moral criticism of the Romantic tradition and William Morris as an alternative to the vulgar materialism of consumer capitalism and labor revisionism. Yet despite Thompson's enthusiasm for the New Left, he was clearly apprehensive about tendencies within it. He was worried, for instance, that the movement would fall under the control of a group of intellectuals without organic ties to the working class. He was apprehensive that the New Left's attempt to rethink socialist strategy would result in the abandonment of the Marxist category of class struggle. And if Thompson was excited about the political involvement of youth, he was disturbed by the anarchist spirit of youth politics. In short, Thompson was critical of aspects of the New Left that would become more manifest in the late sixties.

If Thompson was anxious over certain trends within the original New Left, he was increasingly dismayed by the new lefts that succeeded it. As his debate with Perry Anderson in the mid-sixties demonstrated, he was openly hostile to the growing interest in the Western Marxist theoretical tradition, a tradition that he regarded as a sophisticated form of theology. Eventually, his wrath was turned on the Althusserians; yet initially he was averse to Western European Marxism in general. Thompson was also discouraged by the direction of the new left political movement, for he believed it not only failed to reach out to a wider popular base—especially the working class—but that it also self-righteously made a virtue of its exclusivity. In part, Thompson's hostility to radical politics in the late sixties can be attributed to his disdain for the counterculture. "[T]his New Left had elements within it that could be seen at once by a historian as the revolting bourgeoisie doing its own revolting thing—that is, the expressive and irrationalist, self-exalting gestures of style that do not belong to a serious and deeply rooted, rational revolutionary tradition."[60] Stuart Hall and his Birmingham colleagues, who were more enthused about the radical politics of the late sixties, saw the counterculture in historically specific terms: a result of transformations within the mode of production—a revolt within the superstructure, as it were.[61] For Hall, modes of opposition and resistance took new forms because the cultural and political terrain itself had changed. The counterculture and radical movement developed out of conflicts within the dominant culture, the tension, for instance, between the Protestant work ethic and the hedonism needed to sustain consumer capitalism. Thompson, in contrast, was committed to a specific notion of radical culture, and, insofar as radical culture varied, it was incumbent upon activists like himself to speak out in opposition. Thompson never examined the radical or popular culture of the present with the same degree of sensitivity and sympathy as he did for those cultures inhabiting the past. He never showed the same compassion for the historical situation of the counterculture and new left as he felt for the crowd in the eighteenth century, or the Luddites, or deer poachers. If he "listened," he might have come closer to realizing his own methodological goal of seeing them in their own terms.

Thompson's distance from the student movements of the sixties and early seventies was temporarily broken when he became involved in protests at Warwick University, where he had been head of the newly created Social History Centre since 1966. The 1970 protests grew out of a discovery by students occupying the registry that the administration had been keeping files on David Montgomery, an American radical historian and visiting professor. The Warwick campus revolt originally focused on the violation of Montgomery's civil rights and the implications of the university's actions, but more importantly it grew into a critique of the influence of large-scale corporations on the life of the university. Thompson surfaced as one of the leading spokesmen for the dissenting groups, writing about it in *New Society* and editing a volume of documents and commentary entitled *Warwick University Ltd.: Industry, Management and the Universities*, published in 1970. For Thompson, the issue was not just what had transpired at Warwick, but that universities in general were in danger of losing their traditional independence and being controlled by industrial capitalism. His involvement in the Warwick protest foreshadowed his later attack on the authoritarianism of the British state and his vigorous defense of civil liberties in the late 1970s.

During the Warwick protest, Thompson found himself working closely with student activists. On the whole, he admired their patience, control, and growing ability to adjust their strategy in accordance with the movement of events. But as he admitted, his respect for the students was not to be equated with an admiration for youth culture.

I have been known to lament that young people do not serve for a term in a really well-disciplined organization, such as an Officers' Training Corps or the British Communist Party. Youth, if left to its own devices, tends to become very hairy, to lie in bed till lunch-time, to miss seminars, to be more concerned with the style than with the consequence of actions, and to commit various sins of self-righteous political purism and intellectual arrogance which may be itemized in some other book. [62]

As is evident from this characterization, and the preceding discussion, Thompson caricatured rather than attempted to understand the counterculture, the new left, and youth culture, and his diatribe against youth closely resembled that of reactionary critics of society whose politics he despised.

Although Thompson had shown signs of disappointment in the late sixties and early seventies, it was not until the later part of the 1970s that he showed his discouragement. A major objection to radical intellectuals in the 1970s was that they had forsaken British democratic traditions in the name of revolutionary purity. Seeing the capitalist state as inherently authoritarian, and democracy as a ruse to ensure the continuation of bourgeois hegemony, they welcomed indications that the state was resorting to coercion, for it signaled a hegemonic crisis. For Thompson, this stance represented intellectual Platonism and a simplification and distortion of actual political conflict and struggle, and it could not have appeared at a worse time. Simultaneously, concerted, if surreptitious, attempts by the British state were occurring under the guise of law and order and national security to restrict individual rights won through centuries of popular struggle. This creeping authoritarianism from within threatened freedom of the press, the jury system, and the sovereignty of Parliament. It jeopardized traditions of law, the political culture of the British people, indeed the constitution itself. Appropriating terminology from Matthew Arnold, Thompson saw the tyranny of the modern British State as "anarchy" attempting to destroy "culture." [63]

Thompson's response to these threats was twofold. On the one hand, he saw the state's activities in historical perspective as the most recent chapter in a saga that had lasted for centuries. "We have subjected feudal barons, overmighty subjects, corrupt Lord Chancellors, kings and their courtiers, overmighty generals, the vast apparatus of Old Corruption, inhumane employers, overmighty commissioners of police, imperial adventurers and successive nests of ruling-class conspirators to the rules of law."[64] From this point of view, Thompson could imagine the reawakening of the "people," a democratic surge forward that sprang up at every level of society. Yet if he could envision a popular movement reclaiming its democratic heritage, he also could foresee a bleaker scenario: the end of British political culture as he knew it and the full emergence of a "foul authoritarian State." "I must say, in honesty, that I can see no reason why we should be able to bar [bear] that foul storm out. I doubt whether we can pass our liberties on and I am not even confident that there will be a posterity to enjoy them. I am full of doubt. All that I can say is that, since we have had the kind of history that we have had, it would be contemptible in us not to play out our old roles to the end."[65]

Thompson's pessimism reached beyond the British political scene. Disturbed by the renewal of the nuclear arms race, the prospect of cruise missiles in Britain, and the hawkish pro-American stance of the Thatcher government, Thompson returned to one of his favorite topics—the Cold War. For him, the latest round of the arms buildup represented a new stage in a thirty-year stalemate. Where he had previously believed that the Americans and Soviets used the Cold War as a means of maintaining control over their respective power blocs, he was now convinced that the superpowers, rather than controlling global politics, were in fact subject to a power that was overtaking both of them. He described it as "exterminism," a logic—or perhaps more accurately an illogic— that was autonomous and that overdetermined superpower action and response. Exterminism grew out of the drive for domination and control, but it was not a new form of imperialism. "It does not exploit a victim: it confronts an equal. With each effort to dominate the other, it calls into being an equivalent counter-force. It is a non-dialectical contradiction, a state of absolute antagonism, in which both powers grow through confrontation, and which can only be resolved by mutual extermination."[66] Thompson did not rule out the possibility that an international coalition of popular forces involving every manifestation of affirmative values could turn back the exterminist tide. Short of that, it was difficult for him to imagine anything other than an American-Soviet nuclear confrontation and the end of civilization in any recognizable form.

Thompson's historical work following *The Making of the English Working Class* concentrated on eighteenth-century English society before the Industrial Revolution. Just as his approach to the working class was connected to his political involvement in the late 1950s, his study of the eighteenth century related to his activism in the 1970s. Thompson's historical writings during this period mirrored his growing disaffection with the intellectual Left and his feeling that he was fighting an isolated battle for the libertarian tradition in Marxist thought. In opposition to those who saw the masses as bearers of productive relations and passive victims of hegemony and ideology, Thompson emphasized the creativity and robustness of eighteenth-century popular culture and its contributions to British democratic traditions. But his writings on the period also showed signs of his less optimistic evaluation of the current political situation. While *The Making of the English Working Class* was a tribute to human beings as authors of their own history, his later work represented a thoroughly structural (though not structuralist) analysis of eighteenth-century social relations which paid greater attention to the stubborn obstacles that confronted historical actors. While recognizing the independent spirit of eighteenth-century popular culture, he argued that it was mediated by the gentry's cultural hegemony. It was as if his belief that human beings could transform history was kept in check by the more limited political horizons of eighteenth-century politics and his own doubts about the present.

For Thompson, eighteenth-century popular culture was simultaneously rebellious and conservative; it persistently resisted capitalism, but it evoked "tradition" as a means of defending itself and attacking the gentry. He emphasized that the "people" never actually threatened to overthrow the system, and, as a matter of fact, that they accepted the then existing order of things as natural. He viewed this culture in class terms. Eighteenth-century plebs had not developed the type of class consciousness typical of industrial workers, nor were their political practices based only on their position in the productive process. "But one cannot understand this culture, in its experiential ground, in its resistance to religious homily, in its picaresque flouting of the provident bourgeois virtues, in its ready recourse to disorder, and in its ironic attitudes towards the Law, unless one employs the concept of the dialectical antagonisms, adjustments, and (sometimes) reconciliations, of class."[67] Thompson viewed the culture of the people as part of a "field-of-force."

The gentry stood at one pole and the plebs at the other; between them was the commercial and professional middle class, its members "bound down by lines of magnetic dependency to the rulers, or on occasion hiding their faces in common action with the crowd."[68] For Thompson, this metaphor helped explain not only the existence of frequent rioting and the limited aspirations of the rioters, but it suggested the reasons that the force used by the powerful against lawbreakers never exceeded certain bounds. Hence, there were eighteenth-century class struggles, yet the popular classes only sporadically displayed class consciousness. Thompson described this phenomenon as "class struggle without class," and he proceeded to argue that it was indeed "class struggle" rather than "class consciousness" that was to be found universally in history.

Thompson's theoretical defense of "class struggle" was closely related to his adaptation of Gramsci's concept of hegemony. We have noted Thompson's belief that many among the intellectual Left equated hegemony with ideological domination and consequently shunned democratic politics and traditions. But only in analyzing the nature and limits of the eighteenth-century gentry's power did Thompson produce an alternative viewpoint. According to him, the gentry's hegemony consisted of its ability until the 1790s to avoid a challenge to the basis of its rule. This hegemony limited protest and criticism to either constitutional channels or sporadic violent outbursts that *influenced* its actions but did not *contest* its authority. While the gentry's power ultimately rested on coercive force or the threat of it, to a large extent that power became manifest through symbolic manipulation, theatrical gesture, and the legal system. Yet if Thompson believed the gentry had achieved cultural hegemony, he rejected the idea that the popular classes absorbed ruling-class values or assented to the worldview disseminated from above. Despite the hegemony of the ruling class, the popular classes created, maintained, and defended their own way of life. Hegemony did not imply an all-embracing domination upon the ruled; it represented a way of understanding forms of class struggle in relatively stable historical moments.

In framing the gentry's rule in hegemonic terms, Thompson simultaneously engaged in a contemporary political debate. Just as the eighteenth century could be regarded as a period in which class struggle was mediated by the gentry's cultural hegemony, the postwar years, and more specifically the 1970s, could be seen as a historical moment in which deep-rooted social and political conflicts were mediated by bourgeois hegemony and the Cold War. In arguing that class struggle preceded the idea of class, Thompson was simultaneously rejecting an Althusserian view—"sophisticated Newtonian Marxism in which classes and class fractions perform their planetary or molecular evolutions"—and underscoring the centrality of political resistance and the agency of the popular classes.[69] In opposition to the claim that hegemony was the equivalent of ideological domination, Thompson maintained that hegemony implied struggle and resistance, and, as a consequence, the term argued for contesting bourgeois definitions of democracy, the state, and the law. His own writings on the British state from the point of view of a libertarian tradition challenged the hegemonic definition of the state's role in society. Yet a discernible shift occurred in the tone of his historical writing after *The Making of the English Working Class*. In taking on board the language of hegemony, Thompson implicitly acknowledged constraints on the field of human agency. He might have believed in general terms that the "people" were the authors of their own history, but in his later historical work, as in his political writings, he more straightforwardly portrayed the barriers, limits, and restraints on their actions.

In the conclusion to *Whigs and Hunters* (1975), his most ambitious historical investigation of the process of hegemony, Thompson within the context of current debates reflected on the nature of law in general and the way it functioned in the eighteenth century. Here, he revealed the same feelings of isolation and disenchantment as he expressed in some of his late political writings. He depicted himself as standing on a precarious ledge with the old mainstream historiographical consensus crumbling on either side of him. In one direction, he looked out on a resurgent conservative history that saw the ruthlessness of the eighteenth-century English state as insignificant when compared to the atrocities committed by twentieth-century governments. In the other, he beheld the structuralist Marxists, for whom the law was an integral component of the ideological superstructure and a means of legitimizing ruling-class power and reproducing productive relations. "I sit here in my study, at the age of fifty," wrote Thompson, "the desk and the floor piled high with five years of notes, xeroxes, rejected drafts, the clock once again moving into the small hours, and see myself, in a lucid instant, as an anachronism. Why have I spent these years trying to find out what could, in its essential structures, have been known without any investigation at all?"[70] Yet just as Thompson had resolved to play out his old political role, he defended the crumbling mainstream, or at least his own position, and launched a polemic against structuralist Marxists whom he saw as representing a more sophisticated version of orthodox Marxism.

Thompson acknowledged that the primary function of law in the eighteenth century was to solidify the gentry's hegemony and mystify its class power, and in *Whigs and Hunters* he condemned the coldhearted and pernicious rule of the Hanoverian Whigs. Yet he believed that the structuralist conception of law was reductive. For him, the gentry's attempt to erect an elaborate code of laws to naturalize and perpetuate its rule had been a limited success because the law had a life of its own. If the law were to mask the class rule of the gentry, it had to give the impression of impartiality and justice, which meant that at times it must actually be impartial and just. Otherwise, it would be revealed as pure coercion and force.

> *[I]mmense efforts were made . . . to project the image of a ruling class which was itself subject to the rule of law, and whose legitimacy rested upon the equity and universality of those legal forms. And the rulers were, in serious senses, whether willingly or unwillingly, the prisoners of their own rhetoric; they played the games of power according to rules which suited them, but they could not break those rules or the whole game would be thrown away.*[71]

Nor could those who held the reins of power prevent the people from using the law to their own advantage. "[P]eople are not as stupid as some structuralist philosophers suppose them to be," Thompson observed.[72] Rather than dismiss the law as sheer hypocrisy, the plebs appropriated its rhetoric. They invoked the tradition of the freeborn Englishman, the right to privacy, equal treatment before the law, and habeas corpus for their own purposes, and they sometimes emerged as victors. Thus, while he saw eighteenth-century law as a critical component of the hegemonic process, he did not believe that the propertied classes could simply use it as they pleased. Hegemony was inseparable from class struggle; the rule of law entailed a continual process of negotiation and conflict.

These reflections on the eighteenth century led to more general considerations. For Thompson, structuralist Marxists rendered the historical investigation of law unnecessary, for they theoretically understood the law in advance. If they had engaged in an empirical investigation, they would have discovered that a real distinction existed between arbitrary rule and the rule of law and, above all, that law was a universal human good. Their failure to recognize the beneficial contributions of the law was a major intellectual blunder with dire political consequences. Thompson described it as "a self-fulfilling error, which encourages us to give up the struggle against bad laws and class-bound procedures, and to disarm ourselves before power. It is to throw away a whole inheritance of struggle *about* law, and within the forms of law, whose continuity can never be fractured without bringing men and women into immediate danger."[73] But if Thompson rightly condemned a priori theoretical judgments, he never explained how a historical investigation in the empirical mode could avoid the problems to which the "theoreticist" ones succumbed. Evidence did not exist naturally nor in a neutral state but had to be produced, and producing it was impossible without theoretical assumptions. While it may have been true that good historians knew how to "listen," what they listened to and how they understood it depended on a theoretical framework.

Indeed, Thompson no less than his structuralist adversaries employed assumptions that predigested the evidence. His investigation of eighteenth-century English society powerfully demonstrated that a legal system, even at that time, could be conceived of as a site of struggle. But did this evidence warrant his assertion that the rule of law was a universal good? Such a claim needed a comparative dimension, one in which the English system would be compared alongside others. What was more, Thompson assumed that the achievement of law was a universal good, but he never explained how despotic and authoritarian states that contained elaborate legal systems advanced the cause of civil liberties or, for that matter, could be regarded as historical exceptions.[74] If structuralists' cynicism about law in bourgeois society led them to underestimate its elasticity and hence its democratic potential, Thompson's optimism about, and faith in, English democratic legal traditions was responsible for overly positive conclusions.

By the end of the seventies, then, Thompson was deeply discouraged about the state of the Left, the condition of England, and the direction of international politics. Although he had sporadic moments of great enthusiasm and accordingly reaffirmed his faith in human agency, signs of resignation and submission to forces beyond his control became tangible. There was an irony in this surrender. After years of attacking numerous fractions of the Left, particularly the Althusserians, for embracing a fatalistic view of social reality, Thompson himself at moments capitulated before a

vision of inexorable necessity. Of course, socialists had many reasons to be discouraged, and serious socialist thought has explicitly
or implicitly acknowledged a political and theoretical crisis. But
Thompson's gloomy forecast, albeit a powerful warning, exaggerated the crisis in both the domestic and international arenas. Indeed, it says as much about the man as it does about the situations
he analyzed. Indeed, the question might be asked: how was the
disciple of William Morris and the defender of the utopian ideal
also the prophet of the apocalypse?

At one level, of course, Thompson's pessimism resulted from his
political disappointments. His image of a socialist transformation
depended on a weakening coalition of workers and middle-class
sympathizers. The political and cultural forms of resistance that
emerged in the sixties and seventies—the student movement, the
counterculture, working-class youth subcultures, the feminist and
gay rights movements, and antiracist politics—were never seen by
him as suitable substitutes. Furthermore, the Cold War gave every
indication of escalating, thus further ossifying movements of dissent in both East and West. Thompson never swayed from seeing
the Cold War as the major obstacle to a revival of the international
progressive movement.[75]

These disappointments were accentuated by Thompson's way of
thinking. When he evoked "human agency" and "experience," he
was not discussing them as concepts in general; instead, they were
historical categories pertaining to the working-class movement
and its ancestors. Indeed, he first employed these two terms as part
of his critique of Stalinism and his defense of socialist humanism in
1956. Against the deterministic formulas of orthodox Marxism,
Thompson reaffirmed the ability of human agents to make their
own history. In opposition to the Leninist claim that the Party must
rescue workers from the false consciousness of ideology, he appealed to "experience." For Thompson, socialist movements must
be founded on the "experience" of the working class rather than
on some imposed notion from above. This insistence on "agency"
and "experience" provided the foundation for a populist politics.
Thompson saw the working class in heroic terms: an authentic
radical culture that resisted ideology and embodied democratic
traditions. His was a moral vision in which the "people"—human
agents in the process of making history—challenged the power of
evil capitalists and landlords.

If this made it possible for Thompson to appreciate many of the achievements of working-class people ignored by others, and if it justified constructing the social order from the bottom up, it did not allow for a portrayal of the "people," warts and all. Despite the grandeur of *The Making of the English Working Class*, Thompson seldom if ever considered working people who defended their employers' interests, supported ruling-class imperialist wars, preferred compromises to dreams of radical transformation, or treated their wives and lovers like property. Similarly, Thompson's political analysis did not acknowledge contemporary workers who preferred the Tories to Labour, were preoccupied with consumer goods, and harbored racist resentments against their immigrant neighbors. To take these aspects of working-class culture into account would have required the concept of ideology. Rather than celebrate human agency or the creativity of the working class, he would have had to rethink people's lives in connection with the dominant institutions of cultural and ideological production. He seemed to assume that the choice was between experience or ideology—democracy or Stalinism. But this was a false dichotomy; experience and ideology were not so easily separated.

The same is true, though perhaps to a lesser degree, of Thompson's writings about the eighteenth century. His later historical writings contained a structural, if not structuralist, interpretation of eighteenth-century social relations, and in employing the concept of hegemony he displayed a greater awareness of the mutual determination of structure and human agents in the historical process. Yet if he correctly argued that hegemony did not imply the total subordination of the masses to the dominant ideology, in another sense he was less than faithful to the original spirit of the concept. Gramsci had developed another idea of hegemony as a means of understanding why the working class in the advanced capitalist West had failed to revolt on the scale of the Russian Revolution in the East. Gramsci used "hegemony" to capture the process whereby the working class had come to feel a stake in the institutions of civil society, and he emphasized the role of the church and the schools in cementing these bonds. In Gramsci's terms, hegemony might have been inseparable from "class struggle" but it entailed "consent." In *The Prison Notebooks* he defined hegemony as "the 'spontaneous' consent given by the great masses of the population to the general direction imposed on social life by the dominant fundamental group."[76] Thompson glossed over this aspect of hegemony's definition.

At one level, then, Thompson's thought was limited by his refusal to see the "people" in anything but the most positive light. But it was not just his reluctance to be critical. He never truly defined who the "people" were or where the line between the "people" and the "non-people" was to be found. This definition was important because, as the fascists of the thirties and Right-wing populists since the seventies have demonstrated, the "people" did not automatically end up on the Left. Or as Stuart Hall aptly observed: "We can be certain that *other* forces also have a stake in defining 'the people' as something else: 'the people' who need to be disciplined more, ruled better, more effectively policed, whose way of life needs to be protected from 'alien cultures,' and so on."[77] From this point of view, the "people" are never simply lying inert at the margins of history waiting to be rescued. They have to be constructed by theoretical labor. The "people," by its nature, is a contested concept, part of the ideological and political battlefield.

As the crisis of the Left became more apparent, Thompson's theoretical commitment to "agency" and "experience" impeded his ability to analyze setback, defeat, and loss of political momentum. The fact that he equated radical politics with traditional working-class culture made it difficult for him to be enthused about subcultural and movement politics in the sixties and seventies. Rather than adapt his thinking to changing conditions, Thompson at times seemed to lose faith. His humanist trust in ordinary people was transformed into a resignation to "playing our old roles out to the end." His attempt to invigorate socialist thought and practice by reviving utopian aspiration was turned into its opposite—a prophecy of apocalypse. Yet through it all, he never lost his zeal for launching polemical attacks on those he perceived to be his opponents and enemies, Left and Right. Nowhere is this more true than in his passionate attack on Althusserian Marxism, "The Poverty of Theory."

SIX The Politics of Theory

In the 1970s the writings of Louis Althusser and his followers spurred a major intellectual movement in Britain, affecting socialist and Marxist scholarship in sociology, literature, film criticism, cultural studies, education, philosophy, and history. For some of those who embraced it, Althusserianism was more than an intellectual and political position; it was a commitment to the one and only true faith, a commitment as crucially formed in opposition to other positions as in affirmation of its own. Carrying the banner of theoretical practice, these devout Althusserians condemned all forms of intellectual and political commitment tainted by economism, humanism, and empiricism. It is easy to exaggerate the magnitude of Althusser's appeal among the intellectual Left in 1970s Britain. But something of the mood of the time was captured by the Marxist and anti-Althusserian economist Simon Clarke who wrote: "Even marxists from non-Althusserian backgrounds were abdicating, either espousing Althusserianism or, tacitly or explicitly, abandoning hope for Marxism."[1]

No universal stampede developed, however, to jump on the Althusserian bandwagon. Many proponents of older or alternative versions of Marxist practice ignored the assault on their disciplines, while others eventually fought back. They defended their own modes of intellectual and political work, and they condemned Althusserianism with the same intensity as had been reserved for them. Indeed, significant segments of the British intellectual Left in the last half of the 1970s were like two unyielding armies engaged in interminable trench warfare. One was humanist and libertarian, declaring its faith in the "people," the empirical mode, and history. The other championed structuralism, was hostile to all forms of culturalism and empiricism, and advocated theory with a capital T. In this strained and polarized climate, historians and cultural theorists of the Marxist tradition attempted to debate issues raised by structuralism and humanism.

I

The Birmingham Centre for Contemporary Cultural Studies was among those that refused to accept these polarities. The Centre's work in the 1970s can be regarded as a sustained attempt to break down the opposition between structuralism and humanism, oppositions that, as Stuart Hall argued, had become "the prison-house of thought."[2] Typically, Hall imagined a third way, a position that built on the strengths of both traditions, while avoiding the pitfalls that had made neither of them "adequate to the task of constructing the study of culture as a conceptually clarified and theoretically informed domain of study."[3]

Hall and the Centre attempted to overcome the structuralist/humanist dichotomy by undertaking a critical appraisal of both traditions in the hope of salvaging their legitimate theoretical contributions, while discarding their deficiencies and failings. Here, the most prominent figure (in addition to Hall) was the historian Richard Johnson who had filled the vacancy at the Centre left by Richard Hoggart's departure. In many respects Johnson was ideally suited for the task. Before coming to the Centre, he had taught in the University of Birmingham history department and worked closely with, and was influenced by, Dorothy and Edward Thompson.[4] (Dorothy Thompson taught in the same department.) Although *The Making of the English Working Class* was a fairly late influence on his intellectual formation, Johnson's work on educational conflicts in the early nineteenth century owed a considerable debt to it. At the same time, Johnson was deeply affected by the events of 1968 and beyond, including the Birmingham sit-in, and he was open to the new, mostly French avant-garde intellectual currents that followed. As a consequence of his appointment to the Centre in 1974, Johnson developed an interest in Althusser. Although he acknowledged that Althusserianism tended to create simplified and distorted polarities, he regarded Althusser's theory as an indispensable way of posing fundamental theoretical questions about the process of knowledge. Trained in a tradition critically shaped by Thompson and indebted to an approach that was in crucial respects that tradition's antithesis, Johnson was in an excellent position to interrogate both Althusser's and Thompson's frames of thought. The intellectual atmosphere at the Centre provided the perfect support system.

If in principle Johnson was committed to scrutinizing both traditions, in practice he and his colleagues in the Centre's Cultural

History Group devoted the greater part of their energies to re-thinking Marxist history.[5] The Group's project can be broken down into three categories. First, Johnson and his colleagues critically examined the tradition of British Marxist and socialist historiography: late nineteenth- and early twentieth-century labor history, the Communist Party's Historians' Group, and the theoretical contributions of Maurice Dobb.[6] They argued that Dobb's theoretical and historical analysis of modes of production in *Studies in the Development of Capitalism*, despite a tendency toward economism, corresponded to Marx's own methodological protocols in *Capital*. These protocols shaped the project of the Historians' Group, but were partially abandoned in the Group's later work and unequivocally displaced by the "culturalist" and "socialist-humanist" historiography of the sixties. The Cultural History Group advocated that the mode of production analysis initiated by Dobb—and improved upon by Althusser—should be restored to its rightful position in Marxist historical analysis.[7]

Second, the Group returned to Marx. With all the uproar about what Marx *really* meant—or what he should have meant—that was initiated by Althusser's return to the original texts, Centre researchers found it necessary to develop their own understanding of Marx's method. They viewed Marx's thought as operating at various levels of abstraction, evidence in their view that the antagonism between "history" and "theory" was false. For Johnson, Marx never doubted that abstraction was necessary for historical investigation; his concern was with finding the level or levels of abstraction appropriate to understanding a given historical object.[8] For Stuart Hall, whose essay on the 1857 introduction was immensely influential on the Centre's understanding of Marx, his method, in contrast to that of Hegel or as portrayed by Althusser, was not exclusively a "mental operation." "It is to be discovered in real, concrete relations: it is a method which groups, not a single 'essence' behind the different historical forms, but precisely the many determinations in which 'essential differences' are preserved."[9]

The most controversial aspect of the Cultural History Group's project was Johnson's critical analysis of culturalist historiography, mainly Thompson's *The Making of the English Working Class*, but also Eugene Genovese's *Roll Jordan Roll*. The analysis was originally published in *Economy, Culture and Concept*, and it appeared in a slightly revised version in *History Workshop* in 1978.

In view of the earlier discussion of History Workshop, the

group's publication of Johnson's essay might appear surprising, for it is difficult to imagine a group more opposed in spirit to Althusser and his followers. As a matter of fact, History Workshop was itself undergoing changes. We have noted that feminist historians' equation of the personal and the political posed difficult questions for objectivist notions of historical methodology. In addition, feminists associated with the group were accustomed to taking Althusserian concepts seriously as a result of their involvement in socialist feminist theoretical debates. Althusser's emphasis on the relative autonomy of the superstructure, the discontinuities between the various levels of the social formation, the connection between ideology and social reproduction, all were potentially useful in explaining women's role within capitalism. His use of Lacan's notion of interpellation to explain the ideological construction of subjectivity was germane to theoretical discussions on the social construction of gender. It was possible to acknowledge that Althusser himself had been blind to the category of gender, his account of ideology functionalist, and still conclude that his ideas were important for socialist feminist theory.

The composition of the collective was also in flux. While the group had been founded by both professional historians and Ruskin students, the balance began to shift toward the historians. The creation of a journal in 1976 signaled the change in the overall center of gravity, not only because the journal was produced primarily by full-time historians, but because it was aimed primarily at a Left-wing academic audience. Among the most influential figures in this later phase of the Workshop's development was the social historian Gareth Stedman Jones, a member of the faculty of Kings College, Cambridge. Stedman Jones was by no stretch of the imagination an orthodox Althusserian. However, he used Althusserian concepts in his own historical work, believed that Althusser had posed fundamental questions regarding historical methodology, and attacked the narrow empiricism of the British historical profession.[10]

While the History Workshop collective was generally enthusiastic about Johnson's article, Stedman Jones seems to have been particularly excited. He had "been worried about the lack of sufficient theoretical discussion in *HWJ* [*History Workshop Journal*], but hamstrung by the scarcity of available texts written in a non-hermetic language."[11] And he thought that Johnson's presentation and critique was "very clearly written and cogent." As for Johnson, he was as enthused as Stedman Jones since "it will enable the argument to reach a wider historical audience, but one predisposed to take problems in Marxist historiography seriously."[12]

Johnson's overall goal might have been to overcome the structuralist/humanist dichotomy, but the essay he wrote for *History Workshop* was, by his own admission, a "limited preemptive strike versus Thompson on Althusser"—a reference to the imminent publication of "The Poverty of Theory."[13] This intention was evident in the essay's premise, which seemed certain to antagonize an audience of historians who had been formed to a great extent by *The Making of the English Working Class*, however open they might have been to discussing history and theory in general. "It is through the theoretical categories of Louis Althusser (and their extension by neo- and post-Althusserians) that we are best able to *place* these histories within the range of contemporary marxisms and to assess them critically. To put it another way, Althusser's work provides a privileged vantage-point from which to survey our object."[14] The justification for this position was no less provocative. According to Johnson, an Althusserian critique had attained its privileged status because it represented a double opposition against humanism and economism, while culturalism was only founded in opposition to one of these—economism. Johnson qualified this statement by asserting that structuralism was neither logically superior to, nor likely to supersede, culturalism, but such a qualification was unlikely to appease an audience that was invariably beginning from the opposite starting point.

Johnson's critique of culturalism was not nearly as explosive as his initial position might have suggested, and it raised important issues about the nature of Marxist history and theory. He criticized culturalist histories for avoiding abstraction, emphasizing only the "experiential" and the "lived," equating class with the experience of class, and regarding the social relations of productions as relations between people. It was Johnson's contention that culturalism (like structuralism) was as reductionist as economism, but in an upward direction. "The economic as a set of objectively present relations only appears in an attenuated form, *through* the cultural, *through* the 'inwardness of experience.'"[15]

Johnson certainly appreciated the accomplishments of culturalist historians. In conformity with a more general Centre position, he acknowledged culturalists' decisive contributions to socialist and Marxist historiography. Texts like *The Making of the English Working Class*, he acknowledged, permanently reminded us that any account of social life that did not acknowledge intentionality or subjective experience easily slipped into mechanical concepts of society or "fundamentally conspiratorial ideas of 'control.'"[16] However, he believed that socialist historians should strive to be more "authentically Marxist." Historical accounts should move back and forth between different levels of abstraction, fusing theory and description, and they should be founded on a structural analysis of the relationship between the mode of production and the social formation. Johnson never clarified how this prescription translated into actual historical practice.

Both History Workshop and the Birmingham Centre viewed Johnson's essay as an initial step in fostering a working relationship between the two groups: a dialogue founded on common intellectual and political interests, made possible by the Centre's move toward "history" and History Workshop's growing interest in "theory." Johnson talked of the essay as part of a wider rapprochement; Stedman Jones thought of it as an example of the practical cooperation between them.[17] However, the anticipated dialogue never took place. The feedback of History Workshop readers was almost universally negative. Critics were enraged by Johnson's structuralist reading of culturalism; they rejected his negative assessment of Thompson's masterpiece; and they violently disagreed with his contention that culturalist approaches were insufficiently Marxist or, worse yet, outmoded. They wondered why structuralism, supposedly an equally limited mode of thought, was not granted the same critical examination as had been reserved for culturalism, and they were dissatisfied with Johnson's explanation that the essay represented one part of a larger project. More than one commentator totally rejected Johnson's portrayal of culturalism. Yet while critics pointed to some real failings in Johnson's argument, they also badly caricatured his position, thus making it possible to avoid the legitimate questions that the essay raised. They portrayed him as an orthodox Althusserian and a history hater who, as Stedman Jones observed, "might just as well have copied down chunks of Althusser and left it at that."[18] The reactions to Johnson's essay indicated just how much passion could be generated by the conflict over history and theory in the 1970s. But this was just the beginning.

II

Between the publication of Johnson's essay and his critics' responses in *History Workshop*, Thompson's nearly 200-page denunciation of Althusserianism, "The Poverty of Theory," appeared in print. Arguably more passionate and inspired than anything he had ever written—no small feat given his other writings—the essay was the most influential critique of Althusser's thought ever produced in English, as well as the most cogent statement of Thompson's own theoretical and political principles. The book provoked one of the most impassioned and bitter debates and some of the best intellectual theater that ever took place among British Left-wing academics.

"The Poverty of Theory" contained little that was new in the way of criticism of Althusser's theoretical practice. Its power and impact can be attributed to the relentlessness of its attack, the electricity of its prose, its humanist politics, and its hilarious parody of Althusserian theoretical practice. The essay, to use Stuart Hall's phrase, scored "palpable hits" against some of the most well-known failings of Althusser's mode of thought.[19] Thompson convincingly demonstrated that Althusser's theoretical practice was idealist, self-confirming, and theoreticist—in violation of the dialogue between theory and evidence so critical to the process of acquiring knowledge. He showed that Althusser's notion of structuralist causality was hyperrational, giving rise to a conception of the social formation that was static and mechanical, unable to account for social change and transformation. He correctly observed that, in condemning empiricism, Althusser had conflated the ideology of empiricism and the empirical mode of thought, though the two were not always as distinct as Thompson thought. And he successfully attacked Althusser's refusal to acknowledge the contributions of consciousness, experience, and human agency to historical outcomes.

While Thompson cogently portrayed the weaknesses in Althusser's thought, he was less persuasive in other respects. Carried away by polemical zeal, he continually overshot his target. Thus, whatever might be said about Althusser's conception of the social formation, it was not, as Thompson claimed, a sophisticated form of economism. If anything, it emphasized discontinuities between base and superstructure, economic structure and ideologies. Ironically, while Thompson shunned the language of base and superstructure, his view of social dynamics, which emphasized the interpenetration of economic and cultural practices, seemed closer to a traditional Marxist position than Althusser's. Moreover, despite their vast differences, Althusser's and Thompson's projects were formed in common opposition to the ossification of Marxist thought that occurred during the Stalin era. Althusser's emphasis on the semiautonomy of ideology was as opposed to economism as Thompson's insistence on the interdependence of social being and consciousness.

In "The Poverty of Theory" Thompson not only strove to destroy the foundation of Althusserian theory, but he proposed an alternative to it—historical practice. His portrayal of what historians did—or thought they did—and their justification for their methods was, if anything, conventional. It represented a traditional defense of the historian's ability to produce objective knowledge. Historians, he maintained, had developed theoretical and critical methods capable of gleaning knowledge from determinate, objective evidence. Although historians excavated the facts and recognized their significance to the historical process, the facts themselves existed independently of any particular perspective. "[T]he facts will disclose nothing of their own accord, the historian must work hard to enable them to find 'their own voices.' Not the historian's voice, please, observe: *their own voices*, even if what they are able to 'say' and some part of their vocabulary is determined by the questions which the historian proposes."[20] Similarly, Thompson argued that the historical process itself was unitary, existing independently of the historians' point of view. New perspectives could reshape historical understanding, but, unless historians accepted their involvement in a common discipline whose purpose was objective knowledge, their dialogue remained "mere exchanges of attitude, or exercises of ideology."[21]

While Thompson's defense of the historian's craft might have been a welcome contrast to Althusser's crude antiempiricism, his own alternative also was deficient. Thompson offered a choice whereby historians could accept that they were producing objective historical knowledge corresponding to a unitary historical process or they could abandon the project altogether. Yet this was a poor choice based on simplified oppositions and divisions. Thompson ignored such basic questions as whether "objectivity" and "neutrality" were the same. He also closed his eyes to more than thirty years of work on objectivity and relativism undertaken by historians, anthropologists, psychoanalysts, literary critics, and legal scholars, including the historian of science Thomas Kuhn, the art historian Ernst Gombrich, the anthropologist Clifford Geertz, and the philosopher Richard Rorty.[22] Although posing a serious threat to objectivist claims, this literature was by no means univocal; it demonstrated the potential for a range of positions besides extreme forms of objectivism and relativism.

Indeed, Thompson's ability to discuss the anatomy of historical practice without so much as a mention of these important contributions to the understanding of historical, cultural, and social investigation suggested that his thought was closer to the ideology of empiricism than he himself recognized. In opposition to Althusser's conception of Marxism as a self-sufficient science, he counterposed the practice of the historian, though conceding that it could not produce knowledge in the same way as the natural sciences. However, no less than did Althusser, he placed science on a pedestal; he regarded it as a privileged domain of knowledge, an ideal that historical investigation must emulate—in spirit if not in fact. The problem was that Thompson's concept of science was itself being called into question, a result of the revolution in the history of science launched by Kuhn and others. Ironically, Thompson did not have to look far to find an alternative model of science. Robert Young and his associates, producers of the London-based *Radical Science Journal*, were engaged in a persistent effort to demystify the scientific enterprise by placing it in its historical and ideological context. As a *Radical Science Journal* editorial stated: "We have broad agreement that we want to develop a marxism that does not recognize science as a specially privileged form of knowledge. Indeed, the only special status we would allow to science is its historically specific relation to the capitalist social order. We do not regard the notion of 'scientificity' as being exempt from political criticism."[23]

In fact, Thompson was able to sustain his view of the historian's enterprise with only the greatest difficulty. For instance, he argued that historical theory and practice were to be judged by a court of appeal, presumably consisting of those versed in historical discourses and protocols, that is, members of the profession. This position was somewhat surprising for a radical historian who had been a major actor in the interminable ideological disputes of British historiography. But Thompson was less committed to this position than he appeared to be at first glance. He was willing to accede to the profession's judgment as to the veracity of historical materialism. (He noted that the verdict was still out, though it is hard to imagine who it was that remained undecided.) And he was enthusiastic about J. H. Hexter's "reality rule"—the idea that reasonable people could agree on the most likely story sustainable by the evidence. Yet he conceded that the court's judgment had indeed been mediated by ideological prejudice and that Hexter himself had used his own rule "in increasingly unhelpful ways, in support of a prior assumption that *any* 'Marxist' story *must* be unlikely."[24] Thompson, in effect, recognized the persistence of ideological division within the historical community, but he seemed unwilling to accept that this division was intrinsic to it. It would have meant acknowledging that the historical court of appeal was unable to transcend ideology and that historical knowledge was mediated by ideological conflict. For Thompson, such acknowledgment would mean abandoning all faith in the objective basis of his enterprise.

Ironically, Thompson's professed commitment to historical objectivity contradicted his own practice as a historian. He insisted that "in showing how causation actually eventuated, we must, insofar as the discipline can enforce, hold our own values in abeyance. But once this history has been recovered, we are at liberty to offer our judgement upon it."[25] That is, only after historians had reached objective conclusions were they legitimately entitled to make moral and political evaluations of them. Yet while Thompson might have thought this was an accurate description of his own and other historians' ambitions, his work suggested otherwise. Indeed, works like *The Making of the English Working Class* and *Whigs and Hunters* contained a rich fusion of moral and political commitment and analytical procedure; and his historical analysis was continuously mediated by contemporary political debates and agendas.

In fact, no better example of how Thompson's practice as a historian was rooted in political and moral engagement exists than "The Poverty of Theory." While the essay was a refutation of Althusserian theory, it was, perhaps more importantly, an attack on the political culture of the British intellectual Left from which Thompson felt deeply alienated. "In the much-publicised 'revival of Marxism' in Britain in the last two decades," he wrote, "a mountain of thought has not yet given birth to one political mouse. Enclosed within the intelligentsia's habitual elitism, the theorists disdain to enter into any kind of relation with a Labour movement which they know (on *a priori* grounds) to be 'reformist' and 'corporative.' "[26] By exposing the political errors of the younger generation of Marxist intellectuals, Thompson hoped that he might revive interest in the libertarian tradition of socialist thought and practice.

We can see this target in Thompson's attack on the political credentials of structuralist and Althusserian thought—in his terms, "the illusion of this epoch." Thompson situated structuralism within the history of twentieth-century ideology. For him, twentieth-century political thought could be divided into three chronological stages: the "progressivism" of the early twentieth century based on a faith in the inevitable triumph of the working class; a "voluntarist" spirit that developed in response to the rise of fascism in the thirties, culminating in the heroic sacrifices of the Popular Front and the resistance movements of the Second World War; and "structuralism," which grew out of the stasis and political paralysis induced by the Cold War. According to Thompson, while progressivism and voluntarism involved elements of self-deception, they represented social and political challenges to the dominant order. Structuralism, in contrast, "in its most pervasive accents . . . has been a *bourgeois* vocabulary, an apologia for the *status quo* and an invective against 'utopian' and 'mal-adjusted' heretics."[27]

Thompson's account of twentieth-century ideology was polemical, designed to show structuralist thought in the worst possible political light. As Perry Anderson argued, it was a thinly disguised autobiography, a historical projection of Thompson's own political anguish.[28] While many political setbacks occurred during the postwar epoch—among others, Allende's Chile, Prague Spring, 1956 itself—Thompson's dismal portrait reflected his own disappointments and anticipations. How otherwise (to cite Anderson again) can we explain his failure to take into account the Chinese Revolution, the civil rights movement, May 1968, the worldwide crusade against American involvement in Vietnam, and the development of an international women's movement?

Thompson's comparative analysis, which contrasted structuralist stasis with earlier activist political mentalities, was misleading. For Thompson, while the progressivist and voluntarist stages referred to modes of Left-wing thought, the structuralist phase involved a broader spectrum of political stances. In other words, the first two stages described a narrower and, in fact, different phenomenon than the third. To be consistent, he was obliged to either compare post-World War II Left-wing ideas with analogous earlier movements or to chart the history of a wider spectrum of thought. In the first case, he was obliged to characterize the postwar period very differently from what he had done, including, for instance, existential Marxism, the situationists, the *Argument* group, and later Frankfurt School thinkers such as Jürgen Habermas. In the second case, it was incumbent upon him to widen his terms in depicting earlier historical phases, including fascism as well as the Popular Front, avant-garde modernism as well as the Second International's faith in inevitable progress. That a historian as sophisticated as Thompson could have established such inconsistent categories—and, thus, in effect, rigged the results in advance—suggests the extent to which his political hatred of Althusserianism affected his analytical judgment.

This bias was even more apparent in what may be the most dramatic and startling argument in "The Poverty of Theory," Thompson's attempt to demonstrate that Althusser was a Stalinist and that Althusserianism was not only an impoverished theoretical paradigm, but the perfected form of Stalinism itself. The claim of Stalinism was based on bits and pieces of biographical information. Thompson implied that Althusser's membership in the Jeunes Étudiants Catholiques connoted his attraction to dogmatic systems of belief. He regarded Althusser's decision to join the PCF in 1948, a time when the Cold War was establishing itself, as evidence of a distance from Popular Front and Resistance principles and an affinity for high Stalinism. His refusal to speak out in 1956, in contrast to Thompson's own public declarations and activism, only confirmed this view. It is because of Althusser's silence during the crisis precipitated by the Twentieth Congress that Thompson could regard his subsequent critique of socialist humanism "as an ideological police action *against* any fundamental socialist critique of Stalinism."[29] In Thompson's words: "When the illusions were finally dispelled, in 1956, it was Althusser's business to sew up people's eyes and block their ears, to put the whole corrupt structure of falsehood back in a more sophisticated form."[30]

Thompson's portrayal of Althusser's politics was inadequate, because it failed to take seriously the immediate political context of his project—the world of French and international communism in the early 1960s. Rather than being in the forefront of a Stalinist police action against the socialist-humanist opposition of 1956, Althusser supported the Chinese position during the Sino-Soviet split in the early sixties.[31] He was clearly no friend of socialist humanism, and his silence during the crisis of 1956 was certainly not to his credit. But by the time Althusser wrote *For Marx*, socialist-humanist principles were not only being espoused by dissidents, but they had become part of the official language of Communist parties. Althusser's critique of humanism, then, was not primarily aimed at those who left the Party like Thompson, but those who remained within it, for instance, the French Communist philosopher Roger Garaudy, who had adopted the new language for purely opportunistic reasons. Althusser was not endorsing Stalinism; he was reaffirming the philosophy of Marxism-Leninism as formulated by Mao. His writings were not endorsed by Party leaders.

Thompson's most substantive argument connecting Althusser and Stalin was not his effort to link them directly, but his assertion that they possessed common attitudes. For Thompson, Stalin and Althusser shared a comparable indifference to the plight of individuals, were political elitists who believed that the working class by itself was condemned to ideology, and expressed this elitism theoretically. Their disregard for flesh-and-blood human beings manifested itself in an abstract theoretical language in which individuals were given no other role than as supports to structural relations or in meaningless slogans such as "the masses make history." Because of their total disregard for human agency, they could justify blatant inhumanities undertaken in the name of History with a capital "H." Althusser's thought represented a systematization of what was scattered and half-articulated in Stalin. In his words, "Althusserianism *is* Stalinism reduced to the paradigm of Theory. It is Stalinism at last, theorised as ideology."[32]

Althusser had qualities that might be conceivably defined as Stalinist. His thought was antidemocratic; he was a political elitist who believed that only Party intellectuals possessed scientific theory; he saw the working class as being eternally condemned to ideology; and his notion of theory was replete with authoritarian implications. But was this specifically Stalinist? This equally describes Leninism, and Althusser never denied that he was anything but a Marxist-Leninist. Thompson, though consistently anti-Leninist since 1956, never systematically confronted Leninism, nor did he discuss it in relation to Stalinism. A political attack on Althusserianism would have been far more compelling if it had been framed as a democratic critique of Leninism.

Thus, despite successfully exposing the most glaring weaknesses in Althusser's theoretical system, Thompson's "The Poverty of Theory" proved disappointing. He unsuccessfully defended the objectivity of historical knowledge. He unsuccessfully characterized structuralism as politically reactionary and Althusserianism as a sophisticated form of Stalinist ideology. His representation of Althusser's politics was nothing more than caricature. Thompson projected his own experience of 1956 onto Althusser, ignoring the specific historical context of international communism in the early sixties.

What is truly astounding is that Thompson undertook this "out of compassion for the innocence of a 'post-Stalinist generation.' " He wrote it for those "who have agonised over Balibar and Lacan but who have not acquainted themselves with the elementary history of socialism in this century." They might at least, he observed, "postpone their theoretical practice until they have dried themselves behind the ears."[33] Given his belief in the centrality of the political issues at stake, it is remarkable that he displayed so little intellectual caution.

Paradoxically, in spite of Thompson's fervent hatred for Stalinism, he deployed some of the same polemical strategies that it had perfected. Thompson might have recalled the Communist smear tactic of discrediting socialist humanists because of their "bourgeois" origins when he wrote of Balibar: "I fall into a reverie, and wonder whether M. Balibar also came to intellectual maturation with the Jeunes Étudiants Catholiques? And then, by random association, I recall that Stalin served his own intellectual apprenticeship in a seminary of the Greek Orthodox priesthood."[34] Whether it was guilt by class association or guilt by religious association, this style of argument has no place in serious political and intellectual debate. In attempting to defeat the political ideology that he hated the most, Thompson assumed some of its character.

III

By the time that "The Poverty of Theory" was published in 1978, the Althusserian onslaught in Britain and elsewhere was already beginning to recede, a result of an accumulation of critiques, including many from the crumbling ranks of theoretical practice itself. The appearance of Thompson's essay coincided with the first visible signs of a surging conservative revival coalescing around the person of Margaret Thatcher. For those post-1968 socialist intellectuals attracted to various forms of theoreticism, awareness was growing of the importance of historical modes of analysis to understand the current political moment. Gramsci, not Althusser, was the Marxist theorist whose thought was becoming the most avidly discussed by leftist intellectuals. In such a climate "The Poverty of Theory" was greeted with great enthusiasm and acclaimed not only by British Left-wing students and academics but by leftist intellectuals throughout the English-speaking world. Many regarded it as a welcome vindication of empirically based social investigation, a devastating blow to the autocratic pretensions of structuralist abstraction, and an inspiring defense of human agency and experience. It was an essay, as Stuart Hall noted, that students were "clutching to their hearts" and that "raised the dust in intellectual circles."[35]

Undoubtedly, the most sustained response resulting from this dust-raising was Perry Anderson's *Arguments Within English Marxism*, a critical study devoted to the arguments of "The Poverty of Theory" and Thompson's historical work as a whole. Anderson's book represented a balancing act. As he admitted, an Althusserian would have been a more appropriate respondent, someone he certainly was not. But "in the absence for the moment of more indicated candidates," Anderson found himself thrust into the position of defending Althusser without actually embracing him.[36] While he acknowledged that Thompson and Althusser were separated by an unbridgeable theoretical divide, he pointed out that their politics were not that far apart, especially since Althusser had embraced Eurocommunism. Anderson contrasted his own commitment to "classical Marxism," rooted in the idea that the state must be overthrown as a precondition for a socialist transformation, with Thompson's and Althusser's support for social democratic strategies. Yet unlike their initial encounter, which produced bad feelings on both sides, Anderson now called for an open dialogue with Thompson, "to leave old quarrels behind, and to explore new problems together."[37] Every indication is that Thompson responded to this appeal.

One of the most important aspects of Anderson's critique was his examination of Thompson's notion of "experience" in "The Poverty of Theory." Anderson suggested that Thompson's use of the term was inconsistent. On the one hand, he meant it as a response by a group or individual to a series of intertwined or repeated events; on the other hand, he used the term to describe an intermediary stage between objective processes and the handling of them. To use his own terminology, Thompson vacillated between locating experience within social consciousness and finding it between social being and consciousness. Anderson attributed

Thompson's inconsistent usage to the word's dual connotation in ordinary language. "Experience" could refer either to occurrences and events that one lived through or to the trial-and-error process of learning that followed repeated incidents and episodes. Anderson argued that Thompson often was "unconsciously transferring the virtues and powers of the (more restricted) second type to the (more general) first type of experience. The efficacy of the one is fused with the universality of the other, to suggest an alternative way of reading history as a whole. The generic category that results inevitably conflates very different problems."[38] Moreover, while Thompson acknowledged that experience was valid within certain prescribed limits, he implicitly argued that the lessons that it taught were mostly the right ones. Anderson correctly observed that diametrically opposed conclusions could be drawn by agents living through the same events.[39] Thompson never gave any indication of how to distinguish valid from invalid experience.

Anderson's critique of Thompson's notion of agency was less convincing. Anderson did not deny the role of human agency in history, but he argued that Thompson consistently magnified its role, especially in regard to earlier historical epochs. Anderson argued that according to the tenets of historical materialism most of the past was part of the kingdom of necessity, meaning that historical agents had minimal impact on historical outcomes. It was only with the rise of the socialist movement and the Russian Revolution that the masses began to play a major role in shaping their destiny. Ironically, it was Althusser the philosopher rather than Thompson the historian who came closer to sharing Marx's vision of the past. It is true that the "people" in earlier historical phases did not play as conspicuous a role in the political arena as in modern times, and, in fact, they rarely challenged the dominant order in a systematic way. Yet this did not mean that their actions had no effect on historical outcomes, or that they did not play critical roles at more localized levels. Indeed, Marxist historians in Britain have demonstrated that events like the Peasant Rebellion of 1381, the Civil War, and the actions of bandits and millenarians were manifestations of human agency on an intermediary scale. Thompson's work on the eighteenth century was itself an illustration.

Thompson's essay also raised the intensity of the debate in History Workshop, and it established the ground for subsequent discussions between the disciplines of history and cultural studies. These exchanges reached a climax at the group's annual meetings in 1979 when Thompson, Johnson, and Hall debated the theoretical and political issues that the essay raised. In view of Thompson's intense hatred for Althusserianism and his passion for debate, sparks might have been expected to fly, but the event exceeded expectations. It "resolved itself," as Raphael Samuel recalled, "into something resembling a gladiatorial combat."[40]

To appreciate the drama of the event, it is necessary to say something about the setting and tone of the meeting and of the speakers. The debate was held on a Saturday evening in early December at St. Paul's, a dilapidated and cavernous neoclassical church in Oxford, which until the late seventies had been boarded-up. "Crammed with an audience of hundreds, the temperature boosted by the biggest blow heater imaginable, with a public address system installed. . . . Bright spotlights increased the sense that a theatrical performance was demanded, not a closely-knit discussion."[41] The tone of the evening was initially established by the social historian, Stephen Yeo, who acted as chairman. In his opening remarks Yeo all but declared Thompson to be the leading intellectual of the British Left. He paid tribute to Thompson for having "made inroads into the wide-open spaces of the capitalist culture in which we live."[42] And he praised "The Poverty of Theory" as a magnificent contribution that took great risks and deserved everybody's gratitude. No wonder that Stuart Hall jokingly remarked in the introduction to his paper that discussing Edward Thompson at a History Workshop was "like trampling on the carpet in hobnail boots." Another important ingredient involved the participants' speaking styles. While Stuart Hall and Edward Thompson were charismatic speakers used to addressing large audiences, Richard Johnson was uncomfortable in front of a large group and delivered his paper in a monotone. The speakers' ability to play to the audience certainly had an impact on the evening's events—in surprising ways.

The program was divided into three parts. Opening and closing presentations by the protagonists sandwiched an open discussion from the floor. Hall and Johnson began by giving papers with common themes. Hall acknowledged that Thompson had successfully dismantled the most vulgar forms of Althusserianism, but he objected to Thompson's method of going about it. Thompson might have been a master of polemic, and certainly occasions arose when it was appropriate to conduct political debate in this way; Hall insisted, however, that when difficult issues were at stake, the polemical mode was a form of overkill, continually creating artificial oppositions and evading serious political and theoretical problems. Johnson echoed this critique, arguing that "The Poverty of Theory" exemplified a more general tendency of the Left to hold its debate in crippling, absolutist terms. In the current political moment—when the Left was in disarray—he advocated an "accumulative mode of critique": a form of argument that would be critical yet constructive, preserving theoretical gains as well as abandoning mistaken and obsolete positions. The Centre had employed—or tried to employ—this mode of critique in the debate over structuralism and humanism.

While Hall and Johnson criticized Thompson's use of the polemical mode, they articulated their own distinctive positions. Johnson recapitulated his analysis of the historical development of Marxist theory in Britain, distinguishing between two of its phases, "the moment of culture" and "the moment of theory." The moment of culture referred to the culturalism of the early New Left, the theoretical contributions of Hoggart, Thompson, and Williams; the moment of theory described the 1970s, the period when the post-1968 generation of Left intellectuals gravitated toward Continental Marxism and French structuralist thought. Here, of course, Althusser was the major figure. Johnson argued that the time was now ripe to move beyond these too often opposed moments, to create a new phase retaining their strengths and discarding their weaknesses. The problem was how to conceptualize the subjective moment in politics in such a way that human beings are seen as "constructed and fragmented in the relations in which they are actively implicated" and yet viewed as being "involved in conscious and integral struggles to transform them." [43]

Hall discussed the alternatives that Thompson put forth in opposition to theoretical practice and the implications of these alternatives for socialist thought and politics. He viewed Thompson's defense of the historian's enterprise, his stress on the category of "experience," and his privileging of the "concrete" over the "abstract" and the "theoretical" as suggestive but problematic. For Hall, Thompson and History Workshop tended to invert Althusser's mistakes and errors. Thompson and the Workshop viewed the historical process as speaking for itself, hypostatized historical practice, fetishized the concrete, and confused theory with theoreticism. "There is a poverty of theoreticism, but for socialists and Marxists there cannot be a poverty of theory. There is, of course, never theory without practice, but there is never adequate practice that is not informed by theory. What Marx teaches us is that there are by necessity different kinds of work with different levels of abstraction." Hall also objected to Thompson's concept of experience. While he paid tribute to the British Marxist historiographical tradition for having made giant strides toward recovering the experience of the dominated classes and the oppressed, Hall believed that the concept of experience often employed in this tradition had its problems. Marxists could never embrace "experience" wholesale, nor could they understand it apart from the concept of ideology. He was not suggesting that historians should reproduce the Althusserian stupidity of denying the importance of experience, only that they not repeat this stupidity in reverse. "Experience," he observed, "cannot be an authenticating witness to the reality of the historical evidence that we have."

Hall pointed to two political problems resulting from the notion of experience as articulated by Thompson and his followers. First, he suggested that it tended to underwrite a politics whereby the socialism of the future was guaranteed by summoning up and celebrating the experiences of the past. Second, he believed that it endorsed a conception of the "people" that no longer was productive for socialist politics. In the 1970s, he argued, a political strategy could not be based on the way that capital united the working class. He rejected the notion of the "common people." In his words, socialism

> would have to start from the difference in contradictions that operate in such a way as to forge oppositions between feminism and socialism as much as those which unite them. It would have to be a socialism that began with difference so as to look at the forms of struggle and organization that might create unity. It is close but radically different from a politics of populism.

Hall no longer believed in a populist politics which assumed that the common people could simply be called upon, beckoned as it were. His reading of Althusser helped him realize that popular forces could be constructed only as a result of a unity of differences. Despite his respect for Thompson's politics, he could not say that "The Poverty of Theory" was politically useful.

In his talk Thompson responded to his critics. He believed that Hall's critique could not be sustained by a close reading of his work. Of course he saw problems with empiricism, and, no, he did not refuse the concept of structure—only structuralism. He was "astonished" to discover that ideology was an "absent category" in his work and "enraged" to learn that he believed in transhistorical values.

In response to a more general critique of his work, he accepted that his formulation of "experience" was ambiguous. Acknowledging that the term had more than one meaning, Thompson distinguished between "experience I" (lived experience) and "experience II" (perceived experience). Thus, a pattern of events in social being gave rise to "experience I," which was then not simply reflected in "experience II," but pressed upon the "whole field of consciousness" in such ways that it could not "be indefinitely diverted, postponed, falsified or suppressed by ideology." How else, he asked, "are we to suppose that there can ever be any human remedy to the hegemonic domination of the mind, the false descriptions of reality reproduced daily by the media?"[44] This was one of the few instances in which Thompson ever specifically recognized that the relationship between ideology and experience was problematic. But even here Thompson did not really address the problem as much as he asserted his faith in the fact that experience could overcome ideology.

Thompson did not restrict himself to discussing theoretical and political issues on such a high plane. He attacked—in what some of his targets took to be personal terms—both Johnson and others who had either written position papers for the evening's debate or had contributed to the *History Workshop* discussion. He distanced himself from the cult of Thompsonianism that had begun to surface, but he used his immense prestige to dismiss his critics.

Thompson was extremely tough, for instance, on the sociologist Philip Corrigan, who wrote that History was "a cultural form engaged in practices of regulation" in which the dominated classes were "encouraged to agree to their own confinement." While conceivably Corrigan had meant the dominant ideological practice of history (thus the capital H), Thompson believed he was referring to history in the broadest sense. Pronouncing judgment as if he were some religious authority deciding a heresy case, Thompson told the audience: "How on earth does his typewriter encompass that sentence, the most defeatist and terrorist of all? . . . Now, I hope that Phil is going to withdraw this formulation or at least qualify it. For if he does not, I must come to regard him as . . . one who thinks that theory is no more than a seminar game in which one can say any damn thing one likes."[45] The mixed response of the audience to this mode of attack presaged the discussion that followed.

Thompson's primary objection to Johnson's paper and his article in *History Workshop* was the conception of the "moment of culture." He saw it as sloppy and impressionistic history, a distorting conflation of the New Left debates on culture. This categorization obliterated Thompson's theoretical differences with Hall, Hoggart, and Williams, which had been precisely over the question of culture and culturalism. Thompson rebuked Johnson for accusing everyone except himself of being theoretical absolutists, while Johnson created false oppositions and categories that had their own absolutist implications. But Thompson went even further: "What Richard Johnson doesn't seem to be interested enough in, what scarcely, and this is perhaps part of the conditions of our academic work today . . . what scarcely doesn't seem to enter the door of the Birmingham Centre is *politics.*"[46] Thompson had either simply ignored what the Centre had been doing for the past ten years, or he had become so caught up in the heat of battle that the desire to score a polemical point overtook the need to be precise and accurate.

The ensuing discussion then focused on what one speaker described as Thompson's "offensive and hurtful criticism." Indeed, while the evening began by recognizing Thompson's immense stature and authority, by the time he finished speaking, many in the audience felt he had abused it. Ironically, what had begun as a debate about Althusser was transformed into a debate about Thompson.

As he had done at the start, Yeo established the tenor of what followed. Observing that power could be personal, he distanced himself from Thompson's debating style. He suggested that Thompson had not been intentionally malicious but that he was oblivious to the power which he wielded over others. This explained why it was possible for him to "ad hominem pillory" some comrades on the platform. Yeo was referring to Johnson, who felt deeply pained by Thompson's attack and was unable to play an active role for the rest of the evening.

Thompson, of course, had his defenders. John Saville, his old comrade from the *Reasoner* group, mocked what he perceived as the chairman's grandstanding. "It was all really charitable and generous and sisterly and brotherly." In an impromptu speech delivered at maximum volume and interrupted by more outbursts of dismay than approval, Saville portrayed the audience's distaste for Thompson's hard-hitting style of argument as symptomatic of the "arid theorizing" that characterized recent Marxist debates. In Saville's terms, the intellectual Left misunderstood the way forward. At a History Workshop, where it was assumed that everyone present was a comrade, theoretical advance was possible only as a result of the "kind of hard and firm polemic that has come from this platform."

Saville believed that the objections to a hard-hitting debate were connected to the growth of academic Marxism in the 1970s. The congenial discourse of the academy had displaced the spiritedness of the political meeting. However, Yeo's equation of power with personal power called attention to the impact of an entirely different perspective on radical intellectuals than Saville imagined. Yeo's suggestion alluded to a suppressed dimension in the debate that then came rushing to the surface—feminism.

Indeed, the objections to the polemical mode set forth by Johnson and Hall, and echoed by later speakers, were rooted in the alternative modes of political organization and discussion developed by the women's movement. Thus, a male speaker did not view Thompson's mode of argument as Stalinist, as others had implied, but as a "very antiquated Oxford liberalism, the Oxford Union debating team tactic of slugging off the enemy instead of answering their substantive questions." He believed that political knowledge was created along the lines of the feminist movement—by large numbers of people in small groups confronting problems independently, collectively, and quietly. "Not hectoring at one another. And waiting for those experiences to become shared across a wide spectrum of society."

Similarly, a female speaker could not find one sisterly aspect in the debate. She attributed "the booming of certain people's voices" and "a sort of contempt in the air" to an absolute failure to absorb the last ten years of the women's movement. As a result, she asserted, the debate never got off the ground. "Everyone who has studied undergraduate history knows that we wouldn't be here if it wasn't for E. P. Thompson's *The Making of the English Working Class*, but the discussion shouldn't end there. And we shouldn't allow ourselves to be painted into corners." Moreover, she wanted to know why, with so many accomplished feminist historians present, not one woman was on the platform. In fact, Jane Caplan was originally asked to speak but had decided against it. Later, Caplan explained to the group that silence sometimes was a creative moment, and the events that transpired on the platform only confirmed her in this view. The form of the event, she said, was masculinist to its core. By participating, she would be endorsing it. Alluding to Thompson's contention that Althusser was a Stalinist, she stated: "We've had odd socks on the line tonight, and I want to ask which foot the Stalinist boot is on as well."

After this period of audience participation, Hall and Thompson returned to the podium to reflect on the evening's events. In his closing remarks Thompson addressed those who criticized his performance. He acknowledged that the group objected to his style of argumentation—but he saw no reason to change it. He accused them of being a "little bit soft" and justified the severity of his critique on the grounds that he was addressing friends and comrades. It was especially necessary to be tough on Johnson, for his concept of culturalism suppressed the distinctive voice of the Marxist historiographical tradition in New Left debates. Like Saville, Thompson viewed the group's dislike for polemics as causally linked to the growth of academic Marxism in the 1970s. He argued that the intellectual Left, despite its achievements, had retreated to a ghetto and was cut off from the political world. In this context, Thompson accepted the characterization that both he and Althusser used Leninist tactics on opponents. If sharing nothing else, they, along with Saville, came from a common tradition: a tradition where theory was closely related to political practice, where people were accountable in terms of results.

Thompson wrote "The Poverty of Theory" because he viewed Althusserianism as a threat to the Marxist historiographical tradition, but by the time of the Workshop debate two years had passed. His scholarly interest in theoretical questions had been supplanted by his concern with the growing authoritarianism of the state and the erosion of civil liberties in Britain. This concern provided the background for his final remarks. Thompson complained, as he had in *Writing by Candlelight*, that because the intellectual Left knew the capitalist state to be coercive a priori, they lacked "the sensitivity of response" necessary to launch the struggle to oppose it. Sounding the alarm, Thompson reminded his audience that because Britain lacked a written constitution, the breakdown of accepted legal norms threatened the historical gains of the working class. Indeed, he would be "very surprised if some people in this room" did not "serve terms of imprisonment in the next five or six years in the very sharp confrontation with an authoritarian state." Thompson called for historians to take a leading role in protecting legal rights in Britain.

Thompson alerted historians to the gravity of the political crisis, and he exhorted them to become involved in politics. But for Stuart Hall, the evening's final speaker, Thompson's plea only added insult to injury. Hall did not disagree with Thompson's analysis of the state, although he would have undoubtedly portrayed the crisis in a different way. Nor did he lack an appreciation of Thompson's own writings on the subject. However, as one of the authors of *Policing the Crisis*, he found it difficult to accept Thompson's obliviousness to his own and others' political writings and struggle. After all, he asserted, Thompson's writings had been founded on the struggle of "people who have for a very long time—the last ten years—been drawing attention to the problem of the state, and the law as a force—for disciplining the class and for disciplining Blacks." It was a difficult moment for Hall. As he recalled, he realized that Thompson had no understanding of what the Centre had been up to for the last ten years.[47] With more than a hint of sarcasm, he welcomed Thompson to the ranks.

Hall proceeded to reflect again on the use of polemics in intellectual and political debate. The evening's events had only reconfirmed his view that polemics had no place in debates between socialists. "The problems are politically too serious; the intellectual problems are too difficult to be conducted in this way for much longer." He observed that he could have been more critical than Thompson of the work of the Birmingham Centre, but he could never say about it, as Thompson had, that "politics never entered the door." Nor could he say that the Centre had ever engaged in the kind of theoretical argument that required Thompson's work to be excluded. "Whatever else the Centre has done, we have stood for being able to do intellectual work without reading people into corners or excommunicating them from the field." The dialogue between Hall and Thompson that had existed since the days of the first New Left had broken down.

Hall was not content to conclude by discussing the form of political and theoretical argument. He returned to theory. He admitted his disappointment that Thompson refused to address his critique of "The Poverty of Theory," for differences between them remained. Yet he was heartened that Thompson acknowledged a problem with the concept of experience, that, in fact, the term had different meanings. Hall agreed that the problem was precisely as Thompson had formulated it, that is, as the relationship between social being (experience I) and social consciousness (experience

II)—experience and ideology. Yet Hall rejected Thompson's solution. He argued that theoretical confusion could not be averted when one term referred to two separate concepts. "If both things are experience, how are socialists to understand how to operate on experience I so as to produce without ideological distortion experience II in order to bring about some change in practice." In other words, how were they to know what Thompson meant from sentence to sentence? Hall concluded that historians might know in their private thoughts what they meant or intended, but this understanding was not adequate. The problem could be solved only theoretically.

The stormy History Workshop session produced bad feelings and confusion among the principal participants. Afterward, Yeo wrote of the "bewilderment" and "sadness" of those trying to make sense of the event. "The meeting was not full enough of controversy, as well as being (more obviously) empty of sisterly/brotherly qualities."[48] It was still very unclear to Richard Johnson "whether the conflicts there or their modes were important, organic, formative or really quite accidental, ephemeral and superficial."[49] Thompson was also confused by the "bad vibes" that permeated the evening, though he was certain they would subside. But he thought that Yeo's and Johnson's continued preoccupations with the session were further evidence of the self-isolation of the intellectual Left. "They are full of self-examinations," he wrote, "pulse-takings, ruminations on style, private inner-left references, excessive awareness of 'positions' within the left, and numb and null towards all the rest of the world."[50]

While the debate on history and theory might have been confusing to the participants, its meaning, in retrospect, is more apparent. Disputes over the polemical mode, the concept of experience, socialist political strategy, and history and theory suggested deep and enduring theoretical and political divisions that had been growing throughout the 1970s.

Certainly, one of the most fundamental differences resulted from the growing influence of feminist theory and practice on the post-1968 generation of socialist intellectuals. This influence was apparent in disagreements over the debate's form and style. Thompson (and Saville) had every right to be concerned about the isolation of intellectuals from the working-class movement, though the problem of theory and practice had not begun in 1968, nor was it as easy to bring the two concepts together as his rhetoric suggested. Yet

Thompson seemed unable to understand the meaning of the criticism. More was involved than his being nicer. Feminists were conceiving of new forms of politics and organization. They were, in effect, arguing that Thompson's mode of intellectual and political argumentation represented a form of masculine power and domination that resulted in the silencing of women's voices, among others. Polemics were part of the problem, not the solution.

Feminism's impact was also partially responsible for divisions over socialist strategy. Although Thompson did not specify the concept of the "people" underpinning the struggle against the authoritarian state, that concept recapitulated his notion of the common people expressed throughout his writings. He conceived of the political struggle against the state as another chapter in the historical saga of the oppressed. For Hall (and Johnson), socialists faced new challenges as a result of the growth of feminism, the emergence of antiracist politics, and the fragmentation of the traditional working-class movement. Socialist politics no longer could be conceived in terms of the common experience of the "people." Not only was the experience of the "people" not necessarily shared, but it was not in any sense—even an ultimate sense—necessarily leftist. Thatcher's reconstruction of popular consciousness rendered previous assumptions obsolete. Hall argued that socialists must recognize the combined and uneven effects of race, class, and gender in a social formation; political unity must be produced out of irreducible difference. Socialist strategy must be founded on a new theory of subjectivity. This theory viewed experience and ideology as being intertwined rather than opposed and conceived of "culture" as a field of signification rather than an expression of a group's consciousness.

Finally, what surfaced at the History Workshop debate was the unbridgeable divide that had opened up between the Marxist historiographical tradition as exemplified by Thompson and the cultural studies of the Centre. From the beginning, a creative tension had been present between cultural theorists such as Hall and historians such as Thompson, a tension evidenced in the original debates over culturalism. Thompson's early writings were a major source of inspiration for the Centre's work until the mid-seventies. The Centre's critical adaption of Althusser (and semiotics as well) led to the reevaluation of its own culturalist and humanist past, and this fueled conflicts and friction. It became clear at the Workshop debate that the two traditions were unable to communicate and that the communication for a long time had been one way. Thompson, in effect, had dismissed the Centre as being part of an amorphous Althusserianism, while giving virtually no indication of following or understanding the Centre's work in the 1970s. After twenty years of active if sometimes strained dialogue, Hall severed the ties between them.

The audience, however, was more interested than Thompson was in what Hall had to say. Many of those present, including historians, were as impatient and weary with the polarities of the debate as Hall himself. He was seen as offering a positive alternative, an attempt to engage in the national political arena as well as taking account of the political and social changes of the past ten years. Hall not only had objected to the terms of the debate, but he was beginning to create the new theoretical ground that would supplant it. A phase in historical and cultural theory was coming to an end.

Conclusion

The subject matter of intellectual history tends to resist neat parameters; frequently, where to begin and end a given historical narrative is partially arbitrary. Yet in the case of British cultural Marxism abundant reasons can be found to conclude a narrative in 1979 (or at least in the late seventies and early eighties) on the ground that this point in time represents the end of a decisive phase in cultural Marxism's development.

Marxism's position in intellectual debates had undergone fundamental shifts. Since the thirties, Marxism played a major role in radical intellectual discussions in Britain. The same held true even in the late fifties, when Hoggart and Williams, despite their attempts at establishing a critical distance, made assumptions about the class basis of society and politics that were indirectly indebted to Marxism. In the 1970s a post-Stalinist generation reaffirmed the necessity of a more systematic Marxist practice. Under the influence of French structuralism and semiotics, of Western Marxism, especially the study of Althusser and Gramsci, and of a rereading of Marx himself, this generation helped build a Marxist intellectual culture whose scope was unparalleled in Britain. Never had so many leftist intellectuals overtly thought and wrote in Marxist categories.

The Ruskin debate represented the culmination of several years of impassioned discussions on the epistemological basis of Marxist theory and practice. Several hundred people attending a History Workshop conference simply confirmed the existence of a flourishing socialist intellectual culture. But the session was perhaps the last time that historians and cultural theorists were so resolute in their support of Marxism as a theoretical and historical practice. The evening signified the end of a phase in historical and cultural theory and the end of a dialogue between different versions of cultural Marxism. It also symbolized the beginning of the end of Marxist hegemony in Left-wing intellectual discussions.

To be sure, such a change did not come to pass only because of what was said on a particular night, on a platform at Oxford, in late 1979. The conflicts aired on that stage were informed by deeper historical shifts—shifts that were redrawing the political map used by the Left to understand itself and its relationship to the political and social world. The net effect of these changes contributed to a crisis in Marxist thought of unprecedented dimensions in Britain and elsewhere.

Internationally, the rise of Solidarity in Poland and the beginning of the end of existing socialism in Eastern Europe and the Soviet Union raised the issue of whether the democratic alternative was necessarily Marxist. The Iranian Revolution defied Marxist expectations of radical social transformation in the Third World. Rather than the driving revolutionary force being anticapitalism, it was religion, a social practice thought by Marxists to be residual. In Britain, Thatcher's victory in 1979 ushered in a new era of politics that resulted in the dissolution of the 1945 social contract and signaled a simultaneous assault on the state-controlled economy, the welfare state, and trade unionism. Such changes were made possible by Thatcher's extraordinary reconstruction of the "popular" along conservative lines. But these changes were founded on the fragmentation, defection, and shrinkage of the Left's traditional working-class base. Labour's vote in the 1979 election fell to its lowest since 1931, one-third of all trade union members voting Conservative.[1]

Indeed, British identity itself was being reshaped. Although historically a country where people's principal self-identification was their class, the impact of postwar emigration was changing Britain's character. The country was becoming an increasingly multiracial and multiethnic society, its growing pains made abundantly clear in street confrontations in Bristol, Brixton, and Liverpool in the spring and summer of 1981. For Marxist theory and practice, the emergence of these new social subjects in conjunction with those being created by the feminist movement posed difficult if not insurmountable problems.

In such a transformed atmosphere it is not surprising that socialist and feminist historiography and cultural studies in the 1980s manifested new concerns, priorities, and agendas. In general, these changes involved problematizing the connection between class position and cultural expression without rejecting the material basis of culture, focusing on the material impact of language and discourse on subjectivity and cultural identity while simultaneously insisting that cultural life was underpinned by political and social struggle. In cultural studies, where structuralism and semiotics were deeply ensconced, the shift was expressed through an intensified interest in feminism, theories of race and ethnicity, and critical appropriations of poststructuralist and postmodernist theory. An ongoing influence was a reformulated reading of the Gramscian notion of hegemony. Extending the view that surfaced in the Centre's work of the late 1970s, Gramsci's notion was viewed as representing the "articulation" of a ruling bloc's diverse and contradictory interests within a continuously shifting cultural and political field. Crucial here, according to Tony Bennett, was the idea that "the political and ideological articulations of cultural practices are *movable*—that a practice which is articulated to bourgeois values today may be disconnected from those values and connected to socialist ones tomorrow."[2]

In social history (as represented by History Workshop) a rethinking of established paradigms took place. The idea that language played a constitutive role in social behavior directly challenged the cultural materialism of social historians such as E. P. Thompson, for whom social consciousness was represented through language, not produced by it. This shift is evident in the pages of *History Workshop* since the early 1980s—its exploration of discourse, gender, race, ethnicity, and Foucault's philosophical history.[3] It is perhaps best captured in Gareth Stedman Jones's pathbreaking analysis of Chartism, which challenged the prevailing notion that Chartism could exclusively be explained in terms of the experience and conditions of the early Industrial Revolution. According to Stedman Jones, this past outlook assumed a simplistic view of the relationship between consciousness and language and was unable to explain either why Chartist consciousness took the form it did or why it later became less compelling. He reformulated the relation between consciousness and experience.

> Class consciousness— "a consciousness of identity of interests between working men of the most diverse occupations and levels of attainment" and "consciousness of the identity of interests of the working class or productive classes as against those of other classes," as Thompson defines it—formed part of a language whose systematic linkages were supplied by the assumptions of radicalism: a vision and analysis of social and political evils which certainly long predated the advent of class consciousness, however defined.[4]

An in-depth analysis of the transformation in history and cultural studies is beyond the scope of this book. In part, the historical dust has insufficiently settled to bring into focus the meaning and significance of what has transpired. However, most important, in my judgment, is the complexity of what must be taken into account. One major change that affected the contours of both radical historiography and cultural studies is its complex interaction with counterparts in North America, Europe, Australia, and elsewhere. While British historians and cultural theorists have continually been influenced by scholars and writers outside Britain, the level of the dialogue greatly intensified in the 1980s. This intellectual exchange was made possible through the growth of international conferences and transnational journals. It also has taken place as a result of the increasing migrations of British scholars. Sometimes these migrations have been short-term, involving periodic lecture tours or visiting appointments at foreign universities. However, they also have been more sustained, resulting in full-time academic positions, notably in Australia and North America. All of these elements have resulted in intellectual dialogues and exchanges immensely more varied and complex as well as lines of communication more fragmented and difficult to trace.

What I propose to discuss here is more modest in ambition, but, I believe, more consistent with the nature of this project. I have argued throughout these pages that we can learn a great deal about cultural Marxism—both radical historiography and cultural studies—by situating it in the context of radical politics, particularly that of the new left. I have suggested that it represents an implicit and explicit response to the postwar crisis of British socialism. This role of cultural Marxism was no less true of the era of Conservative triumph since the 1979 election. I will conclude this discussion by examining responses of historians and cultural theorists to the historical transformations that have characterized the eighties. Whether or not these responses have been explicitly Marxist is open to debate, and their impact on mainstream politics remains peripheral, but they continue to be part of an ongoing struggle to fuse theory and practice, academic work and political activism.

Striking similarities are apparent between the situation faced by the intellectual Left in the 1980s and that in which it had found itself in the 1950s. In both decades the Left was confronted by an array of forces—a culture of consumption, a rapidly developing and changing mass media, the expansion of a world market, and new technologies—that were redefining class relationships, cultural life, and the language and substance of politics. As in the 1950s, the politics of the 1980s were dominated by a resurgent Conservative Party that defined the political agenda and consistently defeated the Labour Party in elections. Just as Marxism found itself in retreat and dissolution in the fifties, it was plagued by an unparalleled crisis thirty years later. In the fifties this condition resulted from the crumbling of Stalinist orthodoxy and the emergence of socialist humanism in 1956. Thirty years later it was connected to the demise of socialist states in Eastern and Central Europe, the proliferation of various strains of critical theory, and the political demands of new social subjects.

The end of the Soviet empire, and the crisis of Marxism associated with it, was responsible for soul-searching among British Marxist intellectuals. Stuart Hall detected a state of depression among the Labour-aligned Left, including socialist feminists and those in the new social movements, who were forced to confront "the unpleasant truth" that "some part of what has been understood as 'socialism' by the world in general, and by much of the Left itself, is indeed crumbling to dust in Eastern Europe."[5] Reaffirming his commitment to the principles of socialism, Eric Hobsbawm freely admitted that those who believed that the Russian Revolution was "the gate to the future of world history"—which of course included himself—had been proved wrong.[6] And Stedman Jones argued that Marxism, though not synonymous with Leninism, could not isolate itself from the end of communism in Europe. It was as ludicrous to blame Marx for the gulags as Nietzsche for Auschwitz. But nonetheless "the one social and political alternative to capitalism constructed on the basis of Marx's ideas, although arguably more egalitarian, has also proved itself to be more authoritarian, less efficient and less desirable than the system it was supposed to replace."[7]

Yet at the same time events in Eastern Europe caused great exhilaration. After all, the new left, with which many intellectuals discussed in this study identified themselves, had been founded partially to oppose the regimes that later disintegrated. "We should not be alarmed," wrote Stuart Hall, "by the collapse of 'actual existing socialism' since, as socialists, we *have been waiting for it to happen for three decades.*"[8] Edward Thompson echoed these sentiments, viewing the collapse of the Soviet regime from the perspective of the "third way" created by the New Left politics of the fifties and more recently articulated by European peace movements of the 1980s. "I remain worried less," he wrote,

> by the manifest crisis of Marxism (which had that deservedly coming to it) than by the loss of conviction, even on the Left, in the practices and values of democracy. But the end of the Cold War has—and on both sides—seen a revival of these practices and a reaffirmation of these values, in the self-activity of masses who moved outside orthodox ideological and political stockades. And we should still see this as a moment of opportunity, not defeat.[9]

These intellectuals were clearly dismayed by the celebration of the death of Marxism in the West, but for more than thirty years they had viewed official Marxism as intellectually and morally bankrupt, and they had taken pains to distance themselves from it. Writing in early 1990, Stedman Jones conveyed this feeling in words recalling the spirit of the original New Left: "[I]t is time that the Left abandoned its adherence to marxism as an indivisible unity of theory and creed. Ideas, not creeds, are what is wanted. Marx is only one of many sources from which a renewal of socialist thinking might come about, and the need for that thinking is as pressing as ever."[10] Stedman Jones's plea for a heterogeneous Left captured the evolving spirit of the cultural Marxist tradition in the 1980s. If cultural Marxists continued to be inspired by Marx—and particularly by Gramsci—that influence was less overtly and self-consciously Marxist. Hall and Dick Hebdige spoke of a "Marxism without guarantees." Ernesto Laclau and Chantal Mouffe, Argentinean and French political theorists who were involved in British debates, vigorously defended post-Marxism—a radical democratic politics that both acknowledged and rejected its roots.[11] Indeed, the cultural Marxist tradition continued to thrive, and it remained committed to radical change, but whether it remained Marxist in any conventional sense is debatable. That tradition perhaps is best described as an eclectic mode of theoretical and political radicalism.

International developments undoubtedly played a critical role in highlighting the crisis of the Left in the eighties, but the principal issue, as in the 1950s, was the future of socialism in Britain so powerfully called into question by Thatcherism's triumph and Labour's precipitous decline. The broad-based participation of Left-wing writers and academics in radical political debates so characteristic of the New Left was likewise present in the eighties. The rethinking of socialist theory and practice characteristic of *Universities and Left Review*, the *New Reasoner*, and the early issues of *New Left Review* was revived in magazines such as *New Socialist* and *Marxism Today*, sponsored, respectively, by the Labour and Communist Parties. (Because of the reform of the British CP along Eurocommunist lines, *Marxism Today* contained the voices of many non-Communist writers.) As in earlier ventures, historians and cultural theorists associated with the cultural Marxist tradition assumed leading roles.

Even before Thatcher's first electoral victory, the process of re-examination was under way. In 1978, Sheila Rowbotham, Lynne Segal, and Hilary Wainwright published *Beyond the Fragments*, a pamphlet (and later a book) which, from a socialist feminist perspective, openly confronted the segmentation and divisions within the radical Left and the lethargy of the socialist movement in Britain.[12] The initiative recalled the original New Left's attempt to bring together disparate tendencies and interests into a grassroots and democratic movement. For Rowbotham and company, the cultural revolt of the late sixties—including feminists, gay rights activists, antiracist groups, environmentalists, numerous community organizations, a new generation of radical academics, and post-1968 revolutionary groups—had produced a radical movement unparalleled in its richness and diversity but whose component parts were frequently isolated from one another. "That is, we are without a sustained way of organizing beyond our specific oppressions and experiences. We lack the means to develop a general theory and programme for socialist change from these varied experiences. And we do not have adequate ways of convincing people of the wider political changes which need to be fought for if their specific demands and needs are to be met."[13] Like the New Left of the fifties, *Beyond the Fragments* sought to bring together these many strands into an organized force that would reshape the direction of the labor movement. It advocated a strategy that recognized the centrality of the Labour Party, argued for the necessity of reinventing it, was aware of the structural obstacles impeding this goal, and in the end insisted that reinvention must come from a political formation on the outside.

Beyond the Fragments caused "a furor," sparking extensive debates, a bulletin, and a 1980 conference in Leeds.[14] But in the present context its importance is not as a political movement, which like other "third way" efforts never achieved its goals, but as a contribution to debates on political strategy founded on the authors' experiences in the women's movement. For the *Beyond the Fragments* authors, the women's movement had accomplished more than helping women to achieve the power to organize and fight for control over the direction of their lives. First, its attention to the "private" and "inward" dimension of women's oppression had made possible a wider notion of politics, touched people who usually did not consider themselves to be political, and created a movement not dominated by hard-core political activists. Second, as part of its struggle against "inequalities of power" and a "hierarchical division of labor," it produced organizational forms which prefigured in miniature the society that it was fighting to make possible. As Rowbotham pointed out, the practice of the women's movement did "not assume that we will one day in the future suddenly come to control how we produce, distribute and divide goods and services and that this will rapidly and simply make us new human beings," but involved an ongoing process of personal and collective renewal.[15] For Hilary Wainwright, the values that it embodied gave the women's movement its importance.

> *The values underlying our ways of organizing have been ones which put emphasis on local control and autonomy; on small groups within wider co-ordinating structures; on local centres and social and cultural activities; on relating theory to practice; on discouraging forms of procedure and of leadership which make others feel inadequate or uninvolved; on recognizing that different views on strategy and tactics come from some real experience and are worth listening to and discussing.*[16]

At its best, the women's movement united on "major practical issues of the day," while continuing to openly debate and respect political differences. This synthesis of unity and diversity represented a potential model for socialist renewal.

Rowbotham was not the only radical historian to become involved in debates on the Left's future. In 1978, Eric Hobsbawm used the occasion of the Communist Party's annual Marx memorial lecture to question one of the oldest tenets of socialist faith—the linear progression of the workers' movement. Rather than looking at the socialist crisis in the context of the political climate of the late seventies, in "The Forward March of Labour Halted?" Hobsbawm viewed it from a historical perspective. He argued that Labour's decline must be seen in terms of structural shifts in postwar capitalism, and he located its earliest symptoms in the 1950s.

Hobsbawm defended his approach by evoking the opening lines of *The Eighteenth Brumaire*. He reiterated his belief in the ability of human agents to make their own history, but he stressed the centrality of understanding the historical terrain on which action took place. In effect, Hobsbawm distanced himself from Marx's historical prophecies about the future of socialist advance, while reiterating his faith in the spirit of Marx's method.

> *But if the labour and socialist movement is to recover its soul, its dynamism, and its historical initiative, we, as Marxists, must do what Marx would certainly have done: to recognise the novel situation in which we find ourselves, to analyse it realistically and concretely, to analyse the reasons, historical and otherwise, for the failures as well as the successes of the labour movement, and to formulate not only what we would want to do, but what can be done.[17]*

Hobsbawm approached the problem through the base/superstructure framework. He attributed Labour's decline to the combined impact of mass production, larger economic units, the growth of monopoly capital, a greatly enlarged public sector, and a greater number of female workers. The net result was increased sectional divisions, the breakup of the common working-class way of life, and an atmosphere that hindered unified class action. This fragmentation was especially true of the public sector where the class enemy was no longer a capitalist and where militant action was frequently based on creating public havoc. Not only did such action create conflicts among groups of workers, but it threatened the solidarity of the labor movement as a whole. As Hobsbawn also pointed out: "The sense of class solidarity may be further weakened by the fact that the real income of a family may no longer actually depend on a worker's own job alone, but even more on whether their wives or husbands also work and what sort of jobs they have, or on various other factors not directly determined by the union struggle."[18]

In the present context, Hobsbawm's analysis is significant for at least two reasons. It is noteworthy because of the wide-ranging debate that it provoked and the diversity of contributors that participated in it: the discussion included supporters of the Labour, Communist, and far-Left parties; shop stewards and a member of Parliament; intellectuals and trade union leaders.[19] The breadth of these contributions underscored the potential for intellectual exchange between socialist academics and labor movement activists in Britain. Hobsbawm's views are likewise significant because of the moment when the lecture was delivered and subsequently published. Appearing on the eve of Labour's worst electoral defeat in more than fifty years, the lecture achieved instant credibility in the election's aftermath. Yet for Hobsbawm, "The Forward March of Labour Halted?" was just the beginning. In the 1980s he emerged as one of the most prolific analysts of the Left; his insights into events and trends were major points of departure for debate and discussion. Of these, most controversial was his strategy for ending the Tories' rule during a period when the labor movement was in retreat. Returning to his Popular Front roots, he argued that nothing was more important than defeating Thatcher, and he was willing to accept an electoral pact between Labour and other smaller parties if that was what it would take.[20]

Like Hobsbawm's, Hall's contribution to the debate on the Left's decline began before Thatcher's first victory dramatically confirmed it. Hall and others at the Birmingham Centre portrayed the late seventies in *Policing the Crisis* as a time that was ripe for exploitation by Right-wing populism. Beginning in 1978, Hall elaborated on this position in an evolving analysis and commentary that spanned the 1980s. In contrast to Hobsbawm, whose rethinking commenced with his analysis of the impact of structural transformations in the economic base, Hall concentrated on shifts in the political and ideological field. He analyzed Thatcherism: what held it together, why it had succeeded, what its limits and weaknesses were, and (sure to stir up controversy) what the Left could learn from it.

Hall's analysis of Thatcherism owed a theoretical—even spiritual—debt to the writings of Gramsci. For Hall, Gramsci's importance was not that his statements and utterances could be grafted onto contemporary Britain. He passionately argued that this kind of unreflective practice had for too long hindered genuinely new perspectives on the Left. Rather, Gramsci was important because of how he posed questions and how he attempted to answer them. In interwar Italy, Gramsci faced a situation analogous to late twentieth-century Britain. A capitalist crisis failed to corroborate classical Marxist predictions; the radical Right rather than the Left seized the historical moment. Instead of insisting that Marxist prophecies would eventually assert themselves, he came to terms with the real movement of history. "Gramsci had to confront the turning back, the failure, of that moment: the fact that such a moment, having passed, would never return in its old form. Gramsci, here, came face to face with the revolutionary character of history itself. When a conjecture [conjuncture] unrolls, there is no 'going back.' History shifts gears. The terrain changes. You are in a new moment."[21] Gramsci's relevance for the present-day Left in Britain was that he would have resisted the orthodox Left's tendency to see Thatcherism as a chimera, a temporary shift in the electoral pendulum, or as an ideology in the sense of false consciousness. He would have yielded to the "discipline of the conjuncture."

Hall's Gramscian spirit permeated his understanding of Thatcherism. He viewed it as an ongoing and unfinished hegemonic project. Thatcherism was built on the ground that Labour governments since the late sixties had worked themselves—disciplining the working class, declaring war on the minority fringe, hemming in the largesse of the welfare state. But it had extended and twisted these initiatives into new and contrary directions, displacing both postwar conservatism and labourism as the major voice in the political and ideological field. Its redefinition of political and cultural reality—the creation of a new "common sense"—reshaped the rapidly eroding consensus that had been created in the aftermath of the 1945 elections. Thatcherism lumped together social democracy, the Labour Party, the unions, and the state, portraying them as authoritarian, responsible for lawlessness, wasteful and inefficient, anti-individualist, indeed, un-English. Most important, it transformed pivotal notions of public welfare.

> It has changed the currency of political thought and argument. Where previously social need had begun to establish its own imperatives against the laws of market forces, now questions of "value for money," the private right to dispose of one's own wealth, the equation between freedom and the free market, have become the terms of trade, not just of political debate in parliament, the press, the journals, and policy circles, but in the thought and language of everyday calculation. There has been a striking reversal of values: the aura that used to attach to the value of the public welfare now adheres to anything that is private—or can be privatized.[22]

Yet if Hall stressed Thatcherism's hegemonic and ideological dimensions, he did not mean to imply that this was the only ground on which Thatcherism fought, or that it was a coherent ideology, or that its reach was total. Following Gramsci, he argued that ideologies were neither consistent nor logical when held up to close scrutiny, and indeed they quite often turned out to be made up of seemingly incompatible components. Thatcherism, itself, which Hall described as a project of "regressive modernization," stitched together two, by no means agreeable traditions: "the resonant themes of organic Toryism—nation, family, duty, authority, standards, traditionalism—with the aggressive themes of a revived neo-liberalism—self-interest, competitive individualism, anti-statism."[23] Thatcherism, Hall insisted, contained fault lines on which it could be contested.

Hall viewed Thatcherism's attempt to re-create popular consciousness as an instance of "authoritarian populism": it furthered the interest of capital and consolidated and extended state power, retaining "most (though not all) of the formal representative institutions in place" and simultaneously had "been able to construct around itself an active popular consent."[24] But in contrast to the orthodox Left, who tended to view Thatcher's project as duping the people and who seemed to be waiting for the "natural ideology" of the working classes to reassert itself, Hall argued that Thatcherism had made real inroads into popular consciousness, had made connections with people's experience and found a way to articulate it. "People don't vote for Thatcherism, in my view, because they believe the small print. . . . What Thatcherism as an ideology does, is to address the fears, the anxieties, the lost identities, of a people. It invites us to think about politics in images. It is addressed to our collective fantasies, to Britain as an imaginary community, to the social imaginary."[25]

This analysis led Hall to reflect theoretically on the way that ideology worked in the historical world. He refused the idea that Thatcher's colonization of important elements within the dominated classes could be explained by the classical Marxist concept of "false consciousness." In Hall's words: "The first thing to ask about an 'organic' ideology that, however unexpectedly, succeeds in organizing substantial sections of the masses and mobilizing them for political action, is not what is *false* about it but what about it is *true*."[26] Yet Hall was equally unwilling to accept the poststructuralist tendency to uncouple ideologies from material social relations completely.[27] Rather, Hall wanted to rethink the relationship between ideology and materialism without being pulled in by either extreme.

> *It is therefore possible to hold both the proposition that material interests help to structure ideas and the proposition that position in the social structure has the tendency to influence the direction of social thought, without also arguing that material factors univocally determine ideology or that class position represents a guarantee that a class will have the appropriate forms of consciousness.*[28]

Hall's effort at creating a "third way" in the theory of ideology was in keeping with his tendency, observed throughout this book, to create his own theoretical position by combining aspects of seemingly opposing ones.

The obverse of Hall's analysis was exploring what the Left must do to dislodge Thatcherism from its dominant position in the field. Hall believed that Thatcherism had altered the rules of the political game. It had redefined politics such that the Left must fight against it on the same multiple fronts—economic, political, cultural, and ideological—that Thatcherism itself had captured. It was not a matter of putting forth specific policies, but offering an alternative vision which would engage the political imagination of the British people. As Hall explained:

> *The question is whether the left can also operate on the same ground and turn these popular experiences and emergent attitudes and aspirations to its advantage. Or whether its only alternative is to become aligned with important but increasingly minority and traditional constituencies which need defence in the face of the current onslaught, goodness knows, but which are no longer where the mass experience of the common people is at.*[29]

At the same time Hall and others associated with *Marxism Today* became increasingly convinced that part of displacing Thatcherism involved coming to grips with the global transformations that were affecting Britain. While he and his colleagues had previously tended to view the changes in Britain as synonymous with Thatcherism, it now seemed more likely that such shifts provided the basis on which Thatcherism worked its spell. Whether described as postindustrialism, postmodernity, postfordism (the latter inspired by Gramsci's analysis in "Americanism and Fordism") or a combination of these terms, these shifts were profoundly reshaping consciousness, experience, and the very fabric of everyday life. The result was the *New Times* initiative that appeared in *Marxism Today* in October 1988, its goal to explore the meaning and implications of the new changes and to put forward a leftist response to them.

[T]he ambition of the 'New Times' project is not only to make sense of the new world—to appreciate the tendencies and limits of post-Fordism, to unravel the emergent postmodern culture, to understand the new identities and political subjects in society—but also to provide the parameters for a new politics of the Left, a politics beyond Thatcherism, which can give a progressive shape and inflexion to New Times.[30]

The *New Times* initiative was the subject of a wide-ranging discussion, and it was published as a book edited by Hall and Martin Jacques, editor of *Marxism Today*, the following year. At one level, Hall's understanding of "new times" was a contribution to the postmodernism debate of the eighties. Hall, true to form, resisted either being wildly ecstatic or somberly pessimistic about the "postmodern condition." He acknowledged both the importance of the description of the postmodern world as put forward by Fredric Jameson and Jean-François Lyotard, while aligning himself with Jameson's contention that the postmodern was "the new cultural logic of capital." Yet he was critical (in another context) of how postmodernism, especially in the United States, seemed to be about "how the world dreams itself to be 'American.'"

[I]t not only points to how things are going in modern culture, but it says, first, that there is nothing else of any significance—not contradictory forces, and no counter-tendencies; and second, that these changes are terrific, and all we have to do is to reconcile ourselves to them. It is, in my view, being deployed in an essentialist and un-critical way. And it is irrevocably Euro- or western-centric in its whole episteme.[31]

Hall regarded "new times" as a deeply contradictory phenomenon whose imperatives both potentially foreclosed and made possible democratic initiatives. His way of thinking about "new times" can be seen in terms of the *longue durée* of his intellectual and political career. From this point of view, "new times" represented another stage in an ongoing and long-term preoccupation with understanding the nature of postwar transformations. This preoccupation was visible as early as his *ULR* essay, "A Sense of Classlessness," with its analysis of the impact of consumer capitalism, the new media, and changing patterns of work and industrial organization on popular consciousness. As he did at that time, Hall argued that the new changes could not be understood through a rigid application of base/superstructure, for in modern societies the economic and the cultural were deeply intertwined. Or as he stated it: "Modern culture is relentlessly material in its practices and modes of production. And the material world of commodities and technologies is profoundly cultural."[32] Just as the changes of the 1950s reshaped working-class consciousness, "the proliferation of models and styles, the increased product differentiation which characterizes 'post-Fordist' production" were connected to the "wider processes of cultural diversity and differentiation" and "multiplication of social worlds and social 'logics'" which characterized the contemporary West.[33] Most important, such shifts gave rise to increasingly complex and fragmented identities among social subjects. "The 'self,'" Hall wrote, "is conceptualised as more fragmented and incomplete, composed of multiple 'selves' or identities in relation to the different social worlds we inhabit, something with a history, 'produced,' in process."[34] For Hall, the challenge of "new times" was to create a politics that recognized this proliferation of differences, accepted their irreducibility, and could operate as a unified political front. Critical to the new politics of identity were the theoretical and political insights produced within and around both the women's and new black movements.

Taken together, Hall's writings on Thatcherism and "new times" exemplify the British cultural Marxist tradition at its best. His understanding of the relationship between the economic and the cultural was part of a long-term effort to move beyond the simplistic polarities of the base/superstructure metaphor. His insistence that language was determined by and determining of material social relations, integral to hegemonic politics, and fought over in social and cultural struggles extended the tradition of cultural studies and radical historiography. His attention to objective social and political conditions and his exploration of the potential that they held for a new politics of the democratic Left was characteristic of the cultural Marxist tradition as a whole. His attempt to define the social forces that might give rise to such politics was part of an ongoing process of political struggle rooted in the Popular Front, developed in the New Left politics of the 1950s, and further elaborated in the new lefts that followed. Such a definition was founded on providing a theoretical space for human agency—arguably the most important contribution of the cultural Marxist tradition to the social sciences and the humanities.

Hall's writings likewise point to the connection between cultural Marxism and the wider crisis of the Left. Despite his enthusiasm for "new times," Hall's work, undertaken during the dark days of Thatcherism, was part of a wider project of rethinking whereby segments of the Left were urgently trying to revive both the substance and style of socialist politics. His efforts at bridging the gap between theoretical and scholarly work and a wider political practice were emblematic of both the tradition of cultural studies and radical historiography in Britain: from Christopher Hill to Raphael Samuel, E. P. Thompson to Sheila Rowbotham, Raymond Williams to Paul Gilroy, Rodney Hilton to Catherine Hall.

Notes

Introduction

1 "Introduction: The Territory of Marxism," Lawrence Grossberg and Cary Nelson, eds., *Marxism and the Interpretation of Culture* (Urbana: University of Illinois Press, 1988), p. 1.

2 Meaghan Morris cited in the introduction to Lawrence Grossberg, Cary Nelson, and Paula A. Treichler, eds., *Cultural Studies* (New York: Routledge, 1992), p. 1. As the volume's editors suggest, this description conveys the magnitude of the popularity of cultural studies and points to the faddishness surrounding it. Whether the rule of speculation—for every boom there is a bust—applies to cultural studies remains to be seen.

3 The first type includes Patrick Brantlinger, *Crusoe's Footprints: Cultural Studies in Britain and America* (London: Routledge, 1990); Harvey J. Kaye, *The British Marxist Historians: An Introductory Analysis* (Cambridge: Polity Press, 1984); and Graeme Turner, *British Cultural Studies: An Introduction* (Boston: Unwin Hyman, 1990). The second includes David Harris, *From Class Struggle to the Politics of Pleasure* (London: Routledge, 1992); Bryan D. Palmer, *E. P. Thompson: Objections and Oppositions* (London: Verso, 1994); and Julia Swindells and Lisa Jardine, *What's Left: Women in Culture and the Labour Movement* (London: Routledge, 1990). A notable exception is Lin Chun, *The British New Left* (Edinburgh: Edinburgh University Press, 1993). Although Chun and I have written about many of the same things, we have done so from distinct perspectives. She analyzes the history of the new left to "help us with the difficult task of recasting socialism in the years to come" (ibid., p. xviii). My analysis of the new left focuses on understanding cultural studies and Marxist history.

4 Stuart Hall, "Cultural Studies and Its Theoretical Legacies," Grossberg, Nelson, and Treichler, eds., *Cultural Studies*, p. 279.

5 My generalizations here as elsewhere are primarily derived from the introduction to Martin Jay, *Marxism and Totality: The Adventures of a Concept from Lukács to Habermas* (Berkeley: University of California Press, 1984), pp. 1–20. Jay writes about Western Marxism more generally, but his understanding of this phenomenon seems to apply best to the Frankfurt School.

6 Ibid., p. 11.

7 This point has been reiterated by Raymond Williams, "The Future

of Cultural Studies," *The Politics of Modernism: Against the New Conformists* (London: Verso, 1989), pp. 154–55.

8   As Martin Jay wrote: "One very important distinction between continental and English Marxism was, in fact, the far greater importance accorded by the former to the concept of totality. Aside from several suggestive references to culture as a 'whole way of life' in the early work of Williams, totality did not really enter the English debate until the Althusserian wave of the 1970s. Many English Marxists were historians with that discipline's characteristic distaste for generalizing concepts." Jay, *Marxism and Totality*, p. 4.

1. Lost Rights

1   According to official Party statistics, membership at the end of 1934 was 5,800. In July 1939 it stood at 17,756. Kenneth Newton, *The Sociology of British Communism* (London: Allen Lane, 1969), p. 159.

2   Noreen Branson and Margot Heinemann, *Britain in the 1930s* (New York: Praeger, 1971), pp. 275–78.

3   Raphael Samuel, "British Marxist Historians, 1880–1980," *New Left Review (NLR)*, no. 120 (March–April 1980): 41. See also Harvey J. Kaye, "Our Island Story Retold: A. L. Morton and the 'People' in History," in Kaye's *The Education of Desire: Marxists and the Writing of History* (London: Routledge, 1992), pp. 116–24.

4   For an excellent overview of the social relations of the science movement, see Gary Werskey, *The Visible College: The Collective Biography of British Scientific Socialists of the 1930s* (New York: Holt, Rinehart and Winston, 1978).

5   Samuel, "British Marxist Historians," p. 50.

6   Christopher Hill, interview at Balliol College, Oxford University, 9 May 1984.

7   Samuel Beer, "Christopher Hill: Some Reminiscences," in *Puritans and Revolutionaries: Essays in Seventeenth-Century History Presented to Christopher Hill*, ed. Donald Pennington and Keith Thomas (Oxford: Oxford University Press, 1978), p. 4.

8   Hill, interview, 9 May 1984.

9   Victor Kiernan, interview, Edinburgh, Scotland, 18 June 1984.

10 Rodney Hilton, "Christopher Hill: Some Reminiscences," in Pennington and Thomas, eds., *Puritans and Revolutionaries*, p. 7.

11 Rodney Hilton, interview at the University of Birmingham, 2 May 1984. At one point Hilton's mother was nominated to be a justice of the peace by the local Labour group. Hilton also remembers as a little boy going to see his grandfather, who lived in a tiny cottage in the countryside. Above the door was a sign stating that Samuel Bamford, one of the Peterloo heroes, was arrested there. Such memories had a considerable influence on Hilton; he grew up with a "sense" of the Lancashire labor movement.

12 Hilton, "Christopher Hill," p. 7.

13 Eric Hobsbawm, "Intellectuals and the Class Struggle," in his *Revolutionaries* (New York: New American Library, 1973), p. 250.

14   Ibid., pp. 251–52.

15   Eric Hobsbawm, interview at Birkbeck College, University of London, 4 May 1984.

16   The following discussion of the Historians' Group is based on several sources, the main one being Eric Hobsbawm, "The Historians' Group of the Communist Party," in *Rebels and Their Causes: Essays in Honour of A. L. Morton*, ed. Maurice Cornforth (Atlantic Highlands, N.J.: Humanities Press, 1979). Unless otherwise stated, information given about the Historians' Group is derived from this memoir. A second source is the minutes of the Committee of the Historians' Group, the British Communist Party Archives (hereafter Minutes of the Historians' Group). The minutes are handwritten summaries of meetings, hard to decipher at times. It is difficult to know who kept them, certainly more than one person. Although George Matthews and Betty Matthews showed me every courtesy when I studied the minutes at the Party's headquarters, they would not allow me to copy them. This made my task much more difficult. A third invaluable source included interviews with the principal participants.
      The only secondary account of the group is Bill Schwarz's valuable study, " 'The People' in History: The Communist Party Historians' Group, 1946–56," in *Making Histories: Studies in History Writing and Politics*, ed. Richard Johnson et al. (Minneapolis: University of Minnesota Press, 1982), pp. 44–95.

17   In 1947, Hobsbawm was hired as a history lecturer at Birkbeck College, University of London; he later was promoted to professor of economic and social history. From 1949 until 1955 he was also a fellow of King's College, Cambridge. John Saville was appointed to an assistant lectureship in economic history at the University College of Hull and spent his entire academic career there. Rodney Hilton also taught at only one institution. After World War II, Hilton was appointed as a lecturer in the School of History at the University of Birmingham. He was later made a professor of medieval social history in recognition of his unique contributions to the field.

18   R. H. S. Crossman, "Towards a Philosophy of Capitalism," in *New Fabian Essays*, ed. R. H. S. Crossman (London: Fabian Society, 1970), pp. 5–6.

19   A useful summary can be found in Robert Hewison, *In Anger: British Culture in the Cold War, 1945–60* (New York: Oxford University Press, 1981), pp. 1–31.

20   E. P. Thompson, introduction to *There Is a Spirit in Europe: A Memoir of Frank Thompson*, ed. E. P. Thompson and T. J. Thompson (London: Victor Gollancz, 1948), p. 13.

21   E. P. Thompson, interview with Mike Merrill, in Henry Abelove et al., eds., *Visions of History* (New York: Pantheon Books, 1984), p. 11.

22   Thompson, introduction to *There Is a Spirit in Europe*, p. 20.

23   E. P. Thompson, interview, Worcester, England, 10 May 1984; E. P. Thompson, "The Secret State," *New Statesman*, 10 November 1978, p. 618.

24 E. P. Thompson, preface to *The Railway: An Adventure in Construction*, ed. E. P. Thompson (London: British-Yugoslav Association, 1948), p. viii.

25 E. P. Thompson, "Omladinska Pruga," ibid., p. 2.

26 E. P. Thompson, "An Open Letter to Leszek Kolakowski," in his *The Poverty of Theory and Other Essays* (London: Merlin Press, 1978), p. 160.

27 Thompson, "The Poverty of Theory," in *The Poverty of Theory and Other Essays*, p. 265.

28 See for instance, Eric Hobsbawm, "Where Are British Historians Going?" *Marxist Quarterly* 2 (January 1955): 25–26.

29 Eric Hobsbawm, interview with Pat Thane and Elizabeth Lunbeck, in *Visions of History*, p. 33.

30 Christopher Hill, "Storm Over the Gentry," *Encounter* 11 (July 1958): 76.

31 Christopher Hill, R. H. Hilton, and E. J. Hobsbawm, "Past and Present: Origins and Early Years," *Past and Present*, no. 100 (August 1983): 4–5.

32 Ibid., p. 5.

33 Ibid.

34 Minutes of the Historians' Group, 1 April 1950.

35 Hill, Hilton, and Hobsbawm, "Past and Present," p. 9.

36 The reconstituted editorial board included Norman Birnbaum, Dobb, J. H. Elliot, S. S. Frere, Hill, Hilton, A. H. M. Jones, Brian Manning, Lawrence Stone, Joan Thirsk, and Peter Worsley. (Of these, Manning and Thirsk had been on the board earlier.) Morris remained editor. Joining Hobsbawm as assistant editor was T. H. Ashton.

37 Hill, Hilton, and Hobsbawm, "Past and Present," p. 12.

38 Lawrence Stone, interview at Princeton University, Princeton, N.J., 13 May 1985.

39 Hobsbawm, "The Historians' Group," p. 33.

40 Hill, interview, 9 May 1984.

41 Hilton, interview, 2 May 1984; Hobsbawm, interview, 4 May 1984.

42 J. D. Bernal, "Stalin as a Scientist," *Modern Quarterly* 8 (Autumn 1953): 133.

43 Christopher Hill, "Stalin and the Science of History," *Modern Quarterly* 8 (Autumn 1953): 209.

44 When interviewing Hill, I remarked that I was embarrassed to bring up this essay. Hill responded that he should be embarrassed, not me. Hill, interview, 9 May 1984.

45 E. P. Thompson, *William Morris: Romantic to Revolutionary*, rev. ed. (New York: Pantheon Books, 1977), p. 769.

46 E. P. Thompson, *William Morris: Romantic to Revolutionary* (London: Lawrence and Wishart, 1955), p. 760.

47 Thompson, interview with Mike Merrill, p. 11.

48 Anonymous, "A Marxist View of Byzantium," *TLS*, 12 December 1952, p. 816.

49   Hill's letter was published in *TLS*, 19 December 1952, p. 837; Lindsay's letter appeared—with the reviewer's response—in *TLS*, 26 December 1952, p. 853.

50   G. Wilson Knight, "Freedom and Integrity," *TLS*, 2 January 1953, p. 9.

51   Ibid.

52   Curiously, the eighteenth century attracted only limited interest, the exception being George Rudé, a "lone explorer," in Hobsbawm's words. Hobsbawm, "The Historians' Group," p. 35. I can surmise only that such restrained interest can be explained by the eighteenth century's lack of some of the heroic qualities of other periods. Edward Thompson later attended to this lacuna.

53   Daphne May, "Work of the Historians' Groups," *Communist Review*, May 1949, p. 541.

54   Ibid. To achieve this goal, the Group held many conferences, lecture series, and debates on historiographical issues. Conferences included science and ideology in the seventeenth century (1949); the Reformation (1950); nineteenth-century radicalism (1949); Communism and liberty (1949); and the history of British capitalism (1954). Debates were held on the decline of antiquity and the transition to feudalism (1947–48); the transition from feudalism to capitalism stimulated by Dobb's *Studies* (1947) and the Dobb-Sweezy debate (1952); the nature of the Tudor and early Stuart state (1947–48); agrarian changes in early modern England (1947–48); the relationship between Protestantism and the rise of modern science (1949); and the origins of reformism in the nineteenth-century British labor movement.

55   May, "Work of the Historians' Groups," p. 542.

56   This project found various expressions. The first series of lectures sponsored by the Historians' Group was in five parts: Sir Thomas More; the Levellers and Diggers; Robert Owen and Chartism; Tom Mann; and the present-day Communist Party. The "History in the Making" series made primary sources (edited by members of the Historians' Group and overseen by Dona Torr) available to a nonspecialist Left-wing audience with the purpose of showing the democratic and revolutionary historical perspective of the Group and therefore the Party. It failed because, as Hobsbawm noted, "They were designed for a public of trade union and adult education readers, which did not take them up, and for a public of students which did not yet exist." Hobsbawm, "The Historians' Group," p. 29.

57   Minutes of the Historians' Group, 8 July 1950.

58   Ibid.

59   Ibid. In the early fifties, branches of the Historians' Group were set up in Manchester, Nottingham, and Sheffield to promote local historical work. In October 1951 the *Local History Bulletin* was first published. (It was renamed *Our History* in 1953.)

60   Ibid.

61   Hobsbawm, "The Historians' Group," p. 27.

62   Ibid., p. 26.

63   Ibid.

64   Hobsbawm, interview with Pat Thane and Elizabeth Lunbeck, in Henry Abelove et al., eds., *Visions of History*, pp. 32–33. Only after the collapse of the Soviet Union and the end of the Cold War did Hobsbawm write as a historian about the post-1914 period, notably in *The Age of Extremes: A History of the World, 1914–91* (New York: Pantheon Books, 1994).

65   See Hobsbawm, "The Historians' Group," pp. 31–34.

66   Ibid., p. 32.

67   "Introduction," *Past and Present*, no. 1 (February 1952): iii.

68   Hill, interview, 9 May 1984.

69   John Saville, interview, London, 8 June 1984.

70   Hilton, "Christopher Hill," p. 9.

71   Hobsbawm, "The Historians' Group," pp. 25–26.

72   Hobsbawm, interview, 4 May 1984.

73   James Klugmann, "Introduction: The Crisis in the Thirties, A View from the Left," in *Culture and Crisis in the Thirties*, ed. Jon Clark et al. (London: Lawrence and Wishart, 1979), pp. 26–27.

74   Karl Marx, *The Eighteenth Brumaire of Louis Bonaparte*, in Robert C. Tucker, ed., *The Marx-Engels Reader*, 2d ed. (New York: W. W. Norton, 1978), p. 595.

75   Christopher Hill, "Marxism and History," *Modern Quarterly* 3 (Spring 1948): 58.

76   Rodney Hilton, "Capitalism—What's in a Name?" (1952), in *The Transition from Feudalism to Capitalism*, ed. Rodney Hilton (London: Verso, 1978), pp. 157–58.

77   Hill, "Marxism and History," p. 54.

78   Ibid., p. 64.

79   Karl Marx and Frederick Engels, *Selected Correspondence: 1846–1895*, trans. with explanatory notes by Dona Torr (New York: International Publishers, 1942).

80   Or as John Saville told me, "We were accustomed to raising questions in the style of the *Selected Correspondence*." Saville, interview, 8 June 1984.

81   Hill, "Marxism and History," p. 63.

82   Ibid., p. 52.

83   John Eatwell, "Maurice Dobb," *Cambridge Journal of Economics* 1 (March 1977): 1.

84   Eric Hobsbawm, "Maurice Dobb," in *Socialism, Capitalism, and Economic Growth: Essays Presented to Maurice Dobb*, ed. C. H. Feinstein (Cambridge: Cambridge University Press, 1967), p. 6.

85   Ibid.

86   Hilton, interview, 2 May 1984.

87   Hobsbawm, interview, 4 May 1984.

88   In Dobb's words: "The justification of any definition must ultimately rest on its successful employment in illuminating the actual process of historical development: on the extent to which it gives a

shape to our picture of the process corresponding to the contours which the historical landscape proves to have." Maurice Dobb, *Studies in the Development of Capitalism*, rev. ed. (New York: International, 1963), p. 8. Dobb's tautological defense of this definition indicates the difficulties that arise in using "history" as empirical proof for "theory."

89   Ibid., p. 54.

90   For Robert Brenner, Dobb's contention that class struggle played a secondary role in determining the outcome of the feudal crisis was inconsistent with the logic of his own argument. Surely the reason for this perceived inconsistency is that Brenner was attempting to develop the "class struggle" side of Dobb's work. In *Studies in the Development of Capitalism*, Dobb, on the other hand, adhered to a productionist historical model. Robert Brenner, "Dobb on the Transition from Feudalism to Capitalism," *Cambridge Journal of Economics* 2 (June 1978): 128.

91   Dobb, *Studies in the Development of Capitalism*, p. 123.

92   The debate has been summarized and collected in the *Transition*. In the eighties the debate was revived as a result of the work of Robert Brenner. See T. H. Aston and C. H. E. Philpin, eds., *The Brenner Debate: Agrarian Class Structure and Economic Development in Pre-Industrial Europe* (Cambridge: Cambridge University Press, 1987).

93   Joseph Needham, foreword to *The Levellers and the English Revolution*, by Henry Holorenshaw (New York: Howard Fertig, 1971), pp. 5–6. This text by Needham, written in 1939, appeared under the pseudonym of Henry Holorenshaw.

94   Christopher Hill, "Marx's Virtues," *Listener*, 10 August 1967, p. 172.

95   Ibid.

96   Hill, interview, May 9, 1984.

97   According to one of Hill's classmates, Max Beer (later a well-known political scientist): "The idea of using Marx to study history was still new in England. I recall my sense of daring and novelty when, during a tutorial with Humphrey Sumner in Hilary Term, 1935, I blurted out something to the effect that I thought the conflict of the seventeenth century was 'a class war.' 'Of course, but what else?' was Humphrey's sensible rejoinder." Beer, "Christopher Hill," p. 3.

98   Christopher Hill, "The English Civil War Interpreted by Marx and Engels," *Science and Society* 12 (Winter 1948): 133.

99   Hill, interview, 9 May 1984.

100   Ibid. In retrospect he believed that he mistook the relative absence of class barriers—at least in comparison to England—for egalitarianism.

101   Christopher Hill, "Soviet Interpretation of the English Interregnum," *Economic History Review* 8 (May 1938): 159.

102   Originally published in Christopher Hill, ed., *The English Revolution, 1640: Three Essays* (London: Lawrence and Wishart, 1940); the 1955 edition in which Hill's essay was published alone is the one cited hereafter. Hill, *The English Revolution 1640: An Essay*, 3d ed. (London: Lawrence and Wishart, 1955).

103   Ibid., p. 61.
104   Hill, interview, 9 May 1984.
105   P.F., "England's Revolution," *Labour Monthly* 22 (October 1940): 558–59.
106   Douglas Garman, "The English Revolution 1640: A Reply to P.F.," *Labour Monthly* 22 (December 1940): 653.
107   Hill, interview, 9 May 1984.
108   The years of Pokrovsky's precipitous decline were 1936–40. Paul H. Aron, "M. N. Pokrovskii and the Impact of the First Five-Year Plan on Soviet Historiography," in *Essays in Russian and Soviet History: In Honor of Geroid Tanquary Robinson*, ed. John Shelton Curtiss (New York: Columbia University Press, 1963), p. 302.
109   Kiernan's position on the period of English absolutism and its significance—and the debate that followed—are to be found in three unpublished documents that I obtained from Kiernan (henceforth known as the Kiernan Papers). He first formulated his view in "Theses for Discussion on Absolutism," 1947–48, Kiernan Papers. It was subsequently discussed in a Historians' Group meeting (early modern section), henceforth referred to as "Absolutism Discussion," 10–11 January 1948, Kiernan Papers. And Kiernan replied to his critics in "Postscript: Appendix J," 1948, Kiernan Papers. The final position was published by the sixteenth- and seventeenth-century section of the Historians' Group of the Communist Party as "State and Revolution in Tudor and Stuart England," *Communist Review*, July 1948, pp. 207–14.
110   Hill, interview, 9 May 1984.
111   Kiernan, interview, 18 June 1984.
112   Kiernan, "Postscript: Appendix J," p. 2.
113   Ibid., p. 1.
114   "Absolutism Discussion," p. 4.
115   Ibid.
116   Ibid., p. 6.
117   These conflicting viewpoints are found in Kiernan, "Theses," pp. 4–5.
118   Kiernan, "Postscript: Appendix J," p. 3.
119   Christopher Hill, "Historians on the Rise of British Capitalism," *Science and Society* 14 (Fall 1950): 320.
120   Dona Torr, *Tom Mann and His Times*, vol. 1 (London: Lawrence and Wishart, 1956).
121   Hill, quoted in Kaye, *The British Marxist Historians*, p. 14.
122   Hill, interview, 9 May 1984; Thompson, interview, 10 May 1984.
123   Saville, interview, 8 June 1984.
124   Thompson, *William Morris* (1955), p. 8.
125   Hill, quoted in Kaye, *The British Marxist Historians*, p. 14.
126   Hilton, interview, 2 May 1984.
127   Hobsbawm, interview, 4 May 1984.
128   Hill, interview, 9 May 1984.

129   R. H. Hilton, "Peasant Movements in England before 1381," *Economic History Review* 11 (1949): 136.
130   Christopher Hill, "The Norman Yoke," in John Saville, ed., *Democracy and the Labour Movement: Essays in Honour of Dona Torr* (London: Lawrence and Wishart, 1954), p. 12.
131   Ibid., p. 28. The following sentence is also important. "Previous constitutions proclaimed the rights of man, *ad nauseam*; the Soviet constitution however guaranteed them."
132   Kiernan, "Wordsworth and the People," in John Saville, ed., *Democracy and the Labour Movement*, p. 240. This essay has been reprinted with its 1973 postscript in Victor Kiernan, *Poets, Politics, and the People*, ed. Harvey J. Kaye (London: Verso, 1989), pp. 96–123. All references are to the original (1954) publication.
133   Ibid., p. 261.
134   Ibid., p. 252.
135   Thompson, *William Morris* (1955), p. 841.
136   Hill, "Marxism and History," p. 63.
137   Kiernan, "Wordsworth and the People," p. 270.
138   Raymond Williams, *Politics and Letters: Interviews with "New Left Review"* (London: NLB, 1979), p. 85.
139   Christopher Hill, "The Pre-Revolutionary Decades," in *The Collected Essays of Christopher Hill*, vol. 1 (Amherst: University of Massachusetts Press, 1985), p. 3.
140   Victor Kiernan, *Shakespeare: Poet and Citizen* (London: Verso, 1993).
141   Hobsbawm wrote several short stories in the late thirties and early forties. One, "The Battle," was published in *Punch*, 1 February 1939. He also published several articles for *Die Zeitung* in 1944 on writers, including William Hazlitt, Sean O'Casey, and William Morris. For a nearly complete bibliography of Hobsbawm's writing, see Keith McClelland, "Bibliography of the Writings of Eric Hobsbawm," in *Culture, Ideology and Politics: Essays for Eric Hobsbawm*, ed. Raphael Samuel and Gareth Stedman Jones (London: Routledge and Kegan Paul, 1982), pp. 332–63.
142   Saville, interview, 8 June 1984.
143   Thompson, interview, in Henry Abelove et al., eds., *Visions of History*, p. 13.
144   Thompson, *William Morris* (1977), p. 810.

2. Socialism at Full Stretch

1   In the initial stage of research I benefited greatly from Richard Holden, "The First New Left in Britain: 1956–62," Ph.D. diss., University of Wisconsin, 1976.
2   Quoted in John Saville, "The XXth Congress and the British Communist Party," in Ralph Miliband and John Saville, eds., *Socialist Register 1976* (London: Merlin Press, 1976), p. 7.
3   Eric Hobsbawm, "1956: Gareth Stedman Jones Interviews Eric Hobsbawm," *Marxism Today*, November 1986, p. 19.

4   Hill, interview, 9 May 1984.

5   Malcolm MacEwen, "The Day the Party Had to Stop," in Miliband
    and Saville, eds., *Socialist Register 1976*, pp. 29–30. Of the commis-
    sion's fifteen members, ten were full-time Party officials, five of
    them members of the executive committee. The opposition con-
    sisted of Hill, Peter Cadogan, and Malcolm MacEwen.

6   Eric Hobsbawm et al., *New Statesman and Nation*, 1 December
    1956, p. 701. The list of signatories (in the order signed) consisted of
    Chimen Abramsky, E. J. Hobsbawm, Hyman Levy, Robert Brown-
    ing, Paul Hogarth, Jack Lindsay, Henry Collins, George Houston,
    Hugh MacDiarmid, Christopher Hill, V. G. Kiernan, Ronald L.
    Meek, R. H. Hilton, Doris Lessing, and E. A. Thompson.

7   John Saville, "Problems of the Communist Party," *World News*, 19
    May 1956, p. 314.

8   Edward Thompson, "Winter Wheat in Omsk," *World News*, 30
    June 1956, pp. 408–9.

9   Saville, "The XXth Congress," p. 4.

10 George Matthews, "A Caricature of Our Party," *World News*, 30
    June 1956, pp. 409–10.

11 John Saville and Edward Thompson, "Why We Are Publishing,"
    Reasoner, no. 1 (July 1956): 2.

12 E. P. Thompson, "Reply to George Matthews," *Reasoner*, no. 1
    (July 1956): 15.

13 Saville, "The XXth Congress," p. 12.

14 "Editorial," *Reasoner*, no. 3 (November 1956), p. 2. At the time
    of the Soviet invasion, the third issue of the *Reasoner* was substan-
    tially completed. The original editorial was replaced, and Thomp-
    son's passionate "Through the Smoke of Budapest" was added.
    An abridged version of this essay can be found in David Widgery,
    ed., *The Left in Britain, 1956–68* (Harmondsworth: Penguin Books,
    1976), pp. 66–72.

15 Hobsbawm, interview, 4 May 1984.

16 Hobsbawm, "1956," p. 23.

17 Hobsbawm, interview, in *Visions of History*, p. 33.

18 Saville and Thompson, "Why We Are Publishing," p. 5; Saville,
    "The XXth Congress," p. 8.

19 Editorial, *New Reasoner*, no. 1 (Summer 1957): 2.

20 E. P. Thompson, "Socialist Humanism: An Epistle to the Philis-
    tines," *New Reasoner*, no. 1 (Summer 1957): 108.

21 Ibid., p. 109.

22 Ibid., p. 122.

23 Ibid., p. 114.

24 Thompson, "Postscript: 1976," *William Morris* (1977), p. 810.

25 E. P. Thompson, *The Communism of William Morris* (London: Wil-
    liam Morris Society, 1965), p. 18. A lecture given to the Morris
    Society, 4 May 1959.

26 Ibid., p. 17.

27 Ibid., p. 18.

28   Stuart Hall, "The Politics of Adolescence," *Universities and Left Review (ULR)*, no. 6 (Spring 1959): 2.

29   Stuart Hall, interview, London, 22 June 1984.

30   Stuart Hall, "The 'First' New Left: Life and Times," in *Out of Apathy: Voices of the New Left Thirty Years On*, ed. the Oxford University Socialist Group (London: Verso, 1989), pp. 14–15.

31   Ibid., p. 17.

32   Editorial, *ULR*, no. 1 (Spring 1957): ii.

33   Stuart Hall, "The 'First' New Left," p. 20.

34   In addition, Stuart Hall (by now an adult education teacher in South London) and Samuel (a graduate student at the London School of Economics) were living there anyway. Stuart Hall, interview, University of Illinois, Champaign, 25 June 1983.

35   Editorial, *ULR*, no. 1 (Spring 1957): i–ii.

36   See Perry Anderson, "The Left in the Fifties," *New Left Review*, no. 29 (January–February 1965): 3–18.

37   Editorial, "*ULR* to *New Left Review*," *ULR*, no. 7 (Autumn 1959): 1.

38   Editorial, *ULR*, no. 4 (Summer 1958): 3.

39   Ibid.

40   Stuart Hall, "In the No Man's Land," *ULR*, no. 3 (Winter 1958): 87.

41   Anderson, quoted in "Conference Scrapbook," in Oxford University Socialist Group, ed., *Out of Apathy: Voices of the New Left*, p. 140.

42   Lynn Segal, "The Silence of Women in the New Left," in Oxford University Socialist Group, ed., *Out of Apathy: Voices of the New Left*, p. 115.

43   Stuart Hall, "In the No Man's Land," *ULR*, no. 3 (Winter 1958): 87.

44   E. P. Thompson, "Commitment and Politics," *ULR*, no. 6 (Spring 1959): 51.

45   Raymond Williams, "The New British Left," *Partisan Review* 27 (Spring 1960): 344.

46   Charles Taylor, "Marxism and Humanism," *New Reasoner*, no. 2 (Summer 1957): 98.

47   E. P. Thompson, "The Politics of Theory," in *People's History and Socialist Theory*, ed. Raphael Samuel (London: Routledge and Kegan Paul, 1981), p. 398.

48   E. P. Thompson, "A Psessay in Ephology," *New Reasoner*, no. 10 (Very Late Autumn 1959): 8.

49   Editorial, "*ULR* to *New Left Review*," *ULR*, no. 7 (Autumn 1959): 1.

50   For a detailed account of the CND, see Christopher Driver, *The Disarmers: A Study in Protest* (London: Hodder and Stoughton, 1964). For a historical overview of the peace and nuclear disarmament movement in Britain, see James Hinton, *Protests and Visions: Peace Politics in 20th Century Britain* (London: Hutchinson Radius, 1989).

51   David Widgery, "Don't You Hear the H-Bombs' Thunder?" in *The Left in Britain*, p. 104.

52   At the time the peace movement was labeled a Communist front. Although the CP was certainly one of its supporters, this accusation

was always a simplification. Thompson described the movement in West Yorkshire as a "genuine alliance" including people from the Labour Party, Left-wing pacifists, Communists, and trade unionists. E. P. Thompson, interview, in Henry Abelove et al., eds., *Visions of History*, p. 13. Thompson's view was confirmed by a non-Communist socialist historian, Asa Briggs, interview at Worcester College, Oxford University, 30 May 1984.

53   Thompson, "Socialist Humanism," p. 143.

54   Peter Worsley, "Non-alignment and the New Left," in Oxford University Socialist Group, ed., *Out of Apathy: Voices of the New Left*, pp. 88–89.

55   E. P. Thompson, "NATO, Neutralism and Survival," *ULR*, no. 4 (Summer 1958): 51.

56   The exception was the Fife Socialist League, one of the few New Left connections to the radical working-class movement. The league was a socialist organization, independent of Labour and the British CP, in one of the most radical areas of Scotland. Its founder, Lawrence Daly, who later became president of the National Union of Miners, unsuccessfully ran for a parliamentary seat in 1959 under its banner. See John Saville, "A Note on West Fife," *New Reasoner*, no. 10 (Very Late Autumn 1959): 9–13.

57   "Letters to Our Readers," *New Reasoner*, no. 6 (Summer 1958): 137.

58   Stuart Hall, interview, London, 12 May 1984.

59   Retrospectively, Miliband believed "that the demise of the *New Reasoner* was an opportunity forsaken to develop something important in and for the labour movement." Ralph Miliband, "John Saville: A Presentation," in *Ideology and the Labour Movement: Essays Presented to John Saville*, ed. David E. Martin and David Rubinstein (London: Croom Helm, 1979), p. 27.

60   Stuart Hall, interview, 22 June 1984; Thompson, interview, 10 May 1984. Saville came over to Miliband's view and believed his own papers at the time proved his view was much the same. Saville, interview, 8 June 1984. Not only did Hall disagree with this contention, but Miliband seemed to as well. "I also recall Saville arguing with me that I was wrong, simply on the grounds of practicality: the journal, he believed, could not have been kept going." Miliband, "John Saville," p. 27.

61   Stuart Hall, interview, 12 May 1984.

62   Holden, "The First New Left," p. 249.

63   E. P. Thompson, "A Psessay in Ephology," p. 5.

64   This number was small, however, when compared to the *Tribune*, the Labour Left newspaper, which had a circulation approximately four times greater. Holden, "The First New Left," p. 325.

65   The original editorial board consisted of Ken Alexander, D. G. Arnott, Michael Barratt Brown, Norman Birnbaum, Alfred Dressler, Alan Hall, Mervyn Jones, Michael Kullmann, Doris Lessing, Alan Lovell, Malcolm MacEwen, Alasdair MacIntyre, Ralph Miliband, Ronald Meek, Gabriel Pearson, John Rex, Raphael Samuel,

John Saville, Charles Taylor, Dorothy Thompson, Edward Thompson, Raymond Williams, and Peter Worsley. Additions in the first two years included Paul Hogarth, Lawrence Daly, Nick Faith, Paddy Whannel, and Dennis Butt.

66 In a 1961 memorandum to the editorial board and Left Clubs Committee, Thompson vividly portrayed the hectic life of the *NLR* editor. "To many people, especially in London, the Editor *is* the New Left; and his telephone number is the only means of communication with the New Left. If CND wants co-operation, they ring Stuart. Contributors, London Club members, foreign visitors or provincial readers may ring or drop in. Correspondence comes in to Stuart or Frances [*NLR*'s business manager] which may contain matters which need to be dealt with under a dozen heads: the same letter might have subscription details, proposals on activities, information about Left Clubs, editorial comment and so on. Stuart himself is on demand seven days a week to speak, to talk over Club or student problems, to meet contributors, to visit provincial Clubs or student societies, and so on." E. P. Thompson, Memorandum to the Editorial Board, 1961, Alan Hall Papers. (These papers were made available to the author by Mr. Hall.)

67 The details of the relationship between this triumvirate were derived mainly from conversations with Stuart Hall, but nothing he told me was contradicted by either Thompson or Saville.

68 Simon Rosenblat, "Report on New Left Clubs," 1960, Hall Papers.

69 Minutes of the *NLR* Editorial Board, 8 and 9 October 1960, Hall Papers.

70 Editorial, *NLR*, no. 1 (January–February 1960): 2.

71 John Saville, Memo to Editorial Board on Board Meetings, 1960, Hall Papers.

72 Editorial, *NLR*, no. 1, p. 1.

73 E. P. Thompson, "Revolution Again! Or Shut Your Ears and Run," *NLR*, no. 6 (November–December 1960): 19.

74 Thompson acknowledged the disappointment that readers felt with the book. "Insiders—readers of *NLR* and members of Left Clubs— were no less impatient to find a standard around which to rally—a crisp statement of aims—something to join, something to fight for, something to *do*. And hence the cloudburst of frustration which descended on our heads" (ibid).

75 "Revolution" appeared in both *Out of Apathy* and *NLR*, no. 3. The *NLR* edition will be cited.

76 E. P. Thompson, "Revolution," *NLR*, no. 3 (May–June 1960): 7.

77 Ibid., p. 8.

78 Ibid., p. 9.

79 Ibid.

80 Thompson, "Revolution Again!" p. 30.

81 Although Thompson had probably read some Gramsci at this point, it was not until the 1970s that he was really influenced by him. This is underscored by his inexpert critique of Perry Anderson's inter-

pretation of Gramsci in "The Peculiarities of the English" (1965), *The Poverty of Theory and Other Essays* (London: Merlin Press, 1978), pp. 72–74.

82   Thompson, "Revolution," p. 8.

83   See Hinton, *Protests and Visions*, pp. 163–65.

84   Richard Taylor, *Against the Bomb: The British Peace Movement, 1958–65* (Oxford: Clarendon Press, 1988), p. 222.

85   Peggy Duff, *Left, Left, Left: A Personal Account of Six Protest Campaigns, 1945–65* (London: Allison and Busby, 1971), p. 128.

86   Stuart Hall, interview at the University of Wisconsin, Madison, 23 September 1985.

87   "Missing Signposts," *NLR*, no. 6 (November–December 1960): 9.

88   Alston, quoted in E. P. Thompson, Memorandum to Editorial Board and Left Clubs Committee, 1961, Hall Papers.

89   "Notes to Readers," *NLR*, no. 12 (November–December 1961): inside cover.

90   Stuart Hall, interview, 23 September 1985. According to Raphael Samuel and Dennis Butts, the circulation of the journal was even less—about half of *ULR* and the *New Reasoner* combined, which would place it at about 5,000. Samuel and Butts, A Letter to Members of the *NLR* Editorial Board, 14 July 1961, p. 2, Hall Papers.

91   Ibid., p. 4.

92   According to Samuel and Butts, Saville and Thompson offered their resignations at the same time. They, too, were dissuaded. Ibid.

93   Stuart Hall, interview, 23 September 1985.

94   Perhaps the most successful consisted of Perry Anderson, Butts, Mervyn Jones, Gabriel Pearson, and Samuel, a collection of different generations and points of view. Despite division and conflict, this team was able to produce one of the most stimulating early issues of *NLR*, a double issue concerned with Britain's critical housing problems. *NLR*, no. 13–14 (January–April 1962).

95   *NLR* was running deficits of between £1,000–2,000 a year. It was saved from bankruptcy in 1962 by a contribution of £1,500 by an anonymous donor, presumably Perry Anderson. Minutes of the *NLR* Editorial Board, 26–27 January 1963, Hall Papers.

96   Undoubtedly, Anderson thought of the *NLR* editorship as representing a radical intellectual and political practice, but it was perhaps also true, as he once told Alan Hall, that it was a means of acquiring a profession. Alan Hall, interview, London, 20 June 1984.

97   Edward Thompson to Alan Hall, 22 May 1962, Hall Papers. In the same letter Thompson wrote: "All I *think* I am trying to do now is effect some kind of transition which leaves a continuing journal, a stronger London group, and which does not just sign over the review lock-stock-and-barrel to Perry: which *does* seem to me to be somehow wrong and irresponsible."

98   Minutes of the *NLR* Editorial Board, 7 April 1963, Hall Papers. The minutes of the meeting were produced by Edward Thompson. They were in fact a summary of the two sessions, though the quotes

surrounding Anderson's feelings about the board suggest an actual phrase used.

99 I am indebted to Stuart Hall's discussion of the New Left in "Then and Now: A Re-evaluation of the New Left," in Oxford University Socialist Group, ed., *Out of Apathy: Voices of the New Left*, pp. 150–53.

100 Hall is cited speaking at a preelection CND meeting in 1964 by Peggy Duff in *Left, Left, Left*, p. 197.

101 Michael Rustin, "The New Left as a Social Movement," in Oxford University Socialist Group, ed., *Out of Apathy: Voices of the New Left*, p. 126.

3. Culture Is Ordinary

1 See Perry Anderson's essay, "Components of the National Culture" (1968), *NLR*, no. 50 (July–August 1968): 3–57.

2 See Francis Mulhern, *The Moment of "Scrutiny"* (London: NLB, 1979), pp. 63–72.

3 T. S. Eliot, *Notes Towards the Definition of Culture* (New York: Harcourt Brace Jovanovich, 1949), p. 30.

4 See also Richard Hoggart, *The Uses of Literacy* (Harmondsworth: Penguin Books, 1958), p. 82.

5 Ibid., p. 340.

6 Richard Hoggart, "Speaking to Each Other," in *Conviction*, ed. Norman Mackenzie (London: MacGibbon and Kee, 1958), p. 124.

7 Hoggart, *The Uses of Literacy*, p. 323.

8 Ibid., p. 64.

9 I am indebted here to a new introduction to Hoggart's book: Andrew Goodwin, introduction to *The Uses of Literacy* (New Brunswick, N.J.: Transaction, 1992), pp. xiii–xxxix.

10 Hoggart, *The Uses of Literacy* (1958), p. 232.

11 Reyner Banham, "The Atavism of the Short-Distance Mini-Cyclist" (1964), in *Design by Choice*, ed. Penny Sparke (New York: Rizzoli, 1981), p. 84.

12 Raymond Williams, "Notes on Marxism in Britain Since 1945" (1976), in his *Problems in Materialism and Culture: Selected Essays* (London: Verso, 1980), p. 242.

13 Editorial, "For Continuity in Change," *Politics and Letters* 1 (Summer 1947): 4.

14 Raymond Williams, "The Soviet Literary Controversy in Retrospect," *Politics and Letters* 1 (Summer 1947): 25.

15 Williams was never clear as to what these differences were. He did, however, make it clear that the journal did not collapse because of editorial differences. Williams, *Politics and Letters: Interviews with "New Left Review"* (London: NLB, 1979), p. 74.

16 Ibid., p. 77.

17 Ibid., p. 97.

18 Raymond Williams, *Culture and Society, 1780–1950* (New York: Harper and Row, 1966), p. 328.

19   Williams, *Politics and Letters*, p. 99.

20   Ibid., p. 97.

21   See, for instance, Raymond Williams, "Our Debt to Dr. Leavis," *Critical Quarterly* 1 (Autumn 1959): 245–47.

22   Raymond Williams, "Culture Is Ordinary" (1958), in his *Resources of Hope* (London: Verso, 1989), p. 9.

23   Williams, *Culture and Society*, p. 256.

24   Ibid., p. 260.

25   Later, Williams's view of the conflict between *Scrutiny* and Marxism was that the former had decisively won the thirties' cultural debate. See Williams, "Literature and Sociology: In Memory of Lucien Goldmann" (1971), *Problems in Materialism and Culture: Selected Essays* (London: Verso, 1980), pp. 18–19.

26   Williams, "Culture Is Ordinary," p. 7.

27   Williams, *Culture and Society*, p. 283.

28   Ibid., p. 300.

29   Williams, "Culture Is Ordinary," p. 13.

30   Raymond Williams, *The Long Revolution* (London: Chatto and Windus, 1961; reprint ed., Westport, Conn.: Greenwood Press, 1975), p. x.

31   Raymond Williams, *Communications*, 3d ed. (Harmondsworth: Penguin Books, 1976), p. 10.

32   Williams, *The Long Revolution*, p. 46.

33   Ibid., p. 48. Williams introduced the concept in "Film and the Dramatic Tradition," in Michael Orrom and Raymond Williams, *Preface to Film* (London: Film Drama, 1954), pp. 21–22. Williams wrote the essay just cited, while Orrom was responsible for the book's other essay, "Film and Dramatic Techniques."

34   Williams, *The Long Revolution*, p. 63.

35   Raymond Williams, "London Letter," *Partisan Review* 27 (Spring 1960): 345.

36   The extent to which a book like *Culture and Society* fulfilled a genuine need on the Left can be seen from Asa Briggs's comments written before he read Williams's book. Briggs called for "a critical study of values, of the re-shaping of modern society as a whole, at least since the time of the double shock of the French and Industrial Revolutions. It was then that the context of commitment was radically changed, and in the writings of the early romantics many issues which remain fresh and relevant were posed for the first time." Briggs, "The Context of Commitment," *New Statesman*, 4 October 1958, p. 453.

37   Introduction to "The Uses of Literacy: Working Class Culture," *ULR*, no. 2 (Summer 1957): 29.

38   Ibid., p. 31.

39   Ibid., p. 32.

40   Stuart Hall, "A Sense of Classlessness," *ULR*, no. 5 (Autumn 1958): 27.

41   Ibid., p. 29.

42 Ibid., p. 31.

43 Thompson, "Commitment and Politics," *ULR*, no. 6 (Spring 1959): 51, 55.

44 C. Wright Mills, "The New Left" (1960), *Power, Politics and People: The Collected Essays of C. Wright Mills* (New York: Oxford University Press, 1963), p. 256.

45 The review was published in two parts: E. P. Thompson, "The Long Revolution," *NLR*, no. 9 (May–June 1961): 24–33; and "The Long Revolution II," *NLR*, no. 10 (July–August 1961): 34–39. In the second part, between pp. 34 and 35 as printed in *NLR*, a page is missing; it appeared at the end of *NLR*, no. 11 (September–October 1961), without a page number.

46 Thompson, "The Long Revolution," p. 27.

47 Thompson, "The Long Revolution II," p. 39.

48 Thompson, "The Long Revolution," p. 30.

49 Thompson, "The Long Revolution II," p. 35.

50 See Williams's comments in *Politics and Letters*, p. 363.

51 Ibid., p. 135.

52 Ibid., pp. 135–36.

53 Thompson, "The Long Revolution II," p. 38.

54 Thompson, *The Making of the English Working Class* (Harmondsworth: Penguin Books, 1980), p. 9.

55 Ibid., p. 8.

56 Thompson, "Revolution Again! Or Shut Your Ears and Run," *NLR*, no. 6 (November–December 1960): 24.

57 Thompson, *The Making of the English Working Class*, pp. 230, 214.

58 Thompson, "The Long Revolution," p. 25.

59 Ibid., p. 24.

60 Thompson, *The Making of the English Working Class*, p. 915.

61 Ibid., p. 213.

62 Victor Kiernan, "Culture and Society," *New Reasoner*, no. 9 (Summer 1959): 79.

63 Robin Blackburn, "A Brief History of *New Left Review*, 1960–1990," in *Thirty Years of "New Left Review": Index to Numbers 1–184* (London: New Left Review, 1992), p. vi.

64 Perry Anderson, *Arguments Within English Marxism* (London: Verso, 1980), p. 151.

65 For Nairn's complementary approach, see his "The Nature of the Labour Party," in *Towards Socialism*, ed. Perry Anderson and Robin Blackburn (Ithaca, N.Y.: Cornell University Press, 1966), pp. 159–217, and "The English Working Class," in *Ideology in Social Science: Readings in Critical Social Theory*, ed. Robin Blackburn (London: Fontana, 1972), pp. 187–206. Nairn's importance to the development of Anderson's ideas is recalled in the foreword to Perry Anderson, *English Questions* (London: Verso, 1992), p. 3.

66 Anderson, "The Left in the Fifties," *NLR*, no. 29 (January–February 1965): 17.

67 Anderson, foreword to *English Questions*, p. 3.

68   Ibid., pp. 2–3.
69   Perry Anderson, "Origins of the Present Crisis," in Anderson and Blackburn, eds., *Towards Socialism*, p. 15.
70   Ibid., p. 36.
71   Ibid., p. 29.
72   Ibid., p. 21.
73   Ibid., p. 30.
74   Minutes of the *NLR* Editorial Board, 27 January 1963, Hall Papers.
75   Edward Thompson to Perry Anderson, 10 May 1963, Hall Papers.
76   Anderson, *Arguments Within English Marxism*, p. 135.
77   Minutes of the *NLR* Editorial Board, 7 April 1963.
78   Thompson to Anderson, 10 May 1963.
79   Alan Hall's position was made clear in a letter to Thompson. "Your proposals overlook two salient features of our history. First, the Review was saved from collapse and bankruptcy a year ago by Perry becoming Editor and paying the immediately pressing debts. Second, his subsidies continue to keep the Review going. In the face of this, has any group of 'old Board' members the right to demand that the Review be hived off, and a proportion of the total remaining resources allocated to their projects?" Alan Hall to Thompson, 21 May 1963, Hall Papers.
80   Edward Thompson to Ralph Miliband and Alan Hall, 5 December 1963, Hall Papers; Thompson, interview, 10 May 1984.
81   Anderson, *Arguments Within English Marxism*, p. 138.
82   Edward Thompson to Alan Hall, 25 February 1963, Hall Papers.
83   E. P. Thompson, "The Peculiarities of the English," in *Socialist Register 1965*, ed. John Saville and Ralph Miliband (New York: Monthly Review Press, 1965), pp. 311–62. A slightly altered version appeared in *The Poverty of Theory* (1978). It includes passages the editors convinced Thompson to omit because they were too inflammatory (p. 399). I have quoted from the 1978 version.
84   Thompson, "The Peculiarities of the English," p. 86.
85   Anderson, "The Left in the Fifties," p. 16.
86   Anderson, "Socialism and Pseudo-Empiricism," *NLR*, no. 35 (January–February 1966): 33.
87   Ibid., p. 34.
88   Ibid., p. 39.
89   Thompson, "The Peculiarities of the English," p. 64.
90   Ibid. In the 1965 version the sentence reads slightly differently, specifying "Sartreian neologisms," p. 337.
91   Ibid., pp. 87–88.
92   Despite his interest in Western Marxism, Anderson's analysis of political power echoed Marxists of the classical age from Marx and Engels to Lenin, Luxemburg, and Trotsky. One of his early influences was Isaac Deutscher, a historian with roots in the classical tradition. Robin Blackburn, interview, London, 4 May 1984.
93   Stuart Hall, "Cultural Studies: Two Paradigms," *Media, Culture and Society* 2 (1980): 57.

94 Richard Hoggart, "Literature and Society," in *Speaking to Each Other*, vol. 2: *About Literature* (New York: Oxford University Press, 1970), p. 34.

95 This is recalled by Stuart Hall, "Cultural Studies and the Centre: Some Problematics and Problems," in *Culture, Media, Language: Working Papers in Cultural Studies, 1972–79*, ed. Stuart Hall et al. (London: Hutchinson, 1980), pp. 21–22.

96 F. R. Leavis and Denys Thompson, *Culture and Environment: The Training of Critical Awareness* (London: Chatto and Windus, 1933).

97 Stuart Hall and Paddy Whannel, *The Popular Arts* (Boston: Beacon Press, 1967), p. 24.

98 Ibid., p. 47.

99 Ibid., p. 273.

100 Ibid., p. 302.

101 Ibid., pp. 311–12.

102 Centre for Contemporary Cultural Studies (hereafter CCCS), *Third Report: 1965–66* (Birmingham: CCCS, 1966), p. 8.

103 Among the thinkers considered by the Centre to be part of this tradition were Saint-Simon, Comte, Marx, Durkheim, Weber, Tönnies, and Mannheim. Why it is described as solely a German tradition is not completely clear. Richard Hoggart and Stuart Hall, introduction to Alan Shuttleworth, *Two Working Papers in Cultural Studies*, Occasional Paper no. 2 (Birmingham: CCCS, 1966), p. 2.

104 Ibid., p. 24.

105 Ibid., p. 44.

106 Hall, "Cultural Studies and the Centre," pp. 23–24.

107 CCCS, *Fourth Report: 1966–67* (Birmingham: CCCS, 1968), p. 29.

108 See, for instance, Tim Moore, *Claude Lévi-Strauss and the Cultural Sciences*, Occasional Paper no. 4 (Birmingham: CCCS, 1968).

109 CCCS, *Sixth Report: 1969–71* (Birmingham: CCCS, 1971), p. 5.

110 A. C. H. Smith with Elizabeth Immirzi and Trevor Blackwell, *Paper Voices*, with an introduction by Stuart Hall (Totowa, N.J.: Rowman and Littlefield, 1975).

4. Between Structuralism and Humanism

1 Rustin, "The New Left as a Social Movement," in Oxford University Socialist Group, ed., *Out of Apathy: Voices of the New Left Thirty Years On* (London: Verso, 1989), p. 125.

2 Eric Hobsbawm, "The Forward March of Labour Halted?" in *The Forward March of Labour Halted?*, ed. Martin Jacques and Francis Mulhern (London: Verso, in association with *Marxism Today*, 1981), pp. 1–19.

3 See Ronald Fraser, *1968: A Student Generation in Revolt* (London: Chatto and Windus, 1988), p. 251; David Widgery, *The Left in Britain, 1956–68* (Harmondsworth: Penguin Books, 1976), p. 479; and Tariq Ali, *The Coming British Revolution* (London: Jonathan Cape, 1972), p. 140. I found Nigel Fountain's *Underground: The London Alternative Press, 1966–74* (London: Routledge, 1988), espe-

cially useful. Significantly, the first issue of *Black Dwarf* began with vol. 13, no. 1, continuing the numbering of its predecessor—a sign of its wish to extend an earlier phase of British radicalism.

4   In addition to Ali (an IMG member and a leader of the student movement) the editorial board included Rowbotham, Bob Rowthorn, and Fred Halliday (members of the *NLR* editorial board), Clive Goodwin, and Adrian Mitchell (a libertarian socialist).

5   Ali, *The Coming British Revolution*, pp. 140–42; and John Callaghan, *British Trotskyism: Theory and Practice* (Oxford: Basil Blackwell, 1984), p. 133.

6   See David Caute, *The Year of the Barricades: A Journey Through 1968* (New York: Harper and Row, 1988), pp. 349–50, and Robert Hewison, *Too Much: Art and Society in the Sixties, 1960–75* (New York: Oxford University Press, 1987), pp. 155–57.

7   Elzey, quoted in Hewison, *Too Much*, p. 156.

8   According to Birmingham Centre researchers, 1969 marked the "partial politicization" of the counterculture, an example of which was the 144 Piccadilly Squat by the London Street Commune. "It was consciously planned as an 'improvisation' designed to bring together several different tributaries of the counterculture: quasi-anarchists, political 'hard men,' hippie drop-outs, working-class lay-abouts, hard-core bohemians, and the Hell's Angels." Stuart Hall et. al., *Policing the Crisis: Mugging, the State, and Law and Order* (New York: Holmes and Meir, 1978), p. 252.

9   Anderson, *Arguments Within English Marxism*, p. 152.

10   Ibid.

11   Quoted in Caute, *The Year of the Barricades*, pp. 355–56. See also Fraser, *1968*, p. 251, and Widgery, *The Left in Britain*, pp. 382–88.

12   See Caute, *The Year of the Barricades*, pp. 346–48. But also see David Triesman, "Essex," *NLR*, no. 50 (July–August 1968): 70–71.

13   Caute, *The Year of the Barricades*, p. 371.

14   David Fernbach, "Strategy and Struggle," *NLR*, no. 53 (January–February 1969): 41.

15   I am indebted here to the discussion in Caute, *The Year of the Barricades*, pp. 33–38.

16   The most notable instances were the activism of Robin Blackburn (discussed above) and Tom Nairn, who was involved in Hornsey College protests and (like Blackburn) lost his position as a result. But contributors to *NLR* also were involved in the VSC and the Revolutionary Socialist Students' Federation (RSSF) among other activities.

17   Widgery, *The Left in Britain*, p. 513.

18   The editorial board in 1968, in addition to its editor, Perry Anderson, included Anthony Barnett, Robin Blackburn, Ben Brewster, Alexander Cockburn, Ronald Fraser, Jon Halliday, Nicolas Krassó, Branka Magas, Juliet Mitchell, Roger Murray, Tom Nairn, Lucien Rey, Bob Rowthorn, Gareth Stedman Jones, and Tom Wengraf. In 1968, Anderson was twenty-eight; Nairn was thirty; Stedman

Jones was twenty-six; Blackburn was twenty-seven; Rowthorn was twenty-five; Mitchell was twenty-eight; Cockburn was twenty-eight. I am indebted here to the research buried in the notes of Lin Chun, *The British New Left* (Edinburgh: University of Edinburgh Press, 1993).

19 This view of *NLR* was not universally shared. To quote Widgery again: "Although the ostensible aim of these analytical imports was to raise the lamentable theoretical level of British Marxism, the educational operation was carried out with such pomp, pretentiousness and deliberate obscurity that it probably served to retard, distort and discredit Marxist thinking, and was indeed positive incitement to philistinism." Widgery, *The Left in Britain*, p. 512.

20 Nairn quoted in "Editorial Introduction," *NLR*, no. 52 (November–December 1968): 7.

21 "Themes," *NLR*, no. 50 (July–August 1968): 1.

22 Mandel, quoted in Peter Shipley, *Revolutionaries in Modern Britain* (London: Bodley Head, 1976), p. 115.

23 Perry Anderson, "Components of the National Culture," *NLR*, no. 50 (July–August 1968): 3.

24 Ibid., p. 4.

25 Ibid., p. 3.

26 Richard Merton, "Comment," *NLR*, no. 47 (January–February 1968): 31.

27 Robin Blackburn, "A Brief Guide to Bourgeois Ideology," in *Student Power: Problems, Diagnosis, Action*, ed. Alexander Cockburn and Robin Blackburn (Harmondsworth: Penguin Books in association with *NLR*, 1969), p. 163.

28 Ibid., p. 213.

29 Gareth Stedman Jones, "History: The Poverty of Empiricism," in *Ideology in Social Science: Readings in Critical Social Theory*, ed. Robin Blackburn (London: Fontana, 1972), p. 115.

30 Ibid.

31 Anderson, "Components of the National Culture," p. 6.

32 Ibid., p. 13.

33 The two notable exceptions where English thinkers dominated their fields were Keynes in economics (although Anderson noted that he had no clear successors) and Leavis in literary criticism, whose influence was critical to the development of Raymond Williams's thought. Ibid., pp. 35–36, 50, 55–56.

34 Ibid., p. 19.

35 Many of them were subsequently collected in *Western Marxism: A Critical Reader*, ed. New Left Review (London: Verso, 1978). Indeed, it was this volume that Anderson's *Considerations on Western Marxism* was originally to serve as an introduction.

36 Perry Anderson, *Considerations on Western Marxism* (London: NLB, 1976), pp. 52–53.

37 Chun, *The British New Left*, p. 110.

38 Anderson, *Considerations on Western Marxism*, p. 69.

39   Ibid., p. 96.

40   Ibid.

41   Anderson, *Arguments Within English Marxism*, p. 155.

42   Wainwright, quoted in Fraser, *1968*, p. 326.

43   Blackburn, quoted in ibid., pp. 325–26.

44   "Radical Philosophy Group," *Radical Philosophy*, no. 3 (Winter 1972), inside cover.

45   Editorial, *Radical Science Journal*, no. 6/7 (1978): 3.

46   Paul Q. Hirst, "Anderson's Balance Sheet," in *Marxism and Historical Writing* (London: Routledge and Kegan Paul, 1985), p. 5.

47   Stuart Hall, "A Critical Survey of the Theoretical and Practical Achievements of the Last Ten Years," *Literature, Society and the Sociology of Literature: Proceedings of the Conference Held at the University of Essex, July 1976*, ed. Francis Barker et al. (Essex: University of Essex, 1977), p. 6.

48   Stuart Hall, "The Formation of Cultural Studies," to be included in Stuart Hall (with J. Slack and L. Grossberg) *Cultural Studies* (forthcoming), ms. p. 30.

49   Stuart Hall, *The Hippies: An American "Moment,"* Stencilled Occasional Paper no. 16 (Birmingham: CCCS, 1968), p. 29.

50   The Centre's move from "idealism" to "materialism" was at first controversial. See the debate between Alan Shuttleworth, "People and Culture," and Stuart Hall, "A Response to 'People and Culture,'" in *Working Papers in Cultural Studies*, no. 1 (Spring 1971).

51   Hall, "Cultural Studies and Its Theoretical Legacies," in Lawrence Grossberg, Cary Nelson, and Paula Treichler, eds., *Cultural Studies* (New York: Routledge, 1992), p. 280.

52   Graeme Turner, *British Cultural Studies: An Introduction* (Boston: Unwin Hyman, 1990), p. 15.

53   See, for instance, Bob Lumley and Michael O'Shaughnessey, "Media and Cultural Studies," in *Developing Contemporary Marxism*, ed. Zygmunt G. Baránski and John R. Short (New York: St. Martin's Press, 1985), pp. 268–92; Janet Woollacott, "Messages and Meanings," in Michael Gurevitch et al., eds., *Culture, Society and the Media* (London: Methuen, 1982), pp. 91–111.

54   See, for instance, Peter Golding and Graham Murdock, "Ideology and the Mass Media: The Question of Determination," in *Ideology and Cultural Production*, ed. Michèle Barrett et al. (London: Croom Helm, 1979), pp. 198–224. For a concrete example of this approach, see Graham Murdock, "Large Corporations and the Control of the Communications Industries," in Gurevitch et al., eds., *Culture, Society, and the Media*, pp. 118–50.

55   Anthony Easthope, *British Post-Structuralism Since 1968* (London: Routledge, 1988), p. 35.

56   Colin MacCabe, "Class of '68: Elements of an Intellectual Autobiography," in his *Tracking the Signifier: Theoretical Essays: Film, Linguistics, Literature* (Minneapolis: University of Minnesota Press, 1985), p. 16.

57 There were important divisions among *Screen* contributors. Indeed, the adoption of Lacanian psychoanalysis produced intense disagreements and led to the resignations of several board members. For the background to these arguments, see ibid., pp. 11–12.

58 Laura Mulvey, "Visual Pleasure and Narrative Cinema," *Screen* 16 (Autumn 1975): 11–12.

59 Ibid., p. 12.

60 Ibid., p. 18.

61 Rosalind Coward, "Class, 'Culture' and the Social Formation," *Screen* 18 (Spring 1977): 87, 90.

62 Iain Chambers et al., "Marxism and Culture," *Screen* 18 (Winter 1977–78): 115.

63 Rosalind Coward, "Response," ibid., p. 122.

64 Marx, *The Eighteenth Brumaire of Louis Bonaparte*, in Robert C. Tucker, ed., *The Marx-Engels Reader*, 2d ed. (New York: W. W. Norton, 1978), p. 595.

65 Williams, quoted in Alan O'Connor, *Raymond Williams: Writing, Culture, Politics* (London: Basil Blackwell, 1989), p. 20.

66 See O'Connor's discussion in ibid., pp. 22–23. But also see Fred Inglis, *Raymond Williams* (London: Routledge, 1995), pp. 196–209.

67 Raymond Williams, "Literature and Sociology: In Memory of Lucien Goldmann," *Problems in Materialism and Culture: Selected Essays* (London: Verso, 1980), p. 18.

68 Raymond Williams, *Marxism and Literature* (Oxford: Oxford University Press, 1977), p. 5.

69 I have benefited here from Stuart Hall's reading of this essay in "A Critical Survey of the Theoretical and Practical Achievements of the Last Ten Years," p. 2.

70 Williams, "Literature and Sociology," p. 22.

71 Raymond Williams, "Base and Superstructure in Marxist Cultural Theory," in his *Problems in Materialism and Culture*, p. 34.

72 Ibid., p. 31.

73 Williams, *Marxism and Literature*, pp. 87–88.

74 Ibid., p. 110.

75 Williams, "Base and Superstructure in Marxist Cultural Theory," p. 41.

76 CCCS, *Eighth Report: 1974–76* (Birmingham: CCCS, 1976), p. 6.

77 Stuart Hall, "Cultural Studies: Two Paradigms," *Media, Culture and Society*, no. 2 (1980), p. 69.

78 Some of the publications associated with the group are Stanley Cohen, ed. *Images of Deviance* (Harmondsworth: Penguin Books, 1971); Ian Taylor, Paul Walton, and Jock Young, *The New Criminology: For a Social Theory of Deviance* (London: Routledge and Kegan Paul, 1973); and Ian Taylor, Paul Walton, and Jock Young, eds., *Critical Criminology* (London: Routledge and Kegan Paul, 1975).

79 Stanley Cohen, "Criminology and the Sociology of Deviance in Britain," in Paul Rock and Mary McIntosh, eds., *Deviance and Social Control* (London: Tavistock, 1974), p. 28.

80   Paul Willis, *Profane Culture* (London: Routledge and Kegan Paul, 1978), pp. 84–85.

81   Ibid., p. 177.

82   Ibid., p. 182.

83   Paul Willis, "The Cultural Meaning of Drug Use," in Stuart Hall and Tony Jefferson, eds., *Resistance Through Rituals: Youth Subcultures in Post-War Britain* (London: Hutchinson, 1977), p. 107. Although an expanded version of this essay appears in *Profane Culture*, I have chosen to quote from this early version, which was published in 1975 and is probably closer to Willis's dissertation.

84   Ibid., p. 115.

85   The two notable exceptions to this were Willis's "The Cultural Meaning of Drug Use," pp. 106–18, and Paul Corrigan, "Doing Nothing," pp. 103–7.

86   For the sake of convenience, I am quoting from the more widely available, though edited, version of the essay: Phil Cohen, "Subcultural Conflict and Working-Class Community," in Stuart Hall et al., eds., *Culture, Media, Language* (London: Hutchinson, 1980), pp. 82–83.

87   John Clarke, "Skinheads and the Magical Recovery of Community," in Hall and Jefferson, eds., *Resistance Through Rituals*, p. 99.

88   Ibid., p. 100.

89   John Clarke, *The Skinheads and the Study of Youth Culture*, Stencilled Occasional Paper no. 23 (Birmingham: CCCS, 1973), p. 12.

90   John Clarke and Tony Jefferson, *The Politics of Popular Culture: Culture and Sub-Culture*, Stencilled Occasional Paper no. 14 (Birmingham: CCCS, 1973), p. 9.

91   See the critique of the Centre's work made by Graham Murdock and Robin McCron, "Consciousness of Class and Consciousness of Generation," in Hall and Jefferson, eds., *Resistance Through Rituals*, pp. 203–7.

92   Paul Willis, *Learning to Labor: How Working-Class Kids Get Working-Class Jobs* (New York: Columbia University Press, 1981), p. 113.

93   See Michael Apple's review of *Learning to Labour*, "What Correspondence Theories of the Hidden Curriculum Miss," *Review of Education* 5 (Spring 1979): 101–12.

94   Angela McRobbie, "Settling Accounts with Subcultures: A Feminist Critique," *Screen Education*, no. 34 (Spring 1980): 41.

95   Clarke et al., "Subcultures, Cultures and Class: A Theoretical Overview," in Hall and Jefferson, eds., *Resistance Through Rituals*, p. 10.

96   Ibid., p. 66.

97   Coward, "Class, 'Culture,' and the Social Formation," p. 88.

98   Ibid., p. 95.

99   I am indebted to Lawrence Grossberg for pointing me toward this line of thought.

100 Dick Hebdige, *Subculture: The Meaning of Style* (London: Methuen, 1979), p. 56.

101 Ibid., p. 121.

102   Ibid., p. 126.

103   Ibid., p. 140.

104   I have relied on Paul Willis's account in "What Is News: A Case Study," *Working Papers in Cultural Studies*, no. 1 (Spring 1971): 14–16. I have also benefited from conversations with Lawrence Grossberg and Stuart Hall.

105   Willis, "What Is News," p. 13.

106   Stuart Hall, "Deviancy, Politics, and the Media," in Rock and McIntosh, eds., *Deviance and Social Control*, p. 277.

107   Ibid., p. 300.

108   Stuart Hall, "Encoding/Decoding," in Hall et al., eds., *Culture, Media, Language*, p. 134.

109   Frank Parkin, *Class Inequality and Political Order* (London: Macgibbon and Kee, 1971).

110   Hall, "Encoding/Decoding," p. 135.

111   Stuart Hall, "The Rediscovery of 'Ideology': Return of the Repressed in Media Studies," in Gurevitch et al., eds., *Culture, Society and the Media*, p. 78.

112   Hall et al., *Policing the Crisis*, p. 60.

113   I was reminded how remarkable this insight was by Michael Bérubé, "Pop Goes the Academy: Cult Studs Fight the Power," *Village Voice Literary Supplement*, no. 104 (April 1992): 11.

114   This is recalled by Stuart Hall in "Cultural Studies and Its Theoretical Legacies," p. 282.

115   Hall et al., *Policing the Crisis*, p. 394.

116   Ibid., p. 393.

117   Lawrence Grossberg, "The Formations of Cultural Studies: An American in Birmingham," in *Relocating Cultural Studies: Developments in Theory and Research*, ed. Valda Blundell, John Shepard, and Ian Taylor (London: Routledge, 1993), p. 49. I have benefited from this essay as well as Grossberg's "History, Politics and Postmodernism: Stuart Hall and Cultural Studies," *Journal of Communication Inquiry* 10 (Summer 1986): 68–70.

118   Stuart Hall, "Notes on Deconstructing 'the Popular,'" in Raphael Samuel, ed., *People's History and Socialist Theory* (London: Routledge and Kegan Paul, 1981), p. 239.

119   Stuart Hall, "Cultural Studies and Its Theoretical Legacies," pp. 282–83. For a firsthand account of the impact of feminism at the Centre, see Charlotte Brunsdon, "A Thief in the Night: Stories of Feminism in the 1970s at CCCS," in David Morley and Kuan-Hsing Chen, eds., *Stuart Hall: Critical Dialogues in Cultural Studies* (London: Routledge, 1996), pp. 276–86. For Hall himself, the eruption of feminism at the Centre would prove not only theoretically and politically challenging, but it would play an important role in his decision to leave the Centre in 1979. See "The Formation of a Diasporic Intellectual: An Interview with Stuart Hall by Kuan-Hsing Chen," in ibid., p. 500.

120   Editorial Group, "Women's Studies Group: Trying to Do Feminist

Intellectual Work," in Women's Studies Group, *Women Take Issue: Aspects of Women's Subordination* (London: Hutchinson, 1978), pp. 7, 11.

121   Ibid.

122   Ibid., p. 7.

123   Helen Butcher et al., *Images of Women in the Media*, Stencilled Occasional Paper no. 31 (Birmingham: CCCS, 1974), p. 31. The other contributors were Ros Coward, Marcella Evaristi, Jenny Garber, Rachel Harrison, and Janice Winship.

124   See Leslie G. Roman and Linda K. Christian-Smith, introduction to *Becoming Feminine: The Politics of Popular Culture*, ed. Leslie G. Roman and Linda K. Christian-Smith (London: Falmer, 1988), pp. 1–34.

125   Dorothy Hobson, "Housewives and the Mass Media," in Hall et al., eds., *Culture, Media, Language*, p. 114.

126   Ibid., p. 109.

127   Dorothy Hobson, *Crossroads: The Drama of Soap Opera* (London: Methuen, 1982), p. 111.

128   Angela McRobbie and Jenny Garber, "Girls and Subcultures: An Exploration," in Hall and Jefferson, eds., *Resistance Through Rituals*, p. 221.

129   McRobbie, "Settling Accounts with Subcultures," p. 39.

130   Ibid., p. 49.

131   John Solomos et al., "The Organic Crisis of British Capitalism and Race: The Experience of the Seventies," in Centre for Contemporary Cultural Studies, *The Empire Strikes Back: Race and Racism in 70s Britain* (London: Hutchinson, 1982), p. 28.

132   Ibid., p. 35.

133   Hazel Carby, "White Women Listen! Black Feminism and the Boundaries of Sisterhood," in CCCS, *The Empire Strikes Back*, p. 214.

134   Hazel Carby, "Multi-Culture," in *The Screen Education Reader: Cinema, Television, Culture*, ed. Manuel Alvarado et al. (New York: Columbia University Press, 1993), p. 266.

5. History from Below

1   Alan Dawley, "E. P. Thompson and the Peculiarities of the Americans," *Radical History Review*, no. 19 (Winter 1978–79): 39.

2   Saville, interview, 8 June 1984.

3   Christopher Hill, "Men as They Live Their Own History," in his *Change and Continuity in Seventeenth-Century England* (Cambridge, Mass.: Harvard University Press, 1975), pp. 241–42.

4   Eric Hobsbawm, "The Making of the Working Class, 1870–1914," in his *Workers: World of Labor* (New York: Pantheon Books, 1984), p. 194. For Hobsbawm's original critical review of Thompson's book, see his "Organised Orphans," *New Statesman*, 29 November 1963, p. 788.

5   Rodney Hilton, *Bond Men Made Free: Medieval Peasant Movements and the English Rising of 1381* (London: Methuen, 1977).

6   Hilton, interview, 2 May 1984.

7   Christopher Hill, *The World Turned Upside Down: Radical Ideas During the English Revolution* (Harmondsworth: Penguin Books, 1975), pp. 16–17.

8   Raphael Samuel, "History Workshop, 1966–80," in Samuel, ed., *People's History and Socialist Theory* (London: Routledge and Kegan Paul, 1981), p. 410.

9   Dave Douglass, "The Durham Pitman," in *Miners, Quarrymen and Saltworkers*, ed. Raphael Samuel (London: Routledge and Kegan Paul, 1977), p. 288.

10 Samuel, "History Workshop, 1966–80," p. 410.

11 Ibid., p. 414.

12 Raphael Samuel, "General Editor's Introduction: People's History," in Samuel, ed., *Village Life and Labour* (London: Routledge and Kegan Paul, 1975), pp. xx–xxi.

13 "The Attack," *History Workshop: A Journal of Socialist Historians*, no. 4 (Autumn 1977): 3.

14 Samuel, "General Editor's Introduction," p. xix.

15 See Douglass, "The Durham Pitman," pp. 205–95. See also Jennie Kitteringham, "Country Work Girls in Nineteenth-Century England," pp. 75–138; Raphael Samuel, "'Quarry Roughs': Life and Labour in Headington Quarry, 1860–1920: An Essay in Oral History," in Samuel, ed., *Village Life and Labour*, pp. 141–263; and Frank McKenna, *A Glossary of Railwaymen's Talk*, History Workshop Pamphlets, no. 13 (Oxford: Ruskin College, undated). In a case where a pamphlet also appeared as a book I have cited the book.

16 Raphael Samuel, foreword to Jerry White, *Rothschild Buildings: Life in an East End Tenement Block, 1887–1920* (London: Routledge and Kegan Paul, 1980), p. x.

17 Samuel, "General Editor's Introduction," p. xv.

18 Raphael Samuel, "Local History and Oral History," *History Workshop*, no. 1 (Spring 1976): 201.

19 Samuel, "General Editor's Introduction," p. xix.

20 Thompson, "E. P. Thompson: Recovering the Libertarian Tradition," *Leveller*, no. 22 (1978): 22. Thompson's critique of the Workshop was reported by Samuel, "General Editor's Introduction," p. xix.

21 Dave Marson, *Children's Strikes in 1911*, History Workshop Pamphlets, no. 9 (Oxford: Ruskin College, 1973), p. 35.

22 Ibid., p. i.

23 Ken Worpole, "A Ghostly Pavement: The Political Implications of Local Working-Class History," in Samuel, ed., *People's History and Socialist Theory*, p. 24.

24 Raphael Samuel, "The Workshop of the World: Steam Power and Hand Technology in Mid-Victorian Britain," *History Workshop*, no. 3 (Spring 1977): 58–59.

25 Samuel, "'Quarry Roughs,'" p. 234.

26   In the 1980s, Samuel's work has been no less nostalgic, attempting
      to recover the lost Communist milieu of his youth. See Raphael
      Samuel, "The Lost World of British Communism," *NLR*, no. 154
      (November–December 1985): 3–53; and Samuel, "Staying Power:
      The Lost World of British Communism, Part Two," *NLR*, no. 156
      (March–April 1986): 63–113.

27   My account of the early women's movement and feminist history is
      based on discussions in the spring of 1984 with Sally Alexander,
      Anna Davin, Sheila Rowbotham, and Barbara Taylor, and talks with
      Catherine Hall in early 1987. I have also benefited from Sheila Row-
      botham, "The Beginnings of Women's Liberation in Britain," in her
      volume of collected essays, *Dreams and Dilemmas: Collected Writings*
      (London: Virago Press, 1983), pp. 32–44; Juliet Mitchell, *Woman's
      Estate* (New York: Pantheon Books, 1971); and Anna Coote and
      Beatrix Campbell, *Sweet Freedom: The Struggle for Women's Liberation*
      (Oxford: Basil Blackwell, 1982).

28   Juliet Mitchell, "Women: The Longest Revolution," in her *Women,
      The Longest Revolution: Essays in Feminism, Literature and Psycho-
      analysis* (London: Virago Press, 1984), pp. 17–76.

29   This paragraph is based on the discussion in Hewison, *Too Much*,
      pp. 216–17.

30   Sally Alexander, "Women, Class and Sexual Difference in the 1830s
      and 1840s: Some Reflections on the Writing of a Feminist History,"
      History Workshop, no. 17 (Spring 1984): 127.

31   Alexander, quoted in Campbell and Coote, *Sweet Freedom*, p. 21.

32   Alice Clark, *Working Life of Women in the Seventeenth Century* (Lon-
      don: Routledge and Kegan Paul, 1982).

33   Sheila Rowbotham, *Women, Resistance and Revolution: A History of
      Women and Revolution in the Modern World* (New York: Vintage
      Books, 1974), and *Hidden from History: 300 Years of Women's Oppres-
      sion and the Fight Against It*, 3d ed. (London: Pluto Press, 1977);
      Catherine Hall, "Gender Divisions and Class Formation in the
      Birmingham Middle Class, 1780–1850," in Samuel, ed., *People's
      History and Socialist Theory*, pp. 164–75, and *White, Male and Middle
      Class: Explorations in Feminism and History* (New York: Routledge,
      1992); Leonore Davidoff and Catherine Hall, *Family Fortunes: Men
      and Women of the English Middle Class, 1780–1850* (Chicago: Univer-
      sity of Chicago Press, 1987); Sally Alexander, "Women's Work in
      Nineteenth-Century London," in *The Rights and Wrongs of Women*,
      ed. Juliet Mitchell and Anne Oakley (Harmondsworth: Penguin
      Books, 1976), pp. 59–111; Barbara Taylor, "Socialist Feminism:
      Utopian or Scientific?" in Samuel, ed., *People's History and Socialist
      Theory*, pp. 158–63; and *Eve and the New Jerusalem: Socialism and
      Feminism in the Nineteenth Century* (New York: Pantheon Books,
      1983).

34   Sally Alexander and Anna Davin, "Feminist History," *History Work-
      shop*, no. 1 (Spring 1976): 5.

35   The following discussion of Sheila Rowbotham is based on an

interview conducted in London on 15 June 1984. I have also benefited from Sheila Rowbotham, interview with Dina Copelman, in
Henry Abelove et al., eds., *Visions of History* (New York: Pantheon
Books, 1983), pp. 47–69, and her introduction to the American
edition of *Hidden from History*, published in Britain for the first time
as "Search and Subject, Threading Circumstance," *Dreams and Dilemmas*, pp. 166–89.

36 Eric Hobsbawm, *Primitive Rebels: Studies in Archaic Forms of Social Movement in the Nineteenth and Twentieth Centuries* (New York:
W. W. Norton, 1965). The book was originally published in 1959.

37 Rowbotham, interview, 15 June 1984.

38 Rowbotham, *Hidden from History*, pp. 168–69.

39 Rowbotham, "Search and Subject, Threading Circumstance," p.
171.

40 Ibid., p. 172.

41 Rowbotham, interview, 15 June 1984.

42 Rowbotham, *Women, Resistance and Revolution*, p. 158.

43 Rowbotham, *Hidden from History*, p. 109.

44 Catherine Hall, "Feminism and Feminist History," *White, Male and
Middle Class*, p. 11.

45 The two essays are Eric Hobsbawm, "Man and Woman in Socialist Iconography," *History Workshop*, no. 6 (Autumn 1978): 121–38,
and Sally Alexander, Anna Davin, and Eve Hostettler, "Labouring
Women: A Reply to Eric Hobsbawm," *History Workshop*, no. 8
(Autumn 1979): 174–82.

46 Ibid., p. 182.

47 Joan Wallach Scott, "Women in *The Making of the English Working
Class*," in her *Gender and the Politics of History* (New York: Columbia
University Press, 1988), p. 79.

48 Alexander, "Women's Work in Nineteenth-Century London," p.
111.

49 Taylor, "Socialist Feminism: Utopian or Scientific?" p. 161.

50 Taylor, *Eve and the New Jerusalem*, p. xvi.

51 Catherine Hall, "Feminism and Feminist History," p. 4.

52 Ibid., p. 6.

53 Ibid., p. 11.

54 Ibid., p. 11, 16.

55 Catherine Hall, "Gender Divisions and Class Formation in the
Birmingham Middle Class, 1780–1850," *White, Male and Middle
Class*, p. 94.

56 Davidoff and Hall, *Family Fortunes*, p. 29.

57 Catherine Hall, "The Early Formation of Victorian Domestic Ideology," *White, Male and Middle Class*, p. 92.

58 An example being Catherine Hall's "The History of the Housewife," *White, Male and Middle Class*, p. 48.

59 See, for instance, Thompson, interview with Mike Merrill, in Abelove et al., eds., *Visions of History*, p. 10.

60 Ibid.

61   See Stuart Hall et al., *Policing the Crisis: Mugging, the State and Law and Order* (New York: Holmes and Meir, 1978), pp. 255–58.

62   E. P. Thompson, *Warwick University Ltd.: Industry, Management and the Universities* (Harmondsworth: Penguin Books, 1970), p. 155.

63   E. P. Thompson, "The State of the Nation," in his *Writing by Candlelight* (London: Merlin Press, 1980), p. 247.

64   Ibid., p. 232.

65   Ibid., p. 246.

66   Edward Thompson, "Notes on Exterminism: The Last Stage of Civilization," *NLR*, no. 121 (May–June 1980), p. 26.

67   E. P. Thompson, "Eighteenth-Century English Society: Class Struggle Without Class?" *Social History* 3 (May 1978): 151.

68   Ibid.

69   Ibid., p. 149.

70   E. P. Thompson, *Whigs and Hunters: The Origins of the Black Act* (New York: Pantheon Books, 1975), p. 260.

71   Ibid., p. 263.

72   Ibid., p. 262.

73   Ibid., p. 266.

74   See Perry Anderson, *Arguments Within English Marxism* (London: Verso, 1980), p. 198.

75   Even as late as 1980, Thompson could write: "Give us victory in this, and the world begins to move once more. Begin to break down that field-of-force, and the thirty-year-old impediments to European political mobility (East, South and West) begin to give way. . . . A new space for politics will open up" ("Notes on Exterminism," p. 31). A new space, of course, has opened up, but it is certainly not the one that Thompson imagined.

76   Antonio Gramsci, *Selections from the "Prison Notebooks,"* trans. and ed. Quintin Hoare and Geoffrey Nowell Smith (New York: International Publishers, 1971), p. 12.

77   Stuart Hall, "Notes on Deconstructing 'the Popular,' " in Samuel, ed., *People's History and Socialist Theory*, p. 239.

6. The Politics of Theory

1   Simon Clarke, "Althusserian Marxism," in Simon Clarke et al., *One-Dimensional Marxism: Althusser and the Politics of Culture* (London: Allison and Busby, 1980), p. 7.

2   Stuart Hall, "Cultural Studies: Two Paradigms," *Media, Culture and Society*, no. 2 (1980): 67.

3   Ibid.

4   Richard Johnson and Dorothy Thompson taught a graduate seminar on historiography. Richard Johnson, interview, CCCS, 6 June 1984.

5   In addition to Johnson the Cultural History Group included Gregor McLennan, Dave Sutton, and Bill Schwarz. The notable exception to their examination of British Marxist historiography was their critique of Hindess and Hirst in Johnson, McLennan, and

Schwarz, *Economy, Culture, and Concept: Three Approaches to Marxist History*, Stencilled Occasional Paper no. 50 (Birmingham: CCCS, 1978).

6   See ibid.; David Sutton, "Radical Liberalism, Fabianism, and Social History," pp. 15–43; Bill Schwarz, " 'The People' in History: The Communist Party Historians' Group, 1946–56," in Richard Johnson et al., eds., *Making Histories: Studies in History Writing and Politics* (Minneapolis: University of Minnesota Press, 1982), pp. 44–95; and Richard Johnson, "Culture and the Historians," pp. 41–71, and "Three Problematics: Elements of a Theory of Working-Class Culture," pp. 201–37, in *Working-Class Culture: Studies in History and Theory*, ed. John Clarke, Chas Critcher, and Richard Johnson (London: Hutchinson, 1979).

7   In addition to *Economy, Culture, and Concept*, see Richard Johnson, "Histories of Culture / Theories of Ideology," in *Ideology and Cultural Production*, ed. Michèle Barrett et al. (London: Croom Helm, 1979), pp. 49–77.

8   See Richard Johnson, "Reading for the Best Marx: History-Writing and Historical Abstraction," in Johnson et al., eds., *Making Histories*, pp. 153–201.

9   Stuart Hall, "Marx's Notes on Method: A 'Reading' of the '1857 Introduction,' " *Working Papers in Cultural Studies*, no. 6 (Autumn 1974): 139.

10   For Stedman Jones's debt to Althusser, see his introduction to *Languages of Class: Studies in English Working Class History, 1832–1982* (Cambridge: Cambridge University Press, 1983), p. 12.

11   Gareth Stedman Jones to Richard Johnson, 19 June 1978. This and other related documents were obtained from Richard Johnson; hereafter Johnson Papers. Stedman Jones (anticipating the imminent publication of Thompson's "The Poverty of Theory") also wrote that "with the threat of Edward's text on Althusser hitting us at any moment, to publish your piece will be very timely and distance us from any uprush of anti-gallicism."

12   Richard Johnson to Gareth Stedman Jones, 1 June 1978, Johnson Papers.

13   Richard Johnson to Gareth Stedman Jones, n.d. [Summer/Autumn 1978], Johnson Papers.

14   Richard Johnson, "Edward Thompson, Eugene Genovese, and Socialist-Humanist History," *History Workshop*, no. 6 (Autumn 1978): 82.

15   Ibid., p. 91.

16   Ibid., p. 96.

17   Johnson to Stedman Jones, n.d.; Stedman Jones to Gregor McLennan, 21 May 1978, Johnson Papers.

18   Gareth Stedman Jones, "History and Theory," *History Workshop*, no. 8 (August 1979), p. 198. The major responses to Johnson's article were Keith McClelland, "Some Comments on Richard Johnson, 'Edward Thompson, Eugene Genovese, and Socialist-Humanist

History,' " pp. 101–15 and Gavin Williams, "In Defence of History," in *History Workshop*, no. 7 (Spring 1979): 116–24. They were followed by Simon Clarke, "Socialist Humanism and the Critique of Economism," pp. 137–56, and Gregor McLennan, "Richard Johnson and His Critics: Towards a Constructive Debate," pp. 157–66, in *History Workshop*, no. 8. Letters by Tim Putnam, Robert Shenton, and Tim Mason appeared in *History Workshop*, no. 7, and by Johnson in *History Workshop*, no. 8.

19 Stuart Hall, "In Defence of Theory," in Raphael Samuel, ed., *People's History and Socialist Theory* (London: Routledge and Kegan Paul, 1981), p. 379.

20 Thompson, "The Poverty of Theory," in his *The Poverty of Theory and Other Essays* (London: Merlin Press, 1978), p. 222.

21 Ibid., p. 233.

22 See Peter Novick, *That Noble Dream: The "Objectivity Question" and the American Historical Profession* (Cambridge: Cambridge University Press, 1988), pp. 524–72. Although specifically about the American historical profession, the implications of Novick's account are wider.

23 Editorial, *Radical Science Journal*, no. 6/7 (1978): 3.

24 Thompson, "The Poverty of Theory," p. 387.

25 Ibid., p. 234.

26 Ibid., p. 383.

27 Ibid., p. 265.

28 I have benefited from Anderson's discussion of this issue in *Arguments Within English Marxism* (London: Verso, 1980), pp. 100–103.

29 Thompson, "The Poverty of Theory," pp. 327–28.

30 Ibid., p. 324.

31 Perry Anderson originally argued this in *Arguments Within English Marxism*, pp. 105–10. It has now been thoroughly documented by Gregory Elliot, *Althusser: The Detour of Theory* (London: Verso, 1987), esp. chap. 2.

32 Thompson, "The Poverty of Theory," p. 374.

33 Ibid., pp. 327, 329.

34 Ibid., pp. 336–37.

35 Hall, "In Defence of Theory," p. 379.

36 Anderson, *Arguments Within English Marxism*, p. 2.

37 Ibid., p. 207.

38 Ibid., p. 27.

39 Ibid., pp. 28–29.

40 Raphael Samuel, "Editorial Note," in Samuel, ed., *People's History and Socialist Theory*, p. 376.

41 Martin Kettle, "The Experience of History," *New Society*, 6 December 1979, pp. 542–43.

42 The following account of the entire debate is based on a tape recording acquired from the archives of Ruskin College, Oxford. Unless otherwise noted, the remarks attributed to the speakers are quotations based on my own transcription. The papers of the three principal speakers were later published in lightly edited versions in

People's History and Socialist Theory. Unless otherwise stated, I have quoted from the original debate.

43   Richard Johnson, "Against Absolutism," in Raphael Samuel, ed., *People's History and Socialist Theory*, p. 394.

44   Thompson, "The Politics of Theory," in Raphael Samuel, ed., *People's History and Socialist Theory*, p. 406.

45   Appropriately, Corrigan retorted that if he was to be excommunicated, this occasion was a proper one because he had no intention of withdrawing what he wrote.

46   In the published version of the essay it was changed to "What Richard Johnson is not interested in—what scarcely seems to enter the door of the Birmingham Centre for Cultural Studies—is any consideration of the *politics* of his 'moments.' " Thompson, "The Politics of Theory," p. 399.

47   Stuart Hall, interview, 12 May 1984.

48   Stephen Yeo to Richard Johnson, 8 December 1979, Johnson Papers.

49   Richard Johnson to Stephen Yeo, 29 December 1979, Johnson Papers.

50   Edward Thompson to Richard Johnson, 9 January 1980, Johnson Papers.

Conclusion

1   James Hinton, *Labour and Socialism: A History of the British Labour Movement, 1867–1974* (Sussex: Wheatsheaf Books, 1983), p. 197.

2   Tony Bennett, "Introduction: Popular Culture and 'the Turn to Gramsci,' " in *Popular Culture and Social Relations*, ed. Tony Bennett, Colin Mercer, and Janet Woollacott (Milton Keynes: Open University Press, 1986), p. xvi.

3   See these articles that appeared in *History Workshop*: Jeffrey Weeks, "Foucault for Historians," no. 14 (Autumn 1982): 106–19; Sally Alexander, "Women, Class and Sexual Differences in the 1830s and 1840s: Some Reflections on the Writing of a Feminist History," no. 17 (Spring 1984): 125–49; Sonya O. Rose, " 'Gender at Work': Sex, Class and Industrial Capitalism," no. 21 (Spring 1986): 113–31; and Peter Schottler, "Historians and Discourse Analysis," no. 27 (Spring 1989): 37–65.

4   Gareth Stedman Jones, "Rethinking Chartism," in his *Languages of Class: Studies in English Working Class History, 1832–1982* (Cambridge: Cambridge University Press, 1983), p. 102.

5   Stuart Hall, "Coming Up for Air," *Marxism Today*, March 1990, p. 22.

6   Eric Hobsbawm, "Goodbye to All That," in *After the Fall: The Failure of Communism and the Future of Socialism*, ed. Robin Blackburn (London: Verso, 1991), p. 117.

7   Gareth Stedman Jones, "Marx After Marxism," *Marxism Today*, February 1990, p. 3.

8   Hall, "Coming Up for Air," p. 25.

9 Edward Thompson, "The Ends of Cold War: A Rejoinder," in Robin Blackburn, ed., *After the Fall*, p. 107.

10 Stedman Jones, "Marx after Marxism," p. 3.

11 See Stuart Hall, "The Problem of Ideology: Marxism Without Guarantees," in *Marx: A Hundred Years On*, ed. Betty Matthews (London: Lawrence and Wishart), pp. 57–85; Dick Hebdige, *Hiding in the Light: On Images and Things* (London: Routledge, 1988); Ernesto Laclau with Chantal Mouffe, "Post-Marxism Without Apologies," in Ernesto Laclau, *New Reflections on the Revolution of Our Time* (London: Verso, 1990), pp. 97–132.

12 The original edition was published by the Tyneside Socialist Centre and the Islington Community Press, and it was expanded into a book published by Merlin Press a year later. The present discussion uses the Merlin Press edition.

13 Hilary Wainwright, "Moving Beyond the Fragments," in Sheila Rowbotham, Lynne Segal, and Hilary Wainwright, *Beyond the Fragments: Feminism and the Making of Socialism* (London: Merlin Press, 1979), p. 224.

14 See Sheila Rowbotham's remarks in the introduction to "Stretching," the third section of *Dreams and Dilemmas: Collected Writings* (London: Virago Press, 1983), pp. 312–13.

15 Sheila Rowbotham, "The Women's Movement and Organizing for Socialism," in Rowbotham et al., *Beyond the Fragments*, p. 140.

16 Hilary Wainwright, "Moving Beyond the Fragments," in Rowbotham et al., *Beyond the Fragments*, p. 251.

17 Eric Hobsbawm, "The Forward March of Labour Halted?" in *The Forward March of Labour Halted?* ed. Martin Jacques and Francis Mulhern (London: Verso, in association with *Marxism Today*, 1981), p. 19.

18 Ibid., p. 14.

19 The full debate is collected in ibid.

20 See Eric Hobsbawm, "Labour's Lost Millions" (1983), in his *Politics for a Rational Left: Political Writing, 1977–1988* (London: Verso in association with *Marxism Today*, 1989), pp. 63–76.

21 Stuart Hall, "Gramsci and Us," in *The Hard Road to Renewal: Thatcherism and the Crisis of the Left* (London: Verso, 1988), p. 162.

22 Stuart Hall, "The Toad in the Garden: Thatcherism Among the Theorists," in Lawrence Grossberg and Cary Nelson, eds., *Marxism and the Interpretation of Culture* (Urbana: University of Illinois Press, 1988), p. 40.

23 Stuart Hall, "The Great Moving Right Show," *The Hard Road to Renewal*, p. 48.

24 Ibid., p. 42.

25 Hall, "Gramsci and Us," p. 167.

26 Hall, "The Toad in the Garden," p. 46.

27 Hall distanced himself here from Laclau and Mouffe's *Hegemony and Socialist Strategy* (London: Verso, 1985). "I do not believe that just anything can be articulated with anything else and, in that sense, I

stop short before what is sometimes called a 'fully discursive' position." Hall, introduction to *The Hard Road to Renewal*, p. 10.

28 Hall, "The Toad in the Garden," p. 45.

29 Stuart Hall, "The Culture Gap," *The Hard Road to Renewal*, p. 219.

30 Stuart Hall and Martin Jacques, introduction to *New Times: The Changing Face of Politics in the 1990s*, ed. Hall and Jacques (London: Verso, 1990), p. 15.

31 Stuart Hall, "On Postmodernism and Articulation: An Interview with Stuart Hall," ed. Lawrence Grossberg, *Journal of Communication Inquiry* 10 (Summer 1986): 46.

32 Stuart Hall, "The Meaning of New Times," in Hall and Jacques, eds., *New Times*, p. 128.

33 Ibid., p. 129.

34 Ibid., p. 120.

Selected Works

Abelove, Henry, Betsy Blackmar, Peter Dimock, and Jonathan Schneer, eds. *Visions of History*. New York: Pantheon Books, 1983.

Alexander, Sally. "Women, Class and Sexual Differences in the 1830s and 1840s: Some Reflections on the Writing of a Feminist History." *History Workshop*, no. 17 (Spring 1984): 125–51.

Alexander, Sally, and Anna Davin. "Feminist History." *History Workshop*, no. 1 (Spring 1976): 4–6.

Alexander, Sally, Anna Davin, and Eve Hostettler. "Labouring Women: A Reply to Eric Hobsbawm." *History Workshop*, no. 8 (Autumn 1979): 174–82.

Ali, Tariq. *The Coming British Revolution*. London: Jonathan Cape, 1972.

Anderson, Perry. "The Left in the Fifties." *New Left Review*, no. 29 (January–February 1965): 3–18.

———. "Origins of the Present Crisis." In *Towards Socialism*, edited by Perry Anderson and Robin Blackburn, pp. 11–52. Ithaca, N.Y.: Cornell University Press, 1965.

———. "Socialism and Pseudo-Empiricism." *New Left Review*, no. 35 (January–February 1966): 2–42.

———. "Components of the National Culture." *New Left Review*, no. 50 (July–August 1968): 3–57.

———. *Considerations on Western Marxism*. London: New Left Books, 1976.

———. *Arguments Within English Marxism*. London: Verso, 1980.

———. *English Questions*. London: Verso, 1992.

Anonymous. "A Marxist View of Byzantium." *Times Literary Supplement*, 12 December 1952, p. 816.

Banham, Reyner. "The Atavism of the Short-Distance Mini-Cyclist." In *Design by Choice*, edited by Penny Sparke, pp. 84–89. New York: Rizzoli, 1981.

Bennett, Tony. "Introduction: Popular Culture and 'the Turn to Gramsci.'" In *Popular Culture and Social Relations*, edited by Tony Bennett, Colin Mercer, and Janet Woollacott, pp. xi–xix. Milton Keynes: Open University Press, 1986.

Bernal, J. D. "Stalin as a Scientist." *Modern Quarterly* 8, no. 4 (Autumn 1953): 133–43.

Bérubé, Michael. "Pop Goes the Academy: Cult Studs Fight the Powers." *Village Voice Literary Supplement*, no. 104 (April 1992), pp. 10–14.

Blackburn, Robin. "A Brief Guide to Bourgeois Ideology." In *Student Power: Problems, Diagnosis, Action*, edited by Alexander Cockburn and Robin Blackburn, pp. 163–213. Harmondsworth: Penguin Books, in association with *New Left Review*, 1969.

———, ed. *After the Fall: The Failure of Communism and the Future of Socialism*. London: Verso, 1991.

———. "A Brief History of *New Left Review*, 1960–1990." In *Thirty Years of "New Left Review": Index to Numbers 1–184, 1960–1990*, pp. v–xi. London: New Left Review, 1992.

Branson, Noreen, and Margot Heinemann. *Britain in the 1930s*. New York: Praeger, 1971.

Brantlinger, Patrick. *Crusoe's Footprints: Cultural Studies in Britain and America*. London: Routledge, 1990.

Butcher, Helen, Ros Coward, Marcella Evaristi, Jenny Garber, Rachel Harrison, and Janice Winship. *Images of Women in the Media*, Stencilled Occasional Paper no. 31. Birmingham: CCCS, 1974.

Callaghan, John. *British Trotskyism: Theory and Practice*. Oxford: Basil Blackwell, 1984.

Carby, Hazel V. "Multi-Culture." In *The Screen Education Reader: Cinema, Television, Culture*, edited by Manuel Alvarado, Edward Buscombe, and Richard Collins, pp. 263–74. New York: Columbia University Press, 1993.

Caute, David. *The Year of the Barricades: A Journey Through 1968*. New York: Harper and Row, 1988.

Centre for Contemporary Cultural Studies. *Third Report: 1965–66*. Birmingham: CCCS, 1966.

———. *Fourth Report: 1966–67*. Birmingham: CCCS, 1968.

———. *Sixth Report: 1969–71*. Birmingham: CCCS, 1971.

———. *Eighth Report: 1974–76*. Birmingham: CCCS, 1976.

———. *The Empire Strikes Back: Race and Racism in 70s Britain*. London: Hutchinson, in association with the CCCS. Birmingham: CCCS, 1982.

Chambers, Ian, John Clarke, Ian Connell, Lidia Curti, Stuart Hall, and Tony Jefferson. "Marxism and Culture." *Screen* 18, no. 4 (Winter 1977–78): 101–19.

Chun, Lin. *The British New Left*. Edinburgh: Edinburgh University Press, 1993.

Clarke, John. *The Skinheads and the Study of Youth Culture*. Stencilled Occasional Paper no. 23. Birmingham: CCCS, 1973.

Clarke, John, and Tony Jefferson. *The Politics of Popular Culture: Culture and Sub-Culture*, Stencilled Occasional Paper no. 14. Birmingham: CCCS, 1973.

Clarke, Simon, Terry Lovell, Kevin McDonnell, Kevin Robins, and Victor Jeleniewski Seidler. *One-Dimensional Marxism: Althusser and the Politics of Culture*. London: Allison and Busby, 1980.

Coote, Anna, and Beatrix Campbell. *Sweet Freedom: The Struggle for Women's Liberation*. Oxford: Basil Blackwell, 1982.

Coward, Rosalind. "Class, 'Culture' and the Social Formation." *Screen* 18, no. 1 (Spring 1977): 75–105.

———. "Response." *Screen* 18, no. 4 (Winter 1977–78): 120–22.

Crossman, R. H. S. "Towards a Philosophy of Capitalism." In *New Fabian Essays*, edited by R. H. S. Crossman, pp. 1–32. London: Fabian Society, 1970.

Davidoff, Leonore, and Catherine Hall. *Family Fortunes: Men and Women of the English Middle Class, 1780–1850*. Chicago: University of Chicago Press, 1987.

Dawley, Alan. "E. P. Thompson and the Peculiarities of the Americans." *Radical History Review*, no. 19 (Winter 1978–79): 33–60.

Dobb, Maurice. *Studies in the Development of Capitalism*. Rev. ed. New York: International Publishers, 1963.

Douglass, Dave. "The Durham Pitman." In *Miners, Quarrymen and Salt-workers*, edited by Raphel Samuel, pp. 207–95. London: Routledge and Kegan Paul, 1977.

Duff, Peggy. *Left, Left, Left: A Personal Account of Six Protest Campaigns, 1945–65*. London: Allison and Busby, 1971.

Easthope, Anthony. *British Post-Structuralism Since 1968*. London: Routledge, 1988.

Eatwell, John. "Maurice Dobb." *Cambridge Journal of Economics* 1, no. 1 (1977): 1–3.

Eliot, T. S. *Notes Towards the Definition of Culture*. New York: Harcourt Brace Jovanovich, 1949.

Fernbach, David. "Strategy and Struggle." *New Left Review*, no. 53 (January–February 1969): 37–42.

Fraser, Ronald. *1968: A Student Generation in Revolt*. London: Chatto and Windus, 1988.

Garman, Douglas. "The English Revolution 1640: A Reply to P. F." *Labour Monthly* 22, no. 12 (December 1940): 651–53.

Gramsci, Antonio. *Selections from the "Prison Notebooks."* Edited and translated by Quintin Hoare and Geoffrey Nowell Smith. New York: International Publishers, 1971.

Grossberg, Lawrence. "History, Politics and Postmodernism: Stuart Hall and Cultural Studies." *Journal of Communication Inquiry* 10, no. 2 (1986): 61–77.

———. "The Formations of Cultural Studies: An American in Birmingham." In *Relocating Cultural Studies: Developments in Theory and Research*, edited by Valda Blundell, John Shepard, and Ian Taylor, pp. 21–66. London: Routledge, 1993.

Grossberg, Lawrence, and Cary Nelson, eds. *Marxism and the Interpretation of Culture*. Urbana: University of Illinois Press, 1988.

Grossberg, Lawrence, Cary Nelson, and Paula A. Treichler, eds. *Cultural Studies*. New York: Routledge, 1992.

Gurevitch, Michael, Tony Bennett, James Curran, and Janet Woollacott, eds. *Culture, Society, and the Media*. London: Methuen, 1982.

Hall, Catherine. *White, Male and Middle Class: Explorations in Feminism and History*. New York: Routledge, 1992.

Hall, Stuart. "In the No Man's Land." *Universities and Left Review*, no. 3 (Winter 1958): 86–87.

————. "A Sense of Classlessness." *Universities and Left Review*, no. 5 (Autumn 1958): 26–31.

————. "The Politics of Adolescence." *Universities and Left Review*, no. 6 (Spring 1959): 2–5.

————. *The Hippies: An American "Moment."* Stencilled Occasional Paper no. 16. Birmingham: CCCS, 1968.

————. "Marx's Notes on Method: A 'Reading' of the '1857 Introduction.'" *Working Papers in Cultural Studies*, no. 6 (Autumn 1974): 132–71.

————. "A Critical Survey of the Theoretical and Practical Achievements of the Last Ten Years." In *Literature, Society and the Sociology of Literature: Proceedings of the Conference Held at the University of Essex, July 1976*, edited by Francis Barker, John Combes, Peter Hulme, David Musselwhite, and Richard Osborne, pp. 1–7. Essex: University of Essex, 1977.

————. "Cultural Studies: Two Paradigms." *Media, Culture and Society*, no. 2 (1980): 57–72.

————. "On Postmodernism and Articulation: An Interview with Stuart Hall," edited by Lawrence Grossberg. *Journal of Communication Inquiry* 10, no. 2 (Summer 1986): 45–60.

————. *The Hard Road to Renewal: Thatcherism and the Crisis of the Left.* London: Verso, 1988.

————. "Coming Up for Air." *Marxism Today*, March 1990, pp. 22–25.

Hall, Stuart, Chas Critcher, Tony Jefferson, John Clarke, and Brian Roberts. *Policing the Crisis: Mugging, the State and Law and Order.* New York: Holmes and Meir, 1978.

Hall, Stuart, Dorothy Hobson, Andrew Lowe, and Paul Willis, eds. *Culture, Media, Language: Working Papers in Cultural Studies, 1972–79.* London: Hutchinson, 1980.

Hall, Stuart, and Martin Jacques, eds. *New Times: The Changing Face of Politics in the 1990s.* London: Verso, 1990.

Hall, Stuart, and Tony Jefferson, eds. *Resistance through Rituals: Youth Subcultures in Post-War Britain.* London: Hutchinson, 1977.

Hall, Stuart, and Paddy Whannel. *The Popular Arts.* Boston: Beacon Press, 1967.

Hebdige, Dick. *Subculture: The Meaning of Style.* London: Methuen, 1979.

Hewison, Robert. *In Anger: British Culture in the Cold War, 1945–60.* New York: Oxford University Press, 1981.

————. *Too Much: Art and Society in the Sixties, 1960–75.* New York: Oxford University Press, 1987.

Hill, Christopher. "Soviet Interpretation of the English Interregnum." *Economic History Review* 8, no. 2 (May 1938): 159–67.

————. "The English Civil War Interpreted by Marx and Engels." *Science and Society* 12, no. 1 (Winter 1948): 130–56.

————. "Marxism and History." *Modern Quarterly* 3, no. 2 (Spring 1948): 58–64.

————. "Historians on the Rise of British Capitalism." *Science and Society* 14, no. 4 (Fall 1950): 307–21.

Hill, Christopher. "Stalin and the Science of History." *Modern Quarterly* 8, no. 4 (Autumn 1953): 198–212.

———. *The English Revolution: 1640.* 3d ed. London: Lawrence and Wishart, 1955.

———. "Storm Over the Gentry." *Encounter* 11, no. 1 (July 1958): 76.

———. "Marx's Virtues." *Listener*, 10 August 1967, pp. 172–73.

———. "Men as They Live Their Own History." In *Change and Continuity in Seventeenth-Century England*, pp. 239–47. Cambridge, Mass.: Harvard University Press, 1975.

———. *The World Turned Upside Down: Radical Ideas During the English Revolution.* Harmondsworth: Penguin Books, 1975.

———. *The Collected Essays of Christopher Hill.* Vol. 1. Amherst: University of Massachusetts Press, 1985.

Hill, Christopher, R. H. Hilton, and E. J. Hobsbawm. "Past and Present: Origins and Early Years." *Past and Present*, no. 100 (August 1983): 3–14.

Hilton, Rodney. "Peasant Movements in England before 1381." *Economic History Review* 11 (1949): 117–36.

———. "Capitalism—What's in a Name?" In *The Transition from Feudalism to Capitalism*, edited by Rodney Hilton, pp. 145–58. London: Verso, 1978.

Hinton, James. *Labour and Socialism.* Sussex: Wheatsheaf Books, 1983.

———. *Protests and Visions: Peace Politics in Twentieth-Century Britain.* London: Hutchinson Radius, 1989.

Hirst, Paul Q. "Anderson's Balance Sheet." In *Marxism and Historical Writing*, pp. 1–28. London: Routledge and Kegan Paul, 1985.

Historians' Group of the Communist Party. "State and Revolution in Tudor and Stuart England." *Communist Review*, July 1948, pp. 207–14.

History Workshop. "The Attack." *History Workshop*, no. 4 (Autumn 1977): 1–4.

Hobsbawm, Eric. "Where Are British Historians Going?" *Marxist Quarterly* 2, no. 1 (January 1955): 14–26.

———. "Maurice Dobb." In *Socialism, Capitalism, and Economic Growth: Essays Presented to Maurice Dobb*, edited by C. H. Feinstein, pp. 1–12. Cambridge: Cambridge University Press, 1967.

———. *Revolutionaries.* New York: New American Library, 1973.

———. "Man and Woman in Socialist Iconography." *History Workshop*, no. 6 (Autumn 1978): 121–38.

———. "The Historians' Group of the Communist Party." In *Rebels and Their Causes: Essays in Honour of A. L. Morton*, edited by Maurice Cornforth, pp. 21–47. Atlantic Highlands, N.J.: Humanities Press, 1979.

———. "The Forward March of Labour Halted?" In *The Forward March of Labour Halted?* edited by Martin Jacques and Francis Mulhern, pp. 1–19. London: Verso, in association with *Marxism Today*, 1981.

———. "The Making of the Working Class, 1870–1914." In *Workers: World of Labour*, pp. 194–213. New York: Pantheon Books, 1984.

———. "1956: Gareth Stedman Jones Interviews Eric Hobsbawm." *Marxism Today*, November 1986, pp. 16–23.

Hobson, Dorothy. *Crossroads: The Drama of Soap Opera*. London: Methuen, 1982.

Hoggart, Richard. "Speaking to Each Other." In *Conviction*, edited by Norman Mackenzie, pp. 121–38. London: MacGibbon and Kee, 1958.

———. *The Uses of Literacy*. Harmondsworth: Penguin Books, 1958.

———. "Literature and Society." In *Speaking to Each Other*. Vol. 2: *About Literature*, pp. 19–39. New York: Oxford University Press, 1970.

Holden, Richard. "The First New Left in Britain: 1956–62." Ph.D. diss., University of Wisconsin, Madison, 1976.

Holorenshaw, Henry. *The Levellers and the English Revolution*. New York: Howard Fertig, 1971.

Inglis, Fred. *Raymond Williams*. London: Routledge, 1995.

Jay, Martin. *Marxism and Totality: The Adventures of a Concept from Lukács to Habermas*. Berkeley: University of California Press, 1984.

Johnson, Richard. "Edward Thompson, Eugene Genovese, and Socialist-Humanist History." *History Workshop*, no. 6 (Autumn 1978): 79–100.

Johnson, Richard, Gregor McLennan, Bill Schwarz, and David Sutton, eds. *Making Histories: Studies in History Writing and Politics*. Minneapolis: University of Minnesota Press, 1982.

Kaye, Harvey J. *The British Marxist Historians: An Introductory Analysis*. Cambridge: Polity Press, 1984.

Kettle, Martin. "The Experience of History." *New Society*, 6 December 1979, pp. 542–43.

Kiernan, Victor. "Culture and Society." *New Reasoner*, no. 9 (Summer 1959): 74–83.

Klugmann, James. "Introduction: The Crisis in the Thirties, A View from the Left." In *Culture and Crisis in Britain in the Thirties*, edited by Jon Clark, Margot Heinemann, David Margolies, and Carole Snee, pp. 13–36. London: Lawrence and Wishart, 1979.

Knight, G. Wilson. "Freedom and Integrity." *Times Literary Supplement*, 2 January 1953, p. 9.

MacCabe, Colin. "Class of '68: Elements of an Intellectual Autobiography." In *Tracking the Signifier: Theoretical Essays: Film, Linguistics, Literature*, pp. 1–32. Minneapolis: University of Minnesota Press, 1985.

Marson, David. *Children's Strikes in 1911*. History Workshop Pamphlets no. 9. Oxford: Ruskin College, 1973.

Marx, Karl, and Frederick Engels. *Selected Correspondence, 1846–1895*. Translated by Dona Torr. Vol. 24, Marxist Library: Works of Marxism-Leninism. New York: International Publishers, 1942.

Matthews, George. "A Caricature of Our Party." *World News*, 30 June 1956, pp. 409–10.

May, Daphne. "Work of the Historians' Groups." *Communist Review*, May 1949, pp. 538–42.

McRobbie, Angela. "Settling Accounts with Subcultures: A Feminist Critique." *Screen Education*, no. 34 (Spring 1980): 37–49.

Merton, Richard. "Comment." *New Left Review*, no. 47 (January–February 1968): 29–31.

Miliband, Ralph. "John Saville: A Presentation." In *Ideology and the Labour Movement*, edited by David E. Martin and David Rubinstein, pp. 15–31. London: Croom Helm, 1979.

Miliband, Ralph, and John Saville, eds. *Socialist Register 1976*. London: Merlin Press, 1976.

Mills, C. Wright. "The New Left." In *Power, Politics and People: The Collected Essays of C. Wright Mills*, pp. 247–59. New York: Oxford University Press, 1963.

Mitchell, Juliet. "Women: The Longest Revolution." In *Women: The Longest Revolution: Essays in Feminism, Literature, and Psychoanalysis*, pp. 17–76. London: Virago Press, 1984.

Morley, David, and Kuan-Hsing Chen, eds. *Stuart Hall: Critical Dialogues in Cultural Studies*. London: Routledge, 1996.

New Left Review. "Themes." *New Left Review*, no. 50 (July–August 1968): 1–2.

———. "Editorial Introduction." *New Left Review*, no. 52 (November–December 1968): 1–8.

———. *Western Marxism: A Critical Reader*. London: Verso, 1978.

Newton, Kenneth. *The Sociology of British Communism*. London: Allen Lane, 1969.

O'Connor, Alan. *Raymond Williams: Writing, Culture, Politics*. London: Basil Blackwell, 1989.

Oxford University Socialist Group, ed. *Out of Apathy: Voices of the New Left Thirty Years On*. London: Verso, 1989.

Pennington, Donald, and Keith Thomas, eds. *Puritans and Revolutionaries: Essays in Seventeenth-Century History Presented to Christopher Hill*. Oxford: Oxford University Press, 1978.

Radical Philosophy. "Radical Philosophy Group." *Radical Philosophy*, no. 3 (Winter 1972), inside cover.

Radical Science Journal. Editorial. *Radical Science Journal*, no. 6/7 (1978): 3.

Rock, Paul, and Mary McIntosh, eds. *Deviance and Social Control*. London: Tavistock, 1974.

Rowbotham, Sheila. *Women, Resistance and Revolution: A History of Women and Revolution in the Modern World*. New York: Vintage Books, 1974.

———. *Hidden from History: 300 Years of Women's Oppression and the Fight Against It*. 3d ed. London: Pluto Press, 1977.

———. *Dreams and Dilemmas: Collected Writings*. London: Virago, 1983.

Rowbotham, Sheila, Lynne Segal, and Hilary Wainwright. *Beyond the Fragments: Feminism and the Making of Socialism*. London: Merlin Press, 1979.

Samuel, Raphael , ed. *Village Life and Labour*. History Workshop Series. London: Routledge and Kegan Paul, 1975.

———. "Local History and Oral History." *History Workshop*, no. 1 (Spring 1976): 191–208.

———. "The Workshop of the World: Steam Power and Hand Technology in Mid-Victorian Britain." *History Workshop*, no. 3 (Spring 1977): 6–72.

———. "British Marxist Historians, 1880–1980: Part One." *New Left Review*, no. 120 (March–April 1980): 21–96.

———, ed. *People's History and Socialist Theory*. History Workshop Series. London: Routledge and Kegan Paul, 1981.

Saville, John, ed. *Democracy and the Labour Movement: Essays in Honour of Dona Torr*. London: Lawrence and Wishart, 1954.

———. "Problems of the Communist Party." *World News*, 19 May 1956, p. 314.

Saville, John, and Edward Thompson. "Why We Are Publishing." *Reasoner*, no. 1 (July 1956): 1–3.

Scott, Joan Wallach. "Women in *The Making of the English Working Class*." In *Gender and the Politics of History*, pp. 68–90. New York: Columbia University Press, 1988.

Shipley, Peter. *Revolutionaries in Modern Britain*. London: Bodley Head, 1976.

Shuttleworth, Alan. *Two Working Papers in Cultural Studies*, Occasional Paper no. 2. Birmingham: CCCS, 1966.

Smith, A. C. H., with Elizabeth Immirzi and Trevor Blackwell. *Paper Voices*. Totowa, N.J.: Rowman and Littlefield, 1975.

Stedman Jones, Gareth. "History: The Poverty of Empiricism." In *Ideology in Social Science: Readings in Critical Social Theory*, edited by Robin Blackburn, pp. 96–115. London: Fontana, 1972.

———. *Languages of Class: Studies in English Working Class History, 1832–1982*. Cambridge: Cambridge University Press, 1983.

———. "Marx After Marxism." *Marxism Today*, February 1990, p. 3.

Taylor, Charles. "Marxism and Humanism." *New Reasoner*, no. 2 (Summer 1957): 92–98.

Taylor, Richard. *Against the Bomb: The British Peace Movement, 1958–65*. Oxford: Clarendon Press, 1988.

Thompson, E. P. *William Morris: Romantic to Revolutionary*. London: Lawrence and Wishart, 1955.

———. "Winter Wheat in Omsk." *World News*, 30 June 1956, pp. 408–9.

———. "Reply to George Matthews." *Reasoner*, no. 1 (July 1956): 15–19.

———. "Socialist Humanism: An Epistle to the Philistines." *New Reasoner*, no. 1 (Summer 1957): 105–43.

———. "NATO, Neutralism and Survival." *Universities and Left Review*, no. 4 (Summer 1958): 49–51.

———. "Commitment and Politics." *Universities and Left Review*, no. 6 (Spring 1959): 50–55.

———. "A Psessay in Ephology." *New Reasoner*, no. 10 (Very Late Autumn 1959): 1–8.

———, ed. *Out of Apathy*. London: Stevens and Sons, 1960.

———. "Revolution." *New Left Review*, no. 3 (May–June 1960): 3–9.

———. "Revolution Again! Or Shut Your Ears and Run." *New Left Review*, no. 6 (November–December 1960): 18–31.

———. "The Long Revolution." *New Left Review*, no. 9 (May–June 1961): 24–33.

———. "The Long Revolution II." *New Left Review*, no. 10 (July–August 1961): 34–39.

———. *The Communism of William Morris*. London: William Morris Society, 1965.

———. "The Peculiarities of the English." In *Socialist Register 1965*, edited by Ralph Miliband and John Saville, pp. 311–62. New York: Monthly Review Press, 1965.

———. *Warwick University Ltd.: Industry, Management and the Universities.* Harmondsworth: Penguin Books, 1970.

———. *Whigs and Hunters: The Origins of the Black Act.* New York: Pantheon Books, 1975.

———. *William Morris: Romantic to Revolutionary,* revised ed. New York: Pantheon Books, 1977.

———. "E. P. Thompson: Recovering the Libertarian Tradition." *Leveller*, no. 22 (1978): 20–22.

———. *The Poverty of Theory and Other Essays.* London: Merlin Press, 1978.

———. "Eighteenth-Century English Society: Class Struggle Without Class?" *Social History* 3, no. 2 (May 1978): 133–65.

———. "The Secret State." *New Statesman*, 10 November 1978, pp. 612–18.

———. *The Making of the English Working Class.* Harmondsworth: Penguin Books, 1980.

———. "Notes on Exterminism: The Last Stage of Civilization." *New Left Review*, no. 121 (May–June 1980): 3–31.

———. "The State of the Nation." In *Writing by Candlelight*, pp. 191–256. London: Merlin Press, 1980.

Thompson, E. P., ed. *The Railway: An Adventure in Construction.* London: British-Yugoslav Association, 1948.

Thompson, E. P., and T. J. Thompson, eds. *There Is a Spirit in Europe: A Memoir of Frank Thompson.* London: Victor Gollancz, 1948.

Torr, Dona. *Tom Mann and His Times.* Vol. 1. London: Lawrence and Wishart, 1956.

Triesman, David. "Essex." *New Left Review*, no. 50 (July–August 1968): 70–71.

Tucker, Robert C., ed. *The Marx-Engels Reader.* 2d ed. New York: W. W. Norton, 1978.

Turner, Graeme. *British Cultural Studies: An Introduction.* Boston: Unwin Hyman, 1990.

White, Jerry. *Rothschild Buildings: Life in an East End Tenement Block, 1887–1920.* History Workshop Series. London: Routledge and Kegan Paul, 1980.

Widgery, David. *The Left in Britain, 1956–68.* Harmondsworth: Penguin Books, 1976.

Williams, Raymond. "The Soviet Literary Controversy in Retrospect." *Politics and Letters* 1, no. 1 (Summer 1947): 21–31.

———. "The Uses of Literacy: Working Class Culture." *Universities and Left Review*, no. 2 (Summer 1957): 29–32.

———. "Our Debt to Dr. Leavis." *Critical Quarterly* 1, no. 3 (Autumn 1959): 245–47.

———. "London Letter." *Partisan Review* 27, no. 2 (Spring 1960): 341–47.

———. *The Long Revolution*. London: Chatto and Windus, 1961.

———. "The British Left." *New Left Review*, no. 30 (March–April 1965): 18–26.

———. *Culture and Society, 1780–1950*. New York: Harper and Row, 1966.

———. *Communications*. 3d ed. Harmondsworth: Penguin Books, 1976.

———. *Marxism and Literature*. Oxford: Oxford University Press, 1977.

———. *Politics and Letters: Interviews with "New Left Review."* London: New Left Books, 1979.

———. *Problems in Materialism and Culture: Selected Essays*. London: Verso, 1980.

———. *The Politics of Modernism: Against the New Conformists*. London: Verso, 1989.

———. *Resources of Hope*. London: Verso, 1989.

Willis, Paul. "What Is News: A Case Study." *Working Papers in Cultural Studies*, no. 1 (Spring 1971): 9–36.

———. *Profane Culture*. London: Routledge and Kegan Paul, 1978.

———. *Learning to Labor: How Working-Class Kids Get Working-Class Jobs*. New York: Columbia University Press, 1981.

Women's Studies Group. *Women Take Issue: Aspects of Women's Subordination*. London: Hutchinson, in association with the Centre for Contemporary Cultural Studies, University of Birmingham, 1978.

Index

Abramsky, Chimen, 54
Adorno, Theodor, 135, 136
advertising, 58, 60, 84
Agitprop collective, 127
Aldermaston, 54, 64, 73, 202. *See
also* Campaign for Nuclear
Disarmament
Alexander, Ken, 51, 70
Alexander, Sally, 2, 193, 194, 199,
201
Ali, Tariq, 127, 129
Alston, Bob, 75
Althusser, Louis, 135, 136, 138,
142, 143–145, 159, 165, 170,
172, 213, 219, 220, 221, 222,
223, 225–227, 230–231, 234,
236, 237, 239, 241, 244, 246
Althusserianism, 8, 145, 148, 153,
163, 175, 205, 207, 215, 218,
219, 222, 224–226, 228–229,
230–232, 237, 245. *See also* Anderson, Perry; Johnson, Richard; structuralism; Thompson,
E. P.
Anderson, Lindsay, 59; "Stand Up!
Stand Up!" / "Commitment in
Cinema Criticism," 59
Anderson, Perry, 68, 76, 77, 109,
110–116, 129, 133–139, 151,
207, 229, 233–234; *Arguments
within English Marxism,* 112,
233–234; "The Components of
the National Culture," 134–
135; *Considerations on Western
Marxism,* 136–137; and *New
Left Review,* 68, 76, 77, 109, 110,
133, 134–136, 139; "Origins of
the Present Crisis, 110–111,

135; "Socialism and Pseudo-
Empiricism, 114–115; and E. P.
Thompson, 68, 77, 109, 115,
207, 233–234. *See also* Althus-
ser; Althusserianism; New Left;
new left; Western Marxism
Anti-University of London, 128–
129. *See also* "1968"
Argument Group, 230
Arnold, Matthew, 80, 88, 209
Ashton, T. S., 106
Auden, W. H., 11

Bakhtin, Mikhail, 171
Balibar, Etienne, 232
Ball, John, 40
Ballocha, Lil, 193
Banham, Reyner, 85
Barraclough, Geoffrey, 20
Barratt Brown, Michael, 51,
149
Barthes, Roland, 143, 145, 165,
167; *S/Z,* 145
base/superstructure, 26, 28, 41,
52, 53, 90, 98, 100, 104, 110,
137, 142, 144, 151–152, 175,
225, 254, 260
Bateson, Nicholas, 131
Becker, Howard, *Outsiders,* 156
Bennett, Tony, 248
Berger, John, 51, 128
Berger, Peter, 122
Berlin, Isaiah, 135
Bernal, J. D., 11, 21
Bernstein, Edward, 26
Betts, R. R., 20
Birkbeck College. *See* University
of London

About the Author

Dennis Dworkin is Associate Professor of History at the University of Nevada, Reno. He is coeditor (with Leslie Roman) of *Views Beyond the Border Country: Raymond Williams and Cultural Politics* (1993).

Library of Congress Cataloging-in-Publication Data

Dworkin, Dennis L., 1951–
    Cultural Marxism in postwar Britain : history, the new left, and the origins of cultural studies / Dennis Dworkin.
        p.   cm. — (Post-contemporary interventions)
    Includes bibliographical references and index.
    ISBN 0-8223-1909-8 (cloth : alk. paper). — ISBN 0-8223-1914-4 (paper : alk. paper)
        1. Great Britain—History—1945–   —Historiography.   2. Culture—Study and teaching—Great Britain—History—20th century.   3. Historiography—Great Britain—History—20th century.   4. Great Britain—Intellectual life—20th century.   5. Marxist anthropology—Great Britain.   6. Right and left (Political science)   7. Socialism—Great Britain.   I. Title.   II. Series.
DA589.4.D96 1997
941.085—dc20   96-43000
                                                                                    CIP